Jewish and Islamic Philosophy

Jewish and Islamic Philosophy

Crosspollinations in the Classic Age

Lenn E. Goodman

Edinburgh University Press

Edinburgh University Press
22 George Square, Edinburgh

Typeset in Goudy
by Koinonia Ltd, Bury, and
printed and bound in Great Britain

A CIP record for this book is available from the British Library

ISBN 0 7486 1277 7 (hardback)

Contents

Preface

Near the end of the tenth century, Abū ʻUmar ibn Saʻdī, a pious theologian, travelled from Spain to Baghdad. On his way home, he was asked by a colleague, a jurist in Qayrawān, whether he had visited any of the theological conferences that were a well-known feature of intellectual life in the Islamic metropolis. Only twice, he replied, adding that he was glad to have escaped. "Why so?" he was asked. Judge for yourself, he answered: The first meeting I went to was attended not only by members of every sect, orthodox and heretical, but also by miscreants – atheists, materialists, Jews, Christians – unbelievers of every sort. Each sect had a leader to defend its views, and whenever one of these came into the room, they all rose to show respect, and no one sat down until his leader was seated. Soon, the hall was crowded, and when it seemed full, one of the unbelievers took the floor and said: "We have come together here to reason. All of you know the rules. You Muslims are not to bring arguments against us drawn from your scripture or leaning on the authority of your prophet, since we do not believe in either. All of us must rely on arguments based on human reason." Everyone applauded these words. You can hardly imagine the things I heard. I never went back. But I was prevailed upon to visit a different meeting, which proved equally shameful.[1]

The exchanges Abū ʻUmar found disgraceful others found exciting. Still others found such interactions necessary, informative, or useful. Provoking responses as diverse as the individuals it touched, the cosmopolitanism reflected in the Baghdad meetings was, from ancient times, a fact of life in the Middle East. Jaroslav Stetkevych, a scholar of Arablic poetry, writes poetically of Arabic and Hebrew literature as a confluence of rivers:

> Our first river is that of Hebrew literature. It breaks out of rich, distant Mesopotamian subsoil in visions of creation, lost gardens, primeval floods. It is the quiet, bucolic stream of the Patriarchs; it gains strength and drama with Moses and rushes down the slopes of Canaan to the thundering sounds of the

> trumpets of Joshua. It becomes the majestic, harnessed waterway of the Kingdom, only too soon to break up into dangerous, vaporous, cascading rapids of the Prophets of doom, remorse and a too distant promise ... like a real river of the desert ... [it] did not seem to have reached its sea. Its flow was cut, and its waters sank into the vast sands of so many deserts ...
>
> Down under the desert of Arabia, on the spot marked by the black stone of the *Ka'bah*, where Hagar and her son Isma'il took refuge from the jealous eyes of Sarah, the ground waters of the old biblical stream met with a new impatient current which took them in, absorbed them into its own chaos of creative energy, and then burst out into the pristine light of the desert. The first major confluence of two literatures, two cultures, two prophecies, took place – be it in the cultural subsoil of Arabia, or in the mind of Muhammad, or in a world that felt the need for a new religion.[2]

The two streams have joined, mingled, separated and remet repeatedly. To name just one example: when the philosopher poet Judah Halevi refreshes the ancient strains of Hebrew verse with his own earthy and spiritual passions, he draws water both from the ancient Biblical wells and from the freshets of Arabic poetry that lie close at hand. The poetic tropes and rhetorical energies of Hebrew and Arabic verse spring from a common stock whose roots run back into Biblical and pre-Biblical antiquity and whose images still flower in the literatures and rhetorics of today, belying the commonplace vision of a sterile and arid desert landscape.

Turning from images to ideas, we find not just minglings and borrowings but challenges met and alliances sought, often across seemingly impassable boundaries of linguistic, credal and cultic difference and often in defiance of the seemingly forbidding barriers of time and distance. Difference, we learn soon enough, is not indifference. The metaphor that arises most naturally from long study of the materials of philosophical interchange between Jewish and Muslim thinkers is not that of a confluence so much as that of crosspollination. Philosophers loyal to one tradition discern the issues that unite them with philosophers of another time, place or confession, inherit their problematics and creatively adapt their responses.

In the records of thousand-year-old correspondence preserved in the Cairo Geniza documents and other ancient manuscripts,[3] in open acknowledgments, and in the implicit nisus of well worn but ever renewed arguments and illustrations, we can overhear healthy snatches of a sustained conversation that is as old as the cultures themselves, and at least as old as their faiths. What we learn from these conversations, as we cock our ears to listen, is first to doubt and then to deny the stereotypic notions of nineteenth-century scholarship that would assign to each race and nation a particular genius or spirit of its own, uncommunicable and inscrutable to any other, incapable of mixture without adulteration of each distinctive and pristine essence, but transparent, invisible, unexchangeable and uncriticisible by those who share it or who live within its thrall. On the contrary, it is characteristic of human thought in general, and of philosophy in particular that each individual must pursue the argument where it leads and where the philosophical *sitz im leben* seems to demand, without regard to the purisms and pigeonholes that later scholars will concoct or construct for their own convenience, and in imperfect but real freedom from the prevailing nostrums of unquestioning and uncritical faith or prejudice.

Still more importantly, however, we learn something of philosophy itself. For comparative studies in philosophy set up a crosslight in which the great issues can be examined more critically than is possible in the polarising light of a single tradition. Collingwood taught us that the assumptions that run deepest in any philosopher's work are often those of which he is least aware – and therefore, also, those about which he is least critical, least philosophical, To an alien sensibility, raised in a rival tradition or nurtured on alternative assumptions, what is subtlest and most abstruse to others will often be most obvious, and perhaps most glaring. Cross-cultural study of Jewish and Islamic philosophical themes and arguments is especially revealing in this way. It is especially useful in allowing us to get our bearings on the issues themselves by affording us vantage points for triangulation. For the close analogies and kinships among underlying assumptions highlight the differences. And the areas of affinity in turn show up tellingly against the backlight of ancient pagan ideas, or silhouetted by the more glaring lights of post-Enlightenment ways of thinking, be they empiricist, romantic, skeptical, analytic, or post-modern.

The present book is an exploration of a handful of major philosophical issues as they unfold in the historic interplay of Islamic and Jewish philosophy. The problems considered are issues of abiding philosophical interest: freedom and determinism, the nature and meaning of history, the basis of ethical values, the foundations and social implications of friendship, the viability and relevance of the idea of God. The cross-cultural perspective is pursued both for its intrinsic interest and for its aid in overcoming potentially parochial views of the philosophical possibilities. The approach is synthetic rather than descriptive. The object is not to find the "sources" of ideas, as if to credit the philosophical originality of one group or cast aspersions on the philosophical dependency of another, but rather to follow the conversation that continues across the centuries, in hopes that we can learn philosophically from what we overhear.

Appreciation of skilful argumentation is the point of entry that allows us to distinguish genuine philosophy from mere opinion and to learn from and find common ground with past philosophers who may differ from us even more than they differ from one another, but who may yet (and for that very reason) broaden our perception of the live philosophical options. A key premise that I find vindicated in the practice of comparative philosophy is that none of us is entombed or imprisoned in our historical moment or cultural circumstance. Cultures, unlike Leibniz' monads, do have windows. Indeed the relationships that open up when creative individuals look out of those windows at the challenges and achievements of another culture or another age are part of what give life to cultures. For no organism can sustain itself wholly from within, and no population can survive without constantly renewed diversity.

It is often supposed that the political conflict between Israel and her Arab neighbours is an expression of deep philosophical differences, as though the conflict represented a difference in underlying axioms. But the historical record reveals a long symbiosis between Jewish and Islamic philosophical ideas, nourished by kindred scriptures and stimulated by a shared intellectual heritage that runs back not only to a cousinage in scriptural texts and ritual practices but also to a shared patrimony in the great philosophical texts and discussions of classical and Hellenistic antiquity. Readers who examine the fruits nurtured by this symbiosis will discover affinities and interactions between Jewish and Islamic philosophy that run as deep as the deepest philosophical probing will permit. Even in times of persecution, creative interactions continue across temporal, linguistic, cultural, religious and sectarian boundaries. The commerce of ideas, like that of more worldly goods, persists even in time of war. And human nature makes intellectual goods just as much subject to barter, adaptation and exchange as are their material counterparts.

What the ancient texts reveal is that differences in cultural backgrounds do not make for incommensurability. When philosophers of another epoch deal with the great issues of philosophy – God and truth, right and freedom, justice and friendship, goodness and greatness – their thoughts are not incomprehensible to others who grapple with the same questions. And if the questions are phrased in other tongues and terms, the differences in outlook afford a precious if delicate standpoint from which to check unquestioned assumptions. Comparative philosophy in this sense provides us with a touchstone for our philosophical scepticism and a source of controls for use in our own philosophical thought experiments, just as the ancient commerce of ideas afforded a goad and a resource to our predecessors. It allows us, as it allowed them, to see if we have really carried our self-examination and self-critique quite as far as we might.

This book, then, is not simply a celebration of past intellectual achievements but an endeavour to gain insight from philosophical exchanges and the thinking they provoked, as skilled philosophers deeply committed to scriptural monotheism and the life of reason tried to puzzle out viable answers to the larger questions that we humans have to ask ourselves and one another. The seven chapters of the book are case studies of these enquiries.

Our first chapter surveys some of the core philosophical exchanges between Jewish and Islamic thought. Based on papers that I gave at Wayne State University, the University of Haifa, the University of New Mexico, the University of Denver and Vanderbilt University and on an essay of mine that appeared in *Medieval Encounters*, this chapter sounds the book's central theme, the transgenerational, cross-cultural collaboration of Jewish and Muslim philosophers who profited from one another's ideas, arguments and insights in seeking to reconcile the values of their kindred religious traditions with the demands of reason and experience. The three exemplary topics highlighted here regard obligations, self-knowledge and the meaning of history. Taken together they limn the structure of a religious humanism that is the most enduring and valuable product of the collaborations which the balance of the book explores. Thanks are due to Gordon Newby of Emory University, the editor of *Medieval Encounters*, and to Jacob Lassner of Wayne State, Menachem Kellner of the University of Haifa, Seth Ward of the University of Denver, Fred Denny of the University of Colorado, and John Bussanich and Russell Goodman of the University of New Mexico for the stimulating exchanges they opened up with me in connection with this work.

The second chapter, "Rāzī and Epicurus", investigates the ethical, psychological and religious views of the great tenth-century physician and free thinker Muḥammad Ibn Zakariyā' al-Rāzī. It follows up on essays of mine that appeared years ago in *Studia Islamica* and *Philosophical Forum* and in a volume edited by George Hourani and on my more recent article on Rāzī for the *Encyclopedia of Islam*. Rāzī's atomism, his rejection of all prophets as impostors, his democratic ideas about knowledge and education, his theory of pleasure and pain and its use in structuring his distinctive ascetic version of hedonism all echo Epicurean themes in the Islamic environment. Like Rāzī's unusual theory of the "Five Eternals" (God, Soul, Time, Space and Matter), these elements of his philosophy vividly highlight the efforts of a would-be naturalist to acknowledge the transcendent dimensions of value without surrendering religion or philosophy to authorities external to the mind. One philosophical outcome of our investigation is the exposure of some of the peculiar strengths and weaknesses of ethical hedonism that show up clearly in the remarkable synthesis Rāzī makes, with the help of the Galenic writings, between his own version of a Platonic cosmology and his Epicurean ethical thinking. I am indebted to Thérèse Druart of the Catholic University in Washington and to the late Shlomo Pines for their critiques of the early work that is taken up here.

Chapter 3 examines a striking parallel between the thinking of the Jewish pietist Baḥyā ibn Pāqūdā and the philosophy of Immanuel Kant with regard to the problem of free will. Building on an essay of mine that first appeared in the *Journal of the History of Ideas* under the careful editorship of Philip Wiener, this chapter shows how both philosophers, inspired by the pietist agenda – and in particular by the pietist privileging of the practical – relied on skeptical argumentation to dissolve and dismiss the antinomy between freedom and determinism. Again there is a philosophical pay-off, here arising in part from an appreciation of the close complementarity of monotheism with naturalism and in part from a recognition of just how morally fraught are the seemingly disinterested discussions of voluntarism and determinism.

Chapter 4, "Maimonides and the Philosophers of Islam", was originally written for a conference honouring my friend of many years' standing, William Brinner, on his retirement at the University of California, Berkeley. Maimonides grouped the great issues of speculative philosophy under two Talmudic rubrics: the Account of Creation and the Account of the Chariot. These he identified as the problems of physics (that is, philosophical cosmology) and the problems of metaphysics (philosophical theology). The great issues in the first case were the mysteries of the nexus between the Infinite and the finite, the Transcendent and the natural, the Timeless and the temporal. Emblematic of the great questions in the second case was the Rabbinic sensitivity to the strange boldness of the prophet Ezekiel's sensuous description of the divine epiphany he experienced. Gathered under this head were the metaphysical problems of revelation, the confinement of God's infiniteness in modes of expression (the Law, the realm of nature, the language of prophecy) that are apprehensible by finite, human intelligence and, by the same token, incapable of representing adequately what they bespeak. The anthropomorphisms of scriptural language and the particularities of Biblical law are not the only issues brought to light by the disparity between God's infiniteness and the finitude and determinacy of creation. The problem of evil is another. The chapter studies Maimonides' approach to the resolution of the problems of creation and theophany against the background of the work of the Islamic thinkers whose thought informed his powerful efforts toward a resolution of these perennial questions.

From metaphysics we turn to ethical and social philosophy, and in particular to the seemingly familiar terrain of friendship. For Aristotle friendship was a crucial, indeed central philosophical subject, since friendship, generically defined, was the cement that holds together human communities and allows the realisation of our nature as social beings. This chapter follows the evolution of that Aristotelian idea as it was taken up into the humanism of the courtly Persian ethicist Miskawayh, translated into the language of Sufi theory and the conventions of Sufi practice by al-Ghazālī, and synthesised with Biblical and Rabbinic ethical values by Maimonides. Chapter 5, which pursues these developments, began its life as a keynote address at the first meeting of the European Society for Asian Philosophy, chaired by Brian Carr of the University of Nottingham and Indira Mahalingam of the University of Kent. Another version was presented at the Jiminy Peak meeting of the Society for Asian and Comparative Philosophy, where I got helpful feedback from Ben-Ami Scharfstein of the University of Tel Aviv and Walter Watson of the State University of New York at Stony Brook. Speaking on the same topic at Vanderbilt University, I received valuable feedback from Henry Teloh and others who would soon become my colleagues: Jeffrey Tlumak, Robert Ehman, John Post, Donald Sherburne, John Lachs and John Compton. The Jiminy Peak paper was published in *Friendship East and West*, under the editorship of my indefatigable friend Oliver Leaman, who organised the Jiminy Peak panel.

Chapter 6, 'Determinism and freedom in Spinoza, Maimonides and Aristotle", was originally written at the request of the late and much missed Ferdy Schoeman of the University of South Carolina and published in his Cambridge University Press volume *Responsibility, Character and the Emotions*. In the chapter, the three philosophers examined are called to one another's aid, allowing Aristotle to supply the backgrounds and argumentation that Maimonides and Spinoza will take for granted. They in turn help us to see how to complete his argument. These explorations cast special light on the problem of *akrasia* or moral weakness in Aristotle. They also reveal that Spinoza's position on human freedom is not the mass of contradictions that is sometimes laid at his door but an elegant synthesis of determinism with liberty, based on the recognition that we ourselves are among the causes of our own actions and among the chief authors of our own character.

Chapter 7, "Ibn Khaldūn and Thucydides", recasts one of my earliest essays in comparative philosophy, a lengthy paper that I dedicated to John Finley of Harvard and that appeared in the *Journal of the American Oriental Society* at the instance of George Hourani. It examines the philosophies of history developed by two great historians and social thinkers, exploring their commonalities and discovering, in their visions of the meaning of history and the methods of historiography, insights into the human condition that remain as relevant today as they were in the fourteenth century, or fifth century BC. Early comments came from Robert Littman of the University of Hawaii, a friend since 1970, and more recent ones from the formidable analyst of Thucydides' thought Clifford Orwin of the University of Toronto.

Besides all of the friends and scholars mentioned already, I owe special thanks to my student Amani al-Bedah, who read the manuscript of this book more than once and in several stages of its development. Her keen insight and good advice as the argument unfolded contributed qualitatively to my thinking as I worked through the issues with which I had long been grappling. Professors always learn from their students, but it is rare to find a student from whom one can learn so much.

This book is one of the two that I completed in the immediate aftermath of the death of my wife of thirty-one years, Dr Madeleine Goodman, who was lost to me and to the loving community of her friends, colleagues and family in 1996. The other was *Judaism, Human Rights and Human Values* (Oxford University Press, 1998), which was dedicated to her memory. As I write this preface I am embarking on a new journey with my new life's companion, Roberta Walter Goodman, a woman of grace and dignity, profound insight into human character and profound dedication to truth and truthfulness. Her clear-sightedness is a value that the philosophers gathered in this volume would have cherished, as I do. I dedicate this book to her on the occasion of our nuptials.

Nashville *January 1999*

NOTES

1. Abū Umar's report is preserved in al-Ḥumaydī's biographical dictionary (Cairo, 1953). A disciple of the Andalusian polymath Ibn Ḥazm, al-Ḥumaydī (*c.* 1029–95) advocated literalist strict constructionism in Islam. Born in Cordova, he settled in Baghdad and became a key authority on the scholars of the Islamic West.
2. Jaroslav Stetkevych, "The Confluence of Arabic and Hebrew Literature", *Journal of Near Eastern Studies* 32 (1973) p. 216.
3. See, for example, Y. Tzvi Langermann, "Three Singular Treatises from Yemeni Manuscripts", *Bulletin of the School of Oriental and African Studies* 54 (1991) pp. 561–71.

Abbreviations and short titles

Arā'	Al-Fārābī, *K. Mabādi' Arā' Ahlu 'l-Madīnatu 'l-Fāḍila*
B.	Babylonian Talmud
DK	Diels-Kranz, *Fragmente der Vorsokratiker*
DND	Cicero, *De Natura Deorum*
DRN	Lucretius, *De Rerum Natura*
E	Spinoza, *Ethics*
ED	Saadiah Gaon, *Kitāb al-Mukhtār fi 'l-Āmānāt wa-'l-'Iʿtiqādāt (Sefer ha-Nivhar ba-Emunot ve-Deʿot)*
EI_2	*Encyclopedia of Islam* (Leiden: Brill, 2nd ed. 1960–).
Guide	Maimonides, *Guide to the Perplexed*
JHP	*Journal of the History of Philosophy*
JPS	Jewish Publication Society
JQR	*Jewish Quarterly Review*
JTS	Jewish Theological Seminary of America
KD	Epicurus, *Kyriai Doxai*
Kraus	*Al-Rāzī … Opera Philosophica Fragmentaque quae supersunt*, ed. Paul Kraus
MT	Maimonides, *Mishneh Torah*
NE	Aristotle, *Nicomachaean Ethics*
NYU	New York University
PAAJR	*Proceedings of the American Academy for Jewish Research*
SVF	H. F. A. von Arnim, *Stoicorum Veterum Fragmenta*
SUNY	State University of New York
Tahdhīb	Miskawayh, *On the Refinement of Character*
TF	Al-Ghazālī, *Tahāfut al-Falāsifa*
TT	Ibn Rushd, *Tahāfut al-Tahāfut*
TTP	Spinoza, *Tractatus Theologico-Politicus*
VF	Epicurus, *Vatican Fragments*
ZDMG	*Zeitschrift der deutschen Morgenländischen Gesellschaft*

Chapter 1

Crosspollinations

To the Muslim conquerors, scholars used to say, philosophy and its allied sciences appeared at first to be a treasure-house of truth. The intellectual wealth of ancient Greece and Persia and of the Syriac and Hebraic cultures that were folded into the new society of the Islamic empire was now treasured up in the libraries of Muslim princes, warehoused like any other booty. We can still feel Avicenna's elation on entering the Samanid royal library. The books lay piled in cases, with a room for every subject. The philosopher found works he had never seen before – some that in his chequered and too-short life he would never see again. Muslim princes and savants sought manuscripts from Byzantium. Scholars were engaged to translate works on medicine, astrology, statecraft, arithmetic, logic, music, engineering, history, philosophy and poetics. But the value in all these arts was in their use. The heirs learned rapidly that the sciences, like the newly won lands, would lie waste and barren if untended, but yielded fruit if cultivated.

We may suppress a smile when we speak of the treasure-house of truth, as though we knew, and our predecessors did not, that learning is not a store of facts but a way of life, and philosophy not a body of ideas but a path of enquiry. A fashionable scepticism encourages us to discourage students who come seeking wisdom from philosophy. We readily forget that even know-how is information, that culture accumulates ideas, and that the Socratic quest is empty if it has no goal. There is a kind of nihilism in urging self-knowledge and proclaiming the unexamined life not worth living, while almost in the same breath announcing that the point of examining our lives is the examination itself and insisting that no one has an inkling of what it is that self-knowledge knows. The straightforward pragmatism and realism of the ancient quest for truth and understanding are in a way more wholesome and surely far more honest than such a bait and switch. Philosophy, Aristotle said, begins in wonder (*Metaphysics* I 2,

982b 12). But he also insisted that it does not end in wonder but in understanding (*Metaphysics* I 2, 983a 14; *De Anima* I 3, 407a 22–30). Medieval thinkers knew that truth was what they wanted, and they had some sound markers by which truth could be identified – tests of logic and conformance to experience, but also the coherence of ideas in a system and consilience of new ideas with the great themes of a tradition. Critical in gauging the worth of an idea was its power to answer questions and settle issues, to reconcile values seemingly in conflict and to resolve apparent paradoxes.

So wisdom remained a category in the Middle East long after the capital in the treasure-house of truth had been put out at interest and brought home rich returns that doubled and redoubled its worth. Since traditions were cumulative, the latter-day thinkers – the moderns, as they called themselves, *muta'akhirūn* – made it part of their task not only to explicate but to rescue the insights of their predecessors, to synthesise, rationalise and reconcile what they found, if it was the work of exponents of the truth, *muḥaqqiqūn*. The filiation of Islam to Biblical Judaism helped. Islam was conceived as carrying on what Judaism and Christianity had begun. The old fictions that portrayed Greek wisdom as discipleship of the ancient Jewish prophets[1] were used to naturalise philosophic insights as an ancient heritage reclaimed. The protean medium of *ḥadīth* set almost no limit to what could be brought into the house of Islam under the broad cloak of the Prophet.

The problematics guiding the demand for Greek, Persian or Aramaic thought ensured that what was taken up would chime with the great issues of Hebraic thought as well. Not that all would agree in conclusions or even in underlying assumptions. There was no restriction to "one's own paradigm". But clearly all that was conned over, translated and studied was germane. Kindred issues would be debated and old disputes continued in new languages. So when the tradition came full circle and Jewish thinkers fell heir to the works of Muslim thinkers, not by right of conquest but by an intellectual eminent domain, taking up into a new and highly structured Jewish philosophy the ideas of the philosophers – and indeed the pietists, mystics, jurists, and grammarians – of Islam, what the Jewish scholars found was nothing foreign, but theories genuinely useful in addressing Jewish problematics. For the ideas were rooted in Biblical categories. But now the theses were sharpened by Greek analysis, rendered vivid by Greek imagery, and carried to a high pitch of rigour by the dialectic and love of synthesis and dogged hatred for fudging explanations that mark al-Fārābī's and Ibn Sīnā's readings of the Greeks.[2]

Among the Truths that passed in this fashion from Biblical and Qur'anic scripture and Greek philosophical dialogues, treatises, and commentaries, to Muslim and Jewish philosophers, consider three theses that I will express for the moment in rather neutral and generic language:

1. The seemingly ineffable content of religious experience can be articulated through symbols and so made a social reality, as imagery, ritual, myth and law.
2. To know God we must study the world. Since man is made in the image of God, one can learn about God by studying humanity.
3. God executes justice in history by visiting upon us the consequences of our actions, communally and individually.

These are Biblical theses – or would be if the Torah spoke in theses rather than tableaux, vignettes, narratives and norms. They are also theses of Plato, taken up and rendered more conceptual and less mythic in articulation by Aristotle's way of translating Plato's poetry into prose. They are preserved and deepened in the Neoplatonic synthesis of Aristotelian and Platonic thinking that channels the mainstream of medieval Jewish, Christian, and Islamic thought. This book is about comparative philosophy and the long-standing, often continuing dialogue that eddies around such themes as these. In this first chapter I propose to survey the curious collaboration, surmounting confessional, linguistic and temporal barriers, that allowed these bold claims to be philosophically articulated and tested in the crossfire of dialectic to make them progressively more critical. The *Qur'ān* mediates here between the Torah and *kalām* (Arabic dialectical theology). The work of the *falāsifa*, the Greek-inspired philosophers of Islam, similarly mediates between *kalām* and the Jewish philosophers. The play is from Tinker to Evers to Chance. But the ball returns to Tinker with a new conceptual speed and spin.

— 1. HEARING GOD'S VOICE IN WORDS —

The Torah candidly reveals the legislative and cosmological innocence of its founding figures. For the Patriarchs, encounters with the divine (*elohim*) were fleeting visits of seeming mortals bearing news or blessings, promises or warnings, a challenge to wrestle or a chance to offer hospitality. Even for Moses, the message of liberation came wrapped in the old panoply of signs, and the idea of law (*torah*) was at first not far removed from that of teaching or of guidance. The Israelite line of march was directly marked by God: "At God's command they camped and at God's command moved on" (Exodus 9:15–23). Judicial cases awaited oracular determination, until Jethro, Moses' Midianite father-in-law, taught him to let the general decision govern the particular: "Thou wilt surely be exhausted, thou and this people ... Do thou teach them the rules and principles (*et ha-ḥukkim ve-et ha-torot*) ... let them bring every great matter unto thee, but every small matter let *them* judge. Lighten thy load and let them bear it with thee!" (Exodus 18). The great matters are those that involve principles not yet settled. The small are already determined in principle by a prior ruling. Thus the Torah's characteristically graphic narrative schematises the emergence of legal doctrines out of case law and legitimates the use of legal deduction. The revelation of the Ten Commandments follows directly. The legislation comes from God, but the idea of legislation is made accessible by Jethro, the priest of Midian. Without the new-found understanding of the idea of law, God's ten points (*dibrot*) would have been all but unintelligible. The fleeting encounters of humans with the divine lengthen into a sustained, conversation whose subject is the mores and the life of Israel and whose fabric is the panoply of Israel's history.

Mystics, understandably, often hedge their encounters with the absolute in the language of ineffability. But Moses finds a voice in those encounters, and what he hears is normative, for norms are what he needs to know:

> See, Thou sayest to me "Lead this people forward", but Thou hast not made known to me whom Thou wilt send with me. Thou hast said, "I have recognised thee by name, and thou hast found favour in My eyes". Now if indeed I have found favour in Thine eyes, pray make known to me Thy ways, that I may know Thee and continue in Thy favour. And consider that this is Thy people. (Exodus 33:12)[3]

In response, God promises to lighten Moses' burden; and again the Ten Commandments are revealed, engraved in stone, replacing the broken tablets, but now inscribed by Moses (Exodus 34:28), not by God like the lost originals (Exodus 31:18). God's revelation is no mere epiphany but a law for the life of human beings. It accommodates human weakness and inadequacy, just as nature itself, after the Flood, no longer rises up in ire at every human failing (Genesis 8:21).

The cosmology and the historic lore of the Mosaic Torah become a backdrop to the law. Each element has its prescriptive relevance: the genealogies and legacies of the nations ground their rights and define the ethos that binds their destinies. The account of creation gives the Sabbath a cosmological meaning, making this memorial of the liberation from Egypt a universal symbol of the goodness of creation. The story of Adam and Eve situates the primal relations between humanity and nature, and between woman and man ("therefore shall a man leave his father and his mother's house and cleave unto his wife, and they shall be one flesh", Genesis 2:24, showing that men and women are not alien to one another, but, *pace* the misogynists of every age, Eve is Adam's "helpmeet", Genesis 2:20). The accounts of the Patriarchs mark an ongoing trajectory of spiritual awareness that imbues the ethnic identity of Israel with a clear sense of mission.[4]

We may sometimes wonder when it is in Biblical usage that the Hebrew word *devarim* denotes words and when it means "things". But the ambiguity is instructive. Events, divine commands, even charges and accusations are Biblically conceived as discrete items. For the original audience of the Torah, what was critical was the articulacy of Mosaic revelation, overcoming the obscurity that so marks religious experience that specialists have made a dogma of the ineffability of mystical encounters and fused the numinous and even the noumenal with the nebulous and obscure.[5] As Maimonides observes (*Guide* I 54), Moses got more than he bargained for. He did not see God's face, but he did learn God's ways. Specifically, he learned how to govern the people in accordance with the demands made upon their natures by divine perfection itself. So what issued from Moses' encounter with God was no mere paean of ecstasy but words/items, the concrete specifications of a way of life: "These are the words that Moses spoke to all Israel beyond the Jordan" (Deuteronomy 1:1).[6] A foolish lover utters vapid praise, idle promises, cries of rapture, but nature makes a living child.

Maimonides charts the growth of human awareness against the categories of Neoplatonic metaphysics: "A person may receive of this emanation sufficient for his own development alone; or he may receive beyond what his perfection requires, sufficient for that of others" (*Guide* II 37). Adam, after the exile that symbolises the human condition, must judge, like any animal, by his wants and needs, cut off from God's immediate direction (*Guide* I 2; Maimonides, "Eight Chapters", 8). Noah receives promptings and premonitions. The Judges, like Moses before his call, are spurred to generous actions. David, as a poet, like the author of Job, is inspired to articulate a vision of the truth. But a higher inspiration integrates words, dreams or visions into ordered meanings. The ultimately integrated message is legislative: not personal but universal, not mediated by visual symbols but conditioned only by the limits of human reason (*Guide* II 45; Maimonides, "Eight Chapters", 7).

Anyone who is enlightened hopes naturally to share and diffuse what is received. But the intellectual clarity needed to grasp a vision firmly and the imagination needed to articulate it socially are rare gifts. Abraham may have followers, but Moses gives laws to a nation. Jacob may wrestle with an angel – at least in the inwardness of his prophetic consciousness (*Guide* II 42), but only Moses "speaks face to face with God". What they speak about is law, a law showing how human finitude can partake of divine perfection

(*Guide* I 53, II 38, 40, 42, 45, III 13). For what Moses learned in his epiphany was the natural law, which the Torah calls the laws of life. It was in its grasp of human nature, human requirements and deserts, that the Biblical law found the worldly tether to its free-floating evocation of the call made upon all beings by their affinity to the transcendent perfection of the divine.

The progression from private spirituality to the practical and indeed political is paralleled in the careers of Socrates, Plato, and Aristotle. Socrates' meditative piety is linked with his moral insight. His self-discovery comes hand in hand with the inner promptings that warn him against unjust actions and teach him which acts he cannot learn to do. Plato divined here an implicit and unacquired knowledge in Socrates that seemed to hold up before the inner eye of reason a canon of pure and absolute value, the Good itself. The sun that Socrates saluted at the close of his contemplations was its mere ensign. It was a pure insight into the Good itself that guided not only this good man's practical choices but also his seemingly instinctual plunging for the jugular in dialectic, his uncanny grace in dancing around an argument or cutting it keenly at the joints. The Good was not only Right and Beauty, it was Truth, and God. When dialectic cleared a path for intuition, the mind's eye could clearly see not only what was wrong about an action or an argument, but also what was the most human and the most divine way of life. Plato's imaginative articulation of a law that sketched that life was only a matter of linking dialectic to the pure intuition of reason – and giving poetic imagination its philosophic head.

It was Aristotle who named most clearly and explicitly what Plato had discovered in searching for the motive and the means of Socratic courage, honesty, and decisiveness, even in facing death – the inner strength that was the practical expression of the Socratic insight. The word was *ethos*, character. Ethos gave the answer to three of the questions that Socrates professed to ponder all his life: Are the virtues one or many? Can virtue be taught? Does anyone ever knowingly do evil? The virtues are distinct, yet interconnected. For modesty is not justice, and wisdom is not generosity; but piety cannot be hare-brained, and courage cannot be stupid. The virtues are not a unity, but they stem from a unity, in the apprehension that leads us to pure goodness; and they promote a further unity, by integrating our identity as individuals and as communities. So the virtues are linked not merely by similarity or kindred structure but as parts of a larger whole whose adequate functioning depends on their collaboration, and whose collaboration depends on reason. That is, the virtues promote the expression of our humanity. Consciousness is the key to their coordination. For only reason can judge itself and all other things.

Virtue can be taught and learned, but not by precept. The clever formulae of sophists are mere words, and sage proverbs are not much better. There is no rote or recipe for what is always right and fitting, and even having such a recipe would be no promise of its use. Virtue is a form of insight but not mere neutral knowledge. It is the spontaneously reliable insight of those who truly see their interest in terms of goodness. They do not, like Thrasymachus, have a sophisticated idea of power paralysed or addled by a primitive or infantile idea of interest. And they live by what they know, rather than continuously failing to live up to what they believe. Thus those who truly know the Good will choose nothing less. For their actions spring from knowledge, not mere opinion; and their knowledge is the very identity out of which they act, not some separate, isolated thing, kept in the closet of conscience, to be glanced at warily on rare occasions. It is the active core of an ethos and identity, the essence of who the virtuous are.

Virtue is a habit engrained by exercise. The practice of apt acts and considered choices fosters a disposition to choose thoughtfully, reliably and well, by second nature, to use Aristotle's own metaphor for habit. Virtue has its own canon of measurement in weighing pleasures and pains; and it is learned through pleasures and pains – not by mere external association but by discovery of the inner pleasure intrinsic in wise and noble actions and by sensing the pain inherent and consequential in thoughtless acts. It is not conditioned, not in Pavlov's sense. For virtue is always thoughtful, a habit of acting thoughtfully, as reason would direct. It is never a reflex. But the habit is learned, as music or language, or any art is learned. Its teachers, as Plato saw, are parents, peers and institutions. The character of a society reflects and perpetuates the character of its members; it even teaches, beyond the immediate demands of nature, what experiences are worthy to be found pleasurable, and what we shall deem painful, shameful, even loathsome, or revolting. The critical function of the state, then, as the organ of society in pursuit of the good life, is not ultimately the regulation of behaviour but the education of character, from which alone wise and thoughtful choices will reliably emerge.

What al-Fārābī contributes here is the recognition of prophetically mediated law as the very institution Plato had called for when he took the social ethos out of the hands of those who were poets alone and passed it to the philosophers. When the mind is perfected, al-Fārābī writes, that is, when the speculative and the practical are informed by the pure ideas shed upon nature by the hypostatic Active Intellect, then the mind can attain the insight of a prophet:

> This is the man who understands every act conducive to human wellbeing. That is the prime requisite in a leader. Beyond this, he must have the linguistic facility to convey vividly to the imagination all that he knows and the capacity to lead men to their own wellbeing and to the actions by which that wellbeing is attained. (*Arā'*, 245)

The intellectual insight by which a prophet founds a polity is a specification of the general idea of the Good as applied to human nature. But the human virtues themselves must be specified further, into concrete acts productive of specific habits. Laying out institutions that work successfully at so concrete a level demands imagination.

The same is true in conveying ideas. From many a practical standpoint, as Plato saw, sound opinions are as good as knowledge, and far more accessible to those who cannot rise to higher order concepts.[7] What the prophet/philosopher/king knows are the "Principles behind the Beliefs" that will guide the people of an outstanding society. But to convey those principles to an entire nation is impossible without imagination, to translate metaphysical abstractions into symbols. It is here, in the Platonic task of portraying the truth through myth and symbol, instilling beliefs to guide thought non-conceptually, that the poets are reinstated, not on the pretext that the passions bespeak a higher truth than reason knows but on the premise that ritual and symbol can bind allegiance to ideas whose names are too abstruse to be heard as commands by any but the very few.

Imagination brings the philosopher back to the cave, to paint upon its walls images that will allow its denizens to live well, even if they never fly up through the smoke-hole into the clear night air and see moonlit objects, their own reflections in the water, or the image of the daylight sun that the philosopher sees when he floats free. As Richard Walzer was fond of saying, what Avicenna forges here, with his characteristic instinct for the synthesis of Semitic and Hellenic themes, is the idea of the *'aql qudsī*, the sacred intelligence – an idea in which the highest values of two cultures are fused. If we may state the content of these two constituents of Avicenna's synthesis, we have here the Hebraic ideal of holiness as transcendence and the Greek ideal of reason as insight into genuine value. Human intelligence, al-Fārābī writes, can grow so powerful as to intuit pure ideas, without hints or cues, and so without instruction. Such receptivity is the mark of what must be called a sacred intellect, whose rare capacity and openness to the ideas on which reality itself is built allows those ideas to spill over into the imagination and take shape as visions or words. What makes this rare form of reason sacred is its contact with the divine. But its mission is the prophetic one described by al-Fārābī. For here, Avicenna says, we find the highest form of prophecy, the highest reach of human capacity.[8] Maimonides applies the same model to the work of Moses.

Because human interests, abilities, strengths and weaknesses are so diverse, Maimonides reasons, we need divine inspiration to guide us to the highest kind of life. "One man may be so hard that if angry enough he would slaughter his youngest son; another is so softhearted he feels compassion if a bug or other vermin is killed" (*Guide* II 40). "There are people who advance boldly upon a lion while others cower from a mouse, some who go forward against an army and do battle with it, while others quake with fear if a woman shouts at them" (*Guide* II 38). Similarly, just as Ibn Sīnā says, people vary widely in sensitivity and intuitive insight (*Guide* II 38). A prophet can see how the diverse needs and demands of human beings can be met optimally.[9] If politics were simply a matter of providing for human subsistence, or even of optimising our material well-being, then, as al-Fārābī showed,[10] mere cleverness at matching means to ends would suffice for the founding and direction of a state. But if a polity is to foster moral and intellectual perfection, a higher insight is required (*Guide* I 46), to integrate diverse kinds of goods, coordinate and subordinate, choosing among ends as well as means. It is here that prophetic insight becomes essential.[11]

Maimonides shares with al-Fārābī Plato's view that we cannot reconcile and rank disparate goods by finding a lowest common denominator. For such an approach makes all goods commensurate in common coin and (as Kant explains) puts a price on everything and finds real worth in nothing. Rather, we must appeal to a highest good as the standard of all lesser goods, not cheapening or denaturing any to render them commensurate with the rest but ordering all values by reference to the transcendent. It is for this reason that access to the divine becomes a requisite of law for monotheists – not that God decrees norms arbitrarily, but because the very nature of norms, if taken seriously, requires that they not be reduced to some mere empiric good or goal.

The higher aim that all sound values presuppose, Maimonides argues, is the goal of the Torah. It is voiced in the commandment of *imitatio Dei*: "You shall be holy, for I the Lord thy God am Holy" (Leviticus 19:2). Many have thought it futile to attempt to specify, let alone pursue divine transcendence. But in affirming that man is created in the image and likeness of God, Genesis (1:26) assures us that the goal is not beyond our reach. The likeness, Maimonides argues (*Guide* I 1), lies in the divine intelligence within us. The commandment to become like God, then, charges us to perfect our humanity, not to abandon it:

> The height of human virtue is to become like Him, to the extent that this is possible – imitating His acts in our own, as the Sages made clear in commenting on "You shall be holy". They glossed: as He is gracious, so do you be gracious; as He is compassionate, so do you be compassionate.[12]

By echoing Plato's words (*Theaetetus* 176) that the task of man is "to become as like to God *as we can*", Maimonides at a stroke dissolves the worry that our task is to leave our humanity behind, overcomes the seeming lack of specificity in the counsels of perfection, and cuts away from the other-worldly slant that Plato himself gives to the inference when he treats it (loc. cit.) as equivalent to saying "we should make all speed to take flight from this world to the other".

God's glory, Maimonides argues (*Guide* III 13), is in making all things for their own sakes, to pursue their own perfection. Man's perfection is apprehended in an adequate understanding of human nature, which prophetic insight grasps perfectly. We reach for the perfection that is God's by discovering and developing in ourselves the virtues disclosed to us in the experience of human action and potential. Vices, whether moral or intellectual, are the real barriers to understanding of the kind that Plato and al-Fārābī saw is needed in pursuing human fulfilment. Foolishness, witlessness and stupidity, then, are not the only obstacles to spiritual insight. So are excessive sensuality, wrathfulness, arrogance, impudence, greed and self-indulgence. When the Sages say, "Prophecy falls only on the wise, the rich and the brave" (*Nedarim* 38a), they are making the same point that Plato does in deriving justice from the interaction of the other cardinal virtues – courage, wisdom and sophrosyne. For what the Sages are saying is that the prophet must combine the moral virtues of contentment and courage, including poetic courage (*Guide* I 46, glossing Genesis Rabbah 27), with the intellectual virtues of insight and clarity of vision. "It is not improbable that a few moral deficiencies diminish the level of prophecy. For we find that certain character faults like proneness to anger prevent it altogether." But in Moses, "only one barrier remained between him and the apprehension of God as He really is, the transparent barrier of human reason, from which he could not separate himself" (Maimonides, "Eight Chapters", 7). We know the adequacy of the vision granted Moses from the adequacy of the Mosaic Law in integrating the goods that together make for the perfection of human life. For that integration depends on reference to the Highest Good, made relevant in human terms.

Maimonides draws, then, on Ibn Sīnā and on Plato in conceptualising what he calls the highest form of prophecy, just as he draws on al-Fārābī's Platonic account in conceptualising prophecy at large. From al-Fārābī he adopts the idea that a prophet is a person of philosophic insight into the ultimate realities (which are, Platonically, identical with the ultimate values) and endowed with the imaginative capability of translating those insights into institutions – specifically, laws, rituals, symbols and beliefs. Just as Maimonides relies on Plato's epistemology of the Divided Line for the assumption that beliefs are more accessible to those who think in sensuous images than are the pure concepts of the philosopher, so he relies on Avicenna's proof that imagination (in order to display images to the consciousness) must be an embodied faculty.[13] For he uses that assumption in his celebrated argument that certain individuals might have all the intellectual capacities of philosophers yet lack the requisite matter (imagination, cultural/linguistic basis) to become prophets.[14] And just as Maimonides uses Plato's "in so far as possible" to humanise the Platonic and Biblical obligation of *imitatio Dei* and rein in its penchant for excess ("Eight Chapters", 5), so he moderates Ibn Sīnā's intellectualism with the recognition that the moral virtues are critical in the perfection of the intellectual. He insists that we direct all our strengths toward the attainment of a single goal (loc. cit.), identifiable as the goal subtended by the transcendent reach of the mind of which Ibn Sīnā spoke. But he does not urge that we sacrifice our moral strengths to that intellectual goal. Rather, the organicity of his account is a reminder of how crucial the moral virtues remain in reaching and sustaining our intellectual goal. Thus Maimonides' intellectualism is integrative rather than exclusive. It is founded on the recognition that reason finds its métier not just at the contemplative summit of the good life but in every practical, moral, and social step that advances toward that goal.

The most visible impact of the Greek materials on Islamic and Jewish ethics is in the construal of divinely imposed obligations as not as a command ethics but as a virtue ethics. Plato's method of analysis shows how an entire system of legal obligations and social roles can display a single underlying theme or purpose, as when Clinias in the *Laws* (I 625d) infers that Cretan institutions, "have all been made with a military purpose; and it is warfare, if I am to speak my own conviction, which our lawgiver kept in view in all his dispositions". Plato himself, in a broader but comparable sense, sees an educational impact in all laws and cultural institutions. Al-Fārābī follows Plato in treating beliefs as the vehicles of that education. And al-Ghazālī closely follows the Hellenising philosopher-courtier Miskawayh in regarding Islamic law from the standpoint of the virtues it inculcates rather than merely in terms of the Ash'arite notion of the sheer positivity and utter irrefragability of the commands of God as our sovereign Lord. Even when Miskawayh's reading becomes too secular or courtly for his taste and al-Ghazālī strays from Miskawayh's text, it is to follow Ibn Sīnā or al-Fārābī, or perhaps some Sufi theme, but still in the mode of discovering the human virtues, now construed on a pietist or ascetic model.[15] The Platonic assumption, made explicit by Aristotle, remains foundational, that when the Law commands an act it is not merely for the sake of the command or even for the sake of the act but for what such actions and their like will make of us.

Maimonides emphatically agrees and takes to task those who "regard the giving of grounds for any of the laws as something dreadful". He may have Muslim Ash'arites as well as Jewish legal positivists in mind. For he calls the advocates of such views "some among mankind" rather than "some among us". His argument against them is dialectical, but terse and devastating: they deny the goodness that the Law claims for itself (Deuteronomy 6:24) and in effect make God's actions vain, idle or futile (*Guide* III 26, 31). Maimonides himself classifies all the commandments of the Law by the goods they serve (*Guide* III 35). This is an inductive exercise modelled on the method of the Arab grammarians, as developed into a powerful tool of Biblical theology by Saadiah. Out of this method emerge Maimonides' three great works of jurisprudence: *The Book of the Commandments*, the Mishnah Commentary, and the *Mishneh Torah*. The thesis that arises in turn from his exhaustive research is that all the laws serve to organise and stabilise human life, to refine human character in accordance with the human virtues, or to awaken us intellectually. That is, all the laws serve to establish the good life, but their principal means of doing so is that spelled out by Plato, of cultivating the virtues. The moral virtues serve the interests of a stable and secure society in a direct, material way. But they are also ends in themselves, constituents in our higher task of perfecting our humanity. True beliefs and the rituals and symbols that sustain such beliefs again serve the material interests of the good society. But they also lead to higher insights and to the pinnacle of human activity, the contemplation of God and His work in nature, which consummate the fulfilment of our humanity (*Guide* II 36). The scheme is Aristotelian, and ultimately Platonic: virtuous activities root and strengthen virtue in our character. Activity in accordance with the moral and intellectual virtues *is* the good life, variously called happiness, fulfilment, or felicity.

Some may feel uncomfortable at the thought that the Torah is a means to happiness rather than an end in itself. Some may voice surprise at Maimonides' boldness in following a Muslim precedent to treat the *mitzvot* of God as serving a higher end than their mere performance, namely the perfection of man and of human life. But it is only by understanding the good that the *mitzvot* serve that we can appreciate their wisdom (*Guide* III 26, 31), let alone attempt to interpret or apply them. And Maimonides would adamantly deny projecting any external values on to the Torah or subordinating a Hebrew revelation to an alien Greek conception. On the contrary, the Greek method allows us to articulate all the more clearly the inner intention and theme of the Mosaic Law, making explicit those conceptual terms that were too abstract to be voiced (let alone speculatively developed) in the immediate symbolic idiom of the lawgiver.

There is in fact a virtue ethics in the Torah, or Maimonides' reading would be mendacious rather than synthetic. Holiness is set forth as the aim served by the *mitzvot*, and even by justice and love. Yet the command ethics of the Torah is never merely sublated in virtue ethics. The *mitzvot* are ordained not simply for what they will make us but also for the life they will enable us to lead, the life of the *mitzvot*. Those who argue that the Torah offers no reasons for its commands shamelessly ignore the Biblical characterisation of the life of the Law as a life of blessedness, harmony and peace. They ignore the Mosaic fusion of blessing and obligation.[16] And they miss the appeal of the Law to over-arching goals like the ones expressed in the precept "Ye shall be holy, for I the Lord your God am holy", or in the prophetic promise that Israel will become a blessing to the nations (Genesis 22:18), "a kingdom of priests and a holy nation" (Exodus 19:6).

What Maimonides derives from the *falāsifa* in the present case is the explicit concept of virtue as a means to an end, the conception of that end as a congeries of actions that together constitute the good life, and the articulated model by which ordinances are conceived as means to habituating virtue. All of these ideas are implicit in the Torah. And they are voiced symbolically – paradigmatically, in the scriptural image of an ethos as the ways or practices that can sanctify a people or pollute a land.[17] The value of the explicitness becomes clear when we reflect that even today readers, including specialists who have lost touch with the intensionalities of the Biblical idiom, fail to see such ideas as these, or deny their presence, in scripture. Maimonides needs to make explicit the thematic structure and purposive intent of the Law in response to a legal positivism that abstracts the commandments from their moral context. Philosophy must defend and re-establish the integration of act, virtue and outcome that is unquestioned in the Torah.

From our present standpoint, three dichotomies often foisted on Maimonides in contemporary discussion can be fairly but summarily dismissed. The first is the false dichotomy between reason and revelation. For in the Platonic scheme that Maimonides adopts, as interpreted and developed by al-Fārābī, Ibn Sīnā, and himself, revelation is not the disjunct but the summit of reason. Reason is no mere formal schema but a content-bearing intuition. Its Aristotelian object is the middle or causal term that bears a principle of explanation. Its highest content is the highest or Ultimate Explanation, the universal Good, God Himself. There is no secular science here. For the realm of the sacred has not been isolated from cosmology, anthropology or psychology. Ethics itself rests on all of these.[18]

Thus, secondly, we can and should dismiss the chauvinistic dichotomy between the exotic and the home-born. Ethno-centric scholars take umbrage at the discovery of echoes and affinities. Some read borrowings as distortions of some pristine and untranslatable *Rassengeist* or *Urbegriff*. They take comparisons, let alone intellectual alliances or dependencies, as impugning the very integrity of an admired source. Italian scholars pilloried the great Miguel Asín Palacios for discovering not only foreign but indeed Moorish ancestry in the iconography of Dante,[19] and Hellenists still balk at the creativity that gave us the Winged Victory of Samothrace and the philosophies of the Stoics and Epicureans – for getting the true "message" of Greek culture wrong! But no culture has just one message,[20] and no thesis is the property of just one culture. Philosophers of the calibre of al-Fārābī, Ibn Sīnā and Maimonides will follow the advice of al-Kindī and take truth where they find it.[21] Nothing that answers to the demands of reason will seem alien to them. In the present case, the ground was prepared by Biblical thought itself. What the Greek and Islamic thinkers did was to aid in explaining the possibility and the content of prophecy. The ideas were no less relevant or useful for their passing through a diversity of minds and cultures that confronted comparable problems.

Thirdly, I think that in the present instance we can afford to dismiss the esoteric/exoteric dichotomy. The idea has its uses, especially in grasping the implications of an author's expectation that a whole corpus will be studied before any given part of it is well understood. Scripture and law were studied and taught on such an understanding throughout the Middle Ages by Jews, Muslims and Christians alike. And the same assumption was made, quite rightly, about the works of Aristotle, where the esoteric/exoteric distinction finds its most proper use.[22] So the idea is by no means irrelevant in reading authors like al-Fārābī, Ibn Sīnā and Maimonides, who were Aristotelians and, each in his own way, scriptural exegetes and jurists as well. But the notion of the esoteric has been overworked in the jejune and loaded expectations of scholars who see, behind every argument whose premise they cannot share or whose problematic they cannot grasp, a seething if silent resentment against the very thesis that is (often rather ably) defended.

The Maimonidean model of prophecy as intellectual insight brought back to earth by imagination and kept disciplined and honest by the full range of moral virtues is not to be dismissed as insincere because of its Neoplatonising naturalism, any more than it is to be dismissed as inauthentic because it is not home-grown. We have seen enough (and so had our forebears) of intellectual dishonesty to recognise the pertinence of moral virtues in intellectual endeavour. And we know enough about the need for schematism to understand the relevance of imagination even to the purest speculation. Many post-Kantian thinkers deny rational intuition and reduce conceptual thinking to the work of the imagination, if not still further, to the manipulation of symbols. But even without accepting the premises or conclusions of that metaphysical programme, the relevance of images to whatever it is that does the work of thinking is hardly to be denied.[23]

The Maimonidean/Farabian account of insight and inspiration takes its stand between Aristotle's regrouping detachment of troops (*Posterior Analytics* II 19) and James' channelling of a stream of thought out of a "blooming, buzzing confusion". It is a serious and profound attempt to make conceptual sense of what al-Fārābī called higher-order thinking. It is no reduction of prophecy to some familiar and sordid category, preparatory to dismissing or diminishing the authority of scripture, but an honest effort to understand how the Transcendent can be apprehended in terms applicable to our practical and spiritual, indeed imaginative, lives without thereby losing its transcendence. The explanation offered is not reductive at all, although it does place prophecy in a larger epistemic context. Indeed it is not naturalistic in the mechanistic sense, although it does examine prophecy in terms of the human faculties that make receptivity to higher ideas possible. For all of this is done in a Neoplatonic context where abstract ideas themselves are clearly taken to be inaccessible without higher inspiration[24] and where nature is seen to derive its form, which is the very being of things, from a source grounded in the divine. Maimonides' aim is not to diminish but to render intelligible the objects of the Law, just as al-Fārābī and Ibn Sīnā seek to render intelligible the scriptures they inherit. For without such intelligibility one would not understand one's religion well enough even to know whether one was meant to follow or to flout the dictates of the Law.

— 2. "He who knows himself knows his Lord" —

In all three of the monotheistic sister faiths – Islam, Christianity and Judaism – we know our obligations and the nature of the good life as the will of God, specified in Revelation and interpreted in tradition. We know God as the ideal of perfection; we know perfection, as relevant to our obligations, through human nature. What prevents the scheme from collapsing into circularity is our intuitive, Platonic knowledge of the Good Itself, our scientific knowledge of nature, and the junction of the two in our knowledge of the self. As Alexander Altmann showed, monotheists recast the Delphic maxim, "know thyself" into a powerful epistemic tool. The ancient meaning of the motto inscribed at the Pythian oracle of Apollo, was a warning to acknowledge our mortality, to know that we are human, not divine.[25] The same message underlies the ancient Oedipus tragedy: that man, in seeking to escape his destiny, is ignorant of all that mortality portends, and so, despite his seeming understanding, is ignorant of the most elementary fact about himself, graphically represented in the riddle of the Sphinx, that man grows old and dies. Philo preserves this sense, and so does an interjection in the twelfth-century kabbalistic text *Ma'ayan Ganim* by Samuel ben Nissim Masnūt.[26] But for Plato and his successors the Delphic maxim formed the clew to an elaborately woven tissue of glosses and conceits that philosophers cast at higher game.

Ibn Sīnā finds in the maxim an invitation to profound self-scrutiny. The motto, he says, is shared by philosophers and saints – scientists and mystics alike. For it was passed down among the ancients in one of their temples,[27] but it had also entered Islamic tradition as the saying: "He who knows himself knows his Lord". By Avicenna's time it had become a favorite *ḥadīth* of "intoxicated" – i.e. pantheistic[28] – Sufis, for its suggestion of the soul's identity with God. But philosophers and theologians of more sober stamp shied away from the idea that the inner self is divine, preferring another Platonic suggestion, that the mind knows God through an inner likeness.[29] Ibn Sīnā understood this likeness in terms of the realisation of the human intellect, its perfection as an intellect through assimilation to and contact with the hypostatic Active Intellect. It is through such contact that we know the forms of things, i.e. know things as they really are, as God knows them; and it is through such assimilation that we know God. For God is the cynosure of the Active Intellect. As Philip Merlan shows, Alexander of Aphrodisias laid the groundwork for the theory when he argued, in a Peripatetic, intellectualist gloss of Plato's *homoiosis theo*, that man's "material intelligence" is like the unwrittenness of a slate; when it is transformed into active intelligence it achieves a likening to the divine.[30]

The idea of intellectual contact with the divine does suggest not merely a likeness but an identity between man and God. For matter is the Aristotelian principle of individuation: no membrane remains to divide a disembodied soul from its source. The mind for Aristotle *is* what it knows, so to know God seems tantamount to *being* God. Describing the state of the fulfilled human intelligence on such a model, Merlan writes:

> In lieu of the cloud of unknowing, we have in rationalistic mysticism the flood of sheer light ... absolute transparency ... self-knowledge. In an ordinary act of knowledge the object of knowledge is something opaque which knowledge illuminates and makes visible. But in the ecstatic act of knowledge nothing opaque is left, because what is known is identical with what knows ... Omniscience is the ultimate goal ... to know god and to possess divine omniscience coincide ... Aristotle meant literally what he said: there is a kind of knowledge which is in some way all-comprehensive. God possesses it – man should try to acquire it ... Man desires and is able to divinize himself.[31]

Plato's playful references to Empedocles' associative model of the knowing of like by like here become the foreplay to perfect mystic union. But that consummation is not devoutly wished by every exponent of the tradition. Where pagan thought could freely speak of the indwelling of a god or of union with some divine being, strict monotheism must rely on Neoplatonic hypostases that are nothing apart from God, yet are not simply identical with God, if anything is to be distinguished from the Absolute. The preservation of individuality is critical for Neoplatonic metaphysics, if the world is not to collapse into the undifferentiated monism of Parmenides. And the preservation of human individuality is critical to Ibn Sīnā, lest personal immortality collapse into the all-encompassing unity of the Godhead.

Avicenna recognises and values the access to divinity and the forms of all things that the Neoplatonic theory of assimilation to God affords. But by preserving the subject–object distinction he reaps a benefit of rational mysticism that might not have been expected, preserving the individuality of the disembodied soul and protecting his Neoplatonism from a pantheistic reduction. Ibn Sīnā shares al-Fārābī's thought that through contact with the Active Intellect we know (to the extent that this is humanly possible) as God does and thus know God and indeed all things. On Platonic principles it is possible to know anything scientifically only if one knows as God does. But it is crucial for Ibn Sīnā to preserve individual identity as the locus of this knowledge. The immortality of assimilation would come at too high a price if it meant loss of the very identity that is to enjoy the beatific state. Innocent of Stace's dogma of the ineffable and oceanic character of all ecstatic experience, Ibn Sīnā preserves the rational mind even (or especially!) in the height of ecstasy, securing consciousness against an emotive identification of its finitude with God's infinitude and ensuring the continuum between knowing all things in their specificity and knowing God. For without that continuum, mystic experience is made to foster the illusion of the absoluteness of the merely contingent I, and the promised omniscience is evacuated of all concrete content, as the objects of knowledge (and of God's creation) that brought us before the divine throne vanish into nullity.

It was the schematism of the Active Intellect that allowed Ibn Sīnā to frame the logic behind the inference "he who knows himself knows his Lord".[32] To render that inference cogent, articulate its terms and discover their logical relations was an achievement that all reflective monotheists could cherish in their intellectual treasure-houses, precisely because Avicenna set aside the potential for pantheism in the Socratic idea that there is a god within us. He criticised Porphyry for upholding the union of the soul with the Intellect, taking this clearly to imply the loss of individual identity, defeating the very goal of rational mysticism, the attainment of individual immortality. Nor did he accept Plotinus' teaching of the divinity of the soul (*Enneads* V 1; cf. Aristotle, *Eudemian Ethics* VII 1248a 20–39). Rather, he used the full rigour of Neoplatonism to discipline the idea that the fulfilled human intelligence is (in the language of the more sober mystics) in contact (*ittiṣāl*) with divine.

This term too, like so much of the language of mysticism, stems from Plotinus. His word is *aphe*, a term used for the kindling of a flame, contact with a contagious disease, the touching of harp-strings, the contact of a wrestler in a grip (cf. *Genesis* 33:26), the intersection of two lines or surfaces in geometry, or any point of juncture (*Enneads* V 3.17, VI 9.11). Contact allows direct apprehension. At the surfaces contiguous figures do become one. But each retains its identity. Neither is reduced to the other. So in knowledge or in ecstasy, as Ibn Sīnā understands it, the individual is still present as a subject, to receive the higher understanding that gnosis makes possible. And God too does not vanish, swallowed up into the illusory ocean of human consciousness in what the Sufis call its "expansive" mode.

Merlan fuses Avicenna's *ittiṣāl* with the more monistic *ittiḥād*, union with communion. But Avicenna insists on the distinction, for good reason, as Goichon made clear. Avicenna's argument is that if the human mind actually became the Active Intellect, that hypostasis would be divisible; otherwise, the mind that knows anything would know everything. Here Avicenna relies on the primary data of individual consciousness – intensionality, privileged self-access, privacy and inviolability. His reflections lay the groundwork for the Cartesian *sum res cogitans*, just as his Floating Man argument lays the groundwork for the Cartesian *cogito*. The nub of the argument is that there is no consciousness for the intellect, higher or otherwise, without individuality.[33]

The classic danger of pantheism is its liability to equivocation: is nature enlarged and elevated to the sanctity of God, or is God reduced to the fragility and dividedness of nature? In *ḥulūlī* or immanentist varieties of

Sufism in Islam that spring not only from ecstatic emotion but from the incarnationist penchant of charismatic Shiʿism, as in other experiments with pantheism, both sides of the equivocation are essayed, often simultaneously. Symptomatic of the dialectic between the two are the mood-swings of constriction and expansion (*inqibāḍ* and *inbisāṭ*) that call forth the Sufi discipline of the *ṭarīqas* as a means of their direction and control. Ibn Sīnā forestalls the oscillation, not with a spiritual regimen but with the discipline of metaphysics, blocking the equivocation that is its source conceptually if not emotively. He interposes a two-fold safeguard: he sets the Active Intellect firmly between the mind and God, and he pre-empts its identification with the human mind, insisting that the very fact of consciousness, which gnosis should heighten, guarantees our discrete identity and thus precludes the loss of individuality in the wholeness of any hypostasis.

Despite his many criticisms of the philosopher, al-Ghazālī adopts Ibn Sīnā's scheme, even to the point of relying on the Neoplatonic device of an intermediary between man and what he knows. In the *Kitāb Maḍnūn al-Ṣaghīr*, or "Esoteric Minor", al-Ghazālī links a problematic *ḥadīth* based on the Biblical thesis that God created man in his own image with what we might call the Delphic *ḥadīth*, arguing that the man who knows himself knows God because of the inner kinship between man and God. The basis of that kinship, he explains elsewhere, is the human soul.[34] It is this that makes man a microcosm, ruled by the soul as the world is ruled by God. In the *Niche for Lights*, glossing the celebrated Light verse of the *Qur'ān*, a key topos for Neoplatonic fusions of Islamic and Greek thought, al-Ghazālī is most explicit in his Avicennism. There, as Altmann explains, he distinguishes God in His transcendence from his immanent Presence (*ḥaḍra*; cf. the Hebrew *shekhinah*), a hypostasis variously called "*al-Raḥmān*", the Merciful (commonly taken as an epithet of God Himself), or "*al-Muta*'" (He who must be obeyed). Altmann recognises the functional equivalence of such figures to the Philonic *logos* yet wonders along with W. H. T. Gairdner, the translator of the *Niche for Lights*, whether the sensitivity shown here to the immanentist type of pantheism represented by al-Ḥallāj does not mean "that al-Ghazālī considered, albeit for a fleeting moment and with great hesitation, the possibility of understanding the *ḥadīth* about man being in the image of God, and, obviously also the *ḥadīth* about self-knowledge, in terms of an ultimate identity".[35] I suspect that Ibn Ṭufayl caught al-Ghazālī's intent more precisely when he read him as carefully skirting the heretical enthusiasms of an al-Ḥallāj or an al-Bistāmī while not abjuring the access of the mind to the divine that the Neoplatonic theory of assimilation could afford. As Ibn Ṭufayl wrote of al-Ghazālī on just this issue, "his was a mind refined by learning and education".[36] In this case it was what al-Ghazālī learned from Ibn Sīnā, and through him from the Neoplatonic tradition, that allowed him the freedom he exploited: the mind does not become God but comes into intellectual contact or contiguity with the Active Intellect, a hypostasis, to be sure, but the bearer of the form in which man's likeness to the divine subsists.[37]

Jewish thinkers of the Karaite school – Daniel al-Qumīsī, al-Qirqisānī, and Joseph al-Basīr – relied on a line in the Book of Job (19:26), "From my flesh would I behold God", to argue that awareness of my own creation gives me knowledge of God's grace and wisdom. Saadiah does not use the gloss, hewing far closer to what the narrative context requires. But Abraham bar Ḥiyya, Joseph ben Ẓaddiq, and Baḥyā ben Asher do. And Isaac Albalag links it explicitly with the Delphic maxim in its Islamicised wording.[38] A cosmological argument metamorphoses before our eyes into a Platonising argument from introspection: Baḥyā ibn Pāqūdā and Abraham bar Ḥiyya, following a reading of the maxim that was apparently familiar to Porphyry, interpret the self-knowledge that it mandates as the study of human anatomy, uncovering the marks of God's wisdom and design in our corporeal make up. Joseph ben Yehudah even cites the Job verse as an endorsement of medical studies. And Joseph al-Baṣīr writes, "Now our path is laid out: First we must recognize that bodies are created; and from this we can prove that they are in need of a wise Creator".[39] But many kabbalists reject this view, arguing as the *Sefer ha-Mishqal* does, "To say that it is of the body that comes from a fetid drop and is flesh, soon full of worms and maggots it is said, 'In the image of God created He him', is, Heaven forfend, something that will never occur to a wise man".[40] And the *Sefer Sheqel ha-Qodesh* glosses: "'Thou hast clothed me with skin and flesh and knit me together with bones and sinews' (Job 10:11). If skin and flesh are the garment, consider who is the man?" Clearly, "the intellectual form", as the wisest mystics understood![41] It was such a line of reasoning that Maimonides was following when he too, in the opening glosses of *The Guide to the Perplexed* (I 1) interprets the Biblical "image and likeness" as a reference to man's essential and distinctive intellectual awareness, the human rational soul.[42]

Maimonides does not reject the argument from design. Indeed he relies on it in treating all that is intelligible in nature as in effect an "attribute" of God – an expression in terms intelligible to us of the ineffable wisdom that is identical with God's being.[43] But in the case of our own intelligence, we have privileged access to one such expression subjectively rather than as objectified in nature. It is this subjectivity that is the special focus of the Platonic appeal to self-knowledge. As the *Sefer ha-Mishqal* expresses it:

"Even as God sees and is not seen, the soul sees and is not seen." Altmann calls this a "rather homely" analogy. But its seeming simplicity belies its profundity. The reason the soul is not seen (despite the efforts of eagle-eyed inspectors like Hume to spot it) goes to the very nature of its being. The soul as a subject never lays itself out as an object, defined and delimited by the conditions of cognition. Indeed that is one of those conditions. Subjecthood is possible only for what does not take itself as an object. That is why human consciousness is not of or about the brain, why the eye cannot see itself. Subjecthood is the counterpart of objecthood because subjecthood is the very act of setting oneself apart as an identity toward which all other things are as objects.

The soul can objectify the world because it always remains a subject. All things are for it and toward it. But the same is true of God. God acts and creates by objectifying reality, projectively, rather than reflectively as the soul does. But, like the soul, God remains always out of sight, always the subject, never the mere object or thing. Here the analogy of man and God goes deeper than the affirmation of divine intelligence in tandem with our own claim to reason and strikes something like bedrock. The key to the analogy is in the fact that rational subjectivity and subjecthood, human consciousness, are not merely further artefacts from the atelier of some consummate (but not necessarily absolute) creator. Rather, the self-containedness and unabstractable subjecthood of the self, what Plato's Socrates calls the mind's eye, is the fitting mirror of the self-sufficiency and unabstractable subjecthood of God. Here we see a real likeness and no pallid simile or groping conceit. Likeness, as Maimonides teaches, can have a spiritual as well as a physical sense, "For when he says 'I am like a pelican in the desert' (Psalms 102:7), he does not mean that he has feathers and wings like a pelican, but that he is as desolate" (*Guide* I 1).

Maimonides adheres consistently to the reading which finds the likeness between man and God to be spiritual/intellectual. And he consistently recognises the epistemic potential that such a reading opens up for a more direct, less inferential path to God than that afforded by reasoning from natural objects to the craftsmanship responsible for them. Thus he treats the appetitive and passionate "souls" as the "matter" that provides the potential and lays the basis for the emergence of rational consciousness, much as the *Sefer ha-Mishqal* treats the human soul as the "throne" upon which God rests. What Maimonides expresses in terms of Neoplatonic psychology, the kabbalist pictures by rearranging the furniture of the mystical pleroma. But the meaning is the same: that the soul provides a point of access for God into the world distinct from the normal, productive mode of creation, and a point of access for man to God, not by mediated inferences about natural objects but through immediate, if disciplined and informed, introspection. We know that Maimonides held fast to such a view, despite all that is alleged of his distaste for mysticism by writers who assume an incompatibility between rationalism and mysticism. For Maimonides insists that silent meditation is a higher form of worship than even prayer, just as prayer is higher than sacrifice. And he insists that it is only through our intellectual affinity with God that we are subject to individual providence (*Guide* III 17, 32; I 50, 59; II 5, citing Psalms 4:5).

Ibn Sīnā preserved individual identity even in the disembodied state by positing the creation of individual souls and assigning to each its own unique history. The discreteness of each consciousness was then sufficient to sustain the individuality of subjects even once they were deprived of the matter that had kept them distinct. For even a disembodied mind, Ibn Sīnā argued in his Floating Man argument, would be aware of his own existence. Al-Ghazālī followed Ibn Sīnā in adopting the doctrine of the discreteness of disembodied minds. Ibn Bājjah modified Avicenna's view, to allow for the taking up of the rational soul into a hypostatic whole. But he respected the argument, Avicenna's appeal to the intellectual integrity of individual consciousness and the moral integrity of personal history. So he preserved the individual subject even within its hypostatic nest – much as Spinoza preserves particular modes, that is, individuals, in the universal whole, refusing to reduce their particularity to the all, even while refusing to regard them as really separate or separable from it. The synthesis by which Ibn Bājjah united individuality with continuity for the perfected mind of man was a major breakthrough for him, preserved by his disciple in the verbatim transcription of the master's own, almost breathless report.[44]

Maimonides apparently followed Ibn Bājjah. Ibn Rushd seems to have gone further in the direction of monopsychism, accepting the ultimate unity of all human minds and laying the basis for later Romantic theories of collective consciousness, as Merlan showed. But Ibn Ṭufayl, profiting from Ibn Bājjah's ability to differentiate individual subjects within an overarching whole, stood fast with al-Ghazālī and Ibn Sīnā, explaining the unity-in-difference of disembodied human souls as a direct Neoplatonic corollary of their disembodiment, since only in the material world do identity and difference have the senses we familiarly assign them.[45] Baḥyā too shows a profit from Ibn Sīnā's insistence on the individuality of the fully realised human rational soul, by calling on our individual intellects, rather than the universal Intelligence, to engage the soul in dialogue and admonition. We recognise the hypostatic background of that intellect when Baḥyā reminds us of the Farabian basis in argument for its epistemic claims: "We should elucidate the purport of the mind's admonition ... and let us say at the outset that the remonstrance of the intellect is God's inspiration of man through the medium of his intelligence, allowing us to know Him and to discern the marks of His wisdom."[46]

Evidently Maimonides was not as worried as Avicenna was at the thought of the ultimate unity of all intelligences in the Active Intellect. But the reason lies in the work of Ibn Bājjah and in the fact that, like al-Ghazālī and Ibn Ṭufayl, he could rely on the metaphysical interposition of the supernal world, playing the role of the Platonic Intellectual World or the Islamic *Malakūt*, to assure no fusion or confusion between the individual intellect and God. Maimonides could rely upon a long a tradition of domesticating the Neoplatonic texts to monotheistic purposes. In the Hebrew and presumably the prior Arabic version of Alexander of Aphrodisias' *De Anima*, for example, the Pythian oracle becomes "the prophet",[47] in much the way that pagan gods in translated texts regularly become angels. Where Plotinus speaks of "acquiring identity with the Divine" (*Enneads* IV 8.1), the corresponding text in the Arabic *Theology of Aristotle* used by al-Fārābī, Moses Ibn Ezra, Shemtov ibn Falaquera and Ibn Gabirol, substitutes "I rose in my essence ... to the divine world". Moses de Leon paraphrases to similar effect, speaking of access to the World to Come. Altmann finds echoes of the same monotheistic usages in Maimonides' grandson Obadiah's *Treatise of the Pool*.[48]

Despite the differences in setting out the arithmetic of ecstasy, the epistemology remains the same in all these thinkers. Maimonides makes it very clear in his own case how little room is left for pantheistic license. For in discussing the priestly teaching of God's explicit names he argues forcefully that these portend a meaning identical with the highest content of metaphysics, the intellectual grasp of the absoluteness of God's being. Maimonides identifies that knowledge, which gives us mastery in this world and access to the higher world, with apprehension of the Active Intellect (*Guide* I 62, ed. Munk, p. 81a). Mystic experience is rational intuition that brings contact, assimilation, indeed identity, not with God but with the Active Intellect which is the active, formative expression of God within the world.[49]

What the *muḥaqiqqūn* find portended in the Biblical dictum or *ḥadīth* which tells us that man is created in the image of God, and again in the Delphic maxim or *ḥadīth* which tells us that to know the self is to know God, is not a overblown image of man as God and still less an imploded image of God as man, but the divine and ideal pattern of human excellence. Humanity itself, through the affinity of man with God, provides a miraculous metaphor, in the self-containedness of the human subject, of God's Ipseity and subjecthood.

Here, as with our first thesis, we find a mild admonition in the texts. Beyond and beneath the more profound admonition to self-knowledge that they share, there is a soft-spoken rebuke to the orientalist. For both Merlan and Altmann too readily project a monistic metaphysics of the self on Ibn Sīnā and others. Merlan is borne along by an enthusiasm that he in fact disclaims. Altmann's more sober scholarship is tipped by its method, the search for analogies and homologies, the old midrashic oracular method of *Quellenforschung*, towards assimilations. It marks the door from which each thought emerged so carefully that it sometimes fails to note that the emergence was a departure, and the door is closed. Merlan sets aside Ibn Sīnā's actual argumentation and his explicit disavowals in favour of an over-strenuous reading of the text; but Altmann is betrayed into equating *ittiṣāl* with *ittiḥād* by their functional equivalence, although, of course, he knew that the same end could be achieved by diverse means, and divergent ends by corresponding means.

What the philosophers influenced by Ibn Sīnā found most attractive in his arguments here was the opening they afforded to the Neoplatonic account of knowledge and inspiration/ecstasy without commitment to its seeming implications in the direction of pantheism. A delicate balance was struck by Ibn Sīnā's portentous reliance on the temporality of the human soul as a created being with a history that gives each soul a unique intensionality and thus an unsubmergible individuality.[50] But if only the analogies of function and homologies of provenance are followed, Ibn Sīnā and his successors become mere redactors, their solutions to the problems they confronted fused within the matrix of those problematics themselves; their distinctive arguments, set aside as insignificant, and their philosophical creativity, ignored.

— 3. GOD'S ACT IN HISTORY —

Our third thesis is the visiting upon human beings of the consequences of their actions, either communally or individually. The idea is coeval with the sense of justice that regulates the very idea of the God of monotheism.[51] Thus Abraham can argue with God in behalf of Sodom and Gomorrah, "Wilt Thou indeed sweep away the righteous with the wicked? Perhaps there are fifty innocents within the city … Far be it from Thee to slay the innocent with the guilty! Will not the Judge of all the earth do justice?" (Genesis 18:23–5). The same conception of God that sees natural disasters as divine judgements that must discriminate the righteous from the wicked, person by person and city by city, whether in the case of Sodom or in the case of Noah's Flood, also conceives of God as bestowing a just law whose commands are not impossible, incoherent or even unreasonable (Deuteronomy 30:13). God rewards those who keep His covenant and punishes those who fail to do so. The vehicle of that reward or punishment is the character or ethos of the recipients of God's commands.

Thus Balaam is unable to curse the Israelites, because they are already blessed:

> How shall I curse whom God hath not cursed? Or doom those whom God hath not doomed? ... Let me die the death of the righteous; let mine end be like his ... God is not a man to be capricious; nor a mortal to change His mind ... He hath beheld no evil in Jacob and hath seen no wrong in Israel. The Lord his God is with him ... For there is no sorcery in Jacob, nor any divination in Israel. Now is it said of Jacob and of Israel: "What hath God wrought!" How goodly are thy tents, O Jacob, thy dwelling places, O Israel ... Blessed are those who bless thee, accursed are those who curse thee. (Numbers 23:8–9, 19, 21, 23; 24:5, 9)

Israel is blessed by her fair ways, visible even at a distance in the order and fellowship of her camp. Her ethos imparts a blessedness that no arbitrary sentence can take away. Human happiness is the product of human choices, and the mores that preserve that happiness are those of the law whose subjects regard one another's deserts.[52]

A comparable message is conveyed in Heraclitus' admonition that the real "daemon" of human destiny is our own character. The theme is preserved in the Socratic thesis that no one knowingly chooses evil. For to understand our choices is to recognise the true disadvantageousness of evil and the preciousness of honesty and justice. To act on our understanding is simply to do what is right. Any other course must be an error. Plato credits the Socratic thesis and argues at length in the *Republic* that the unjust man is not happy but unhappy, and the supremely unjust man is a tragic figure, even though he may not know it. For the tyrant is an enemy to himself as well as to all around him. He fails to understand the need for justice to integrate conflicting interests and reconcile divergent tendencies even in a single soul. The inner conflict of the tyrant and the corresponding instability of the exploitative or oppressive state express the natural retribution of invidious and thoughtless choices as they become engrained in character and policy, their consequences worked out in the dynamics of psychological and social pathology and that record of fruitful and disastrous choices that we call history.

Plato shows in the *Republic* exactly how our own character can become our daemon. Aristotle sustains his allegiance to the Socratic thesis by supplying the key unstated middle term to Plato's argument, taking it to be rhetorical in appeal and understanding that rhetoric perforce leaves many middle terms unstated: it is because man is a social animal (*zoon politikon*) that the tyrant is an enemy to himself. Our identity is vested in our social relations, and only a god or a beast can live alone. The self-isolated man is denatured by friendlessness, dehumanised. He becomes a monster. Saadiah will use this very argument against the misanthropy of anchorite asceticism and reclusiveness (*ED* X 4, trans. Rosenblatt, pp. 364–7).

Plato dramatises the consequences of moral strength and weakness upon actors and their dependents – that is, their societies and offspring – in his celebrated historical dialectic of characters in individuals and societies: the just society, like the honest man, is inherently stable and self-stabilising, profiting from the fruits of good judgement. But if prestige is substituted for judgement, or wealth for prestige, or mere claims for wealth, or sheer demands for claims, history spirals into a tailspin that each generation wields less power to reverse. The oligarchic man and state are the natural outcomes of the weaknesses of timocracy, just as timocracy itself is the natural perversion of the strengths of the merit state and the well-governed personality that Plato calls aristocratic. Tyranny is the natural outcome of the perversion of democracy; and the anarchic penchant of democracy, when liberty gives way to license, is the natural outcome of the diffusion of oligarchic values and the widespread acceptance of the maxim that desires are self-legitimating – in more modern terms, that value is the object of any interest.

Again Aristotle puts a brake on Plato's rhetoric, reminding us that characters are not mere products of culture, but critically the product of our own choices. And again he finds followers in Saadiah and Maimonides. For when Saadiah reads in the Torah that an evildoer's sins are visited upon his offspring, he hastens to add the Rabbinic caveat: "only if they follow his example, as it is said: 'and also by the sins of their fathers, with whom they shall decline' (Leviticus 26:39)."[53] It is the appropriation of their forebears' mores that brings punishment on the offspring. And that, as Maimonides explains ("Eight Chapters", 8), is a matter of *their* choices, although deficiencies of temperament or environment may render the exercise of wiser choices difficult, and deficiencies of character (arising from our own choices) may diminish our degrees of freedom to the point that our punishment becomes inevitable. The model is Mu'tazilite, perhaps ultimately Stoic. But Maimonides is reading nothing into the text when he recognises that the hardening of Pharaoh's heart was the vehicle of his ultimate downfall. As the Psalmist says, in a passage that poetically encapsulates the Biblical as well as the Greek teaching on this theme: "When the wicked blossom like grass and all sorts of evildoers flourish, it is only to be destroyed forever." This is the subtlety of God's plan of nature that the thick and foolish fail to understand (Psalms 92:7–8).

Biblically, natural justice is sketched in the imagery of pollution: the Canaanites fouled their land, but this pollution did not make it uninhabitable by others. For the pollution was moral. Israelites are warned not to practise divination, idolatry, or child sacrifice. The people must rise up before a hoary head, care for the weak and helpless, champion the widowed and orphaned. It is by these means that they will avoid fouling their land (see Leviticus 19:23–20:27; Deuteronomy 12:29–31; etc.). For a land is polluted not only by failure to give surcease to its soil (Leviticus 26:34–5, 43), but also by the sacrifice of innocent children (Psalms 106:38), the stench of unrequited crimes (Numbers 35:33) and the ethos that such practices express and engender (Deuteronomy 21).

Muḥammad adopts not only the prophetic role of the admonisher but also the moral archaeology of the Torah: the ruins that dot the Arabian desert testify to prior judgements against lost cities and vanished civilisations.[54] Each site is a portent. In the popular philosophy of the Ikhwān al-Ṣafā' the theme is broadened and rationalised into a theory of cosmic revolutions and the emergence, decline and fall of nations, cities, even species and genera, with the turning of the celestial signs that mark the passing of the epochs.[55] Even in its astrological guise the scheme remains moral. For the reasoning is that each era exhausts the powers and the virtues of those who rightly hold dominion for their day. The limits of every virtue in every creaturely kind – animal, human, or *jinnī* – mark the limits of its reign and lead inevitably to its succession. Here the elegiac tones of the Arabic poets are transmuted into a tragic vein that bespeaks the insufficiency of all things mortal.[56] But the acceptance of tragedy does not lead to pagan relativism or pessimism, since God presides over the entire scheme, and every human soul is immortal, in principle exempted, not from the fray but from its ultimacy. Humanity here is liberated by the very weight of human choice and freedom. The inexorable necessity of choice brings with it the recognition of the infinite, ineradicable consequences of each choice we humans make.[57]

Al-Fārābī treats even the succession of forms in elemental matter in moral terms. He writes:

> For any matter it is as proper for it to have this form as its contrary. So each of these bodies has a right and entitlement (*ḥaqq wa isti'hāl*) for its form and a right and entitlement for its matter. What it deserves by its form is to retain the existence it has; but its right by its matter is to have a different sort of existence. Since these two states are incompatible, it must fulfill now one and now the other, alternatingly.[58]

The scheme is that of Anaximander,[59] preserving even his striking thesis that a kind of cosmic justice governs and indeed drives the most fundamental processes of change in nature. Al-Fārābī applies the scheme to political succession and to the succession of one generation by the next: "The kings of virtuous cities who succeed one another at diverse times are all like a single soul, as though they were a single king." For the king is the *hegemonikon* or ruling principle of the city, as the soul is in the body; and if the wholesome and proper regimen does not cease, it is as if the same ruler continued to rule, despite the death of one king and ascension of another.

As in Plato, so in al-Fārābī, the state and the individual do not decline but flourish through virtue. The life of actions in accordance with the virtues is self-reinforcing, since the human virtues are matters of habit. When each member of society acts appropriately, in keeping with Plato's advice that each class must perform the function for which it is best suited, "each acquires by his actions that wholesome and virtuous disposition of the soul. And the more he continues to do so the stronger and more outstanding that virtuous disposition becomes, just as continued practice in writing well makes one an excellent penman".[60] But, as in Plato, divergence from the dispositions that give strength to an individual or a community will lead to a progressive decline in the welfare of either.[61]

Ibn Khaldūn naturalises this Platonic schema still further by rediscovering Plato's dialectic of political/generational decline in the historical and cultural milieu that his own political experience had taught him to understand as intimately as Plato understood the sicknesses and health of the polis. The dialectic of the desert and the sown replaces Plato's succession of constitutions. But the moral judgement of history remains. It is character that builds and conquers, and character that loses and falls. As in the tragic vision of the Greeks and the moralistic historiography of the Ikhwān al-Ṣafā', history becomes cyclical again. The Bedouins may be "closer to being good" than city people, but only city folk can sustain the efflorescence of arts and sciences that Ibn Khaldūn knew and loved as civilisation,[62] and that Aristotle had so much in mind when he argued that man is a creature of the polis and that civil life alone fully humanises our existence. For Ibn Khaldūn no one mode of life attains the adequacy or moral stability to endure, let alone progress, indefinitely. But presiding over the inevitable dying falls of history is an implacable but ultimately fair moral judgement, the judgement written in our own characters, by our choices but also by the limitations of our capabilities. In the words of the *Qur'ān* (48:23, 33:62) repeatedly quoted by Ibn Khaldūn, "This is God's way, established of old, and thou shalt never find alteration in God's way".[63]

In all three of the theses we have considered, there is an enthymeme or a riddle, a middle term to be discovered. The content of the theses is durable and clearly predates the work of the philosophers who gave them voice in abstract terms. For it does not need the apparatus of philosophy to conceive of judgement, or to see the image of the divine in man or nature, or to imagine that the moral law is God's command. But it does require philosophy to make explicit and critically defensible theses of such themes. Philosophy can assign the grounds for regarding a given obligation or system of obligations as divinely inspired and so can regulate the thematic elaboration of the principles of such a law. Philosophy can interpret the dictum that humanity is created in the image of God and so can articulate the dimensions of the sanctity of human personhood, differentiating what is and what is not implied by the idea of an affinity between the finite creature and the infinite Creator. And philosophy can vindicate the operation of divine judgement through the dynamics of individual and communal character by probing the dialectics of human nature and interdependence and rendering explicit the material foundations and constituents of the idea of virtue.

If we trust the insight of the canonical sources and the integrity of their philosophical expositors, we can say that the philosophers whose efforts we have scanned discover the unspoken pivot critical to all three of the theses we have considered. In all three cases it is man, or more precisely, human character. For it is man, human nature and character, that allows the ideal of perfection, as glimpsed in revelatory experience or as conceived by reason, to acquire a humanly relevant meaning. It is the idea of humanity that translates the Good in its transcendent purity into what Aristotle called "the doable good". It is man again, human character and personality, that holds out the mirror in which the face of God is seen – not in the sense that man loses his identity and becomes God, for that would leave no beholder and nothing to behold, but in the sense that human rational and moral subjecthood is the very image of divine subjecthood. The inextinguishable moral identity of man as a unique individual is our only adequate image of divine self-sufficiency and omnibenevolence. Finally, man, human character specifically, is the vehicle by which God's natural justice acts in history, both on individuals and on cultures and societies, through a subtle dynamic that is social on one level and psychological on another.

The three theses that link the *muḥaqqiqūn* – whether their idiom is Biblical or Qur'ānic symbolism, philosophic syllogism, or the Platonic, Aristotelian, Farabian, Maimonidean or Ibn Khaldūnian anthropology – these three theses all portend a humanism. It is not the sort of humanism that sets itself up in opposition to theism. Quite the contrary, it finds adequate dignity for the human person only in the guarantee of a transcendent God. It predicates the very protections it affords to the human image on the relation it discovers between humanity and God. Yet it is a humanism in that it speaks insistently from the role it assigns to man.

The conceptual clarity first brought to perfection in Greek thought is as relevant in formulating the content of this humanism as is the ideal of moral and spiritual purity first brought to perfection in Hebraic thought. The Arabic milieu was a crucible in which these elements were alloyed. Muslim thinkers, writing in Arabic and sometimes Persian, were among the most skilful and systematic to touch the conceptual pestle to stir and blend the contents. The outcome was not a pollution or adulteration of the given, but a fusion that would render the humane and appropriable constituents of the resultant amalgam even more durable than they had been alone. The outcome of that synthesis, and of the critical refining that inevitably accompanies such a process, is a humanism whose work among the recipients of monotheistic scriptures, laws, and essays at philosophy is not yet completed.

— NOTES —

1. See Norman Roth, "The 'Theft of Philosophy" by the Greeks from the Jews", *Classical Folia* 22 (1978) pp. 53–67; Moshe Idel, "Kabbalah and Platonism in the Middle Ages and the Renaissance", in Goodman, ed., *Neoplatonism and Jewish Thought*, pp. 319–51.
2. The potential for alliances between Judaic and Islamic thought based on the achievements of Islamic thinkers in applying Greek philosophical methods is sometimes masked by the Talmudic ethos and Midrashic idiom. Yet the early impact of Greek thought on Judaic understanding was pervasive, and the shifts of idiom betray not only foreignness but also a heavy traffic. As Moses Hadas explains, a word, idea, motif, or argument is most thoroughly naturalised when least marked as exotic; see his *Hellenistic Culture*. The Rabbinic sages neither simply aped nor simply rejected Greco-Roman ideas but sought to respond to them. The outcome was an extended dialogue with pervasive and enduring impacts. See Gedalyahu Alon, *Jews and Judaism and the Classical World*, trans. Israel Abrahams (Jerusalem: Magnes Press, 1977) and *The Jews in their Land in the Talmudic Age (70–640 CE)*, trans. G. Levi (Cambridge: Harvard University Press, 1989); Victor Tcherikover, *Hellenistic Civilization and the Jews* (Philadelphia: JPS/ Atheneum, 1970) pp. 344–55; A. T. Kraabel, William S. Green, Tessa Rajak, John J. Collins and others, in Jacob Neusner and Ernest Frerichs, eds, *"To See Ourselves as Others See Us" – Christians and Jews in Late Antiquity* (Chico: Scholars Press, 1985); Boaz Cohen, *Jewish and Roman Law: A Comparative Study* (New York: JTS, 1966); Urbach, *The Sages*.
3. I translate following the JPS rendering of 1962.
4. Cf. Goodman, *God of Abraham*, chs. 1 and 7.
5. See W. T. Stace, *Mysticism and Language* (London: Macmillan, 1961); Rudolf Otto, *The Idea of the Holy* (Oxford: Oxford University Press, 1969; 1st German ed.

1919); contrast B. K. Matilal, "Mysticism and Reality: Ineffability", *Journal of Indian Philosophy* 3 (1975) pp. 217–52. The sense of ineffability, I suspect, often arises in a healthy self-restraint. But the effects of such chastity are compounded when the imagination is impoverished by a sense of paradox moored in romanticism, obscurantism or discomfort with metaphysical questions.

6. Cf. Exodus 4:15, 30; 19:6–7; 20:1; 34:1, 27–8; 35:1; Leviticus 8:36; Deuteronomy 1:18; 4:13, 30; 5:19; 6:6; 10:2, 4; 12:28; 28:14.
7. See Plato, *Meno* 97; cf. *Philebus* 59a, *Crito* 47, *Symposium* 202; al-Fārābī, *The Book of Letters*, ed. Mahdi, pp. 133–6, 150–3.
8. Ibn Sīnā, *Shifā'*, Psychology, ed. Rahman, pp. 248–50.
9. Cf. *Arā'* V 15.1, ed. Walzer, p. 229.
10. *Arā'*, pp. 255–7; al-Fārābī, *Book of Letters*, ed. Mahdi, pp. 148–9.
11. Not that theology or metaphysics simply serve at the pleasure of law and morals. Alfred Ivry, my friend and colleague since the 1960s, rightly insists that one must not reduce the metaphysical achievement of al-Fārābī to his political purposes. I would add al-Fārābī's equally stunning achievements in logic, on which his work in metaphysics rests. See my "Three Enduring Achievements of Islamic Philosophy" and Majid Fakhry, *Philosophy, Dogma and the Impact of Greek Thought in Islam* (Aldershot, Hampshire: Variorum, 1994), ch. 3. Al-Fārābī himself, however, often brackets metaphysical ideas within a political context, as "principles underlying the beliefs of the inhabitants of the virtuous state". Cf. Joshua Parens, *Metaphysics as Rhetoric: Alfarabi's Summary of Plato's Laws* (Albany: SUNY Press, 1995). Ibn Sīnā more fully disengages metaphysics from its societal context.
12. *Guide* I 54, citing *Sifre* to Deuteronomy 10:12; cf. B. Sota 14a, Leviticus Rabbah 24.
13. *Arā'*, pp. 165–9, 178, 211–13. Cf. Ibn Sīnā, *Najāt*, Psychology, trans. Rahman, pp. 41–5.
14. *Guide* II 36; the argument seems to me to pay deference to Halevi's theme of the historic distinctiveness of the people and the land of Israel.
15. See Goodman, "Morals and Society in Islamic Philosophy" and Chapter 5 below.
16. See Goodman, *On Justice*, Chapter 3.
17. See, e.g., Leviticus 18:24–8, 20:22; Goodman, *God of Abraham*, pp. 219, 224–5, 235.
18. See *Guide* III 29–33; Maimonides, *Eight Chapters*, 1–4, 8. Maimonides assigns determination of the facts about the heavens to astronomy (*Guide* II 8) but does not deem astronomy irrelevant to the cosmological concerns of religion; see *Guide* I 9, 47, II 19, 20. Indeed, like Georg Cantor, he finds a religious relevance even in the study of the mathematics of infinity; see *Eight Chapters*, 5.
19. Asín Palacios, *Islam and the Divine Comedy*, Preface by the Duke of Alba, p. viii.
20. See Goodman, "Six Dogmas of Relativism".
21. Al-Kindī, *Risālah On First Philosophy*, trans. Ivry, pp. 57–8.
22. See D. S. Margoliouth, "On the Esoteric Style", in his *The Poetics of Aristotle* (London, 1911) pp. 21–76.
23. See Arthur I. Miller, *Imagery in Scientific Thought: Creating Twentieth Century Physics* (Boston: Birkhauser, 1984).
24. Al-Fārābī, *Book of Letters*, ed. Mahdi, pp. 76–7; Ibn Sīnā, *Najāt*, Psychology, trans.

F. Rahman, pp. 35–8; Ikhwān al-Ṣafā' *Rasa'il* (Beirut: Dar Sadir, 1957) vol. 1, pp. 391–2.

25. Plato, *Alcibiades I*, 127e, 132b; cf. *Epinomis* 988, *Philebus* 48c, *Charmides* 164d; Aristotle, *Metaphysics* Alpha 2, 982b 22 ff. See Werner Jaeger, *Aristotle*, trans R. Robinson (Oxford: Oxford University Press, 1948, 1962) pp. 164–5.
26. See Philo, *De Specialibus Legibus* I 10.44, *De Sacrificiis Abelis et Caini* 54; Masnūt, ed. Buber, 61, quoted in Altmann, *Studies*, pp. 18, 30.
27. See S. Landauer, "Die Psychologie des Ibn Sīnā", *ZDMG* 29 (1875) pp. 340–1, 374–5.
28. See Goodman, "The Sacred and the Secular".
29. See, e.g., al-Ṭabarī, cited in Franz Rosenthal, "On the Knowledge of Plato's Philosophy in the Islamic World", *Islamic Culture* 14 (1940) p. 410.
30. Alexander of Aphrodisias, *De Anima liber cum mantissa*, ed. I. Bruns in *Supplementum Aristotelicum II* (Berlin, 1887) pp. 84–91; Merlan, *Monopsychism, Mysticism and Metaconsciousness*, pp. 14–16.
31. Merlan, *Monopsychism, Mysticism and Metaconsciousness*, pp. 21–22. Cf. the error described by Ibn Ṭufayl in *Ḥayy ibn Yaqẓān*, trans. Goodman, p. 150 = ed. Léon Gauthier, Beirut: 1936, pp. 123–4.
32. Augustine was well aware of the linkage between self-knowledge and knowledge of God but declined to parse it, writing instead: "I could not find myself: How much less then could I find You (*Confessions* V ii 2; cf. III, vi 11, X vi 9, viii 15); see Peter Brown, *Augustine of Hippo* (London: Faber, 1967) p. 168.
33. Merlan (*Monopsychism, Mysticism and Metaconsciousness*, 25–9) chastises Goichon for projecting a Thomistic orthodoxy on Ibn Sīnā. But this puts the cart before the horse. It is Avicenna's metaphysics that makes possible Thomas' articulation of an orthodox position here. Merlan's reading ignores Avicenna's argument and substitutes an enthusiasm that Merlan disclaims (p. 25) for the insistent clarity of Avicenna's text. See W. Kutsch, ed., *Ein arabisches Buchstück aus Porphyrios (?)*, in *Melanges de l'Université Saint Joseph* 31 (1954) p. 268; *K. al-Shifā*, Psychology, ed. and trans. Jan Bakoš (Prague: Nakladatelstvi Ceskoslovenske Akademie Ved, 1956) Arabic pp. 235–46 = French pp. 169–77; *Kitāb al-Ishārāt wa 'l-Tanbīhāt*, trans. A.-M. Goichon (Paris: Vrin, 1951) 447–8, with her notes pp. 442–43; and her *La Distinction de l'essence et de l'existence d'après Ibn Sīnā* (Paris, 1937) pp. 87, n. 1; 316–28. Merlan relies on a remark in Ibn Sīnā's "Essay on Love", trans. Emil Fackenheim, *Medieval Studies* 7 (1945) p. 225: "The highest degree of approximation to It is the reception of Its manifestation in its full reality, i.e., in the most perfect way possible, and this is what the Sufis call unification (*ittiḥād*)." Merlan takes this to mean that "Avicenna within his system had a place for the 'ecstatic,' highly emotional union of Sufi mysticism and used the term *ittiḥād* to describe it". But this is to confuse use with mention. Ibn Sīnā is describing the real nature of what the Sufis call *ittiḥād*. More strictly translated, and including the opening lines that precede the passage quoted, Ibn Sīnā's words were, "We want to show in this chapter *a*) that every being loves the Absolute Good with an innate love, *b*) that the Absolute Good manifests Itself to all those who love it, although their receptivity to that epiphany and their contact (*ittiṣāl*) with it vary, and *c*) that the highest degree of assimilation to it is in receiving its true epiphany (or manifestation), that

is, as perfectly as possible. This is the meaning (*al-maʿnā*) of what the Sufis call union (*ittiḥād*)", or, more literally, "this is what the Sufis intend by the word 'union'"; Ibn Sīnā, *Risāla fī 'l-'Ishq*, ed. F. Mehren in *Rasā'il … Ibn Sīnā*, (Leiden: Brill, 1899) p. 22. Characteristically, Ibn Sīnā analyses a religious idea for its philosophically workable content. Maintenance of the integrity of the Absolute is a value in his philosophy secured by his most rigorous arguments, those demarcating contingent from necessary being. And finding a way of preserving individuality in the disembodied human soul is one of the foremost and most abiding themes of Ibn Sīnā's philosophy. Ibn Sīnā recognises that the manifestation or epiphany accessible to any being (animate or inanimate, rational or irrational) will depend on that being's capacity. So the manifestation is not identical with the Absolute Good, but is a true (not "real") expression of Him, as perfect as the limitations of each being allow. See Goodman, *Avicenna*, ch. 3. For the fruits of Avicenna's approach in dealing with immortality, see Chapter 4 below, pp. 109–14.

34. Al-Ghazālī, *Iḥyā' 'Ulūm al-Dīn*, IV (Cairo, 1933) p. 263; *K. al-Imlā'* (Cairo, 1927); *Al-Maqṣad al-asnā* (Cairo, 1905) p. 17–27; Farid Jabre, *La Notion de la Ma'rifa chez Ghazali* (Beirut, 1958) p. 86–108, and appendices 11–12.
35. Altmann, *Studies*, 11–12.
36. Ibn Ṭufayl, *Ḥayy Ibn Yaqẓān*, ed. Gauthier, 5; trans. Goodman, p. 96.
37. The kabbalist Alemanno noted the parallel between al-Ghazālī's strategy and the kabbalists' reliance on the *Sefirot*, as Altmann, following Moritz Steinschneider notes, *Studies*, p. 9, n. 57.
38. Altmann, *Studies*, pp. 3–4.
39. Altmann, *Studies*, pp. 24–25. Joseph ben Yehudah, *Sefer Musar*, ed. W. Bacher (Berlin, 1910) p. 75.
40. I translate after Altmann, *Studies*, p. 16.
41. I translate after Altmann, *Studies*, p. 16.
42. Cf. Shemtov ben Joseph Shemtov, *Derashot ha-Torah* (Salonika, 1525) 2ab, quoted in Altmann, *Studies*, pp. 38–40.
43. Cf. Goodman, "Matter and Form as Attributes of God in Maimonides' Philosophy".
44. See Chapter 4 below and Ibn Bājjah, *Opera Metaphysica*, ed. Fakhry, pp. 153–73; M. Asín Palacios, "*Tratado de Avempace sobre la union del Intellecto con el hombre*", *Al-Andalus* 7 (1942) pp. 1–47; Goodman, "Ibn Bājjah" in Nasr and Leaman, eds, *History of Islamic Philosophy*, pp. 294–312. I have translated the *risāla* in my forthcoming anthology, *Philosophical Readings from the Arabic Tradition*.
45. Ed. Gauthier, pp. 123–31; trans. Goodman, pp. 150–3.
46. Baḥyā, *K. al-Hidāya ilā Farā'iḍ al-Qulūb* III 4–5, ed. A. S. Yahuda, pp. 198–9; cf. Chapter 3 below, pp. 72–3; Altmann, *Studies*, pp. 36–7. A. S. McGrade finds metaphysical bulwarks for the idea of natural rights in Thomas Aquinas's "campaign for the individuality of the agent intellect in each person and his parallel contention that God's promulgation of the natural law is not through an illumination above the mind but by the creation in each of us of a capacity for practical reasoning in virtue of which we ourselves may *come up with* dictates for decent, responsible, and personally fulfilling conduct". See McGrade's paper "Righting some Wrongs about Rights", 28 December 1993, American Philosophical

Association, Atlanta; and see the discussion in Goodman, *Judaism, Human Rights and Human Values*.

47. Alexander of Aphrodisias, *De Anima*, ed. Bruns, p. 1; trans. A. P. Fotinis (Washington: University Press of America, 1979) p. iv.
48. Altmann, *Studies*, pp. 32–5.
49. Cf. Aristotle, *De Anima* III 5, 430a 13–15; *Eudemian Ethics* VII 14, 1248a 18–27.
50. I say portentous because of the future significance of this idea, not only as a vehicle of humanist individualism, but also, pointedly, for the impact that the idea of the inextricability of temporality in consciousness will have through the philosophy of Kant. But I must add that Ibn Sīnā himself would not accept the inferences that Kantian and post-Kantian philosophers found upon the temporality of human consciousness.
51. See Goodman, *God of Abraham*, Chapter 1.
52. See Deuteronomy 11:26–28; 12:1, etc. and Goodman, *On Justice*.
53. Saadiah, *The Book of Theodicy*, 301 *ad* Job 21:19; and B. Berakhot 7a.
54. E.g., *Qur'ān* 11:68, 95; 14:9; 22:42; 25:38; 26:141; 29:38; 89:9, etc.
55. See Ikhwān al-Ṣafā', *The Case of the Animals vs Man*, trans. Goodman, pp. 72–5; and my introduction, pp. 5–7, 30.
56. Ikhwān al-Ṣafā', *Animals vs Man*, 99–102.
57. Ikhwān al-Ṣafā', *Animals vs Man*, 201–2.
58. *Arā'* III 9.1, ed. Walzer, p. 145; cf. 9.2, pp. 146–9.
59. Anaximander, *DK* 12a *ap.* Simplicius, *Phys.* 24.17; G. S. Kirk and J. E. Raven, *The Presocratic Philosophers* (Cambridge: Cambridge University Press, 1962) item 112, p. 117 = Kirk and Raven and M. Schofield, *The Presocratic Philosophers* (Cambridge: Cambridge University Press, 2nd ed. 1983) item 110, p. 117.
60. *Arā'*, V 16.2, ed. Walzer, pp. 258–61.
61. *Arā'*, V 15.13–19, ed. Walzer, pp. 250–9.
62. For Ibn Khaldūn's delight in the efflorescence of civilisation, witness his enthusiastic response to Cairo on arriving there in 1383; see Ibn Khaldūn, *Muquddimah*, trans. Rosenthal, p. lviii.
63. Ibn Khaldūn, *Muqaddimah*, trans. Rosenthal, vol. 1, p. 173; vol. 2, pp. 99, 134, 377.

Chapter 2

Rāzī and Epicurus

Rāzī was an atomist but not a materialist. Of the five things that must exist in his universe, three suffice for a purely physical world: time, space and matter. The other two, God and Soul, are transcendent and not physical. Soul finds her embodiment and God, His effect, by projecting themselves into finitude. It is characteristic of Rāzī's eclecticism that he ignores the materialistic agenda of the ancient atomists he so admires. In Democritean atomism sensory properties are subjectivised, reduced to atomic shape, arrangement and position. The tempered atomism of Epicurus makes size too a variable among the real characteristics of atoms. But Epicurus holds to the Democritean aim of reducing all predicates to location, in keeping with the atomists' positivistic dream: to speak only of what Democritus and Leucippus called being and non-being – atoms and void – and never to confuse mere higher order notions (such as secondary qualities) with being itself. Asclepiades (d. c. 40 BC), the Greek physician who may have stimulated Rāzī's atomism, made the denial of teleology a prominent feature of his atomism. But Rāzī follows Galen in upholding teleology[1] and ignores the positivist affinities of atomism.

Rāzī classes matter as inanimate, incapable of action in its own right, the passive "substrate to the forms".[2] Readily crossing his atomism with Platonism, he ascribes the natural order to divine intervention[3] and the motion of matter to the animation of Soul[4] – a far cry from the rigorous materialism that would make all motion an intrinsic property of matter and treat order as the mere pattern of motion.[5] Rāzī snubs materialism again by treating the human soul as an offshoot of Soul at large,[6] and intelligence as an emanation of the Godhead.[7] But he ignores the Neoplatonic derivation of Soul from Mind.

Throughout Rāzī's philosophy materialism and immaterialism intertwine, making rival claims on his allegiance. In this chapter I want to consider the interplay of Epicurean with non-Epicurean motives in the framing of that philosophy. We begin with Rāzī's theories of perception and sensation, pleasure and desire, free will and motivation. From there we turn to his ethical work, and then to his account of the body–soul relation and his view of rationality and immortality.

— 1. PERCEPTION AND SENSATION —

With regard to perception Rāzī is a materialist. Not that materialism can explain our awareness of sensation. But Rāzī does provide a materialistic model for the anatomical effects presumed to underlie that awareness. He treats perception as an irritation arising in the physical contact of two bodies: "Perception is the impinging of the perceived upon the percipient. Impinging means the direct action of that which impinges upon that which is impinged upon."[8] This precious direct quote from Rāzī, as Kraus calls it, canonises the mechanism of Democritus and Epicurus. Process or change is essential to sensation.[9] So Rāzī can explain the self-anaesthesis of certain prolonged sensations as a result of their constancy[10] and can even warrant Epicurus' almost religious faith that sharp pains are brief but lasting pains, bearable.[11] "The natural state", Rāzī, writes, "is insensible. For sensation arises only through impact, which moves what it affects from the state it is in."[12]

In conceiving perception as a result of the stimulus of a physical dislocation in the percipient's body, caused by the impact of (atoms of) the object perceived, Rāzī submerges the distinction between percepts and the bodies that cause them. Such realism is well precedented in the ancient materialists.[13] Plato develops a parallel account of the nexus of bodies with perception in his efforts to use geometry to mediate between the arithmetic of the forms and the solidity of matter (*Timaeus* 61D ff.). Here, as Cornford puts it, addressing the sensations that present themselves to "the mortal part of the soul", Plato seems to adapt Democritus' "attempts to connect the character of a sensation with the shapes of the atoms in the body which yields it".[14] Rāzī evidently knew of Plato's approach, either from the *Timaeus* itself or from Galen's compendium of it.[15] But his departures from it are striking.

Plato had spoken of the systematic elaboration of the possible combinations and permutations of atomic configurations in relation to their perceptual counterparts as a pleasurable "diversion from discourse about eternal things" (*Timaeus* 59c). He sketches a kind of prototype of what we would call physical chemistry as a hypothesis embedded in his cosmology. But he can offer no higher praise for the content of that cosmology than to call it "a likely story" (loc. cit.). Even at the heart of his mechanistic narrative, Plato preserves the distinction between the things perceived (*aistheta*) and the affections of the sense organs. Democritus, as Theophrastus stresses, ironed out that distinction.[16] For, while he famously made secondary characteristics subjective and "conventional",[17] Democritus preserved the absolute reality of the bodies that cause such responses. Plato, by contrast, problematises the physical thing in itself. For the critique of perception is his epistemic highroad to idealism.

Like Democritus Rāzī thinks mechanistically. Thus his model of sensation as an impinging of bodies. It seems doubtful, with his busy schedule and distaste for the impractical,[18] that he had much relish for Platonic "pastimes". He did write a treatise rebutting a critique of Galen's theory of taste[19] – since Galen had taken the evidence here as favouring a departure from his usual opposition to atomism. But the hypothetical framing of Plato's "likely story" and his bracketing of the geometrical models of perceptible objects as "probable accounts" and "plausible explanations" strikes no chord in Rāzī. His penchant is for the elemental Democritean position. Rather than hedge like Plato, Rāzī seems to follow the Epicurean counsel to adopt the "plausible account",[20] not make it a mere placeholder, like one of Plato's myths, or his own[21] – as much as to say, "Here the materialists hold the field".

Materialists favour realism – naïve realism phenomenally, causal realism at the atomic or objective level. For what is must be what is perceived if materialism is to draw empirical support from the axiom that only the physical can make contact with physical organs of perception. Faithful to the realism of the materialists, Rāzī defends the claim that bodies are as they appear. He even links atomism with solidity,[22] much as Epicurus had done when he argued that bodies would lose their claim to solidity and with it their ontic primacy unless they were composed of indivisible particles.[23] Epistemologically solidity rests on the realist's "direct" perception,[24] which privileges touch in materialistic accounts of the senses.[25] Epicurus is the paradigm here. His naïve realism retires in deference to causal realism only when naïve realism begins to joust with atomism.[26] Rāzī faithfully tracks Epicurus in this regard and like him slights the possibility of tension between atomistic reductionism and the artlessness of naïve realism.

One consequence of Epicurean realism was the famous inference that the gods must be real since men have seen them. Rāzī affords a diverting parallel when he ascribes revelatory experience (and thus revealed religion) to demonic apparitions. The demons perceived, he reasons, invoking a Platonising notion of metempsychosis, must be the souls of persons too wicked to have fully shed their matter as yet. They give themselves out as angels and instruct their dupes the prophets to bear messages to mankind, thus fomenting dissension and bloodshed.[27] Rāzī here imports to the Islamic context the Epicurean moral outrage at the works of religion,[28] along with the Epicurean explanation for the generality of the infection.[29] Because the "demons" are not yet clear of the physical, they still fall under the purview of the senses, like the material gods of the Epicureans.

— 2. PLEASURE AND PAIN —

Sensation is crucial in Rāzī's ethics. It links a naturalistic physiology with hedonism, erasing the distinction between right action and the universal and wholesome natural response of animals to their environment. What is perceived is what is real, so the theory of perception naturally grounds both a psychological and an ethical hedonism, the two linked by ethical naturalism. For action flows naturally and directly from apprehension. Sensations bear with them not only the springs of motivation but the justifications of intent. The most basic and naturally the most powerful intent is the avoidance of pain.

Pain is a displacement from the natural state. Rāzī's lost writing on the relation of excessive heat to bodily harm[30] gives us a hint of his view: that pain serves as a safeguard to the body's delicate equilibrium, that is, the physical arrangement (cf. the *concilium* of Lucretius) that makes a body capable of life. Pain is a signal or alarm triggered when disturbance to the natural state rises toward the threshold of permanent damage.[31] Prior to perceptions of the more refined and focused sort, atomic to them, we might say, pain is a biological primitive. As such, pain, like other sheer sensations, is irrefragable. But, as Plato taught and Epicurus understood, the same unstructured, non-propositional character that makes sensations unquestionable also makes their data subject to interpretation and critique.

Pain is defined formally by Rāzī as the sensation of the painful.[32] The definition is not trivial, since it refers to a primary datum of experience. But Rāzī does not define pleasure as the sensation of the pleasurable. Rather he defines it reductively, as a relaxation or release from pain. This Epicurean[33] formulation is crucial to Rāzī's ethics, which is founded on the premise that pleasure is the physiological counterpart of discomfort or dislocation. The account has its origin in Plato's critique of hedonism. It is used by Rāzī to ground his own critical hedonism, a moderate, hedonically grounded asceticism. Rāzī counsels the curbing of desire on grounds that the pleasures that are the specious objects of desire are no more than a return to normalcy from distress. The augmentation of desire means only an augmentation of distress. Our primary object should not be pleasurable sensations but sustained enjoyment of the relaxed or normal state that is the true aim of all desires and the proper consummation of all pleasurable sensations.[34]

Rāzī can put the full weight of his hedonic calculus behind this counsel only to the extent that pleasure is strictly a nought, nothing in itself but only a relief from pain. Only by showing that every pleasure has an equal pain or displacement as its precondition can Rāzī shift the focus of hedonism from pursuit of pleasures to avoidance of pains. Thus the nullity of pleasure is crucial to his ethics.[35] He calls upon his physiological expertise and his mechanistic model of sensation to testify in behalf of the nullity of pleasure.

Physically, Rāzī treats pain as a kind of distension. Pleasure is the release of tension.[36] Pleasure yields sensation at all only because matter is undergoing a process, returning to normal. Without a prior departure from the natural state, no pleasure would be felt. Rāzī grants that some pleasures are not in fact preceded by perceptible pains. But in such cases, he argues, the displacement was gradual and imperceptible; the return, steeper, and thus, perceptually more pronounced. Without the prior displacement, no restoration would have been necessary or even possible. Hunger and thirst are prime examples. The pleasure of eating or drinking presumes a prior depletion. Over time the displacement grows severe enough to be hardly insensible. Alternatively, pain may come suddenly, as by a blow, and fade only gradually, without pleasurable sensation, in the course of healing.[37]

Pleasure cannot be a positive sensation in its own right, Rāzī argues, pursuing his model of sensation as irritation, since the same physical causes (e.g. a cold breeze) that give pleasure now cause pain at another time. What matters is one's prior condition, whether one was warm or cold, comfortable (in a state of nature) or uncomfortable at the outset.[38] What of the pleasures arising from the sight of a lovely face, the sound of a beautiful voice, the taste of some delicious fruit that one has never known before? Do these too involve prior deprivation? Rāzī argues that they do. Our appreciation of a lovely face is heightened by the plainness of our companions, the enjoyment of musical tones grows in proportion to the shrillness and discord of the sounds in one's milieu, and sweet tastes taste sweeter to those who have been deprived of them – even though the particular face, sounds and savours were hitherto unknown. Deprivation, Rāzī urges, is an absolute pre-condition of pleasure. The rule discovered in regard to some sensations properly applies to all. Those who are sated with a particular aesthetic quality will not welcome more of the same but will grow insensible to it. Ultimately they will find it painful, if it persists to the extent of moving them perceptibly from the natural state. Thus light is pleasurable to man, but darkness can seem restful after prolonged exposure to light.[39]

The same considerations, applied systematically to such areas as sexual activity, anger and even reading, yield the "spiritual physic" that forms the core of Rāzī's ethical regime.

— 3. DESIRE, MOTIVATION, AND FREE WILL —

Rāzī keeps pleasure within a mechanistic frame of reference by treating it as the reflex of pain. Conceiving the body as a complex of polyhedrons, spheres, cylinders and other hollow, elastic vessels,[40] Rāzī can readily picture its organs as capable of distension through a range of limits. The presence or absence of specific materials within or the impact of other bodies from without can bring distension or displacement to the threshold of sensation, pain, or harm. Relying on this model, Rāzī treats all desire on the analogy of appetite, reduplicating Epicurus' treatment of hunger as the paradigm of desire and repletion as the model of pleasure.[41] Even money may need to be replenished or "restored".[42]

Atoms lack plasticity, so the void is the condition of all motion. The dislocation responsible for pain, hunger, appetite or desire is no exception. Indeed Rāzī explains appetite mechanistically in terms of the attraction of the atoms by the void, specifically the attraction of the (depleted) organ for the matter proper to it.[43] In itself, of course, the void is wholly indeterminate, but such indeterminacy plays a critical role in Epicurean physics and thus in Epicurean psychology as well. To account for free will[44] and for the rise of complexity, the Epicureans appealed to an uncaused and imperceptible atomic "swerve", the famous *clinamen*. They defended this *ad hoc* foundation of chance and indeterminacy by urging that nothing prevents it.[45] Since the atoms move in the void, this literally was true. Since Epicurean atoms are infinitely elastic (absolutely solid), their collisions are strictly deterministic. But apart from their collisions and the momentum they seem to impart, and apart from the effects of their own weight, insofar as atoms are unimpeded and interact not with one another but with the void, their motions are undetermined. The two governing principles of the Epicurean cosmos, chance and causal law, for this reason, seem to rest on space and matter respectively. It was perhaps by recognising the absolute indeterminacy of space, alongside the absolute determinacy of matter, that Epicurus felt he had unfettered the atomic universe from Democritean determinism.

Like Epicurus, Rāzī needs an arbitrary principle to explain (irrational) choice, spontaneity, error, creativity and (excessive) appetite.[46] And, like

Epicurus, we find, he asserts an uncaused or spontaneous motion[47] and discovers its principle in the empty void. As in the Epicurean universe, the order and pattern of atoms place limits upon this principle of disorder. The void in itself is appetite (as it were) unqualified, the undifferentiated lack of and attraction for any and all matter. The void in a particular bodily organ is more specific. It lacks specifically what will fill or complement its cavity, restore its natural condition. But *qua* void it preserves some measure of indeterminacy.

Desire then, physiologically, is an emptiness, a specific kind and quantity of emptiness, capable of being filled. When its specificity is ignored desire seems without limit, an unqualified or unquantified, ever-changing, ever-increasing demand, by its very nature incapable of satiation.[48] But while specificity is a condition of rational desire, it is the indeterminacy of the void *qua* void that makes possible the arbitrary aspect of choice.[49] Along with rationality, such arbitrariness is, for Rāzī, as for Epicurus, a condition of free will. There is another, Platonic, factor in desire, however, since no mere hole or emptiness by itself, as Rāzī reasons, can actively desire, just as no mere mass of matter can move. Soul is the motive principle in Rāzī's cosmos, the life principle and principle of desire. It was Soul's desire for embodiment, a kind of repletion, after all, that put Rāzī's nature into motion in the first place, allowing Soul to become incarnate and subjecting her to loss and depletion as well as to the joys of restoration and replenishment.[50] But once Soul was embodied, animating those geometric solids and hollows that make up a living body, it was their emptiness that framed her desires.

To ground freedom of the will in any way in the indeterminacy of motions at the atomic level raises a serious problem in the phenomenology of willing. For the inclinations of free will seem to be anything but at hazard. Sir Arthur Eddington, who for a time sought refuge for human freedom in Heisenberg's indeterminacy principle,[51] seems for the nonce to have forgotten that such treatment demands a radically unconventional phenomenology of willing, preserving something of the capriciousness of its natural foundations. The Aristotelian objection to any such strategy would be that it unfetters human choices from the blind force of causal determinism only to shackle them to another blind force, the play of chance. But Epicureans do show some responsiveness to this problem. For in the Lucretian phenomenology of willing (*voluntas*) spontaneity of will is highlighted, linked with the spontaneity of pleasure (*voluptas*) and desire, and foregrounded in the poet's visualisation of the startling burst of energy when racehorses seem to freeze and then bolt from the starting gate:

If cause forever follows after cause
In infinite, undeviating sequence
And a new motion always has to come
Out of an old one, by fixed law; if atoms
Do not, by swerving, cause new moves which break
The laws of fate … where would we get
This free will that we have, wrested from fate,
By which we go ahead, each one of us,
Wherever our pleasures urge? Don't we also swerve
At no fixed time or place, but as our purpose
Directs us? There's no doubt each man's will
Initiates action, and this prompting stirs
Our limbs to movement. When the gates fly open,
No racehorse breaks as quickly as he wants to,
For the whole body of matter must be aroused,
Inspired to follow what the mind desires;
So, you can see, motion begins with will
Of heart or mind, and from that will moves on
Through all the framework. This is not the same
As our advance when we are prodded on
Or shoved along by someone else's force ….
Yet you see, don't you, something in ourselves
Can offer this force resistance, fight against it,
And this resistance has sufficient power
To permeate the body, to check the course,
To bring it to a halt? In atoms also
There has to be some other cause for motion
Beyond extrinsic thrust or native weight,
And this third force is resident in us
Since we know *nothing can be born of nothing* ….
What keeps the mind from having inside itself
Some such compulsiveness in all its doings,
What keeps it from being matter's absolute slave?
The answer is that our free-will derives
From just that ever-so-slight atomic swerve
At no fixed time, at no fixed place whatever.[52]

Will here evidently takes on some of the character of the chance movements to which it is ascribed. Rāzī, however, goes appreciably further in his recognition of the implications of binding free will to chance. He frontally attacks the Aristotelian treatment of free choice as a purely rational process,[53] sharply distinguishes will from reason, placing them, to some extent, at odds with one another, and boldly invokes a model of pure will as spontaneous; arbitrary, capricious and originative[54] – just as its roots at the atomic level would lead us to expect. Will is rational only to the extent that it is curbed and guided by reason, which Rāzī introduces in the role of a governor set upon the limitlessness of pure desire.[55]

Free will as it functions in motivation for Rāzī is not the work of pure chance but caprice moderated by reason. The determinacy of choice is ascribed to rationality; its indeterminacy, to the spontaneity of the soul. No actual material configuration is wholly indeterminate or empty. Correspondingly, no natural choice of the embodied soul is wholly indiscriminate. Like Epicurus, Rāzī links freedom with indeterminacy: the bounds of freedom are the limits of necessity, and the limits of necessity make room for freedom. Appetite, desire, even free will are given scope by the reality of chance and the void alongside atoms and determinacy. But motivation is more complex than the pure principle of freedom, since rationality is needed to define and delimit the bounds of choice.

In explaining human choices as an interplay of spontaneity with reason, Rāzī makes use of the classic Neoplatonic differentiation of Soul from Mind.[56] Mind, he reasons, the principle of rationality, cannot be identical with the principle of spontaneity. Both Mind and Soul are necessary to the individual and to the world. For it was Soul's passionate desire that brought the world to life: "Soul was enamored of matter, passionate to ground her sensory and intellectual perfections in it; thus arose – from the mingling of these two – the race of generated things."[57] The cosmogonic union that gave birth to all things began with the spontaneous and irrational desire of Soul for embodiment. Soul contained no literal void. Yet her desire was indiscriminate, as indeterminate as the matter that was its object. It is because her desire contained nothing to determine or differentiate matter that Soul unaided was powerless to bring her desire to fruition. Rationality was needed; matter needed the determination of form. Mind, in a word, was needed to complete the creative act that Soul would initiate.[58]

The glimpse that Rāzī's account of the cosmic Soul affords us into the relations of reason and desire opens the way to an understanding of the limitations he must have found in materialism in psychology. It thus helps us to see the grounds for his departures from materialism in ethics as well.

— 4. RĀZĪ'S ETHICS AND THE ETHICAL TRANSPARENCY OF HEDONISM —

When Rāzī's contemporaries heard him claiming to have made philosophy his way of life,[59] they naturally expected to find in him a follower of the philosophical school, as they imagined it. Its leaders would be his guides; his life would be modelled on theirs. Socrates would be his *imām*; the ways of the great philosophers would be his *sunna*. This was not the first time, nor would it be the last, that the methods of a field were transmogrified, for outsiders or even participants, into the doctrines or the habits of a school. Nor is it in the tenth century alone that intellectual independence and originality of thought have seemed rather alien notions. Clearly it was politic, among Rāzī's contemporaries, to present new ideas as ancient ones restored. And ideas typically came bundled in a tradition. As propaedeutics to praxis, all thoughts were expected to come branded with legible signs of ritual and manner.

Rāzī's outspoken rejection of traditionalism[60] set him at a distance from his more conformist contemporaries. His medical writings are full of efforts not just to expand but to surpass the received tradition.[61] The same spirit dominates his philosophy. No Muslim claimant to the title of philosopher is less prone than Rāzī to see himself as a follower or commentator, or more eager to engage the live issues of philosophy. For Rāzī's critic and interlocutor Abū Ḥātim al-Rāzī, the assumption that a philosopher must be a follower of philosophical paradigms and paragons was underscored by Shī'ī notions of authority and dogma, the *taqlīd* of the *imām*. But for Muḥammad b. Zakariya', despite his respect for the thinking of Plato and the person of Socrates, the title of philosopher belonged pre-eminently to those who use independent judgement in the search for truth.[62] "You must realise", he told Abū Ḥātim, who reports his words in shocked dismay,

> that every later philosopher who commits himself creatively (*ijtahada*), diligently, and persistently to philosophical inquiry where subtle difficulties have led his predecessors to disagree, will understand what they understood and retain it, and improve on it, having a quick mind and much experience of thought and inquiry in other areas. Because he has the skill to master what his predecessors knew and grasp the lessons that others afford, he readily surpasses them. For inquiry, thought and originality make progress and improvement inevitable.[63]

Philosophy for Rāzī was anything but a closed book, let alone an exclusively Academic or Peripatetic one. His independent spirit shows vividly in his ethics. By his own confession, he modelled his ethical practice not on the example of "the philosophers" but on the pattern set by his own theory. And in ethical theory, to a striking degree, Rāzī turned to Epicurean ideas, both in matters of detail and in demarcating the standard from which, he insists, all his specific moral teachings derive.[64]

Rāzī heartily rejects the ascetic extremes that tradition projected on to the persona of Socrates. He may not know that it was the Cynic Diogenes, not Socrates, who lived in a barrel. But he does know, contrary to the Cynic Apocrypha, that Socrates went to war, fathered children and attended the theatre.[65] Indeed, Socrates is said to have shown off his physiognomy at the first performance of *The Clouds*. This last Rāzī would not know, but he does know that Socrates ate well and drank – sparingly, Rāzī says; and the *Symposium*, in a backhanded way, confirms it. So Rāzī applies the Cynic legend to the early career of Socrates, when the "youthful zeal" for philosophy was strongest and the passions most in need of a damper.[66] For himself, Rāzī prefers the more moderate lifestyle of the mature Socrates to the supposed earlier pattern that he ascribes to a young man's infatuation with novelty.[67]

Rāzī's frequent appeals to moderation[68] may suggest an Aristotelian ethical standard.[69] But the resemblance is superficial. Aristotelian moderation is discovered by practical wisdom. The Aristotelian mean is not simply or even largely a quantitative issue but a matter of appropriateness, as judged by the standards of nobility and by all the relevant considerations of intent, consequence, and circumstance. Aristotle's ethics cannot be demeaned to a mere pleasure-pain calculus. But that, on the whole, is what Rāzī's is.[70] Reason serves; but, in practical decision making, its role is largely instrumental.

Restraint of desire, Rāzī writes, is the noblest of the moral virtues and the key to the rest: all virtue rests on self-control.[71] Yet Rāzī's marshalling of the virtues under the banner of self-restraint is a far cry from Socrates' insistence on the inseparability of sophrosyne from justice, honesty, truthfulness, friendship, courage and wisdom. Rāzī's argument is not that moral integrity outweighs all other presumed advantages, still less that the virtues form an indissoluble unity. What he claims, simply, is that restraint of the passions is our safest and most profitable course.[72] His paradigm of moral choice is a homely medical illustration: an ophthalmic boy whose brief enjoyment of a handful of dates will be outweighed by the bellyache they bring on.[73]

What we have here is not an appeal to Plato's "art of measurement". For Rāzī asserts, contrary to both Plato and Aristotle (*NE* I 3, 1094b 12 ff; cf. *Statesman* 924b), that moral decisions need only a simple rule, a weighing or calculation.[74] And what counts in this calculus, where Plato insists that all goods be included, are simply pleasures and pains.[75] That is why Rāzī can lay all moral virtues to the charge of restraint of desire and ascribe all moral vices to its free play.[76] Rāzī transforms the Platonic rule of justice in the soul, by which reason is meant to govern, into an equilibration (*taʿdīl*) regulating the appetitive impulses of the vegetative soul, the passionate impulses of the irascible soul, and even the intellectual aspirations of the rational soul.[77] Ethics here returns, by a circuitous route, to the hedonic base that Plato and Aristotle had sought to transcend. The Socratic "tendance of the soul" has become a "spiritual physic".

The point needs to be made clearly, since both Shlomo Pines, in a face-to-face exchange, and Majid Fakhry in print have emphasised Rāzī's Platonism, as has Thérèse Druart.[78] Fakhry writes: "That al-Rāzī should be regarded as the outstanding Platonist of Islam, in the fields of metaphysics and cosmology, should be considered established. I wish to reinforce this thesis here by underscoring the chief features of his ethical Platonism."[79] Fakhry goes on to cite Rāzī's "repudiation of hedonism" based on the analysis of pleasure as a return to the natural state. Rāzī's analysis clearly does urge the futility of a life spent in attempts to pile up ever greater pleasures. But Rāzī ascribes the argument, as Fakhry notes, to "the physical philosophers" – the standard Arabic designation of philosophical naturalists or materialists. Rāzī cites them specifically for his rejection of the sybaritic life, calling them "those philosophers who did not assign an independent existence to the soul".[80] That is not a reference to Plato. Yet, as Fakhry reminds us, the analysis is clearly "adumbrated in *Philebus*, 31d and 42c and *Timaeus*, 64d and is reported by Galen in his compendium of the *Timaeus*, extant only in Arabic".[81] The same analysis of pleasure is taken up by al-Āmirī, who ascribes it to Galen.[82] Paraphrasing Rāzī's view, Fakhry writes, "It is because of their ignorance of the genuine nature of pleasure that the incontinent yearn for never-ending enjoyment, little suspecting that the [sustained] duration of the pleasurable condition is impossible, since it can only come in the wake of the condition preceding it, i.e., pain."[83]

The reasoning is indeed Platonic. It is the ancient argument that Plato suggests by imaging the souls of the foolish as a leaky jar that can never be filled (*Gorgias* 493b). Why, then, does Rāzī ascribe it to materialists? We see the hint of an answer in the twist Rāzī gives the argument. Entering into the spirit of Plato's reasoning, he criticises the sybaritic life on hedonistic grounds, arguing that pursuit of maximal intensity or extended duration in pleasures and efforts to accumulate pleasures are inherently self-frustrating. In the hands of Epicurus, who was schooled in Platonism,[84] these arguments of Plato's formed the basis of a trenchant hedonistic critique of the crude hedonism of the Cyrenaic school. Here was the line of argument that captured Rāzī's imagination. For if we note the conclusion Rāzī draws from his analysis of pleasure we find him glancing longingly, almost wistfully, toward Plato's intellectualism but basing his ethical reasoning at every stage and for every practical choice on the prudential considerations he derives from his model of the physiology of pleasure.

Epicurus' argument against the Cyrenaics is the clearest lesson he learned from Plato. Hedonism will never be an ethically serious option as long as it seems merely to urge maximisation of pleasurable sensations. But by adapting

Plato's art of measurement to his own hedonistic programme, Epicurus can set reason in the service of pleasure, as a prudential umpire of pleasures and pains, reminding us of the welcome and unwelcome sensations that loom beyond the horizon of the specious present. Explaining that those who live to gratify their appetites seem only to enlarge those appetites, Plato had aptly compared their toils to attempts to carry water in a sieve or fill a hole with the earth dug out of it. Guided by Plato's analysis of pleasure, Epicurus could replace Cyrenaicism with a more modest and more practical hedonism based on a few home truths about pleasure:

1. That pleasures do not grow in linear progression with the intensity of sensations.
2. That pleasures are not possessions to be amassed or accrued.
3. That the sensation of pleasure results (at least in key paradigm cases) from the process of alleviating pain or lack.[85]
4. That (given 1–3) the optimum of pleasure is to be sought not in unlimited sensory gratifications (the illusory aim of appetite) but in *ataraxia*, peace of mind.

Distinguishing pleasurable sensations or kinetic pleasures from what he calls katastemic or resting pleasures (which are, strictly, not sensations at all), Epicurus can ascribe the sensations of kinetic pleasures to underlying bodily processes, while at the same time preferring katastemic pleasures as the optimum that sybaritic apologists systematically lose sight of.[86] Kinetic pleasures, he says are "a mere tickling (γαργαλισμός) of the flesh".[87] Using these core ideas, Epicurus could develop his own, prudential version of hedonism.[88]

Plato himself was after higher game. His art of measurement was no mere hedonic calculus but arose in the recognition that goods are incommensurate and so need a higher faculty than sensation to judge among them: appetite cannot set its own limits or adjudicate its quarrels, say, with honour, piety or curiosity. Intelligence must do the judging. For intelligence, that is reason, knows itself and its objects; it can test those objects not directly against each other (since they have no common denominator) but against the touchstone of the Good itself, which it must know if it is to judge anything at all, let alone succeed in its political task within the psyche or the state. Plato here takes aim at a moving target, pointing us toward the recognition that reason cannot be a mere umpire of prudence but must be a judge of values, including values that have nothing in common but the fact that they are values, expressions of or declensions from a higher Good. The departure from the realm of sense that follows our recognition of the need for reason to adjudicate among incommensurate goods is, of course, a journey Epicurus does not take. Hence his denial that pleasures are of ultimately different kinds,[89] his insistence that all are physical, and his linkage of that doctrine with the claim that peace of mind is the highest happiness (*KD* 9, *VF* 33). For, in the end, Epicurean peace of mind is a special kind of physical undisturbedness.

Rāzī reconstructs or reinvents the Epicurean position. He does not imbibe the dogmatic materialism, but he does absorb the hedonism. He gives reason the task of moderating the passions and sets philosophy to cool them further, by displacing vulgar notions of pleasure with a more adequate conception.[90] Reason in morals means weighing long-term peace of mind against short-term sensations.[91] Ethical philosophy becomes the application of scientific understanding, that is, the Epicurean physiology of pleasure as a sensation resulting from restoration of the natural state. Rāzī reinstates the Epicurean bifurcation of pleasures into the static and the kinetic, treating the static state as the goal of desire, and the sensation of pleasure as a result of those phases of sensation that reflect movement in that direction. The natural limitation of all (wholesome) desires is a direct corollary of Rāzī's Epicurean physiology of pleasure.[92]

Rāzī knows Plato, but what he makes his own replicates Epicurus' naturalist reduction of Plato's critique of desire. The priggish story Rāzī tells of Plato's rebuke to a tardy student who was losing sleep over a girl gives a pretty good idea of what character reformation means to Rāzī. It means a rap on the knuckles for passion – a crude reduction of Plato's ethical stance. As Druart acknowledges, "al-Rāzī is at pains to provide for his arguments a fairly neutral or minimalist philosophical framework which does not take a stance on difficult issues such as the nature of the soul and its immortality or God's attributes and causation".[93] Rāzī's ethical arguments rest on the standard Epicurean claim that the best way to maximise pleasure is to minimise desire. In the words of Epicurus:

> You must consider that of the desires some are natural, some are vain ... some necessary for happiness, some for the ease of the body, some for life itself. The man who has perfect knowledge of this will know how to make every choice or rejection tend toward gaining health of body and peace of mind, since this is the ultimate goal of the blessed life. For to gain this end, namely freedom from pain and fear, we do everything. When once this condition is reached, all the storm of the soul is stilled .... For we only feel the lack of pleasure when from its absence we suffer pain; but when we no longer suffer pain we are no longer in need of pleasure.[94]

Rāzī is probably following a scent he picks up in Galen. But, as Rāzī says, philosophers are quick learners. The well trodden trailhead from Plato's text should not tempt us to confuse Rāzī's earthy prudentialism with Plato's intellectualist aims or to confound Rāzī's rejection of the all-consuming pursuit of sensations with a rejection of hedonism *tout court*. Rāzī's ethics is far closer in mood to Epicurus than to any other ancient philosopher. Indeed, several authors including Ibn al-Qiftī, Abu 'l-Faraj b. al 'Ibrī, and Hillī attempt to cite Epicurus as the source of Rāzī's hedonism but run aground on an early copyist's or redactor's confusion of Epicurus with Pyrrho. Al-Fārābī and Sā'id al-Andalūsī are among the authors who escape this error.[95]

Rāzī shows his hedonist colours when he defines virtue as moderation regarding the objects of appetite and desire[96] and again when he assigns all vice to some excess of passion or desire.[97] His ethical suasions are anchored in calculations about safety, pleasure, or profit, where safety and profit themselves are understood in terms of potential pain and pleasure. The goods Rāzī cites as standards of action are pleasures; the ills are pains. His ethical norms are applications of the maxim that we should choose long-term pleasures and avoid the long-term pains that so many pleasures bring in train. His analysis of pleasure exposes the futility of a life devoted to sheer sensual gratification.[98] But he does not move on to Plato's conclusion, that the ultimate ethical standard must be sought beyond the hedonic. He is content to point out that it is senseless to seek satisfaction of appetites that can never be finally sated, gratification of desires that can never fully be assuaged.[99]

Philosophically, much of the interest of Rāzī's ethical stance springs from its roots in hedonism and in a dialectic internal to hedonism: like Epicurus, Rāzī replaces a vulgar with a more philosophical hedonic standard. If we knew from the outset, say, that Speusippus was right in condemning pleasure *per se*, or even if we knew of a certainty, with Plato, that there are higher goals than those of the senses, Rāzī's inference that the sheer pursuit of maximal sensuous gratification is misguided would be trivial or otiose, and his counsel to maximise gratification by minimising desire would be more misleading than helpful. But Rāzī rests nothing on Plato's higher claims, knows nothing of Speusippus, and shows no regard for the wholesale rejection of pleasures that was the stock-in-trade of so many of his pietist contemporaries.

Rāzī's high praise for reason[100] may suggest a Platonic intellectualism, although his encomia smack more of Lucretius' proemia than of the Socratic distaste for such fulsome praise.[101] But consider what reason is praised for: practical reason for Rāzī is less a standard of judgement than a form of restraint. Reason is praised for its many profits and benefits, its capacity to save us from harm, provide for our defence and secure our supremacy over all creation.[102] Intellect does open a path to immortality.

But Rāzī does not speak of Plato's forms in this regard. He does not share Plato's love of mathematics (the more abstract the better) but condemns mathematical studies as useless.[103] Reason here is valued for where it takes us, and Rāzī's ethical work seems reticent about the constitutive role of reason in the quest for immortality – the genuinely Platonic argumentation that finds reason capable of making us immortal not just by what it does but by what it is. Practical reason, for Rāzī, must work to earn the authority it holds over human life. Contrast the democratic Rāzī here with the aristocratic Plato, who privileges practical reason on epistemic grounds, because it alone can choose among the disparate and incommensurate goods of appetite, passion and intellect itself.

Despite the capacity of the mind to raise us to a higher world by thoughts of higher things, Rāzī does not whole-heartedly adopt Aristotle's ideal of a life devoted to theory for its own sake, any more than he absorbs Aristotle's analysis of pleasure as a by-product of the sense of completeness in an activity. As a result, there is a vice in Rāzī's accounting that is unknown in Plato or Aristotle, the excess of the rational soul, excessive concern with the things of the mind.[104] The yearning for wisdom, Plato's highest form of *eros*, is here an appetite to be moderated or "treated", like any other. Passions, as such, are not bad in themselves, not sinful, but they can impede our ends, and the passion for understanding is no exception. Contrast Aristotle's care to remove the intellectual virtues from the entire scheme of the mean that maps the moral virtues: one cannot be too wise. Or contrast Plato. Can one, in Plato's scheme, have too much of the intellectual, of the real ideas?

Rāzī's version of the classic "futility" or frustration argument voiced by Plato is continually addressed to issues of health and contentment. Rāzī senses the irony in self-frustrating quests, but he does not, as Kant will do, and as Socrates had done long before, pinion any formal inconsistency between what is sought and what is got by those who seek avidly to serve their appetites and passions. It is Rāzī's earthier analysis that chooses Socrates' "later" over his "earlier" career and blames the younger Socrates for succumbing to over-intellectualism.[105] Similarly, using a purely prudential, hedonic standard to assay the love of wisdom, Rāzī draws the distinction between his own life and that of Socrates as a matter of degree. Contrary to Rāzī's own dictum,[106] reason here has become not the measure but the measured. It is valued not for its own sake but because it sweetens life, gives us seafaring, medicine and our knowledge of God – "our most profitable attainment".[107]

Unlike the Epicureans, Rāzī does not deny an afterlife. Indeed, the avenue he proposes for access to immortality is Platonic. Independent exercise of reason, "even in the slightest degree", is our sole portal to the hereafter. For "souls are cleansed only by thought and inquiry".[108] Thus Rāzī does not affirm a physical resurrection on the Islamic model, with eternal blessing or damnation contingent on prophetic faith. Even when he mentions the bad end, say, of those who are cruel to animals, he brackets the idea, as the view of other philosophers. As for scripture, all prophets are frauds. Faith in their "old wives tales" is not a stepping stone but a stumbling block to the kind of intellectual activity that leads to immortality.[109]

In the story of the young man and the dates, which she calls "simplistic", Druart sees an intention to rely on reasoning accessible to one who does not know that the human animal and vegetative souls exist to serve the rational soul. Similarly with Rāzī's strictures against lying: prudential arguments are used for dialectical reasons. Again with carnal pleasures: "The very coarseness of these desires is matched by the crassness of the arguments al-Rāzī uses."[110] Those who have made some philosophical progress would presumably find nobler arguments, opened to them by their higher and more properly philosophical concerns. What these concerns are is summed up in Plato's admonition (*Theaetetus* 176) that the task of man is to become as like to God as humanly possible. They hinge on recognition of our intellectual access to immortality.

I see some truth in the claim that Rāzī's earthiest arguments have a dialectical intent. Socrates himself, after all, would not have got far in his arguments with the Sophists had he pinned his claims on an idealism they could not share. Far more effective, dialectically, is argumentation that shows the futility and incoherence of Thrasymachus' or Callicles' programmes even in their own terms. But there is another factor as well to consider in Rāzī's case. Not only are the vulgar resistant to higher claims but their very idea of everlasting life is itself mired in sensuality and incoherence. It is with popular piety in mind, I think, that Rāzī problematises immortality. He insulates his purely hedonic ethical standard from the Platonism of his soteriology for much the same sort of reasons that led Plato to isolate his unconditioned ethical standard from any trace of hedonism that it might acquire from his soteriology. To avoid tainting his appeal in behalf of the unconditioned preciousness of justice, Plato in the *Republic* deferred questions about immortality until the intrinsic worth of justice was established. Rāzī, for his part, seems eager to show that a sound ethics can be derived from prudential, hedonic considerations alone, without reference to transcendence. He makes a point of arguing only from hedonic considerations, even as he recognises that stronger ethical injunctions might be derived, say, on Platonic principles.[111] The worldliness he adopts as a result is the heart of Epicurean ethics, where deference to any standard other than pleasure and pain – be that standard social, religious, traditional, or in some other way imported from without into the inner and individual forum of reason and sensibility – is regarded not only as misleading but as unwholesome, heteronomous and in effect, immoral.[112]

Rāzī does think that (independent) thinking is what redeems us from this world, where we are, rather gnostically, trapped. But, within ethics, Rāzī conscientiously suppresses his Platonic scheme for the restoration of the soul to its divine home. Indeed, he treats soteriology itself strictly hedonically, attacking worldly pleasures not by dismissing worldliness but (with a calculating spirit to rival Pascal's in the *Pensées*) by preferring the infinitely greater pleasures that await us in the hereafter.[113] And Rāzī is at pains to leave open the Epicurean alternative, that "death is nothing to us." Taking up the Epicurean topos of the fear of death in the closing chapter of the *Spiritual Physick*, he pleads that a discussion of the soul's fate that could rise above mere hearsay – that is, reliance on received religious traditions – and reach a level of demonstrative force would take far longer than the time available to him, "especially in this book", and would demand a systematic survey of all religious traditions and their views about the manners of life that lead to various sorts of state in various sorts of hereafter.[114] Rather than attempt such a discussion here in his work on ethics, Rāzī offers the Socratic disjunction:[115] either death is dissolution and brings only surcease from life's sufferings, or it is a passage to a higher state, if the promises of one or another of the received religious accounts proves true. One who doubts the veracity of those accounts (as Rāzī does), should use his mind to discover the truth, and that will bring him to his goal. Note the thrust here: the promises of religion are to be doubted, but doubt opens the door to philosophy, and philosophy is the one key, if there is any, to immortality. Clearly Rāzī does hope for immortality of the sort that Plato promised. He affirms that anyone who uses his God-given intelligence independently can reach that goal. But he also believes that any proof of immortality would be difficult, and he refuses to ground his ethics on other-worldly appeals. For the most prominent of those appeals are the suasions of the prophets, and these are old wives' tales at best – when they are not springs of fanaticism.

Druart distinguishes a higher and a lower ethics in Rāzī: an ethics of immortality enunciated in the *Philosophic Life* and a "pre-philosophical" ethics articulated in the *Spiritual Physic*. I think she is right in suggesting that the two works address a somewhat different imagined reader and use different dialectical premises. She rightly points out Rāzī's frequent references to human superiority over the animals, to the divine life of Plato, and to the immortality that religion promises and that reason can bring.[116] But Rāzī never makes a premise of these notions when he seeks to ground ethical injunctions. All of his ethical argumentation appeals to hedonic, prudential concerns. In the *Philosophical Life* these are supplemented by the concerns of justice and of intellect itself. But neither justice nor understanding is treated as an intrinsic good. The goods of the intellect are our means to immortality. They are not constitutive of it. And justice is our means to attaining God's favour and entry to a more blissful state, in so far as the words of the prophets are to be credited. Coupled with his Platonising principles, Rāzī holds fast to the Epicurean affirmation that the world amply provides all that our natures require – thus, all that we genuinely need. His only modifications to this ancient Epicurean thesis are his attribution of such provisions to God's generosity in the act of creation, and the characteristically Rāzīan admonition that our access to such necessities depends on our readiness to exert ourselves to secure them. In the *Ṭibb al-Rūḥānī*, Rāzī's announced ethical standard is hedonic. The appeal is to a pleasure-pain calculus, by which all value choices are to be made, even those that involve reason or the Kingdom of Heaven. We can say that Rāzī's worldly ethics reflects the limitations of a worldly audience, but one must recognise as well that Rāzī himself does not seem to distance himself from the doubts and demands of that audience. Indeed, when scripture comes into play, his motive is to heighten those doubts. Plato's idealism has a spiritual function for Rāzī, to be sure, but in theory and practice the ethics he spells out is the ethics of Epicurus.

Rāzī boasts that all assignments of value within his ethics can be hedonically derived. Is this true? Superficially at least, a rival standard seems to be in play. For in almost every concrete decision, Rāzī counsels the avoidance of pleasure, putting philosophy to work as a discipline or control on the passions: philosophy itself is the spiritual physic that enables us to combat our desires.[117] On this basis can we really speak of Rāzī as a hedonist? Externally his maxims sound more like the voice of duty than like any form of naturalism. But unlike Kant, Rāzī understands moral obligation not in terms of reverence for the moral law but in terms of the repression of desire. And in addressing specific choices, his consistent rule is to maximise pleasure by minimising desire.

Paradigmatically, Rāzī wears his medical hat to warn his reader that over-indulgence in drink or sexual pleasure, or even music, undercuts the very pleasures sought.[118] The argument assumes that a hedonic optimum is the aim, and that such a quest is perfectly legitimate, natural and appropriate. Prudentially and without moralising, Rāzī counsels that the optimum will be found in vigorous avoidance of excess. Similarly when he addresses long-term drawbacks and short-term gains. His talk of the expense involved in various appetitive vices, the risks others may pose to health or reputation – all his claims of this ilk anchor prudential arguments appealing to a primary pleasure–pain principle: vice is irrational, in some way mad. It fails to weigh the advantages of alternative choices or to recognise the locus of one's own interest. There is no way to distinguish the vicious individual from one bent on self-destruction.[119] Pleasure is a baited trap. One who does not see this cannot attain his goal – which is pleasure itself.

What we must do, to complete Rāzī's conceit, is relax the springs of the trap, unset it and gain the bait, now recognised with the abatement of desire, for the modest thing it is. It is not pleasure as an absolute that we seek,[120] but the enjoyment of pleasure. Enjoyment is possible, but only if we understand it in largely negative terms, as a state of rest, not a product but the endpoint of a process. Rāzī's sole argument against sybaritic hedonism, and all forms of perverse seeking of sensation or experience "for its own sake", arises from this analysis. He flatly denies (calling on his medical authority) that any form of excess or perversion (he is prone to identify the two) is enjoyable. Standing fast with his premiss, that it is pleasure that we and all living things do (and should) seek, he insists that specious pleasures be exposed for what they are, with all their dangers and drawbacks: the glutton's maw, as Plato showed, cannot be filled.[121] Besides, gluttony earns its victim disgrace as well as indigestion.[122] Love is degrading[123] – not sinful, but overrated by its literary panegyrists,[124] and fraught with dangers of loss and grief that far outweigh its brief joys.[125]

Sex, Rāzī urges, is harmful to health. It need not be completely avoided, but an awareness of its drawbacks counsels moderation, which in turn will prolong life in the contented state that is our true objective.[126] Like eating, drinking and many another pleasure, sex, not controlled, nurses a self-aggravating desire that leads to harm. Some pleasures, such as drink (and other opiates) are actually addictive – the hook is barbed.[127] Once the destructive processes are in motion, it is hard if not impossible to halt the dialectic that leads ultimately to ruin. But not only appetitive vices are self-defeating. Pride,[128] envy[129] and anger are purged by the same rationale. For pride earns one only contempt – just the opposite of what was desired. Envy may have its pleasures, but they are far outweighed by the bodily and mental damage that this gnawing habit wreaks on those who indulge it. Anger too, in excess, defeats its biological end. Like all forms of lunacy, it is a self-destructive rejection of the basic self-preserving drive that leads all living things to avoid pain and pursue pleasure. Rāzī illustrates by repeating Galen's anecdote about his mother's attempt, in anger, to force a lock with her teeth.[130] In each case, Rāzī works to keep the argument within the boundaries of the concept under investigation – to show that lust or anger is destructive of the very object it intends. Never does he depart from his assumption that the proper object of all desire is the maximisation of pleasure.

Moral vices reduce to errors of calculation, whether through ignorance or through some self-destructive urge.[131] Rāzī's sole arguments against lying are prudential, based on the inconvenience and ultimate disgrace attendant on prevarication[132] – a far cry from Kant's appeal to logic or to a right of all men to know the truth, and still further from Plato's appeal to the higher courts of metaphysics, psychology and politics, in response to the tale of Gyges – or from Saadiah's Rabbinic thought, that to misrepresent reality is an insult to the Creator. Stinginess, for Rāzī, arises from a misapprehension of one's own desires and the proper mode of securing their objects.[133] Anxiety and even enthusiasm in excess are self-defeating, impediments to the very objects they pursue.[134] Even Rāzī's suasion that it is better never to have loved than to have loved and lost[135] rests on purely hedonic standards.

Social vices like excessive ambition, social climbing, fawning and the like are condemned by Rāzī not for their indignity but for their riskiness and futility, and for the dependency they render inevitable.[136] Finally over-intellectualism, a fault that Rāzī's spirit of self-criticism[137] marks, along with excessive ambition, as a factor in his own career,[138] is condemned solely for its harmfulness to health and the unattainability of its goal when set too high or too passionately sought.[139] Pleasure here becomes the judge of reason.

Even benevolence, Rāzī's ground for all positive obligations of man to man and of man to himself,[140] is deduced, as promised, from hedonistic first principles. For Rāzī reads Plato's objective of becoming "as like to God as humanly possible" in the light of the Islamic principle of pleasing God.[141] Here God, not Socrates, is the philosopher's *imām*. In the imitation of God's benevolence and perfection Rāzī finds grounds for those human obligations of benevolence[142] and self-perfection that surpass the Epicurean goal of *ataraxia*.[143] But even here, the ultimate sanction is hedonic, an appeal to the reward that faith holds out for these scriptural obligations.[144]

Every part of Rāzī's ethic, then, is hedonistic. Is this hedonism the reflex of an effort on Rāzī's part to popularise the moral teachings of philosophy? Perhaps in part. But the philosophy popularised here is not that of Plato or Aristotle but that of Epicurus. And the idea that Rāzī could score dialectical points by advancing a hedonism he did not whole-heartedly accept is a notion that can cut at least two ways. For an open hedonism would hardly endear an already "heretical" outlook to Rāzī's contemporaries. By his own testimony and by his philosophical practice Rāzī takes the hedonic principles he elaborates quite seriously as guides to his own practical decision-making. He appeals to those principles as the standard he has followed, and he uses them in the critique of his own ambitions.[145] Can one be said to popularise for his own sake? Rāzī's own explanation may prove more fruitful. He admires Platonism for its spirituality, its rigorous "combating of passions and desires", but he finds its ideals somewhat impracticable; their practice, at times at least, excessive; and their theory, the faith of the philosopher in intellectual immortality, perhaps at times a bit too lofty to be of direct moral use. He sees his own, hedonic principles as a tempering of Platonic zeal, yielding a more balanced (if less god-like) human life.[146] Rāzī presents himself as sharing the aim of the Platonists, but choosing means that are more moderate.[147]

Plato had criticised the crude hedonism made canonical by the Cyrenaics, revealing how sybaritic readings of hedonism rest on a faulty understanding of pleasure. But Epicurus took over Plato's arguments to urge a different conclusion, to show not that ethics needs to move beyond the hedonic but rather that a new and more philosophical hedonism can be grounded on moderating desire in order to maximise its fulfilment. In drawing ascetic practical conclusions from hedonistic ethical assumptions, Rāzī rediscovers and reconstructs the core of Epicurean ethics, its distinctive, Plato-chastened interpretation of hedonism and its distinctive, Platonically charged, analysis of pleasure.

Not surprisingly, then, Rāzī's ethics revives or reinvents numerous Epicurean themes. Rāzī works conscientiously to keep his ethics within the confines of an Epicurean axiom system, rather than make it dependent on any particular vision of the afterlife – even his own.[148] He canonises the traditional Epicurean discussion of the fear of death,[149] the Epicurean misogyny and bias against the erotic,[150] the Epicurean identification of pleasure as the animating and therefore legitimating principle of all desires,[151] the Epicurean democratic (and anti-Platonic) notion that one man is as good as another in judging of good and evil (or anything else he puts his mind to),[152] and the Epicurean relativisation of virtue to the strength of desire and the habituation of "felt need", (expressed in the notion that "it was easier for Socrates to be abstinent than for Plato").[153] Despite these hallmarks of Epicurean ethical thinking, Rāzī's ethic is syncretic, as witness his deference to the Cynic "Socrates"[154] and other pure ascetics who by strict application of Rāzī's own hedonic standard would count as "madmen".[155] The purest sort of philosopher, it seems, may take on a stronger obligation than ordinary men not just to be rational but to curb his desires.[156]

Rāzī embraces the Epicureans' analysis of pleasure at least as whole-heartedly as they, recognising that the treatment of pleasurable sensation as a mere relaxation of tension makes the avoidance of pain the prime ethical desideratum.[157] Pressing further, Rāzī urges that deprivation is easier to bear than loss[158] and argues that ascetic (but not hedonic) excess may be called for therapeutically.[159] He licenses indulging our appetites not wherever it is likely that pleasure will outweigh pain but only where it is certain that pain will not outweigh pleasure.[160] And his approach to moral training looks almost more Stoic than Epicurean,[161] although it serves an Epicurean end. For he counsels us to inure ourselves to losses by considering the objects of our affection already lost.[162] He encourages us to practise for hardships we may never have to undergo, by forcing ourselves to accept privations, as a discipline to body and soul.[163] Perhaps these biases in Rāzī's application of the hedonic programme express a certain risk-averseness on his part. They are clearly not the product, say, of a Platonic intellectualism, nor even of a properly Stoic equation of happiness with virtue and the path of duty. But, regardless of their source, they give Rāzī's ethics a somewhat dour aspect that may seem out of keeping with its hedonistic first principle.

A further problem is posed by Rāzī's repeated (albeit hedonic) reference to an afterlife. For surely the rejection of all such appeals to transcendence is the hallmark of Epicurean ethical and intellectual integrity and the express primary motive for all truly Epicurean philosophy. Rāzī's Epicurean doctrine of the predominance of sufferings in this life jostles awkwardly into place with his optimistic theodicy and his rejection of the Epicureans' absolute denial of providence. His curious *melange* of commitments leads him to a most un-Epicurean soteriology that reintroduces the very otherworldliness that Epicurus thought it the prime task of philosophy to remove.[164]

Finally there is the whole question of Rāzī's motivation in exposing (hedonically, to be sure) the vices he singles out for attention. Like the Epicureans, Rāzī bears an animus against the abuse of appetite and passion, and to this he adds the recognition of an analogous flaw in intellectualism. But Rāzī's choice of targets and his intensity in scouring them do not follow from hedonism alone. The futility analysis might, in fact, have been turned upon many another object besides mere appetitive and passional excesses – for example, it might have been trained on the search for tranquillity itself, as in the *tu quoque* one might address to Buddhists who too avidly and ambitiously pursue the quest for the cessation of all desire. Yet Rāzī takes care to direct his fire only at specific carefully defined targets, even straw men. He is a free-thinker, but the term must be applied in a relative sense, and then with caution. He wrenched free of some of the prevailing presumptions of his age, but it would be hard to say that even his hedonism serves any but rather conventional moral purposes.

I think we can see from the philosophical remains themselves how it is that Platonic intellectualism and ethical hedonism could settle down and live together in Rāzī's mind. Just as Kant made an afterlife a postulate of morals rather than a theorem of metaphysics, Rāzī distinguishes between what philosophy leads him to hope for and what reason enables him to prove. Immortality, at least of a Platonic sort, is the highest reach of reason. But, for that very reason, it is not the ground on which Rāzī will build his earthy ethics. What we see in Rāzī's surviving ethical writings is the work of a living philosopher and no mere plaster cast or doxographic bust of some long-dead exemplar of the stereotypic age of faith.

As for the ascetic biases we find in Rāzī's hedonism, I think they are less exceptions to its purity than assignments of a direction to hedonism itself. For the ascetic outcome is extra-philosophical and perhaps pre-concerted: it steers Rāzī's argumentation but does not directly enter into the argument itself. Formally the philosophy is hedonistic; but its asceticism is evident materially. Rāzī uses every opportunity afforded by the Epicurean analysis of pleasure to expose in its own terms the futility of pleasure-seeking. Although his ethical standard is consistently hedonistic and all the principles of practice he recommends are derived by him from strictly hedonistic tests, at no time does he praise or recommend a life of pleasure. He tests every proposed action hedonically, but the tests he uses have often been pre-judged by traditional or conventional moral standards; and the results he derives almost never vary from conventional prescriptions. Always in the background of his hedonic arguments, as if overseeing the outcomes, lurk Rāzī's notions of human nature, divine law and justice, moral propriety and equity.[165]

Is Rāzī's curiously ascetic hedonism, then, the outcome of an uneasy eclecticism, an incapacity or lack of opportunity to penetrate deeply into a single philosophical tradition or to graft a viable hybrid using Epicurean and Platonic stocks? A better explanation, I think, arises from the nature of the philosophical materials themselves. Perhaps what we have found here is not an ambivalence on Rāzī's part so much as a systemic weakness in hedonism, what I would call its ethical transparency.

To explain: any hedonically oriented ethical system seems to acquire the burden of proof in showing that its counsels mesh with those of other sources – tradition, convention or some rival philosophy. The hedonist who fails to convince on this point risks not being taken seriously as an ethicist. Even to equate the ethical with the prudential is, as Cicero saw,[166] to make an ethical claim, and the hedonist needs to sustain the seriousness of such a claim in his own behalf. For he is not just saying that pleasure feels good but that pleasure and pain are legitimate moral standards. That is why Epicurean philosophy must anchor itself (not only for the sake of others but for its own self-respect and self-conviction) in its distinction from mere Cyrenaicism. This it does by maintaining a certain seriousness and scientific detachment and above all by deriving from within the Epicurean framework all the pertinent non-sensual, intellectual, moral and social values that might be held up as reproaches to Epicurean standards. Bentham similarly endeavours to derive the altruistic principles of benevolence and even self-sacrifice within the framework of his hedonistic assumptions. Indeed, he embeds social responsibility and equality in the greatest happiness principle, in much the way that Epicurus embedded the critique of Cyrenaicism in his version of hedonism and derived a social ethic (of *laissez-faire*) from the paramountcy of *ataraxia*. Mill's famous difficulty over qualitative versus quantitative differences in pleasure is a comparable attempt to reconcile a hedonistic ethical system with extra-hedonic values deeply held by others, and clearly by Mill himself.

The ethical hedonist finds the results of his value inquiry constantly exposed to the touchstones of alternative philosophical and non-philosophical moralities. What he must show (or prove to himself) is that hedonistic analysis yields choices that are at least as acceptable (in conventional terms) as those claiming some rival pedigree. It is this necessity that gives hedonism its ethical transparency. The hedonism of Epicurus is coloured by the value its author placed on the simple pleasures and on friendship and understanding. That of Bentham can no more be free of his distinctive moral evaluations than Mill's can be of the aesthetic claims that were being made in his time, and both Bentham and Mill absorb the prevailing ideas of progressive politics and social responsibility. Indeed, the appeal of suffrage reform is as much an extra-philosophical given for Bentham and Mill as is asceticism for Rāzī.

In none of these cases does hedonism simply dictate the specific course of the divergent material moralities. On the contrary, hedonism (being an ethic of pleasure) is transparent to a variety of external moral notions – not just because pleasures vary from person to person and from age to age (for some common ground might always be found), but because what is valued conventionally, philosophically, popularly, traditionally, extra-hedonically in a given society and age cannot be isolated from any hedonism put forth in that milieu without undermining the ethical authority of that hedonism for those to whom it is addressed, and even for those who seek to make philosophical sense of it to themselves.

Even what people enjoy cannot remain free of such extra-systemic considerations as these. *A fortiori*, what they are prepared to claim or admit they enjoy. This observation, I suspect, will be confirmed in quite a variety of historical and cross-cultural investigations of ethical philosophy. For the ethical transparency of hedonism, I believe, is a socio-historical consequence of the applicability of the "open question" to all forms of ethical naturalism. One doesn't need the sophistication of a G. E. Moore to recognise a problem in naturalism posed by the very openness of the question "But is it really good?" Thinking people who confront any reductive account of the good will readily enough raise that very question about any purported ethical analysis that makes them ethically uncomfortable. And, of course, as Moore shows, whenever there has been a reduction, it will always make sense for that question to be raised. In such a case, we have suggested, it will fall to the ethical naturalist to make his own claims answer to the standards of his milieu – or as many of these as he can respect or stomach.

It is in this light that we should understand Rāzī's ascetic hedonism. Hedonism for Rāzī seemed an adequate basis for deriving all practically necessary ethical principles. If hedonism grounds a critique of those who "sit in mosques all day",[167] or helps undermine the authority of prophets, who claim to know better than their hearers what constitutes the good for man, why so much the better.

Hedonism could never conflict with but only moderate the loftier claims of Platonic asceticism and other-worldliness. For any necessary ascetic principles could be derived from the Epicurean analysis of pleasure. But the excesses of asceticism could be dismissed out of hand on hedonic grounds, just as the spurious claims of prophetic soteriology could be bracketed on epistemic grounds. Thus Rāzī could afford to be a thorough-going hedonist, and in a way he could not afford not to be. But when it came to asking what practices were worthy of hedonic derivation, Rāzī naturally enough succumbed to the ascetic and intellectualist appeals of Philosophy (the Platonic and Aristotelian heritage) and to the powerful backgrounding ascetic impulses of his Islamic environment. For asceticism and intellectualism were the values that Philosophy and Islam, working in tandem, had persuaded him (and many of his contemporaries) could not be neglected in any sound ethical reasoning.

In this sense, then, despite Rāzī's rather outspoken and highly reasoned iconoclasm – that is, his refusal to confine ethical choice within the received Islamic or Platonic paradigm – hedonism is not paramount in his philosophy. It provides a kind of net for gathering up what he and many of his contemporaries deemed all the best and most acceptable ascetic and other-worldly values, reinforcing the claims of such values by prudential reasoning, and putting them within reach of the (ethically) ordinary man, without ever fully subordinating to an alien standard the claims of these "higher", religious and philosophical values, their claims, that is, to intrinsic, autonomous, or even transcendent worth.

— NOTES —

1. The *Fihrist* of al-Nadīm, trans. Bayard Dodge (New York: Columbia University Press 1970) pp. 706–8) cites several titles of Rāzī's in defence of teleology, including a (teleological) justification of the creation of wild beasts. Cf. Rāzī's *Philosophical Life*, which contains a defence of the wisdom of creation, and a (Galenic) teleology of the dilation of the pupil. Rāzī's *Philosophical Life* is translated by A. J. Arberry as "Rhazes on the Philosophical Life", in *Asiatic Review* 45 (1949) pp. 703–13; cited here pp. 707–8.
2. Kraus: Jurjānī p. 189, Isfahānī p. 196, Fakhr al-Dīn al-Rāzī p. 213.
3. Kraus, Fakhr al-Dīn al-Rāzī p. 205, and Qazwīnī ad loc.
4. Kraus: *Munāẓarāt* p. 309, etc.
5. The *Fihrist* of al-Nadīm (trans. Dodge, p. 706) ascribes to Rāzī a title on the inherence of motion in bodies. But body is not the same as matter. Just as motion is made possible by soul, it is soul that make bodies of matter.
6. Kraus: e.g. *Munāẓarāt* pp. 308–11.
7. Kraus: Fakhr a-Dīn al-Rāzī, p. 206; Qazwīnī ad loc.
8. Kraus: Nāsir-i-Khusraw p. 149.3–4.
9. Kraus: Nāsir-i-Khusraw p. 149.4.
10. *Spiritual Physick*, Arberry, p. 25; Kraus: Shīrāzī p. 42; cf. *Fihrist* trans. Dodge, p. 377. Rāzī will have found it impossible to deal fully with coitus without discussing this aspect along the lines proposed in the *Spiritual Physick*; cf. Kraus pp. 142–55.
11. Epicurus, *Vatican Sayings* 4, etc.
12. Kraus: Nāsir-i-Khusraw, p. 149.3–4.
13. Epicurus *To Herodotus* 39b; cf. Leucippus and Democritus ap. Alexander of Aphrodisias *De Sensu* 56.12 (Kirk and Raven no. 588).
14. F. M. Cornford, *Plato's Cosmology* (New York, repr. first ed. 1937) p. 260.
15. Richard Walzer and Paul Kraus edited the Arabic text as *Galeni Compendium Timaei Platonis* in *Plato Arabus I* (London: Warburg Institute, 1951). Rāzī's super-commentary on Plutarch's (quasi-creationist) commentary on the *Timaeus* is listed in *Fihrist* trans. Dodge, p. 706; cf. Kraus, p. 140.
16. Alexander of Aphrodisias, *De Sensu* 61; cf. Cornford, p. 261.
17. Democritus frag. 9, Sextus *Against the Mathematicians* VII 135 (Kirk and Raven item 589 p. 422).
18. *Philosophical Life*, Kraus, p. 109; Arberry, pp. 711–12.
19. *Fihrist* trans. Dodge, p. 705. Rāzī's defence is of special interest. See Rudolf E. Siegel, *Galen on Sense Perception* (Basel, 1970) pp. 158 ff.
20. Epicurus ap. Sextus VII 216, *KD* 24, *Letter to Herodotus* 49–51.
21. See my discussion of "Rāzī's Myth of the Fall of the Soul", in G. F. Hourani, ed., *Essays on Islamic Philosophy and Science*.

22. Kraus: Mīrak p. 219.
23. Epicurus, *To Herodotus* 41.
24. Epicurus, *To Herodotus* 39b
25. See especially *DRN* II 433–6, IV 42–477.
26. *KD* 24, etc.
27. Kraus: Nāsir-i-Khusraw, p. 177; Arabic trans., p. 178. For the claim that the gods must be real, since men have seen them, see Epicurus, *Ad Men.*, in Diogenes Laertius, X 123–4; cf. *DRN* V 1169–82; *DND* I 46.
28. *DRN* 62–135, etc.
29. *DND* I 16.43.
30. *Fihrist* trans. Dodge, p. 704, etc.; cf. e.g. *DRN* II 1945 ff.
31. Kraus: Nāsir-i-Khusraw, p. 149; cf. Epicurus *To Herodotus* 38b.
32. Kraus: Nāsir-i-Khusraw, p. 149.1–2.
33. Epicurus, *To Menoeceus* 130 ff.; *DRN* II 962–6.
34. *Ṭibb al-Rūḥānī*, ii, v, Kraus, pp. 36–7, 70; Arberry, pp. 39, 75–6.
35. *Spiritual Physick* Arberry esp. p. 39; Kraus p. 36.
36. Kraus: Nāsir-i-Khusraw, p. 149, cf. *DRN* II 944–66. The model is still in use today. Masters and Johnson, for example, describe the sexual response cycle as a build up and release of tension.
37. Kraus: Nāsir-i-Khusraw, p. 153.
38. Kraus: Nāsir-i-Khusraw, p. 151. Contemporary physiologists of sensation do find that our perceptions of temperature are based on the prior temperature of the integument.
39. Kraus: Nāsir-i-Khusraw, p. 155.
40. Cf. S. Pines, "*Rāzī Critique de Galien*", Actes du Septieme Congres International d'Histoire des Sciences, Jerusalem, 1953, p. 483.
41. With Epicurus *Vatican Sayings* 9; cf. *Spiritual Physick* Arberry, pp. 40, 75–76; Kraus, p. 70: cf. Kraus: Nāsir-i-Khusraw, p. 143.
42. *Spiritual Physick*, Arberry, p. 29.
43. Kraus: Nāsir-i-Khusraw, pp. 217–18; cf. Fakhr al-Dīn al-Rāzī, p. 265; Pines "*Rāzī Critique de Galien*", p. 484. Apparently Rāzī believed that different sorts of void (as determined by the surrounding atoms) might attract different sorts matter. The notion may have figured in his account of magnetism (*Fihrist* trans. Dodge, p. 706), as the "general" attraction of matter by the void may have figured in what appears to have been his theory of gravitation; see Kraus: Fakhr al-Dīn al-Rāzī, p. 218.
44. Diogenes of Oenoanda frag. 33, William col. ii, end; *DRN* II 223 ff.
45. *DRN* II 235–6; cf. Epicurus' stock phrase "There is nothing to prevent …", e.g. *To Herodotus* 48.
46. For the irrational in Rāzī's cosmos, see Goodman, "Rāzī's Myth of the Fall of the Soul" and Goodman, "Rational and Irrational".
47. *Munāẓarāt*, Kraus, pp. 311–13.
48. *Spiritual Physick*, chapters 1–3; cf. Epicurus *To Menoeceus* 128 and *Vatican Sayings* 60.
49. Cf. Marzuqī's objections to the absolute indeterminacy of the Razian void, Kraus p. 201. Rāzī's void is neither active nor passive (Kraus: Jurjanī p. 189, etc.), like the Epicurean void, which can neither affect nor be affected: *To Herodotus* 67.

50. See Goodman, "Rāzī's Myth of the Fall of the Soul".
51. Sir Arthur Eddington, *The Nature of the Physical world* (Cambridge: Cambridge University Press, 1948), pp. 294–5.
52. *DRN* II 263–93, trans. Rolfe Humphries as *The Way Things Are* (Bloomington: Indiana University Press, 1968).
53. *NE* VI 2, 1139b 4–5: "choice (*prohairesis*) is either desireful reason (*orektikos nous*) or reasonable desire (*orexis dianoetike*)".
54. *Munāẓarāt*, Kraus, pp. 311–12; *Spiritual Physick*, Arberry, pp. 25–33; Isfahānī, pp. 207, etc.
55. *Spiritual Physick*, Arberry, pp. 25–33, 58; cf. Epicurus *KD* 20.
56. Kraus: Fakhr al-Dīn al-Rāzī, pp. 203–4.
57. Kraus: Qushajī, p. 216.
58. Kraus: Fakhr al-Dīn al-Rāzī, p. 206.
59. Rāzī accepted the idea that philosophy is a way of life, as witness the title of his "apologia pro vita sua", as Arberry calls it: *Kitāb al-Sīratu 'l-Falsafiyya*. The title is usually translated "The Philosophical Life", but the force of the term *sīra* might be better conveyed by rendering it: *The Philosophical Way of Life*; see *Sīratu 'l-Falsafiyya*, Kraus, p. 99.
60. *Munāẓarāt*, Kraus, p. 295–301.
61. *Sīratu-'l-Falsafiyya*, p. 110; cf. *Kitāb al-Shukūk 'alā Jālīnūs*; see S. Pines, "Razi Critique de Galien", pp. 480–7.
62. *Munāẓarāt*, Kraus, p. 302.
63. *Munāẓarāt bayna 'al-Raziyayn*, in Kraus, p. 301: *'idh kāna 'l-baḥth wa-'l-naẓar wa-'l-'ijtihād yūjibu 'l-ziyāda wa-'l-faḍl.*
64. *Ṭibb al-Ruḥānī*, Kraus, p. 33; Arberry, p. 35.
65. *Sīratu-'l-Falsafiyya*, p. 99, ll. 14 ff.
66. *Sīratu-'l-Falsafiyya*, Kraus, p. 100, ll. 1–7 with *Ṭibb al-Rūḥānī*, Kraus, pp. 21, ll. 13–22, l. 16; Arberry, pp. 23–4.
67. *Sīratu-'l-Falsafiyya*, Kraus, p. 100, ll. 15 ff.
68. *Sīratu-'l-Falsafiyya*, Kraus, p. 100; Arberry, p. 704; *Ṭibb al-Rūḥānī*, ch. 2; etc.
69. Cf. Meir Bar-Asher, "Quelques aspects de l'éthique d'Abū Bakr al-Rāzī et ses origines dans l'oeuvre de Galien", *Studia Islamica* 69–70 (1989) pp. 5–38, 130–47.
70. Cf. *Sīratu-'l-Falsafiyya*, Kraus, pp. 102–3; Arberry, p. 706.
71. *Ṭibb al-Rūḥānī*, Kraus, p. 21, ll. 9 ff.; Arberry, pp. 22 ff.
72. *Ṭibb al-Rūḥānī*, Kraus, pp. 21–2; Arberry, pp. 23–4.
73. *Ṭibb al-Rūḥānī*, Kraus, p. 22; Arberry, p. 24. Rāzī reintroduces this example at Kraus, p. 82, Arberry, p. 98, with his avowal that his whole substantive ethic can be deduced from the principles he sets out, Kraus, p. 33, Arberry, p. 35.
74. *Sīratu-'l-Falsafiyya*, Kraus, p. 102; Arberry, p. 706.
75. *Ṭibb al-Rūḥānī*, Kraus, pp. 21–2; Arberry, pp. 23–4.
76. *Ṭibb al-Rūḥānī*, Kraus, pp. 33, 21–2; Arberry, pp. 35, 22–3.
77. *Ṭibb al-Rūḥānī*, Kraus, p. 28.
78. See Thérèse Anne Druart, "The Ethics of al-Rāzī", *Medieval Philosophy and Theology* 6 (1997) pp. 47–71.
79. Fakhry, *Ethical Theories in Islam*, p. 71, citing Fakhry's earlier article, "A Tenth-Century Arabic Interpretation of Plato's Cosmology", *JHP* 6 (1968) pp. 15–22.

80. *Ṭibb al-Rūḥānī*, Kraus, p. 24; Arberry, p. 26.
81. Fakhry, *Ethical Theories in Islam*, pp. 72–3, citing Walzer and Kraus, *Galeni Compendium Timaei*, Arabic, p. 19 = Latin, pp. 67–8.
82. Al-Āmirī, *K. al-Sa'ādah wa 'l-Is'ād*, ed. M. Minowi (Wiesbaden, 1957–8) 49.
83. Fakhry, *Ethical Theories in Islam*, p. 73.
84. The only philosopher Epicurus admitted had taught him at Samos was Pamphilus, a student of Plato's (Diogenes Laertius, 10.14). For the relations between Plato's and Epicurus' accounts of pleasure, cf. V. Brochard *La Theorie din Plaisir d'apre Epicure* (Paris, 1912) pp. 252 ff.
85. See Epicurus, *Ad Men*. 129; cf. *DRN* IV 865–76.
86. Epicurus, frag. 1 ap. Diogenes Laertius X 136.
87. Epicurus ap. Athenagoras 12.546e.
88. See *KD* 3, 18–21, 26.
89. See Metrodorus, ap. *DND* I 40.113.
90. Fragments of Rāzī's lost work on the nature of pleasure were preserved by Ibn Abī Uṣaybi'a; see Kraus 139–64. A sample is translated by E. and J. Marmorstein in F. Rosenthal, ed., *The Classical Heritage in Islam*, pp. 103–6.
91. Epicurus' core hedonic concept *ataraxia* denotes peace of mind, the optimal hedonic state, equivalent to sheer and natural undisturbedness. As Epicurus argues: "The magnitude of pleasure reaches its limit in the removal of all pain"; cf. *VF* 14.
92. See Epicurus, *Ad Men*. 128, *VF* 60; *Spiritual Physick*, Arberry, pp. 27, 39.
93. Druart, "The Ethics of al-Rāzī', p. 49.
94. Epicurus, *Ad Men*. 128–9; cf. *DRN* IV 865–76; *KD* 3, 18–21, 26; Epicurus ap. Athenagoras 12.546e; Metrodorus, ap. *DND* I 40.113.
95. See Kraus, p. 141.
96. *Sīratu 'l-Falsafiyya*, Kraus, p. 99; Arberry, p. 704.
97. *Ṭibb al-Rūḥānī*, Kraus, pp. 21–2; Arberry, pp. 22–3.
98. *Ṭibb al-Rūḥānī*, Kraus, p. 73; Arberry, p. 79.
99. *Ṭibb al-Rūḥānī* II.
100. *Ṭibb al-Rūḥānī* I, Kraus, pp. 17–19; Arberry, pp. 20–1.
101. With Plato, *Symposium* 198–9, cf. *DRN* III ll. 1 ff.
102. *Ṭibb al-Rūḥānī* I.
103. *Sīratu 'l-Falsafiyya*, Kraus, p. 109; Arberry, p. 711. Yet Rāzī did write an introduction and defence of algebra.
104. *Ṭibb al-Rūḥānī*, Kraus, pp. 29–30, 62–3; Arberry, pp. 31, 67.
105. *Sīratu 'l-Falsafiyya*, Kraus, p. 100; Arberry, p. 704.
106. *Ṭibb al-Rūḥānī*, Kraus, p. 18.
107. *Ṭibb al-Rūḥānī*, 1.
108. *Munāẓrāt*, Kraus, pp. 295–300, 303.
109. *Munāẓrāt*, Kraus, p. 303; cf. Rāzī's "pity" for theologians, *Fihrist*, trans. Dodge, p. 706. Rāzī's *The Tricks of the Prophets* or *Ruses of the Self-Styled Prophets*, cited in al-Bīrūnī, *Risāla fi Fihrist Kutub M. b. Zakariyā' al-Rāẓī* (Paris, 1936) p. 17; cf. Mutahhar al-Maqdisī's *K. al-Bad' wa-'l-Ta'rīkh*, ed. C. Huart, vol. 4, p. 113. Knowledge of al-Rāzī's theme may have inspired later thinkers and fed the Enlightenment interest in the topos of the Three Impostors.

110. Druart, "The Ethics of al-Rāzī", p. 63.
111. *Ṭibb al-Rūḥānī*, Kraus, pp. 26–7; Arberry, p. 29.
112. Kant took over and turned inside out the Epicureans' ethical claim that our actions must be self-chosen. He reconstrued the self that does the choosing in terms of its rational rather than its hedonic self-constitution. See Goodman, *On Justice*, p. 203.
113. *Sīratu 'l-Falsafiyya*, Kraus, pp. 102–3; Arberry, pp. 705–6; *Ṭibb al-Rūḥānī* II.
114. *Ṭibb al-Rūḥānī* XX.
115. *Apology* 42: "Now it is time that we were going. I to die and you to live, but which of us has the happier prospect is unknown to anyone but God."
116. Druart, "The Ethics of al-Rāzī", pp. 52–5.
117. *Ṭibb al-Rūḥānī* II.
118. *Ṭibb al-Rūḥānī*, Kraus, p. 22, ll. 16 ff.; Arberry, p. 25.
119. *Ṭibb al-Rūḥānī*, Kraus, p. 23; Arberry, p. 25, and *passim*.
120. *Ṭibb al-Rūḥānī*, Kraus, p. 73; Arberry, p, 79.
121. See *Philebus* 31b, 42d, *Phaedo* 60a, *Phaedrus* 258e, *Republic* IX 583b (contrast *Philebus* 51a), etc.; cf. *Ṭibb al-Rūḥānī*, Kraus, p. 71; Arberry, p. 76.
122. *Ṭibb al-Rūḥānī*, Kraus, pp. 70 ff.; Arberry, p. 75.
123. *Ṭibb al-Rūḥānī*, Kraus, p. 36; Arberry, p. 38.
124. *Ṭibb al-Rūḥānī*, Kraus, p. 42; Arberry, p. 44.
125. *Ṭibb al-Rūḥānī*, Kraus, pp. 64 ff., 75–6; Arberry, pp. 69–70, 82. In their romantic mode, the literary dandies Rāzī singles out might readily take up his plaint: "*plaisir d'amour ne dure qu'un moment; chagrin d'amour dure toute la vie.*" But the romantics' delight in their misery only typifies Rāzī's claim as to the perversity of excess. Cf. *Sīratu 'l-Falsafiyya*, Kraus, p. 105; Arberry, p. 708; *Ṭibb al-Rūḥānī*, Kraus, p. 23; Arberry, p. 25. Chief among the cast of poets who celebrate love in the immoderate way Rāzī disparages would be Imru' al-Qays (d. *c*. 550) among the "ancients" and Abū Nuwās (d. *c*. 815) among the "moderns." Imru' al-Qays celebrates lost and forbidden loves; but in Abū Nuwās, as Andras Hamori puts it, life has become "a perpetual Saturnalia in which addiction has supplanted devotion" (*On the Art of Medieval Arabic Literature*, pp. 47–77). Al-Rāzī, whose morals rest on his medical judgement, would naturally see a progression from the excess and abandon of the one to the perversity and self-destructiveness of the other. I translate and discuss Imru' al-Qays's famous *Mu'allaqah* in Goodman, "Sacred and Secular".
126. *Ṭibb al-Rūḥānī* XV.
127. *Ṭibb al-Rūḥānī* XIV.
128. *Ṭibb al-Rūḥānī* VI.
129. *Ṭibb al-Rūḥānī* VII.
130. *Ṭibb al-Rūḥānī* VIII.
131. *Ṭibb al-Rūḥānī*, Kraus, p. 22; Arberry, p. 25. Rāzī is distinctive in postulating a self-destructive drive analogous to Freud's death wish. That this approach to the irrational is not merely a casual or *ad hoc* aspect of his ethics is evident from his treatment of the fall of the soul.
132. *Ṭibb al-Rūḥānī* IX.
133. *Ṭibb al-Rūḥānī* X.

134. *Ṭibb al-Rūḥānī* XI.
135. *Ṭibb al-Rūḥānī* XVII.
136. *Ṭibb al-Rūḥānī* XVII; Kraus, p. 86; Arberry, p. 95.
137. *Ṭibb al-Rūḥānī* IV.
138. *Sīratu 'l-Falsafiyya*, Kraus, pp. 109 ff.; Arberry, p. 711.
139. *Ṭibb al-Rūḥānī*, Kraus, pp. 29–30, 62–3; Arberry, pp. 31, 67; *Sīratu 'l-Falsafiyya*, Kraus, p. 100; Arberry, p. 704.
140. *Ṭibb al-Rūḥānī* XIX; cf. *Sīratu 'l-Falsafiyya*, Kraus, p. 105; Arberry, p. 708.
141. *Sīratu 'l-Falsafiyya*, Kraus, p. 10; Arberry, p. 710.
142. *Sīratu 'l-Falsafiyya*, Kraus, pp. 103–4; Arberry, pp. 706–7.
143. *Sīratu 'l-Falsafiyya*, Kraus, pp. 104–5; Arberry, pp. 707–8. Even the injunction of kindness to animals is not derived from the neo-Platonic thesis that all things exist for their own sakes, still less from any such notion as ahimsa or reverence for life, but rather from strictly utilitarian and anthropocentric, not to say ego-centric considerations: A physician in a hurry, Rāzī argues, has surely a more important role to play in the divine plan than has his miserable riding beast. All who truly believe in transmigration, al-Rāzī argues, will have no fear for the fate of slain animals; indeed they should recognise that souls may be "freed" to reunite with the universal soul only when they have reached the level of rationality.
144. *Ṭibb al-Rūḥānī*, Kraus, pp. 27 ff.; Arberry, pp. 32–3.
145. *Ṭibb al-Rūḥānī* iv; *Sīratu 'l-Falsafiyya*, Kraus, pp. 99–100, 109–11; Arberry, pp. 703–4, 711–12.
146. *Sīratu 'l-Falsafiyya*, Kraus, pp. 109 ff., 100; Arberry, pp. 710, 704; *Ṭibb al-Rūḥānī*, Kraus, pp. 29–30, 62–3; Arberry, pp. 31, 67.
147. *Sīratu 'l-Falsafiyya*, Kraus, p. 100; Arberry, p. 704.
148. *Ṭibb al-Rūḥānī*, Kraus, p. 23; Arberry, p. 26.
149. *Ṭibb al-Rūḥānī*, XX.
150. *Ṭibb al-Rūḥānī* V, XII, XV.
151. With *Ṭibb al-Rūḥānī* II, etc.; cf. e.g. *DRN* I 1 ff.
152. *Munāẓarāt*, Kraus, pp. 295–9. Charles Butterworth in "The Origins of al-Rāzī's Political Philosophy", *Interpretation* 20 (1993) pp. 237–57, makes no mention of Rāzī's outspoken rejection of prophecy and all forms of intellectual authority and hegemony, remarking only on the conventional view that when a human life is at risk, a horse may be ridden hard, and that when two men are in danger, it is best if the one most useful for the well-being of people survive (pp. 244–5).
153. *Ṭibb al-Rūḥānī*, Kraus, pp. 26 ff.; Arberry, p. 27; *Sīratu 'l-Falsafiyya*, Kraus, pp. 105 ff.; Arberry, pp. 708–9.
154. *Sīratu 'l-Falsafiyya*, Kraus, pp. 100–1, 110; Arberry, pp. 703–4, 711–12.
155. See above and cf. *Ṭibb al-Rūḥānī*, Kraus, p. 23; Arberry, p. 25.
156. *Ṭibb al-Rūḥānī*, Kraus, p. 22; Arberry, p. 23.
157. *Ṭibb al-Rūḥānī*, II, with XX, Kraus, p. 109 f.; Arberry, p. 105.
158. *Ṭibb al-Rūḥānī*, Kraus, p. 23; Arberry, p. 24.
159. *Ṭibb al-Rūḥānī*, Kraus, p. 31; Arberry, p. 33; cf. *Sīratu 'l-Falsafiyya*, Kraus, pp. 101, 105; Arberry, pp. 704, 708.
160. *Ṭibb al-Rūḥānī*, Kraus, pp. 23–4; Arberry, p. 25.
161. *Ṭibb al-Rūḥānī*, II.

162. *Ṭibb al-Rūḥānī*, loc. cit., with XI, XIL; cf. al-Kindī's *Essay on How to Banish Sorrow*, discussed below.
163. *Ṭibb al-Rūḥānī*, Kraus, pp. 22–3; cf. p. 31; Arberry, pp. 23–4; cf. p. 33. Mortification is not proposed; but the behaviours recommended may look a lot like mortifications.
164. To put the matter more sympathetically, al-Rāzī has overcome the Epicureans' characteristic distaste for other-worldliness. He moves beyond their somewhat irrational fear of the irrational fear of death, by leaving open the possibility of a reward and letting an optimistic theodicy and Platonic eschatology eliminate any residual fears of death itself.
165. *Sīratu 'l-Falsafiyya*, Kraus, p. 105; Arberry, p. 708; *Ṭibb al-Rūḥānī*, XIX; cf. the analysis e.g. of envy at VII: it is already assumed, before the hedonic arguments are brought to bear, that "the malicious man is hateful in the eyes of God and men". Thus the purpose of these arguments can only be to confirm what is already known or to demonstrate that common values can be derived from hedonic analysis. Just as the derivation of Boyle's Law from Joule's Principle added more strength to the latter than the former, Rāzī's hedonic arguments favouring common values often seem to lend more to hedonism than they add to the (already conceded) principle under discussion.
166. Cicero, *De Officiis*, 111.
167. *Sīratu 'l-Falsafiyya*, Kraus, p. 106; Arberry, p. 708.

Chapter 3

Baḥyā and Kant

In his celebrated *Book of Guidance to the Duties of the Heart,*[1] Baḥyā Ibn Pāqūdā includes a dialogue between the soul and the mind, in which the mind, or reason, seeks to relieve the ills of the soul, including many philosophic doubts and anxieties.[2] Among them are the soul's indecision between believing that God controls and governs all events and believing that we human beings choose our own actions. Both views, the soul finds, are well represented in scripture.[3] And the mind, reviewing arguments culled by Baḥyā from the literature of past controversies, concedes that it is no easier for reason to adjudicate the two ideas by way of critical thinking (*iʿtibār*) than it is for the faithful reader of scripture to find an unequivocal resolution in the ancient texts.[4] The two views thus represent the poles of a classic antinomy, between determinism and human freedom, the same antinomy that Kant would later describe in terms of an opposition between freedom and causal determination. Indeed, Baḥyā's strategy for addressing this antinomy boldly anticipates Kant's approach. It also leads to some distinctive and philosophically instructive outcomes for ethics and cosmology.

— 1. The antinomy —

Among the texts cited in support of predestination are 1 Samuel 2:6, Psalms 104:29, and Job 34:29, which accent God's universal power over life and death; Lamentations 3:37, affirming God's irrefragable sovereignty; Isaiah 45:7, where God describes Himself as the maker of light and darkness, peace and evil; Psalms 127:1, "except the Lord build a house, its builders work in vain"; Psalms 135:6, which affirms that God has made and done all that He pleases, in heaven, on earth, on the sea and in the deep. Cited in behalf of free will are Deuteronomy 30:15 and 19, where all Israel is given the choice between life and death, the blessing and the curse;

Malachi 1:9, where the people are called upon to entreat God's mercy, in the expectation that He will act, since their failing of God's grace was of their own doing; Job 34:11, where Elihu announces the just requital of all human beings in accordance with their own doings; and Proverbs 19:3, where the foolish man who fumes and frets against God is said to spoil his own path – that is, as Baḥyā takes the verse, to be responsible, although blaming God, for his own doings and for their consequences.

Behind each of these passages Baḥyā finds a theological principle readily sustained by rational argument. Thus, the thesis that God is the universal Cause and Creator, which Baḥyā deems necessary in any adequate account of the existence and character of nature,[5] requires in turn that God determine all events, including all human acts. Following the dialectical mode of argument familiar in the *kalām*, Baḥyā argues further that the entire Biblical history presupposes God's control of human destiny. Yet the Deuteronomic texts and others presume human moral responsibility. And human rationality seems to imply free choice – as does the accountability called for by God's justice.[6] Again, as Saadiah urged, in *kalām* style, and as Maimonides would later insist, the entire prescriptive discourse of the Law – its exhortations and commandments – presupposes human freedom.[7]

Human responsibility and divine justice seem to require that God cede some measure of His power and control to man. But God's absolute governance seems to place divine justice beyond human comprehension. Among Islamic theologians these alternatives were represented by the Ash'arite and Mu'tazilite schools.[8] The impact of their debate was felt among Jewish thinkers long before and long after Baḥyā's time. Saadiah alludes to the Islamic dispute to show that the issues of free will and theodicy are perennial.[9] And Maimonides' hearty "thank God!" when he urges that Jewish thinkers have escaped the presumption that God's governance somehow precludes free will (*Guide* III 17.5) shows that the point was still sensitive in his time.[10] But how exactly is the issue to be dealt with?

Among the evidence that reason might offer against voluntarism, the mind mentions that our actions often fail to match our intentions.[11] Slips of the tongue, for instance, show our lack of perfect control over our own acts.[12] Deeper causes might have to be sought beyond the human will – in natural events, perhaps. But the concatenation of such events would be ascribed ultimately to God. Emblematic of arguments in support of free will, the mind cites the proportioning of just requitals to the actions they address: unless God is presumed to be unjust, our actions must be within our own control.[13]

To reconcile divine power (*jabr*) with divine justice (*'adl*), Baḥyā proposes a third alternative to the polarised extremes. This middle ground, he says, was chosen by other thinkers in the past.[14] The *locus classicus* would be the Rabbis' gnomic saying: "All is foreseen, but sway is given" (*Avot* 3:19). Baḥyā's task will be to lay out the philosophic groundworks and parameters of the alternative suggested here. Reason must show the soul how to make sense of the multi-valenced pronouncements of scripture and explain how free will and divine governance coexist and how it is that scripture does not contradict itself when it vehemently employs both voluntaristic and predestinarian language.

— 2. BAḤYĀ'S RESPONSE —

Context is the key to Baḥyā's strategy. The deadlock between the seeming alternatives will be dissolved if a proper sphere of application can be found for each, situating appropriately the arguments, experiences, and evidences urged in behalf of free will and divine determination. Baḥyā calls upon reason to articulate this approach:

> Some, however, have adopted the views of both schools. They uphold both predestiny and justice, asserting that one who presses either notion too far will never be safe from slipping and stumbling, no matter how sound his intentions. The right answer, they say is to act on the conviction that actions are delegated to human beings and that we are rewarded and punished on the basis of our actions. Thus, we should exert ourselves to the fullest in behalf of our interests before God in both the temporal and the spiritual realms. But we should also place ourselves in His hands as one would who knows that the governance of all acts and motions, advantages and injuries is in God's control, occurring by His leave and at His charge – always presuming that God has the clearest arguments against man but man has no argument against God.[15]

Baḥyā commends reason's approach as his own by having the mind call it "the most direct route to release from all the foregoing problems".[16] The soul congratulates the mind on the subtlety of its reasoning, which has freed her from an oppressive choice, by allowing her to see that "the inner nature (Arabic: *sirr*) of the case" is too subtle and abstruse for one to grasp conceptually.[17] Release comes through a sort of fideistic agnosticism – almost a form of pragmatism. For what Baḥyā advocates is setting aside the metaphysical question, as insoluble by human intelligence.[18] In place of a speculative solution he sets a practical maxim: the pious will act on the assumption that predestination affords them no excuse for their lapses or insufficiencies of endeavour; yet they will deem God's will the perfect and irrefragable repository of all hopes and fears. For metaphysics Baḥyā here substitutes an attitude, a pietist hybrid of trust with maximal appropriation of moral responsibility. The Rabbinic precedent can be found in a Talmudic passage, where Raba excoriates Job for trying to hide human culpability in the shadow of God's omnipotence:

> "*Although thou knowest I am not wicked, and there is none that can deliver from Thy hand*" (Job 9:17). Raba said: Job sought to free from judgement the whole world en bloc (*lifṭor 'et kol ha-'olam kullo min ha-din*). He said, in effect, "Sovereign of the Universe, Thou hast created the ox with cloven hoofs and the ass with uncloven hoofs. Thou hast created Paradise and Gehinnom. Thou hast created the wicked and the righteous. Who could stay thy hand?" His friends replied: "*Thou dost undermine piety and constrainest devotion before God*" (Job 15:4). In other words: "Granted God created the evil inclination, He also created the Torah as its antidote." (B. Bava Batra 16a)[19]

In another of his internal dialogues Baḥyā expands on his idea of maximising individual responsibility and minimising what Raba identifies as a human tendency to self-exculpation. Again Baḥyā's s interests are more practical than speculative. The dialectical dramatis personae are the integrated personality (called "you", in keeping with the customary intimacy of writers of spiritual advice) and its inner foe, inclination or caprice:

> You must know, O man, that your bitterest foe here below is your inclination [*hawā*; taking the place here of Raba's *yetzer ha-ra'*]. It is mingled with the powers of your soul and mixed in the temper of your spirit. It shares with you in governing your sensibilities, bodily and spiritual, and sets up its dominion at the heart of your deepest secrets and all that you hold at the inmost core of your being, insinuating its counsels at every movement, overt or inward, which you execute by your choice. It lies in wait for your moments of forgetfulness. You may drowse and lose track of it, but it is never asleep to you. You may seem to toy with it carelessly, but its play is never idle; it is always intently focused upon you. It may clothe itself in sunny and amiable guise, deck itself out in the trappings of love of you, and so, by subtle deceptions, become your trusted advisor and most faithful of seeming friends, fawning, winking, running to please you with specious flattery. But all the while it fires its deadliest darts, aimed at your destruction.[20]

Inclination clearly plays a subtle role in Baḥyā's psychology of action. If evidence of predestination is found in the disparity of actions with intents, in slips of the tongue, hand and foot, lapses of memory and of judgement, then inclination, to which some of these lapses are ascribed, must act at God's behest, as an element in our nature that can actively counter our true interests. Similarly, the rationality thought to underlie our voluntary acts also acts at the command of God. So in both cases God acts through human nature.

The intertwining of causes and motives, divine causality and delegation, human choice and moral appropriation, Baḥyā suggests, is too complex for our unravelling. Kant similarly argues that the pure will, the only thing that is unqualifiedly good, is not to be discovered by self-examination, since one may never know to what extent one's choices have been influenced or suborned by considerations of interest rather than duty:

> In actual fact it is absolutely impossible for experience to establish with complete certainty a single case in which the maxim of an action in other respects right has rested solely on moral grounds and on the thought of one's duty. It is indeed at times the case that after the keenest self-examination we find nothing that without the moral motive of duty could have been strong enough to move us to this or that good action and to so great a sacrifice; but we cannot infer from this with certainty that it is not some secret impulse of self-love which has actually, under the mere show of the Idea of duty, been the cause genuinely determining our will. We are pleased to flatter ourselves with the false claim to a nobler motive, but in fact we can never, even by the most strenuous self-examination, get to the bottom of our secret impulsions; for when moral value is in question, we are concerned not with the actions, which we see, but with their inner principles, which we cannot see.[21]

The argument is characteristically Kantian. But the thesis, the language of inner motives, the discipline of self-scrutiny, all reflect the pietist tradition, in which Baḥyā stood, and in which Kant was raised and educated. Tellingly, Baḥyā locates our ultimate motives in the councils of our inmost being, whose ultimate determinations and inner character (*sirr*), like Kant's noumenal soul, lie beyond the reach of introspection and may harbour the most deceptively tricked-out of specious motives.

Given their phenomenology of choice and choice-making, neither Kant nor Baḥyā can accept the Epicurean claim that there is a phenomenal answer to the problem of free will. Both agree, in opposition to the daylight and democratic thinking of Epicurus (and of Saadiah, who held that self-scrutiny can reveal to us the innocence of our own motives) that we do not know the complexities of our own will well enough to vouch for its freedom as a fundamental datum of consciousness. Human freedom, for Baḥyā as for Kant, is thus inexorably a metaphysical problem in the pyrrhonistic (and fideistic) sense: it is beyond the reach of human knowledge.

Baḥyā lists numerous ploys by which inclination seeks to deceive and betray us. Entering into a kind of *kalām* dialectic of problem and answer, he uses his device of setting out little dialogues to illustrate the impact of these suasions on the soul, carefully supplying the mind's rebuttals and retorts. Structurally, the device is paralleled in al-Ghazālī and al-Makki. It resembles *Pilgrim's Progress* in its dramatisation of the dangers the soul faces. In narrative structure the dialectic works almost like a kind of fable, the Nightingale of Hazaran or some such tale of quest, with a series of trials, traps and portentous challenges to be bested or circumvented. But the hero in such fables typically escapes the dangers and wins through to the goal by wit and courage, aided by luck or grace. Here the dangers are sophistries, specious doubts – intellectual temptations or deceptions. Philosophical arguments and moral/intellectual purity (*ikhlās*) are the requisite virtues and weapons. And the crucial hints and clues come not from some friendly crone or tattered beggar but by way of homily, parable, and anecdote – although never by sheer faith or dogma. Each new trial begins as inclination is foiled in its deadly work and draws another barb from its quiver. In the sixteenth of the "darts" to be parried, the conundrum of free will and predestiny is raised once again:

> Despairing of taking you in by this means, inclination will next cast you into the sea of doubts over the notions of predestination and justice. If he observes any neglect on your part in performing your obligations or any tendency towards disobedience, he will eagerly seek to prove predestination to you, using powerful arguments, Scriptural and rational, intended to expand your grounds for excuses. He will say, for example, "If God wanted you to obey Him, He would have so ordained it and compelled you to obey. For nothing occurs but what He foreordains. Can you counter fate and subvert His sentence? You are only a tool that does what you are wielded to do. Control of all things is in the hands of God, glorified and exalted be He, as it says in the Writ, 'I, the Lord, do all'" (Isaiah 44:24).
>
> But if he sees you doing any work pertinent to this world and its ways, he will say, "Beware of sloth and indolence. Rely on none but yourself. For good or ill depend on you. It's up to you to act or let things go. So exert yourself to the utmost, and put out your best effort to grasp what you set your heart on of this world's delights. Resist with all your might all that you find hateful, and you will be safe from all such things, as the Allwise has said: 'Thorns and snares in the path of the perverse: he who guards himself keeps far from them' (Proverbs 22:5), 'The folly of man disturbs his course, and his heart frets against the Lord' (Proverbs 19:3), 'By their own hand did this befall them' (Malachi 1:9)," and the like.
>
> Thus inclination switches arguments, now maintaining predestiny and determinism, now justice and free choice, as suits his aim of deceiving you and putting you off guard. But if you rouse yourself and call to mind what the Ancients said on this subject: "All is in the hands of Heaven, except the fear of Heaven" (B. Berakhot 33b), then you will strive in matters of religion as one who knows that rewards and punishments depend upon his actions, as the Allwise said, "For man's doing shall be requited" (Job 34:11); and you will conduct yourself in worldly affairs as one who is certain that the reins governing all his movements and all the vicissitudes of his fortune are in the power of God (exalted be He), and who therefore relies upon Him and casts himself into His hands in all such affairs, as it says, "Cast thy burden upon the Lord" (Psalms 55:23).[22]

Speaking through the diaphanous persona of the mind, in its role as champion of the soul, Baḥyā here cites the classic Rabbinic maxim, "All is in the hands of Heaven except the fear of Heaven". The Rabbinic division will help him forge the logical distinction that he will use, as Kant uses the division between science and practical reasoning, to mark off the realm of freedom from that of external determination. For Baḥyā this is a matter of understanding where we should maximise our sense of responsibility and where we should surrender to our sense of creatureliness and rely upon God's grace. Conceptually this strategy of division harks back to the Stoic dichotomy of the things one can control (for which one is therefore responsible) from the things one cannot control – over which, on Stoic reasoning, it is therefore inappropriate, indeed senseless, to concern oneself.[23] What we can control, and that with certainty, on Stoic teaching, is the inclination (the internal movement, as Baḥyā calls it) of the will – that is, one's moral posture. In Rabbinic language, which still chimes in the hearing of pietism, that realm, the moral realm, is spoken of as "the fear of Heaven". For, in the Biblical and Talmudic tradition, all genuine obligations are obligations before God. What the Stoics called our responsibilities as citizens of the cosmos, in Rabbinic parlance is called shouldering the yoke of the kingdom of heaven,[24] the heavenly imperium, to give the phrase its original, more pointedly political edge. Baḥyā's complex psychology does not allow him to say that we do control even the inclination of our own will. But in place of such a question-begging claim, he substitutes the maxim: act (and judge yourself) as if you knew that all your actions in the moral sphere sprang from choices wholly within your own control.

The things one cannot control with certainty are externals in the Stoic model. We do have moral responsibilities in their regard,[25] but intrinsically they are neutral – in Stoic language, indifferent. These Baḥyā calls the things of this world – goods and ills, events and vicissitudes, which, in the Neoplatonic ontology employed by many monotheistic philosophers, are less than fully real and less than worthy of abiding human concern. They are evanescent and (*qua* particulars) unknowable, inherently ungraspable or unkeepable – fit objects in the moral discipline of souls to be regarded as lost even while we yet (to some limited degree and in some borrowed way) possess them.[26] Baḥyā's approach here, no mere ascetic discipline, seeks detachment not by the ploy of treating externals as though they were already lost to us, as the *consolatio* literature advises, but by using fatalism as a hortatory device in the internal councils of the soul. With our worldly interests, our proper stance (a matter of duty and hence rightly treated as an object of free choice) is not avidly to pursue benefits or anxiously to rage at injuries but (except as our obligations require) to accept what befalls and, Baḥyā urges, so to act and comport ourselves as we would had we the knowledge that all events here in the realm of gains and losses, were predestined by God. What will come will come; what will not will not; all hope and fear should repose in God.[27]

This attitude of total trust (Hebrew *bitaḥon*; Arabic, *tawakkul*) is the hallmark of pietist spirituality. The corresponding shouldering of maximal responsibility (and minimal excuse) is pietist as well. It too rests on the Stoic distinction of inner from outer. But it goes beyond even the Stoic premise of our absolute control within the inner citadel of the soul. Here, in our own internal councils and before God, we must act on the assumption that we are free, even though we can never know with clarity and certainty that this is so.

For the Stoics, as for Baḥyā, all human obligations are religious in tenor. But, by embedding all duties in the fabric of religious law, as Rabbinic Judaism expects, Baḥyā heightens the spiritual significance of the moral realm and strengthens the demand for a throughput from sound intentions to acceptable actions. We no longer have the deontologists' privileging of intention, so familiar from Kant and the Stoics. In its place stands the more Socratic (and Rabbinic) idea that sound intentions bear fruit in sound actions and sound lives. Accordingly, there is no longer the philosophic dismissal of regret. In Baḥyā's world there is room for sin as well as sincerity, and the pious will take ownership of their actions, with Kantian dignity, acknowledging without excuses not only failures of intent but failures of performance, when they have lapsed in their obligations.

Setting aside Baḥyā's characteristically medieval valorisation, almost celebration, of repentance and regret,[28] we find a powerful survival of his moral strategy in Spinoza's counsel that "The mind has greater power over the emotions and is less passively determined by them to the extent that it understands all things as necessary" (E5P6). Functionally, the approach matches Baḥyā's plan to accept all events as determined by God. Spinoza even uses the same terms, although he gives them rather new meanings, so as to avoid what he sees as the difficulties of the older version of the approach.

Most strikingly, however, Baḥyā does not profess a doctrinal solution to the speculative antinomy. He makes no claim about what constitutes the most adequate direct answer to the question over free will versus predestination. Rather, like scripture itself, he continues freely to use the categories and assumptions of both realms, trying only to ensure that they are used in the proper places. He surveys the theoretical debate with urbane scepticism, convinced that the metaphysical facts must elude our minds. The arguments, scriptural or rational in appeal, are set aside, as mere ploys of inclination. Baḥyā underscores the point by including obviously sophistical or specious reasoning on both sides among the arguments he ascribes to inclination. For inclination argues both that to try to make ourselves better persons would be striving to overmaster fate and contravene God's decree, and (a moment later) that one who bends every effort to avoid what he finds repugnant will be secure from pain and distress. Inclination even twists the obvious intent of Proverbs (22:5), to make the verse mean that the cautious escapes thorns and snares, rather than simply counselling that we avoid them by avoiding folly. Then inclination manhandles Isaiah (44:24) to transform the affirmation of God's universal agency (or creation) into a smothering control that excludes the very acts that God is said to bring about or make possible – negating the very "all" over which divine creative providence is said range.

Arguing indiscriminately, as a false friend would, now for free will, now for determinism, inclination cares only for the sting of its arguments in damaging the soul. In a moral/spiritual context, that is, in matters of religion (*dīn*), where responsibility is of the essence, inclination urges predestiny and fatalism. The outcome, as Raba would keenly perceive, is a generalised plea for excuses, encouraging a shirking of responsibility and lulling the soul into forgetfulness of the inevitable accounting. With worldly interests (beyond the demands of duty, the *farā'iḍ*, of Baḥyā's title, that is, the *mitzvot*) effort is often futile, excessive, self-defeating, or misplaced. Here anxiety is quite inappropriate, since the objects of concern are not of ultimate worth but are often distractions from goals of genuine value. But here inclination prods us to the utmost exertion and passionately insists that outcomes of real moment depend on our last ounce of energy and concern. Baḥyā uses inclination's two-faced pleas to expose its sophistical and tendentious intent. The exposure of that intent, or of the ethos it represents, gives Baḥyā the leverage he needs in his tussle to reverse the soul's heading and turn it toward *ikhlāṣ*, devotion, or dedication of all one's actions to God. Taken narrowly *ikhlāṣ* means sincerity. But *ikhlāṣ* is a material, not a formal virtue. It denotes not mere conformity of action to intent but purification of our intent as we reach toward God and the highest good. It is thus the counterpart to the worldly entanglements that inclination promotes.

When Baḥyā argues that we should presuppose free will in the moral/spiritual sphere and predestination in the realm of fortune and misfortune, he is offering, in the name of philosophy, not a decision between freedom and fatalism but a criterion for determining the proper spheres of application for responsibility and resignation. True to the pietist tradition, he draws his criterion from the combined concerns of ethics (maximising our moral charge) and theodicy (minimising claims against God). In abandoning the metaphysical issue, he is strikingly modern, anticipating Kant and the pragmatists and departing from the Stoics', or Spinoza's, metaphysical certitude. Like Baḥyā, Kant believed that direct resolution of the metaphysical issue is beyond the human mind, but he held that resolution unnecessary for science or morals. Like Baḥyā, Kant proposed that we simply assign the rival notions to their proper spheres. For him that meant causality in the realm of the understanding, freedom in that of practical reason.[29] Baḥyā does not depart so far from medieval realism as to assign to the principles underlying the diverse modes of discourse and experience the weighty task of constituting objectivity. He is perhaps more content than Kant with a mild scepticism, a familiar concomitant of piety understood as total trust. But the parallel of motive and outcome remains: final assignment of all human actions to the realm of voluntary responsibility or external governance is as irrelevant to Baḥyā's psycho-therapeutics or training for a spiritual odyssey or olympiad as it is to Kant's concerns with building a critical philosophy. The crucial issue in both cases is to recognise the diversity of the domains in which each of the rival perspectives is appropriate. One need not choose between the two. In dodging the horns of this particular dilemma, Baḥyā and Kant share a certain finesse, despite the divergence of their ultimate objectives.

Kant's Christian pietist upbringing and education, whose impact continued through his university years, clearly left its mark on his moral life as well as on his moral theory.[30] Pietism is an old tradition, and pietist authors, like their mystic congeners, often drank at one another's wells. Al-Makki, for instance, a Sufi writer who may have influenced Baḥyā, loved to quote scripture and did not confine himself to the *Qur'ān*. His Arabic citations from the Sermon on the Mount typify the crosspollination and hybridisation of themes found in pietist writings.[31] Al-Muḥāsibi, another Sufi writer, exerted a widespread influence on Muslim, Christian, and Jewish writers of similar spiritual bent.[32] By paths often too complex to trace any longer with certainty, monotheistic mystics and other spiritually inclined thinkers, including those of philosophical inclination, met frequently in the past, as they still do,[33] in their readings and meditations. A man of Kant's background and interests would doubtless encounter themes and arguments of the sort we have reported in Baḥyā.

Of special interest to us here is not simply the pietist tenor of Kant's morals – his strict deontology, his ideas about motives and self-scrutiny, and the like – but his strategy of compartmentalising the realms of morals and science to allow a proper place for both noumena and phenomena, freedom and determinism. The strategy is generalised in Kant, but it is

Kant himself who tells us of the religious motives that spur it. As Copleston wrote:

> [Kant's] delineation of the boundaries of theoretical or scientific knowledge does not show that God, for example, is unthinkable or that the term is meaningless. What it does is to put freedom, immortality and God beyond the range of either proof or disproof. The criticism of metaphysics, therefore, which is to be found in the *Transcendental Dialectic* opens the way for practical or moral faith, resting on the moral consciousness. Thus Kant can say (B xxx) that he has to do away with knowledge to make room for faith.[34]

Long after Kant outgrew his youthful loyalty to pietism as a movement, and long after his thought had moved beyond its particular tenets, we can see pietist ethics setting a standard that Kant upholds, and, so it seems, suggesting elements of his strategy for addressing some of the great philosophical puzzles. For Kant need not remain a pietist in every respect to avail himself of a pietist mode of argument.

One link between the pietist tradition that Kant knew, and the compartmentalisation of freedom and determinism that in some ways encapsulates the strategy of his critical writings, is Erasmus whose celebrated skeptical discussion of free will and determinism, Biblically and rationally, parallels Baḥyā's and draws deeply on the progressive pietist traditions in which Erasmus was raised and educated. Erasmus' polemic with Luther on the question cannot have been unknown to Kant, who was raised in the same tradition and would not have been ignorant of Luther's famous retort to Erasmus' exegetical skepticism: "The Holy Spirit is no skeptic!"

— 3. THE PHILOSOPHICAL IMPACT OF BAḤYĀ'S APPROACH —

Having pointed out the structural convergence of Baḥyā's and Kant's approaches to (or retreats from) the free will-determinism antinomy and suggested that analogous concerns led both men to conclude in the same curious fashion that they could have their cake and eat it too, as long as they did not do both in the same room, I should like now to reflect on the philosophical significance of the posture Baḥyā adopted in the areas of morals and cosmology.

In morals, I note a passage in the writings of the Ikhwān al-Ṣafā', the Sincere Brethren of Basra. In *The Case of the Animals versus Man*, one of the fifty-one *Rasā'il* or Essays composed by the Brethren in the 960s or 970s, human beings, defending the legitimacy of their hegemony over animals, boast of their sciences and arts, their religious, political and social institutions, including medicine, astrology and prayer. The animals retort that these last institutions tend to be the resort of the desperate:

individuals who have not used proper diet and so have suffered illness rush to physicians. Only when that fails do they resort to prayer-slips and petitions – much as tyrants resort to astrology in a vain effort to gain control over a destiny that does not rightfully belong to them. The proper attitude, the beasts argue, echoing the Sermon on the Mount, as al-Makkī does, is to trust God and leave things in His hands. One should rely on the bounties providentially afforded in nature and not seek to enlarge one's portion beyond what is allotted.[35] Baḥyā similarly contrasts the anxieties of the alchemist, who exhausts himself striving to transform and control nature, with the inner peace of the pious, who calmly accept what comes from God.[36]

Baḥyā retraces the thoughts of the Sincere Brethren in his critique of the ethos of "getting and spending", toil and exhaustion, by which human beings make themselves little better than slaves to their arts and industries.[37] But he does not pursue the contrast between trust and self-exhaustion into quietism and passivity, or into obscurantism. He insists that we exert ourselves to the utmost – as our moral/spiritual obligations require;[38] and he takes it to be a core religious obligation that we strive to understand nature in all its aspects.[39] This melding of acceptance with activism is a striking and central feature of Baḥyā's philosophy. His synthesis rests on moral and intellectual engagement; and, crucially, on acceptance of causality as the backstop of one's practical exertions and one's inevitable, wholly acceptable engagement with nature and with nature's laws in both speculative and practical ways.

Far from falling into an ascetic melancholy or a coldly passive response to destiny, Baḥyā proposes a warm and willing activism in pursuit of our authentic interests. The call to adopt such an inward attitude and to effectuate it in one's living is part of the divine challenge or trial that God has tendered us. And the delineation of the proper moral and intellectual response to that challenge is the burden of Baḥyā's work. Paradigmatically, and contrary to the notions of some extreme quietist/pietists, reliance upon God does not in Baḥyā's view demand that we abstain from medical treatment but rather that we humbly accept the possibility of such treatment as a gift from God's hand.[40] Efforts to disrupt the course of nature, to alter or interfere with it or to demand divine intervention in behalf of selfish interests are not only futile but degrading, even self-destructive. These are Baḥyā's clearest cases of misapplied exertion – misappropriation of the idea of free will.

As in the Stoic philosophers, naturalism and trust of providence are subtly blended; respect for the laws of nature, acceptance of *their* decree, and equanimity in their course are marks of wisdom and tantamount to acceptance of the decrees of providence. But we too are actors in the drama we are cast in. Acceptance of *our* role means acceptance of the responsibility to act and choose.

The trust that Baḥyā advocates demands perfect acceptance of God's judgement in regard to merit and reward and all worldly and other-worldly benefits and injuries affecting self and others.[41] It even demands rejecting the idea that medicine (paradigmatically) – or any other human device that might seem to offer an alternative to God's help – can counteract God's will and plan, or obviate reliance upon it. Yet it does not ask us to reject human endeavours or devices but to use the art and materials of technology in full recognition of their provision by God as instrumentalities of His plan.[42]

Accordingly, Baḥyā declines the occasionalist rejection of natural causality that marks the piety or pietism of many *mutakallimūn*. Like other advocates of *tawakkul*, he does argue that proximate causes are too "weak" to execute their effects, without the power imparted to them by God.[43] But the inference is not that natural causes do not act. Where Peripatetics argue that natural causes, being non-voluntary, cannot help but do their work, al-Ghazālī counters that, being non-voluntary, natural causes can *do* nothing. They depend on God.[44] Ibn Rushd will reply by conceding that natural causes may be incapable of effect without the aid of the (timeless) Prime Mover, but resort to natural causes is necessary if the world is to be made intelligible[45] – let alone controlled. Baḥyā's position mediates between the pietist and naturalist views, treating proximate causes as the means by which God acts. There would be no power in nature without God, he writes. But at the same time, "In the absence of all causes, no natural action could complete its emergence to the border of reality".[46]

It is because they are means through which God acts that natural causes are to be accepted (and used) in so far as they conduce to God's plan. Their outcomes are to be read as divine decrees – whether their force is felt within human character or beyond.[47] But we too are agents, so the recognition of natural causes is no derogation of our responsibility. As in Stoicism, acceptance does not preclude response. Baḥyā's conclusion, then, that events are predestined and only our moral stance is free does not result in a denial of human suffering but in a determination to be its moral master, to regard adversity not as a causally contingent, morally arbitrary affront but as a causally necessary, morally welcome challenge to one's intellectual discernment and moral mettle. The posture here is the same that Seneca described (and ultimately adopted) as that of a courageous soldier who takes it as a compliment, not an imposition, when he is ordered to confront exceptional risks and dangers.[48]

Morally, Baḥyā's segregation of free will from predestiny serves to disarm the frantic, futile efforts at changing the course of nature that mark the character of those whose will is governed by inclination. On similar grounds the Sincere Brethren regard some variety of fatalism as morally liberating, since acting on such a model frees us from the frustrating pursuit of what will (*per hypothesi*) never be ours, and the frenetic pursuit of what will be ours in any case.[49] Frantic engagement, the argument proposes, is intrinsically degrading – dehumanising – and while Baḥyā does not propose complete withdrawal as the alternative, he does advise detachment.[50] His grounds are much the same as those on which the Stoics, or Spinoza, believed a variety of determinism, merging nature and providence, to be morally ennobling and capable of imparting a certain dignity.

Fate, the Stoics argued, is like a heavy wagon – and mankind is like a dog tied on behind it. If so, would it not be better to follow with dignity than to struggle against the inevitable?[51] But this leaves an ambiguity. There are times, as all Stoic philosophers – even Seneca – recognised, when it is nobler to kick against the pricks, even if one knows that one can never stop or overturn the wagon. The mark of wisdom for the Stoic is to recognise those times. Baḥyā's division, grounded in the ancient separation of the temporal from spiritual/moral, is designed to draw just such a line of demarcation – not only between the areas where choice is necessary and not necessary but also between the areas where choice is a proper and an improper notion to apply. In drawing this division, Baḥyā places the principles of nature's operation clearly on the side of God's predestination and regards nature as God's instrumentality.[52] The outcome in relation to Kant is to render the distinction between Kant's natural causality and Baḥyā's theistic predestiny largely terminological. The outcome in relation to the Stoics is to underscore the affirmation that the critical line is drawn not between the inevitable and the contingent but between the morally acceptable and the morally unacceptable – or rather, in view of the supererogatory claims that pietists make on themselves, between the morally exemplary and the morally ordinary.

A striking parallel to Baḥyā's approach is found in the teachings of the Chinese humanist philosopher Mencius (fourth century BC). To paraphrase one reading of his teaching:

> The way that the mouth is disposed towards tastes, the eye towards colours, the ear towards sounds, the nose towards odours, and the limbs towards ease is human nature (*hsing*). Yet there is *ming* (the moral law). So the refined person does not choose to say "human nature".
>
> The way that benevolence pertains to fathers and sons, duty to prince and subject, propriety to guest and host, wisdom to the virtuous and wise, and the

> sage to the ways of Heaven is *ming* (divine decree). Yet there is *hsing* (human nature). So the refined person does not choose to say "*ming*".[53]

One may be subject to the frailties and demands of human nature, but the refined person does not appeal for excuses to the all-too-human, since he recognises his moral charge. Likewise, although he knows that virtue, propriety and grace are ordained, the refined person does not arrogantly claim them as his own, since he knows the ways of all flesh. Wisdom here would be the prism that arrays the iridescent hues of fate and freedom, showing us what to accept and claim and what cannot be accepted and must not be claimed, allowing us to build a character that sharply differentiates complaisance from moralism and excludes them both. Baḥyā's wisdom lies in his clarity in drawing that line, allowing piety to maximise our moral charge and to maximise as well our acknowledgment of God's truth and grace.

Baḥyā does not promote predestination as a metaphysical truth but only as a regulative guide, to be applied in specific contexts. In identifying those contexts he includes the general operations of nature. It is not nature's deeds but nature's laws that count among the phenomena we must accept as given rather than struggle to conquer and transform. Thus the contrast between the physician and the alchemist. For the alchemist seeks not merely to use but to bend God's laws, making human desire paramount to God's law. That, for Baḥyā, is the height of self-frustrating impiety. Medicine, as Baḥyā sees it, uses but does not try to bend the laws of nature. It does not demand or seek to coerce God to change the course of nature in the service of human inclination. This brings us to the impact on theology or cosmology of Baḥyā's bifurcation of predestination and morals and his concomitant fusion of naturalism with trust in providence.

Anthony Flew, in a now classic essay,[54] criticised the tendency of theology to resort to what he calls a "God of the gaps". As human knowledge and control expand, Flew reasoned, the complementary areas of ignorance, helplessness and fear contract, and God's active role is ever more diminished, until God becomes vanishingly insignificant. Gods on this model, which is ultimately Democritean, are fictions wishfully devised as notional stays against human helplessness. Their retreat as human cognitive and practical powers advance is a matter of logic. Flew's gods here are the same deities that show themselves in myth by violating or disrupting the course of nature or interfering in the constitution of our moral values – the same gods that Epicurus had in mind when he equated all religion with superstition.

The monotheistic God, however, as presented by Baḥyā, is conceived in a profoundly different way, not as the disrupter of nature or morals or any other positive values but as their founder and ground. This God is not a product of wish fulfilment, a projection of anxieties or guilts, or a reflex of ignorance and fear. That is why worship of the monotheistic God is achieved not in orgiastic celebrations of violence, or the re-enactment of any primal acts of sensate passion or dramas of conflict and guilt – not symbolised by the icons of any archetype and not to be captured in any story. Rather the God of monotheism is worshipped in the peaceful contemplation and admiration of the universal cosmic pattern. We perform God's will not by self-flagellation, scarification, self-immolation or even self-abnegation, but by the thoughtful endeavours of self-development and the aid of others that are the Biblically commanded expressions of the human love of God.[55]

Here the divine is not identified with the extraordinary in the sense of the morally outrageous or the intellectually outlandish. Thus, the God of monotheism is not exiled to the Epicurean *intermundia*, the cosmic gaps between all possible worlds. Accordingly, that God does not retreat before the advance of human understanding and control. The monotheistic God cannot be exiled beyond the call of human concerns, to a realm of moral gaps. There is no teleological suspension of the ethical. Nor do advances in the techniques of controlling violence, illness or suffering render God irrelevant. As a universal God, the monotheistic God is not confined to ground where science cannot or morals dare not tread, as though God became relevant and active only in events so horrible that men naturally or superstitiously call them works of fate or destiny, and insurance agents throw up their hands and speak of acts of God. Rather, the sphere of this God's work is everywhere – that is, God's act is present commonly and normally. For monotheism as classically understood, and as Baḥyā understands it, denies any realm in nature where causes fail to reach (Psalms 19:5–7),[56] and Baḥyā insists that even miracles are wrought not despite causality but through it, through God's mastery of the full repertoire of causal means.[57] As Franz Rosenzweig writes:

> For the consciousness of erstwhile humanity, miracle was based on ... its having been predicted, not on its deviation from the course of nature .... Miracle is substantially a "sign". In a wholly miraculous world, wholly without law, an enchanted world, so to speak ... the individual miracle could hardly strike one as a miracle. It attracts attention by virtue of its predictedness, not of its unusualness .... The miracle is that a man succeeds in lifting the veil which commonly hangs over the future, not that he suspends predestination. Miracle and prophecy belong together .... The prophet ... unveils, as he foresees it, what is willed by providence .... And by pronouncing the portent, the prophet proves the dominion of providence, which the magician denies .... This explains the delight in miracle. The more miracle the more providence. And unlimited

> providence ... is the new concept of God which revelation brings. It is a concept through which God's relationship with man and the world is established in an unequivocal and unconditional manner wholly foreign to heathendom. In its time, miracle demonstrated ... the predestined lawfulness of the world.[58]

Rosenzweig assumes, in the rather unilinear anthropological scheme that was characteristic of his day, that "erstwhile" consciousness lived in an enchanted world increasingly inaccessible to modern consciousness. That depends on whose "erstwhile" and modern consciousness one considers. We find some very naturalistic thinking among the ancients and some very magical/associative thinking among many of our contemporaries. Myth seems never to die but always to change its colours and often to disguise itself as something else. But what I think is sound in Rosenzweig's analysis is that the experience of miracle, understood in his terms, is not incompatible with causal explanation but is indeed fulfilled in the consummation of causal experience, that is, in science – and, dare one say it, in technology.

The extension of naturalistic causal explanation and control progressively excludes magic and the need for magic and may therefore create the illusion that the "erstwhile" experience of the miraculous is irretrievable. But the illusion is based on confusing the miraculous with the magical – the remarkable with the egregious. To the monotheistic sensibility, which looks upon the cosmos as a whole and human existence in particular as expressions of universal providence both in the sheer fact of their existence and in the continued wonders of their vitality and transformations, the miraculous neither was nor is absent from nature and neither was nor will be incompatible with causality, since all of nature is God's miracle. Baḥyā here is a modern. He finds God's act not just where understanding grows dim and control runs dry but everywhere, and perhaps most clearly in what we understand best. And Baḥyā hears the word of God, once again, not just when human conscience falters or morals seem incapable of guiding our steps, but everywhere and always – through morality, not despite it. God's will for choosing beings is understood *as* morality, just as God's will for constancy in nature is expressed in what we call causality.[59]

Despite the pagan survivals that many of its cultural traditions harbour, monotheism, for just the sort of reason that Baḥyā's schematism makes clear, is not the religion of an anti-natural or anti-social God but the religion of the God of nature and morality, in whatever may be found to be their highest recensions. Monotheism finds the extraordinariness of the divine not in the increasingly infrequent irruptions of irrationality into the pattern of experience – as the seeming absurdity of dreams may disrupt a troubled sleep – but in the uniformity of nature itself. Monotheism is predicated on a recognition of the universality of the extraordinary, known to monotheists by the more familiar idea of the miraculousness of creation. Such a religion may be compared to awakening from sleep, or to Plato's image of the cave whose former denizens step forth into the sun and behold things in the light rather than by their shadows. For monotheism finds God not in the negative but in the positive images it captures of the world or experience. The calm arising from the perception of all daily occurrences as acts of God and from regarding human duties as the only legitimate objects of human concern leads Baḥyā to have Soul express her awakening by Mind as a stilling of passions very like the weaning of a child[60] – an apt analogy especially in the religious sphere.

The monotheistic theme of the universality of the extraordinary is captured in the opening verses of Genesis, where God does not erupt upon a world already formed but (without any sign of struggle or conflict) creates the world as a coherent, precious and lovely whole. Adherence to a conception of religion or of nature, where God governs not despite nature but through it and not in violence against the moral counsels of perfection but by their means and for their sake, renders Baḥyā's idea of piety not only tranquil but subtle. The God in whom Baḥyā advises us to place perfect trust is not a God of dread occasions, not the *mysterium tremendum* of obscure passions and unresolved anxieties, but a God of daily moments and seasons who will not arbitrarily disrupt the course of the nature He created for any trafficking in favours.[61] To trust in such a God (in place of what is vulgarly accounted as religion) is not to expect to win prizes or gratuities from a mythic potentate. Nor is it to expect in any way to be guaranteed success in securing one's perceived worldly goals or interests.[62] It is, however, as Baḥyā might have put it, to secure oneself absolutely against the loss of any good of ultimate worth.

— NOTES —

1. *K. al-Hidāya ilā Farā'iḍ al-Qulūb*, ed. A. S. Yahuda, trans. Menahem Mansoor. The translations used here are my own.
2. Yahuda, pp. 150–74; Mansoor, pp. 198–220. John Wisdom, *Philosophy and Psychoanalysis* (Oxford: Blackwell, 1964) similarly treats philosophical difficulties as anxieties and ills of a special sort, susceptible to therapy by way of rational inquiry. See the discussion of Spinoza in Chapter 6, below.
3. Yahuda, p. 162; Mansoor, pp. 209–10.
4. Yahuda, p. 163, l. 46; Mansoor, p. 210 *ad fin.*
5. Yahuda, pp. 40–50; Mansoor, pp. 114–21. The chapter title is not adequately translated as "On the Unity of God". The actual title is "Towards an Explication of Diverse Means of reaching a Purified Affirmation of Monotheism". *Tawhīd* here is

not the unity of God, nor is it even simply the affirmation of the unity of God but (as shown by Baḥyā's arguments and parallels in numerous other pietistic works), it is the affirmation of monotheism. *Ikhlāṣ* is not a semantically transparent or untranslatable word. What it signifies is the process of mental/spiritual self-purification which the mystic adept must undertake and which Baḥyā fuses with the process of refining one's beliefs philosophically, as demanded by critical thinking. Thus 'purified' here, in keeping with Baḥyā's wide ranging claims in behalf of intellectual clarity as a spiritual obligation, indeed the core obligation anchoring the project of *The Duties of the Heart*, means direct, sincere, lucid and coherent, philosophically rigorous and self-critical. See Baḥyā's Introduction, *passim*.

6. Yahuda, p. 163, ll. 19 ff.; Mansoor, p. 211, para. 3.
7. Yahuda, p. 162 l. 22, p. 163 l. 3; Mansoor, p. 210, para. 4.
8. Baḥyā's strong linkage between divine justice and human freedom is Mu'tazilite, and his gloss of Proverbs 19:3 has a Mu'tazilite flavour, since it elicits the Mu'tazilite theme that human choices are requited by their own consequences in limiting or expanding our degrees of freedom.
9. Saadiah's *Book of Theodicy*, Introduction, trans. Goodman, p. 127.
10. See Maimonides, *Eight Chapters*, 8; Goodman, *Rambam*, pp. 242–70.
11. Yahuda, p. 162, ll. 7–11; Mansoor, p. 210, last para.
12. Saadiah glosses Job 9:20 as implying that in slips of the tongue we unwittingly condemn ourselves, a keen anticipation of the notion of the Freudian slip; *ED* X 4.1; trans. Rosenblatt, p. 365; and Goodman trans. and commentary on Saadiah's Job, ad loc., p. 228, n. 14. In Saadiah self-betraying slips are reconciled with voluntarism through the (Mu'tazilite) assumption that the slip results from the wrongdoer's entanglement in the toils of his own wrongdoing. But Baḥyā takes these slips to be paradigmatic of predestinarian claims, in keeping with Job's original complaint, that even his efforts at self-justification would be undermined by God's ultimate control.
13. Yahuda, p. 162, ll. 11–12; Mansoor, p. 211 *ad init.*
14. Yahuda, p. 163; Mansoor, pp. 210–11.
15. Yahuda, p. 163 l. 22–p. 164 l. 5; Mansoor, pp. 211–12.
16. Loc. cit. ll. 5–6.
17. Yahuda, p. 165, ll. 14-15; Mansoor, p. 213, para. 1.
18. Yahuda, p. 164, ll. 6 ff.; Mansoor, p. 212.
19. For the *yetzer ha-ra'* or evil inclination, see Schechter, *Aspects of Rabbinic Theology*, pp. 242 ff.; Urbach, *The Sages*, pp. 471–83. Cf. the Midrashic *sanegor* and *kategor*, and see Asín Palacios, *Islam and the Divine Comedy*, pp. 226 ff.
20. Yahuda, p. 231; Mansoor, p. 276.
21. I. Kant, *Groundwork of the Metaphysic of Morals* (1785), trans. H. J. Paton (New York: Harper and Row, 1956; first ed. 1948) pp. 74–5. T. S. Eliot, in *Murder in the Cathedral* suggests an instance of the need to deal with such self-deception, when he shows his protagonist, contemplating martyrdom and trying to purge from his mind the idea of self-aggrandisement: This, the saint sees, in his self-scrutiny, would be "the greatest treason – to do the right thing for the wrong reason".
22. Yahuda, pp. 250–1; Mansoor, pp. 295–6.
23. Epictetus, *Discourses*, I, i–ii.

24. See Schechter, *Aspects of Rabbinic Theology*, pp. 65 ff.; Urbach, *The Sages*, pp. 400–19.
25. See Cicero *De Finibus*, III, ix, 31, ed. and trans. H. Rackham (London: Heinemann, 1971; 1st ed. 1914) p. 249.
26. See al-Kindī, "Essay on How to Banish Sorrow", ed. H. Ritter and R. Walzer as "Uno Scritto morale inedito di al-Kindi".
27. Cf. al-Ghazālī, *Iḥyā' 'Ulūm al-Dīn*, XXXV Tawḥīd 1; al-Ḥujwīrī, *Kashf al-Maḥjūb*, trans. Nicholson, pp. 274 ff., 278–85, esp. 283; al-Ghazālī *Tawhīd* 2, *bayān* 1, with *Iḥyā* XL, Mawt, *bāb* 8; see Wensinck, *La Pensée de Ghazzali*, p. 184.
28. Baḥyā devotes the seventh of his ten "Gates" in the *K. al-Hidāya* to Repentance. He includes all failed actions here as proper objects of penitence. Regret and repentance are themselves spiritual; but their expressions, as Baḥyā catalogues them, are bodily.
29. See Kant's "Schluss-Anmerkung" in "Muthmasslicher Anfang der Menschengeschichte", *Gesammelte Schriften* (Berlin/Leipzig, 1923) vol. 8, pp. 120–1.
30. See Paul A. Schilpp, *Kant's Precritical Ethics* (Evanston, 1960; 1st. ed. 1938) pp. 49–51 (and its many citations from Koppel Pinson) pp. 2, 43, 58, 169.
31. Al-Makki's title, *Qūt al-Qulūb* ("Sustenance for Hearts") resonates with Baḥyā's. See his Pt. II, ch. 1, *tawakkul* – "total trust" (Cairo, AH 1310), vol. 2, p. 4. Makkī quotes Psalms 118:8 and Matthew 6:25 ff. Cf. al-Ghazālī, *Iḥyā'* XXXV *Tawḥīd*, *bayān* 2, (Cairo, AH 1312) vol. 4, pp. 189–90, which includes a virtual, i.e., imagined, dialogue combining the intimacy of the mystic's intimation of inwardness with the dialectic of *kalām* and the drama of story. Here the interlocutor is the hag *shirk*, or polytheism. The issue, once again, is who will claim responsibility for natural events and human actions. Andras Hamori, *The Art of Medieval Arabic Literature*, pp. 8 ff., 40 ff., points out the value, as a foil, of a stock objector to the poet's moral posture. Parallels run all the way back to the Greek chorus and Hellenistic uses of contrast to define a mood ("some seek ... but as for me ..."); see Horace, *Odes*, I, i, ll. 3 ff., 19 ff., 29 ff.; vii, ll. 1, 5, 10; and, of course, xxii.
32. See Margaret Smith, *Al-Muḥāsibi* (London, 1935; repr. Amsterdam: Philo, 1974) esp. pp. 60 ff., 253 ff., 269 ff.; cf. Asín Palacios, *Islam and the Divine Comedy*.
33. Thus the ongoing project of the Pauline Fathers to publish translations from the "classics of spirituality".
34. Frederick Copleston, A *History of Philosophy*, vol. 6, *Wolff to Kant* (London: Burns Oates, 1968) pp. 232–3; cf. Michel Despland, *Kant on History and Religion* (Montreal: McGill-Queens University Press, 1973) pp. 101 ff.
35. Trans. Goodman, pp. 175–85.
36. *K. al-Hidāya* IV, Introduction, Yahuda, pp. 177 ff.; Mansoor, pp. 223 ff.
37. Cf. Aristotle, *Politics* 1257b 40 and 1260b 1–4.
38. Yahuda, pp. 197 ff.; Mansoor, pp. 244 ff.
39. Yahuda, pp. 41 ff., 237 ff.; Mansoor, pp. 114 ff., 284 ff.
40. Yahuda, pp. 190–1; Mansoor, pp. 237–8; for trials and medicine, Yahuda, p. 200; Mansoor, p. 247.
41. Yahuda, p. 196; Mansoor, p. 243.
42. Yahuda, pp. 188–9; Mansoor, pp. 235–7.
43. Yahuda, pp. 187, l. 8; 189–91, l. 2; Mansoor, pp. 234, para. 1; 236–7; cf. Ghazālī,

TF, ed. Bouyges, 2nd ed., p. 196, ll. 1–9.

44. But see Goodman, "Did Ghazālī Deny Causality", *Studia Islamica*, 47 (1978) pp. 84–120.
45. *TT*, ed. Bouyges, p. 524, ll. 1–4.
46. Yahuda, p. 190, ll. 12–13; Mansoor, p. 237.
47. Yahuda, pp. 187–9; Mansoor, pp. 234–6.
48. Seneca *On Providence*, esp. para. 4; trans. Moses Hadas, *The Stoic Philosophy of Seneca* (New York, 1968; 1st ed. 1958) p. 38.
49. See Ikhwān al-Ṣafā', *Animals versus Man*, trans. Goodman, pp. 150 ff.
50. Yahuda, pp. 186–7, Mansoor, pp. 233–4.
51. Zeno and Chrysippus ap. Hippolytus, *SVF*, vol. 2, p. 975; cf. Seneca, *ad Lucilium Epistulae Morales*, ed. L. D. Reynolds (Oxford: Oxford University Press, 1965) vol. 2, p. 450 l. 9: "*Ducunt volentem fata, nolentem trahunt*". This last is found in verses ascribed by Seneca to Cleanthes. But Epictetus' quotation of the same verses (*Enchiridion* 53) stops one line short of this Stoic disjunction, and it is not attested in the Greek sources. So scholars doubt whether it belongs to Cleanthes' original or is an embellishment added in Seneca's Latin translation. The sentiment is clearly Stoic, however; and the wagon image, authentic old Stoicism, as Hippolytus' attribution to Zeno and Chrysippus attests. That our linkage to fate is compared to a dog's linkage to a wagon suggests a Cynic ambience.
52. Yahuda, pp. 189–90; Mansoor, pp. 236–7. In arguing that angels, which he construes as natural and cosmic forces, make up the third part of the world and mediate between God and particulars, Maimonides gives ontological expression to the synthesis of providence with naturalism that Baḥyā (among others) evinces. See Goodman, *Rambam*, pp. 25 ff., 282 ff., esp. 330 ff. and Goodman, "Maimonidean Naturalism".
53. See Ning Chen, "The Concept of Fate in Mencius", *Philosophy East and West* 47 (1997) pp. 495–520; cited here, p. 496.
54. A. Flew, *God and Philosophy* (London: Hutchinson, 1966) pp. 3, 5, 60; "Theology and Falsification", in A. Flew and Alasdair MacIntyre, eds, *New Essays in Philosophical Theology* (New York: Macmillan, 1955; repr. 1964) pp. 96 ff.
55. See Goodman, *God of Abraham* for the fuller development of this theme.
56. Yahuda, p. 187; Mansoor, p. 234.
57. Yahuda, p. 190; Mansoor, p. 236.
58. F. Rosenzweig, *The Star of Redemption*, trans. William Hallo (Boston: Beacon Press, 1972; German MS, 1919) pp. 94–5.
59. Yahuda, p. 187; Mansoor, p. 234.
60. Yahuda, p. 165; Mansoor, p. 213 *ad init.*, citing Psalm 131.
61. Yahuda, pp. 249, 134–5, 236 ff.; Mansoor, pp. 294; 184–5, 282 ff.; cf. Plato, *Euthyphro* 14b.
62. Yahuda, p. 202; Mansoor, pp. 248–94; cf. Yahuda, p. 250; Mansoor, p. 295 *ad fin.*

Chapter 4

Maimonides and the Philosophers of Islam

Much ink has been spilt in efforts to determine whether Maimonides was a philosopher or some sort of apologist. Uselessly, since the presumed dichotomy overlooks the impact of a conceptual defence in reshaping what is to be defended, to make it not only defensible but worthy of defence. But if we reframe the question in the terms of Maimonides' own time and language, and ask whether he was a philosopher or a *mutakallim*, the answer comes through clearly and in his own words. For just as we must recognise that a sensitive person is not one who knows when he is in pain but one who knows when someone else feels pain or hurt, so a critical thinker, a philosopher, is not one who can spot the weaknesses in another's stance but one who knows the weaknesses in his own. As Maimonides put it: "We cannot believe unless we think. For conviction is the judgement that what is conceived is, independently of the mind, as thought conceives it to be" (*Guide* I 50, ed. Munk, p. 57a, ll. 11–13). "Conviction is not a matter of what is spoken but of what is conceived in the mind when a thing is affirmed to be as it is thought to be" (*Guide* I 50, ed. Munk, p. 56b, ll. 12–14). So it is not enough, as a Jewish *mutakallim* might have supposed, to know "how to give an answer to an *apikoros*". One must also know what can be meant by such an answer and what kinds of answer are workable. Otherwise one risks incoherence, and in matters of faith that means holding on to nothing. As the Rambam puts it: "Many simple souls have their creeds by rote, without attaching any idea to them at all."

What Maimonides observed is equally true today. There is still many a *mutakallim* all too eager to sweep theological problems under the carpet. Paradigmatic of such problems for the Rambam was the discrepancy between strict monotheism and the assignment of multiple attributes to God. The more sensitive *mutakallimūn* of his day might respond to this particular theological embarrassment with a formula equating God's attributes with His identity. "Some even reach the point of saying that 'His attributes are neither the same as nor outside of His Identity'" (*Guide* I 51). For Maimonides it was not an unrelated difficulty that many Christians said that God is both three and one (*Guide* I 50). A more demanding approach seemed also more inviting: "If you are of the sort who are content with mouthing true opinions, or supposedly true opinions, without conviction and without any idea of a meaning behind your words – let alone seeking certainty about them – that is very easy" (*Guide* I 50, ed. Munk, p. 56, ll. 14–17). It is of such people that scripture says, God is "near to their mouths but far from their kidneys" (Jeremiah 12:2). "But if you are one of those who aspires to rise higher, to the level where things are thought out", then study, dispassionate thinking, and setting aside familiar assumptions or customary modes of thought will bring you beyond lip-service, to the intellectual plane.

For many practical purposes, Plato noted, true opinions are as good as knowledge. But not for teaching, explaining or understanding. For mere opinions, even if true, do not explain themselves. Nor do they validate or justify themselves (*Theaetetus* 200e ff.; *Timaeus* 51d). Maimonides understands how narrow Plato's concession must be. For the usefulness of true opinions does require that they be true, and the assurance that they are true depends on knowledge, not opinion. Knowledge, then, as Augustine understood, is indispensable, even to faith. Far removed from those who speak even when they do not understand are those who understand even what they do not speak: "Rather should one be of the sort who understand and grasp the truth, even if they do not voice it – for that is what is demanded of the best, to whom it is said, 'Speak to your hearts in your beds and be silent. Selah' (Psalms 4:5)" (*Guide* I 50, *ad fin.*)

Maimonides finds two major problems in Biblical theology. A Christian thinker might have called them mysteries, and the Rambam's language about silence suggests that he thought of them in some ways as mysteries. But his rejection of obscurantism and his call to study, reflection and fresh thinking, suggest that he did not see these problems as conceptually insoluble. The two were the core theological difficulties of metaphysics and cosmology that Maimonides located under the Rabbinic rubrics of the Account of Creation and the Account of the Chariot: the problem of God's creative act, the emergence of a temporal and conditioned world from an absolute and timeless Reality; and the problem of theophany, the manifestation of the Infinite on a finite scale.

The two problems in fact are one. For theophany is a special case of God's creativity; and creation is a kind of revelation, in which God makes Himself known through His work. For Maimonides the problems of divine knowledge and providence, the problem of evil, and the problem of prophetic language, that is, the prophets' bold depiction in human language of the Transcendent and Unique, all nest within the problem of theophany. Similarly, the creative act of Genesis is only the most striking and demanding case of God's creativity, which appears as well in the governance of nature and provision for its creatures. For Maimonides, as for the ancient Rabbis, *ma'aseh merkavah*, the problematic centred on God's epiphany to Ezekiel and seeming representation in human form, raises broad issues of language and law, the specification of rules and particularisation of rituals out of the absoluteness of the Unbounded. And the Account of Creation broaches wide issues about nature's dependence on God and the access of human creatures to an understanding of their Creator. Both of the passages that the Rabbis linked as problematic raise questions about nature itself – about its sublimity or beauty or order, but also about its apparent disorder and seemingly arbitrary determinations – turbulence, chaos and catastrophe.

Viewed from a human perspective, the two great problem areas reveal further linkages. For life is the peak of God's creative work, and human intelligence above all. The cynosure of theophany is God's manifestation to that intelligence. Thus central to both problematics are questions of how God scales himself to human apprehension, and more pointedly, how there can be a link or bond between the mind of man and God's absolute transcendence.

In confronting his two great problematics, Maimonides could draw upon the work of the prophets and the Rabbis, but only to a limited extent. For scripture spoke in a different idiom from that of men who had read Aristotle. And scripture was the task at hand, to be vindicated, but at the same time to be discovered. Only circularity would result from calling scripture to witness in its own behalf; and scripture could not unravel its own language into a language other than its own. As for the Rabbis, as the Rambam observes (*Guide* I 46), they participate so freely and uninhibitedly in the conceits of prophetic symbolism that they rarely offer a key to its decoding.

Among the "moderns", as medieval thinkers called their recent predecessors, three great Jewish thinkers stood out: Saadiah, Halevi and Ibn Daud (*c.* 1110–80). Maimonides learned from all of them and respected all of them. But Saadiah was, in key respects, a *mutakallim*, as Maimonides plainly stated.[1] Centrally, Saadiah's reliance on the idea of God's created glory did not help to solve the problems the Rambam faced. Rather, it was part of the problem, not an explanation but at the core of what still needed to be explained. Halevi, in his campaign to accentuate the positive – that is, the volitional, material, historical and particular – still used the metaphysics of Ibn Gabirol, supplying the realia of Jewish history, observance and destiny as the arguments (in the mathematician's sense) of the abstractions to which Platonising philosophers like Ibn Gabirol had been committed.[2] The move was brilliant, and Maimonides profited from it. For Halevi's wit, insight and humour helped the Rambam cut through the authority of dogmatic emanationism and the over-confident reification of the Neoplatonic hypostases and their spheres. But Halevi's insouciant bracketing of the emanationist architectonic did not give Maimonides all he needed in confronting the full-blown Neoplatonic Aristotelianism of Avicenna. Ibn Daud appreciated the affinities of Avicennan philosophy with Judaism, but he seems not to have been prepared to respond radically enough to generate a sufficiently independent philosophic synthesis. Specifically, he relied on "mediation" to derive multiplicity from divine Unity. That only pushed back the problem of the world's dependence upon God without showing how the problem could be solved. Ibn Daud laid the materials of Avicennan philosophy and the Biblical axioms side by side on the table but left much of the task of synthesis and radical re-examination still to be done.

To address the real questions that Avicenna's work had set on the agenda of Jewish philosophy, Maimonides would need to draw upon the full range of Islamic philosophy, the tradition we trace from al-Kindī to Ibn Ṭufayl. He could not afford to overlook the free-thinking physician al-Rāzī, the occasionalist *mutakallimūn*, or al-Ghazālī, the principal critic of the philosophy set out by al-Fārābī and brought to fruit by Avicenna. A special asset to him was the philosophical (and astronomical) work of his Andalusian predecessors; not least of them, the respected if philosophically unfulfilled Ibn Bājjah. What did Maimonides learn from these Islamic thinkers? Their work represents the most open and creative phase of Islamic thought. And Maimonides' openness to their ideas made possible the philosophical synthesis he achieved. Here is a fitting case study of crosspollinations.

— 1. CREATION —

Al-Kindī prepares the ground for future defenders of creation by pre-empting the claim that *ex nihilo* creation is an absurdity. The idea that there is something illogical about radical creation harks back to Parmenides' view that non-being is a contradiction. A corollary was the view that reality has no origin:

> For what birth will you seek for it? How and whence did it grow? I shall not allow you to say or to think "From not being". For it is not to be said or thought that it

is not. And what need would have driven it later rather than earlier, beginning from the nothing, to grow.[3]

Here we see the seeds of arguments set out against creation by philosophers from Aristotle to Proclus and beyond: a radical beginning would be arbitrary, uncaused and inexplicable, it would demand the becoming of becoming (and so pull down an infinite regress from the cupboards of logic), it would require a matter from which to make matter itself, or it would treat the very fact of nothingness as if that were matter, making emptiness pregnant with all that would come to birth.

But monotheists who defend *creatio ex nihilo* assign the power of creation not to nothingness but to God. God is not part of the universe that will be accounted for by cosmology but is the ultimate causal principle, the *arche* that Aristotle held all philosophers to have been seeking. The transcendence of this *arche* is expressed not merely in its intellectuality or incorporeality, but in a transcendence of time that places God outside all changes.[4] The God of monotheism transcends nature not only as the goal toward which all striving aims, but as the *ratio essendi*, the originating and existentiating cause of all that is.

Creation was defended by Philoponus in the sixth century. His many rebuttals of Greek eternalism, along with the eternalist retorts, dying embers of pagan piety, were well rehearsed in Arabic before al-Kindī took up the issue.[5] But Kindī caught the savour of creationism when he simply added a fifth kind of change to the four made canonical by Aristotle. Besides locomotion, alteration, growth/diminution and generation/corruption, we must add God's bringing something out of nothing.[6]

Following Philoponus' lead, al-Kindī fashions an argument that al-Ghazālī will echo: no quantity can be infinite, so time itself must be of finite duration; and the bodies presupposed by the very passage of time will perish in the change that marks its passing. Aristotle is right that time is the measure of motion. But "that which is eternal does not move". So, if the heavens move, they are not eternal.[7] Aristotle had found a paradox in the notion of a first beginning, the becoming of becoming. And Aristotelians asked, in the spirit of Parmenides, what matter or potential underlay that purported coming to be. The inference intended was that change and the cosmos as a whole must be eternal and, in general pattern at least, invariant. But Kindī turns the tables: an eternal body, eternal motion – *a fortiori*, an eternal cosmos – are impossible. Whatever moves is temporal; only the incorporeal is eternal. And only the intellectual is incorporeal.

Just as Plato in the *Timaeus* (28D) demands a perfect division of "that which is always real and has no becoming" from "that which is always becoming and is never real", so Kindī draws the Platonic distinction, in behalf of creationism. Transitory things depend on the higher and fuller being of the ideal and divine. We know that God exists, because changeable things are transitory, and transitory things cannot cause themselves.[8] Behind all change and perishing must lie the One, indivisible and unique, indescribable and eternal, whose constancy is the source of all mutability and whose timelessness begets time itself – not as an infinite duration that might rival the eternity of the Original, but as a finite expression of God's infinite power.

I cannot say that philosophers in Maimonides' time regarded al-Kindī more highly than al-Fārābī, or even that Maimonides knew Kindī's work. He does know Philoponus, whom he calls John the Grammarian (*Guide* I 71, ed. Munk, p. 341). Indeed, he argues that the early beneficiaries of Arabic translations from the Greek somewhat over-eagerly exploited the arguments of Philoponus (*Guide* I 73). Kindī, who was among those beneficiaries, had an indirect impact on Maimonides' discussions, laying a groundwork for al-Ghazālī's spirited defence of creation, which Maimonides clearly does know. Maimonides will not use all the arguments of Philoponus, Kindī or Ghazālī. But after Kindī it was no longer credible for philosophers who wrote in Arabic simply to label creation a paradox or a contradiction. The Philosophers' authority as masters of the Greek science of logic simply did not extend so far. By the time the discussion reached Maimonides it was clear that creation and eternity were rival metaphysical hypotheses. Neither alternative, he will argue, can be established demonstratively. For neither is a matter of logic. Indeed, Maimonides argues, it was the misguided attempt to make creation a demonstrative matter that bound Neoplatonists to eternal emanation and *mutakallimūn* to constant and immediate acts of creation for every particular at every instant. Al-Kindī's work helps free Maimonides from the deductivism behind both of those beliefs.

Rāzī is a philosopher about whom Maimonides has little good to say. The Rambam blames Saadiah, albeit not by name, for unwittingly imbibing the hedonistic premises that underlie the Epicurean dilemma and its corollary, Rāzī's doctrine that evils in this life outweigh the goods.[9] But, in keeping with the maxim of Mishnah Avot that the wise learn from every human being, Maimonides adopts Rāzī's medically oriented approach to ethics in his own "Eight Chapters", the brief but systematic sketch of ethics in his Commentary on the Mishnah. Kindī, Galen, and other authors, including Ibn Gabirol, couched ethical discussions in the mode of a Socratic or Aristotelian therapy of the soul. But Maimonides makes distinctive use of Rāzī's Epicurean and Galenic anatomy of the vices. And both Saadiah and Maimonides echo Rāzī's argument that self-denial can be as unwholesome as excess, and is itself a form of excess.[10] Maimonides adopts Rāzī's Epicurean line of argument that natural appetites have natural limits, while appetites not directed by nature are inherently unlimited (*Guide* III 12). He adjusts to his own uses Rāzī's prescription for avarice. For Maimonides therapeutically justifies temporary excess in the pursuit of various ends, where Rāzī had similarly prescribed excess, albeit only in an ascetic direction.[11] Indeed, Maimonides uses his justification of temporary excess to explain (and limit) ritual asceticism, drawing a Rāzīan conclusion from his own version of one of Rāzī's favorite arguments.[12]

Rāzī's cosmology made his philosophy notorious, despite the good repute of his medical writings. But Rāzī, like Kindī, was a defender of creation. He did not, as we have seen, think *creatio ex nihilo* defensible but adopted *formatio mundi*, the ordering of the cosmos from unformed matter, at the impetus of the world Soul and under the oversight of God. The world Soul, as we saw in Chapter 2, was one of five eternal realities by Rāzī's count, along with God, matter, time and space. The fall of Soul, embroiling her in a world where she did not belong and where there was no fulfilment for her, except through escape, resulted from her impetuous desire for embodiment. God knew that such desires would give Soul no rest until she had learned what embodiment really means, not only in terms of pleasures but also in terms of vulnerabilities. He knew that Soul can learn only by experience. So he allowed her fall, neither powerless to prevent it nor compelling it. He softened Soul's fall by imparting something of His own to her and to the nature whose movements her wild vitality stirred up in hitherto inert matter. What He imparted was intelligence, which was not one of the five independent entities that predated the spontaneous act of creation, but something of the divine. It gave order to the motions of the cosmos but also allowed Soul to sense that this world is not her true home. Further, reason gave Soul the means to regain the intellectual world, where she does belong.[13]

Rāzī's dichotomy between the physical and the intellectual is both Kindian and Platonic. His doctrine of the five eternals is his own. But it is a less striking assumption that most resonates for Maimonides: the divine origin of the rational soul. Maimonides never allows that Socratic or Platonic thought to drop from sight.

Rāzī's insistence that matter is inert is a rebuke to Aristotle and the Neoplatonic eternalists.[14] His idea that vulnerability is rooted in our embodiment is a Platonic/Galenic theme that Maimonides too makes his own (*Guide* III 12, citing Galen, *De Usu Partium* III 10). But Rāzī's idea that creation compassed radical changes in the character of emergent nature is vital to Maimonides. It becomes a key premise of his argument against eternalism. For that argument hinges on the recognition that Aristotelians who reject creation project conceptions of matter, potentiality, time and change that derive from our grasp of the settled course of nature and may be quite out of place in the world's formative stages (*Guide* II 17). Maimonides' appeal here is to an empiricism that exposes the apriorism of the Philosophers. He cautions his reader not to dismiss as impossible what has not been shown to be such (*Guide* I 32). Al-Ghazālī raises similar empiricist arguments in behalf of mystic experience, miracles and resurrection.[15] But the root-stock of the empiricism that Maimonides and al-Ghazālī share lies in the medical and alchemical empiricist bent of al-Rāzī, who insists that we should not assume the impossibility of what we cannot explain, lest we assume the impossibility of magnetism and many other natural phenomena.[16]

Maimonides disparages the methods of *kalām* as *ad hoc* and suppositious. He rejects the conclusions of the *mutakallimūn* as theologically unsound, geometrically paradoxical and mechanically absurd (*Guide* I 73.3). But he calls upon his reader to respect the seriousness of the problems that the *mutakallimūn* faced (*Guide* III 17); and he adapts their doctrine of possibility as a bastion of his creationism. This doctrine, which he calls the linchpin or mainstay (*'umda*) of *kalām*, is the view that "whatever is imaginable is acceptable to reason" (*Guide* I 73.10). Two modifications are needed. For Maimonides will not make imagination the criterion of any form of knowledge (*Guide* I 73, ed. Munk, pp. 115–16); and he will not accept the notion that nature imposes no requirements of its own. Nature, as the arguments of Rāzī may have helped him to see, imposes the requirements familiar to us only once it is a "settled order". And reason, rather than imagination, must guide our thoughts about what is and is not conceivable. But the *mutakallimūn* are right, Maimonides argues, in rejecting a priori restrictions (other than those of logic) on the realm of possibility:

> To draw inferences from the nature of a thing that has developed to full maturity about the character it had while developing or from its developmental character as to its state prior to the inception of that process is not always possible. When you err in this regard, pressing attempts to infer from the character of the realised thing to its character while yet potential, you involve yourself in serious difficulties: necessities will seem to you impossible; and impossibilities, necessary.[17]

That precisely was the error of the philosophical defenders of the eternity of the cosmos.

Eternalism is to be rejected, Maimonides explains, not because scripture affirms creation. For many Biblical passages cannot be taken literally, on Saadiah's grounds that reason or experience, tradition, or the dicta of the text themselves exclude their familiar or surface sense and demand that we find a credible alternative. Not least among these are the Biblical anthropomorphisms, which Maimonides deconstructs in a sophisticated application of Saadiah's methods, allowing the Torah itself to explicate the larger intensions of the prophets. Creation too might be allegorised, had reason in fact shown its impossibility (*Guide* II 25). But since all such demonstrations fail, on the grounds that Rāzī's anti-apriorism suggests, namely, that they are suppositious and project our present knowledge on to the wholly unfamiliar originative history of the cosmos, no such allegorisation is needed. Nor is it appropriate. For, by Saadiah's rather chaste hermeneutical methods, alternatives to the familiar sense are to be sought only when that sense has been excluded.

Aristotle well understood that the world's eternity is not demonstrable, Maimonides argues. For it was Aristotle, "who taught mankind the methods, laws, and conditions of demonstration". He would not have blundered about what constitutes a demonstrative argument, and would clearly not have called on dialectical arguments and persuasive language in support of the world's eternity had he known any apodeictic argument for that claim (*Guide* II 15). Maimonides himself proffers less than apodeictic arguments in behalf of creation. He hopes to show that creation is both preferable theologically and more probable cosmologically than the eternalist alternative (*Guide* II 16).

Theologically, he argues that ascription of the world to God's creative act, as the Neoplatonists intend, makes more sense if the world is not conceived as eternal. For if God is the eternal "Author" (*Ṣāniʿ*) of the world, but not its Originator, the question is left open what difference God's act made. For the world, on that account, has always existed and has never altered in its essence. The argument is a milder version of Ghazālī's charge that the Philosophers of Islam are atheists *malgré lui*, since God's acts seems to make no real difference in their world.[18] Al-Ghazālī heads the Third Discussion of the *Incoherence of the Philosophers*: "On their duplicity (*talbīs*) in calling God the Maker and Author of the world and calling the world His work and the product of His authorship – in which it is made clear that this is purely metaphorical on their part and cannot be taken in a real sense." Less censorious than al-Ghazālī, Maimonides avoids calling the eternalist philosophers atheists. He finds a value and validity in al-Fārābī and Ibn Sīnā's approach that al-Ghazālī does not acknowledge. The Neoplatonists' arguments for the existence, unity and incorporeality of God are sound, provided only that one accepts their eternalism, as Maimonides does not (*Guide* II, Introduction and II 1). But the weakness remains that al-Ghazālī had detected in eternalism, signalled by the question: what difference does God's authorship make if the world is eternal?[19]

Maimonides' claim that creation is more probable than its alternative rests on the philosophers' own speculative model of emanation. Ibn Sīnā had called emanation creation. In keeping with al-Fārābī's general allegorical reading of scripture, he thinks of scriptural creation narratives as symbolic or homiletic expressions of the truth of emanation, a concept not readily accessible to a mass audience. Both Maimonides and al-Ghazālī adopt emanation as a foundation of their metaphysics. But both find eternalist emanation too automatic and mechanical. Indeed, the Greek idea of emanation at times goes beyond the image of light flowing from the sun criticised by many monotheistic writers. For emanation is an intellectual act, and the precipitation of specificity out of pure Unity and Goodness leads some Neoplatonists to speak of emanation as a kind of implication: lower beings are entailed into existence, as theorems are implied by axioms.[20]

Merely to complain that such a scheme is too necessary, too automatic, tying God's hands and the like, is to mount no argument against it but only to presuppose, in the face of one's adversaries, the very theological values they dispute.[21] Maimonides does offer an argument here, cosmological rather than theological, playing on the assumptions of his interlocutors. Following al-Ghazālī,[22] he argues from the Philosophers' premise that the logic of emanation allows only one simple product at each stage.[23] So if the aim is to account for multiplicity and change within the world, emanation alone cannot do the job. Indeed, taken strictly, as set forth by al-Fārābī and Ibn Sīnā, emanation will entail the most rigid determinism and will even preclude the possibility of change – consequences entirely abhorrent to the Philosophers:

> You will have observed that the school of Aristotle and all who hold the eternity of the world take the position that the issuance of being from the Creator is a matter of necessity, that God is the Cause and existence the effect, and therefore that the world's existence is necessary ... All existence is thus made necessary – cause and effect alike. Nothing can fail to exist or be other than as it is. But this implies that everything must retain the nature it has forever, that nothing can diverge in any way whatever from the nature which it has. (*Guide* II 19)

Only voluntarism, Maimonides argues, can break the stranglehold of necessity, making emanation itself possible, allowing change, and, crucially, allowing change in the natures of things, that is, evolution, as a means of bringing creation to "maturity".[24] Maimonides' defence of creation relies critically on the idea of evolution, the idea that the fundamental character of things in nature can change. To forego that idea and concede the essentialism of the Aristotelian school would indeed be to concede their eternalism as well. For part of what Maimonides learns from al-Ghazālī is that the eternalism of the Neoplatonic Aristotelians is the reflex of their apriorist intellectualism. It is understanding the apriorism of eternalism that allows him to frame his argument against their position.

The need for a voluntarist alternative to necessitarian emanation is clear in al-Ghazālī's critique of al-Fārābī and Ibn Sīnā. But the voluntarist option, which Maimonides will adopt, was pioneered by the *mutakallimūn*, as he acknowledges when he cites their doctrine of possibility as the linchpin of *kalām* and incorporates voluntarism into his own model of emanation.[25]

Curiously enough, al-Fārābī and Ibn Sīnā aid Maimonides in this important modification of their schemes. For al-Fārābī showed, in his commentary on Aristotle's *De Interpretatione*, why divine omniscience does not entail determinism of the crushing sort that Maimonides warns against. His argument, in a nutshell, was that the mere fact of there being a fact, or knowledge or truth about the future does not make the future necessary, although a fact or truth or item of knowledge does necessarily imply the corresponding state of affairs. For we must distinguish the necessity of that implication from any necessity in the events themselves. Relational necessity does not imply intrinsic necessity. Natural causes and human volitions remain free to do their work, even though divine knowledge may extend to them.[26]

If God's knowledge does not freeze the will or act of any being but allows beings to act, to express and even to alter their natures, Maimonides can be confident that thinking of God's act in terms of volition as well as intellection will not compromise multiplicity, change or freedom within nature. Creation can then be conceived not merely as a single act at the outset of history but as the general nexus of God's ongoing engagement with nature. To generate a credible paradigm of creation, Maimonides unites divine wisdom with divine will. The resultant hybrid, sharply set off from sheerly intellectualist automatism and from the arbitrary interventionism of purely voluntarist occasionalism, becomes the vehicle of Maimonides' distinctive conception of the open future.

Reflecting on the powerful idea of emanation and developing a thought of the Plotinus scholar Jean Trouillard, John Rist remarks: "A germ of the Plotinian doctrine of emanation is to be found in Plato's account of Eros and ... this germ is supplemented by Plotinus' turning Plato's moral rule 'Being good means doing good' into a law of the cosmos."[27] What Maimonides contributes here, following in the footsteps of al-Ghazālī, is a voluntaristic conception of emanation whose fruitfulness for further explorations into immanentist cosmology is by no means exhausted.[28]

Avicenna too aids Maimonides' doctrine of creation, even as his eternalism takes aim against such doctrines as Rāzī's *formatio mundi.* Convinced that the substrate of all change must be eternal, Avicenna still insists that matter depends for its existence upon God. Thus, although he does not uphold a temporal creation, as Rāzī proudly and resolutely does, Avicenna does not treat matter as self-sufficient. The point is crucial for Maimonides. Later thinkers will routinely charge that emanation, by making matter eternal, made it independent of God. But the orthodox Neoplatonic view was that matter depends directly, if eternally, on the act of God.[29] And when Maimonides wants to take the Philosophers to task over their handling of the problem of evil and the related problems of divine providence and knowledge, he does not claim simply that the Neoplatonists have erred in exempting matter (and hence particulars, since matter is the principle of individuation) from divine knowledge and control. Rather, he blames them for inconsistency with their own sound principles:

> The Philosophers strayed grievously regarding God's knowledge of things other than Himself ... The pitfall they fell into is worse than what they sought to avoid! They ignored the very point they were constantly calling to our attention and explaining to us. They are worse off than they started out in that what they were trying to avoid was attribution of unconcern to God, but they ended up by categorically attributing ignorance to Him, making everything here below hidden from Him and unperceived by Him. And they ignored what they were ceaselessly pointing out to us in that they judged existence at large by the situations of individual human beings. (*Guide* III 16)

The error, Maimonides explains, was in trying to avoid the problem of evil by ascribing to God knowledge only of universals, a Peripatetic stance developed by Alexander of Aphrodisias in response to Stoic claims about providence. But adherents of the Peripatetic approach forget the teaching of Aristotle himself that universals are not real but exist only in the individuals and the kinds that exemplify them. Matter itself, Maimonides urges, is not a real or separate thing (as it was in the philosophy of Rāzī). In a consistent Neoplatonism it is a mere principle of otherness or differentiation. That view is commended, Maimonides argues, when the Book of Job treats the figure of the Satan, that is evil, not as one of the "sons of God", which are the formal principles of reality by which divine goodness is mediated into specificity, but as one who came along with them, "also in their midst" (Job 1:6). This means that matter, the basis of evil and of all vulnerability, is not a thing in its own right – the Gnostic view that influenced Rāzī but that Plotinus had combatted. Rather, matter is a concomitant of differentiation, a condition of finitude but not a principle of being (*Guide* III 22).

All that is real then, is, intellectual, as Neoplatonism originally and consistently taught. There is no independent realm of particularities to escape God's ken. On the contrary, the otherness of matter, along with the differentiation that materiality makes possible, is a gift as well as a ground of division and weakness. It is the locus of imagination and of all the creative differentiations that Maimonides ascribes to what we must apprehend as the volitional side of the divine. Even the seemingly arbitrary expressions of God's power – what we take to be chance as well as what we take to be acts of design and intention – are all, in a Biblical perspective, expressions of God's ultimate wisdom and power.[30]

Maimonides' rejection of the Neoplatonic exclusion of matter from the power and ken of God leads directly to Spinoza's inclusion of extension, along with thought, among the attributes of God. But it stems not simply from some arbitrary or apologetic objection to the limitation of providence. Rather it represents Maimonides' demand that Neoplatonists hold fast to the central tenets of their own metaphysics, as to the ultimate dependence of matter upon God and to the recognition that matter, as otherness, is not a form (or a principle of sameness), but is nonetheless crucial to the self-expression of God that we know as the act of creation.

Before turning to *maaseh merkavah*, I want to remark on the striking illustration that Maimonides chooses to bolster his idea of creation. I refer to the fable Maimonides devises to counter the apriorism of his philosophical interlocutors, the story of the "man of perfect nature" brought up "on an isolated island", without any knowledge of women or the origin of men. A sound thinker, this perfect mind dismisses as incredible the stories he is told of human gestation, on the grounds that no human being could survive nine months' confinement, without air or free movement, without eating, drinking, defecating or even opening his eyes (*Guide* II 17). Where Rāzī, in a Galenic mode, had appealed to magnetism as a counter to apriorism, al-Ghazālī had spoken of opium. For the Philosophers, he argues, echoing Rāzī's discontent with the hot and cold, wet and dry of the traditional four element scheme, say that opium puts one to sleep because it is cold. But earth and water are the cold elements, and pounds of earth and water have not the effect of a single dram of opium. Similarly, one who lacked experience might deny that there could be a substance the merest bit of which could devour an entire town and then itself, leaving no trace of the town or of itself. But fire has that nature.[31]

Taking his cue from a larger interest, shared by Ghazālī, in man himself, Maimonides builds his illustration from the premises of the philosophical romance of his Andalusian predecessor Ibn Ṭufayl.[32] The details about the isolated island and the perfect nature of the individual who is to do the a priori reasoning are hallmarks of the origin of his story. And, like Ibn

Ṭufayl's hero, Ḥayy Ibn Yaqẓān, whose phases of intellectual development reflect the stages of human history and reflection, the Rambam's youthful apriorist mildly satirises humanity and the pretensions of pure reason. The fallacy of his reasoning lies in the assumption that the past must be like the present, that natures cannot change, and that the familiar order of nature extends smoothly back in time without cessation. It is this Aristotelian bias that Maimonides believes the Torah calls into question. But when Maimonides does question it, he writes without rancour, without impugning reason, naturalism, or the settledness of the settled order nature, once it is settled.

— 2. THEOPHANY —

In a practical effort to offer philosophical strategies against anxiety and grief, al-Kindī urges Stoic detachment from the evanescent goods of this world and Platonic cleaving to the enduring realities of the intellectual world. His focus, clearly visible in his "Essay on How to Banish Sorrow", displays the movement in the early days of the importation of Greek ideas into Arabic thought, from the pragmatic concerns that may first have urged sponsorship of the translation of Greek works on medicine, alchemy, astral calculations and engineering, to the more speculative studies that underlay such arts. Al-Kindī writes:

> With any illness, where the cause is not known the cure will not be found. We must explicate, therefore, what sorrow is and what its causes are, so that its remedies may be readily found and easily effected. We say, then, that sorrow is psychological suffering that occurs when some object of love is lost or some object of desire eludes us. It is clear, then too, what causes sorrows: either the loss of something loved or the elusiveness of something wished for. So we must inquire whether one can strip oneself of such attachments. For it is not possible for anyone to attain all that he desires or to be proof against the loss of anything he loves, since there is no permanence or enduring in the world of generation and decay, in which we live. These are found, perforce, only in the intellectual world, which it is possible for us to behold. So if we yearn not to lose the objects of our love or see the objects of our desire slip away, we must gain experience of the intellectual world and shift our assets – our desires and affections – to it. If we do this, we are insured not only against anyone's wresting our possessions away from us or preempting the objects of our desire, but also against losing what we love. For these are not subject to injury or death. Nor will the objects of our desire elude us. For intellectual objects do not slip away or vanish but stand fast to be caught, and one leads on to another.[33]

Here the consolations of philosophy call to their aid metaphysical thoughts about what is enduring and of real value, and about what is real at all.

Speculative interests as to the process of definition and the relations, as in medicine, between etiology, diagnosis, prevention and cure, focus the most pragmatic discussion, and when a question of practical, therapeutic philosophy is raised, Platonic metaphysics responds, like a genie from the flask, with ethical assurances about where our rightful loyalties and requited commitments lie. The call to turn toward the transcendent echoes but also explains and in a way corrects in universal, conceptual language the pictorial and seemingly all too corporeal and fabulous after-worldly images of the *Qur'ān*.

The arguments that al-Kindī deploys here in behalf of Platonism spring from the *Timaeus* (29) and its vivid contrast of the changeable and ephemeral with the intellectual and enduring. But the concern that opened the door to welcome such arguments was existential, bound up in thoughts of life and death, loss, endurance and destiny. For Maimonides the Platonism that Kindī welcomed would serve less as a therapeutic device than as an ontic and epistemic framework, a matrix for understanding the soul's capabilities for reason and communion with the divine. Still, the ethical–therapeutic is linked with the cosmological–soteriological pole of Maimonides' interest by the idea of rationality. It was with rationality that Maimonides opened the substantive discussions of the *Guide to the Perplexed*. For his first gloss in that work, as we have noted, resolves the seeming anthropomorphism of the Biblical dictum that humankind was created in God's image and likeness by identifying that likeness with the human intellect. Opening his commentary on the *Guide*, Narboni writes: "*Ṣelem*. He begins with this because it is our ultimate goal, and what is first in thought is last in action."[34]

The large metaphysical scheme of the *Guide* rests on the Platonism underwritten by al-Kindī's contrast of the evanescent, which is never truly ours, with the timeless, that can be ours at any time and for all time. This is the theme Maimonides raises in his "Eight Chapters", where he takes the tree of life in Genesis as an emblem of the uniquely transcendent dimension of the human condition, that is, of reason and the immediacy of its access to immortality and the Timeless. For Adam was the paradigm of the human condition; and his uniqueness, which is the uniqueness of humanity as a species, is reason, here understood as judgement: "By himself and of his own accord he knew good and evil and could do whichever of them he wished to do, unhindered. Once this was so, it was possible for him to reach out his hand and take [from the tree of life] and eat and live forever."[35] Reason imparts freedom, and freedom betokens immortality.

If we ask ourselves, then, how Maimonides can resolve the apparent tension between his negative theology and the license he accords to prophets, who boldly speak of the Creator in the language of His creatures,[36] the answer is that all positive characterisations of God self-deconstruct.[37] All point upward, signifying only the idea of perfection, but excluding any privation entailed in the human notions of perfection to which they appeal and by means of which they point. But what "upward" means here is not just toward perfection, as though that idea must remain vacuous and uninterpreted, but toward permanence and timelessness and thus toward the intellectual. God's perfection is His transcendence of the limitations of physicality, and man's participation in the life of God, man's self-perfection and fulfilment, are possible through our unique linkage with God, the human intellect, in which the rationality imparted by God becomes subjective, self-conscious and able to acknowledge its Source, choose the good, and in so choosing, choose the self.

In Rāzī, as in Kindī and Maimonides himself, moral philosophy adopts a therapeutic role, playing upon the medical authority of the philosophical author in each case, and offering a prince – in Rāzī's case, the Sāmānid ruler al-Manṣūr – a therapy for the soul, to complement Rāzī's medical work, which was titled to honour his patron, *al-Manṣūrī*. Rāzī's ethics, as we have seen, and as Maimonides well knew and sharply criticised accordingly, was hedonistic at bottom, Epicurean in key underlying assumptions. But regarding the fate of the soul, Rāzī, as we have seen, fell back upon an agnosticism borrowed from Socrates (*Apology* 42) to draw a dichotomous future: if those who hold that death is annihilation are right, then death is surcease; and, in the Epicurean phrase, nothing to us – at least nothing to be feared. But if the truth lies in the Platonism that undergirds Rāzī's myth of the fall of the soul and his hope for immortality, to be won by independent thinking, then the fulfilled human soul returns to its true home in the intellectual world of the divine. We have already found Rāzī excusing himself from a systematic defence of immortality. Such arguments, he pleads, would be lengthy and might prove inconclusive, since they would demand an exhaustive survey of all the claims of all faiths on the subject – at least to the point where prophetic claims could be dismissed and philosophic hopes allowed to displace them. The requisite arguments would, of course, prove highly unwelcome to many a Muslim, since Platonic intellectual immortality excludes physical resurrection and seems to deny even individuality after death. If the soul survives, as Plato's *Phaedo* seems to propose, only to the extent that it is akin to the Ideas, it survives as a universal, merged again into its source in the life principle, the world Soul, not as a unique moral personality. Thus the concerns Plato voices about the River Lethe in the afterlife (*Republic* X 621c). For the loss of memory means the loss of personal identity, as Rāzī well understood. It is Rāzī's penchant for the *Phaedo*'s intellectualist monopsychism along with his Platonising references to souls that have not yet escaped this world, that leads his contemporaries to pigeon-hole him as a transmigrationist.[38]

Maimonides, like Rāzī and al-Fārābī, relies on Platonising arguments to establish the credibility (and the meaning) of immortality. Like them, as a result, he is compromised on the question of physical resurrection, which he often seems to regard as the Torah's outward, symbolic way of suggesting spiritual immortality. But can spiritual immortality be personal or individual? Here Maimonides is aided by the arguments we encountered in Chapter 1 from Avicenna, Ibn Bājjah and Ibn Ṭufayl, as I shall show shortly. What Rāzī has to offer him lies elsewhere, in a curious line of argument that may help Maimonides with another part of the problem bequeathed him by Platonic intellectualism about soteriology.

Rāzī, as we know, rejects special prophecy as imposture and worse. But he does, as we have seen, hold that every human being has access to the kind of thinking that is both a necessary and sufficient means to immortality. All of us are given intelligence by God, although various classes and professions of human beings might use it differently. Those who apply themselves to thought can master and surpass the ideas of their predecessors; and even the smallest measure of individual thinking, even if it does not produce absolute and final truth, leads to salvation, since it rejoins the human soul to its timeless intellectual root-stock.[39]

When Plato asked himself how ordinary people, who are not philosophers and are not capable of the abstract speculations that are the sole route to immortality, can benefit from the ideas of philosophers, the question was primarily an ethical and social one for him. He answered it in terms of the ability of the philosopher to enlist the skills of the poet and legislator, to provide laws, institutions, symbols, myths – culture in general and religion in particular – as a surrogate for philosophy, imparting true beliefs to ordinary human beings and thus enabling them, as individuals and as societies, to acquire the character (*ethos*) that would implicitly embody in action the ideas known conceptually by philosophers. In this way, through symbols, ideas could be made available to the populace, if not overtly then in a form just as useful for most practical purposes in this world. Al-Fārābī read the *Qur'ān* as an example of just such a work of concretisation. It is perhaps for this reason that he seemed so equivocal to Muslim authors on the crucial subject of immortality. For al-Fārābī's Platonising model does not explain how character or belief, practice or symbolism can somehow substitute for knowledge in the most important of practical purposes, that of placing us in touch (*ittiṣāl*) with the Eternal.

Plato does propose a moral basis for immortality, by arguing in the *Republic* that the moral virtue of justice integrates the soul, and so makes it proof, if any moral virtue can, against dissolution. But, as I think the Muslim and Jewish philosophers clearly saw, this solution only pushes the problem back a step. For justice, as a moral virtue, rests on the intellectual virtue of wisdom, which enables the integrated soul to resolve its own internal political problems, by choosing intelligently among the disparate goods whose claims can be weighed fairly only by reason. Granted that justice can belong to anyone if wisdom can be shared through symbols, the problem remains how justice can bring immortality to those who gain the requisite powers of judgement not through any wisdom of their own but through a derivative wisdom that becomes explicit for them only at the level of praxis. This is the problem Maimonides receives.

Like Rāzī, Maimonides is a democrat. Not for the Epicurean reasons that spark Rāzī's rejection of Plato's elitism but for very Biblical and Rabbinic reasons: the Torah addresses all Israel and treats the human spirit not as a capability proportioned to intellectual prowess but as a moral identity, sacred in its uniqueness and its subjecthood. Looking to the moral realm, Maimonides argues that only the righteous will be resurrected: "How can the wicked live again, since they are dead even while living?" he asks, citing the Talmud for the proof-text of this claim, which quietly does away with the eternal suffering for the wicked that Saadiah and many others had promised: "Our Sages said, 'The wicked are called dead even in their lifetime, but the righteous, even after death are called living' (B. Berakhot 18ab)."[40]

The Rambam's rhetorical question, "How can the wicked live again?" and its counterpart, his Talmudically sustained affirmation of immortality for the righteous, hark back to Plato's dialectical argument of the *Republic*, that the integration of the righteous soul is what should assure its survival. But Maimonides needs to go further. Like Rāzī, he will rely on the idea that even an inkling of insight suffices to give a human being a share in immortality. Belief, then, can become not just a practical but an intellectual surrogate for knowledge. Or, put more positively, when Maimonides argues that it is their scriptural faith that gives all Israel a portion in immortality, he is treating belief as window upon knowledge, not a surrogate for it. In making that claim he is profiting from ideas like those of Rāzī, that even inchoate thinking, of a kind accessible to anyone who shares in the divinely imparted rational soul, puts one in contact with the divine. Thus, it is Adam, the type of humanity, by Maimonides' account, not Moses, the paragon of humanity, who can reach out at any moment and grasp eternal fruit from the Tree of Life.

For Rāzī, as we know, prophecy is imposture at best – at best, because the prophets themselves are dupes of restless and malevolent spirits bent on seeding human thought with the invidious and chauvinistic claims to special revelation that result only in bloodshed. Al-Fārābī offers a more charitable and receptive reading of revelation, explaining how it is that prophets, through the use of imagination, make their philosophical insights accessible to ordinary human beings, who have no access of their own to reason. Al-Fārābī's theory is adopted and developed by Muslim philosophers from Avicenna to Ibn Ṭufayl, and it is well known that it was adopted by Maimonides.[41] I will not labour that point here. But I will make three comments.

1. Maimonides' derivation of the insights of prophetic revelation from the same epistemic source, that is, contact with the Active Intellect, that is responsible for our conceptual knowledge is sometimes, rather disdainfully, called a form of naturalism. This is misleading. If what is meant is that revelation makes no violation of the divinely ordained natural order, that of course is true. There is no magic in prophecy. A boor or a fool cannot be a prophet (*Guide* II 36–8; cf. "Eight Chapters", 7). But the Psalms (92:7) say as much long before Maimonides. It was part of the Rambam's aim to resolve what might seem merely theatrical in the symbolism of the ancient Biblical and Rabbinic texts to some intelligible, rationally acceptable sense. But if the charge means that revelation in his view is just a product of human psychology, the claim is false. In revelation, both the conceptual ideas that form the body of the message and the symbols and words that give them their imaginative clothing must, of course, be scaled to the capabilities of the individual prophetic recipient and his or her prospective audience (*Guide* III 32). But for Maimonides, as for al-Fārābī and Ibn Sīnā, even the most ordinary conceptual knowledge comes to us from the divine. Such concepts are sound because they represent the real forms of things, the very forms that the Active Intellect imparts in making things what they are.[42] The process is natural in the sense that it relies on our God given intelligence. But it is not natural in the sense of confinement to the physical.

2. Maimonides, following Halevi's lead, makes a virtue of what had seemed a weakness or limitation in prophecy as understood by al-Fārābī. For the imagination that mediates ideas to the people by way of symbols – whether linguistic or institutional, verbal, legal or ritual – is, as Avicenna demonstrated, a physical capability.[43] It maps ideas, which are non-physical, on to representations that must be physically housed or laid out. Imagination is clearly a lower faculty than reason in the ontological hierarchy that Maimonides, Avicenna and al-Fārābī share. But because

matter for Maimonides is as much an expression (or attribute) of God as mind is, Maimonides can treat the confinement of prophetic gifts to certain chosen individuals as a kind of miracle of grace. And matter here is linked with imagination, language, culture, history, and whatever will seem, from a human perspective, arbitrary or subject to chance.

Thus Maimonides can accept al-Rāzī's view that all humanity have (at least some) potential for thought. But he can also recognise that the full exercise of that potential is not demanded of us universally. Humanity is not left (like the soul of Rāzī's myth) simply to sink or swim. Rather, we are provided, by God's grace, with symbols and institutions that can open the minds of those who open themselves to ideas.[44] It follows that there is no static quota of those who will be "saved", but a dynamic capability in each of us of "reaching out" for the fruit of the Tree of Life. Individuals can grow spiritually and intellectually and are not confined to the level they would reach if they had nothing to aid them but their own private efforts. Not everyone need be an Abraham.

Accordingly, while rejecting Rāzī's radicalism, Maimonides accepts his idea of progress. In the transmission of the Mosaic tradition, he writes:

> There never was a time without careful scrutiny of precedents and creative development of principles. The Sages of every generation treated the dicta of their predecessors as axioms, learned from them and went on from there to develop new themes – but on the basic principles they had received they did not part company."[45]

In keeping with his affirmation of the effectiveness of language and other symbols, Maimonides does not confine intellectual progress to the lives of individuals. Whole nations and cultures, he urges, have adopted the core ideas of monotheism from their Jewish sources, spreading the spiritual and moral values that underwrite and give practical expression to those ideas. By his own day, he writes, only the most far-flung nomadic tribes seem unaffected by the diffusion of such ideas (*Guide* III 29).

3. The historisation of prophecy does not result in its diminution. God accommodates His revelation to the intellectual capacities and cultural development of those who receive it.[46] But, by the same token, the underlying ideas remain constant, accessible at all times and always susceptible to further, richer interpretations. That is why we are not, Maimonides insists, to read the Bible as history or literature (*Guide* I 2). If it is to guide humankind in every generation, it cannot be read simply as the expression of one phase of life or stage of human civilisational development.

There is a dynamic in revelation itself, which Maimonides expresses by way of the image of the Israelites being brought to the Promised Land by the long way around, and not "by the way through Philistia, although it was short": Torah accommodates not only the language but the sensibilities and the moral and intellectual capabilities of the people. Time was needed to develop a new ethos before the nation of Israel could win the land and become "a nation of priests and a holy people". Animal sacrifices must precede the idea of prayer; and prayer, that of meditation (*Guide* III 32, citing Exodus 13:17–18 and 19:6). The developmental pattern shows us that the Torah is no more confined to the scrolls on which it is written than it is isolated in the heavens or across the sea. As a living institution, the Torah is found, as its text itself declares, "in thy mouth and in thy heart, that thou mayest do it" (Deuteronomy 30:11–14). That is, its locus is in the thought, action and speech of its recipients. Revelation is not ended when the canon of prophetic writings is complete, but the hermeneutical responsibility of Israel's teachers gives them an authority tantamount to that of prophets. And prophecy itself is not at an end but will be restored when the conditions of its possibility are recovered: the free life of a confident people living righteously on its land.

Returning now to our question about spiritual immortality, we ask: does suspending immortality from the same nexus with God that makes possible prophecy and conceptual knowledge require that immortality be impersonal, as Plato's intellectualist arguments of the *Phaedo* seem to suggest, and as both al-Rāzī and al-Fārābī seem to believe? Avicenna suggests an alternative that Maimonides, and even Avicenna's sharpest critic al-Ghazālī, incline to accept. The key to Avicenna's alternative to monopsychism is the recognition that matter is not the only possible principle of individuation. Thought itself can differentiate individual souls, as Avicenna clearly saw when he argued that we know the soul as a free-standing substance when we consider that the idea of our own consciousness requires no assumption about the existence of any body or sensation.[47] Al-Ghazālī adopts Avicenna's approach when he argues that for finite intelligences, individuation is sufficiently guaranteed by the diverse contents of their consciousness[48] – a distinctness that we might express in terms of intensionality, recognising here, in Avicenna's work, the roots of the modern, Leibnizian distinction between intension and extension as principles of individuation.

The Andalusian philosophers continue fascinated with the idea of a universal soul or life principle. But an insight of Ibn Bājjah shows both Ibn Ṭufayl and his younger contemporary Maimonides how individuality can survive within a universal soul.[49] Maimonides' respect for Ibn Bājjah is clear from the Rambam's acceptance of his doubts as to the adequacy of Ptolemaic astronomy.[50] Here are the passages in which the somewhat over-committed *wazīr* first makes known to a disciple the nature of his insights about the individuation of disembodied souls:

> Peace be unto you, as is only you due, for your zeal to acquire the virtues. I suppose we both know how hard it is for us to meet at this time, so I felt I should come right to the point and get down the understanding whose proof I have found. A person of the discernment I know you have in the natural sciences deserves an orderly exposition. But a technical account would run long and would demand too much exposition and explanation. It would take too much space and too lavish an expenditure on background assumptions. Besides, time constraints and a steady stream of other business preclude that approach. If I do get the leisure to lay out a formal proof, I shall directly communicate it to you. But I wanted to waste no time in apprising you of what I have now, for fear of losing it, seeing how big and unusual it is.[51]

Ibn Bājjah goes on to argue that the rational soul, as the principle of individual identity – and the life principle in general, as the "prime mover" of all animals (and in a lesser sense, even of plants) – is one being, arithmetically identical in all individuals:

> A child's teeth may fall out and new ones come in; he is still the same child. The same would be true if he could grow new hands or feet in place of those he'd lost: he'd still be the same. Just as a carpenter who loses his adz or rule and gets another is still the same carpenter as he was with the old tools, so if it were possible for one to have other organs in place of these that he has he would still be one and the same person.[52]
>
> What this argument shows clearly is that as long as the prime mover is the same, the individual remains the same, whether he loses some instrument and finds no replacement, like the toothless old man, or does find one, like the youngster whose adult teeth are coming in. Once certain of the natural scientists came upon this idea, it led them to the doctrine of metempsychosis, which has been shown elsewhere to be absurd and untenable. But those who held this theory were reaching for a different idea but fell short of it. They held the prime mover of all men to be one undifferentiated whole. As a result they treated as arithmetically one what is not one.[53]

Like Ibn Sīnā, Ibn Bājjah means to preserve the identity of the individual human soul, even when it no longer has any matter to individuate it. Sundered from the body, the rational soul, which Ibn Sīnā had argued would preserve its identity by virtue of its prior history of temporality, retains its individual consciousness, according to Ibn Bājjah, and "becomes one of those lights that gives glory to God. Singing his praise and sanctifying Him, it joins the ranks of the prophets and saints, the martyrs and the blessed".[54] But, although this soul remains unique and individual even without a body, it is (as we might put it) at one with all other souls, by virtue of its contact (*ittiṣāl*) with the Active Intellect.

Likewise, it is at one with the Active Intellect itself. It is not wholly identical with other souls, or with the Active Intellect. But it is not separate from them. As Ibn Bājjah argues:

> What is connected is said to be one as long as it remains connected; once it is divided it becomes multiple. Things that cohere are spoken of in the same way as things that are connected. Things that are linked are treated the same as those that cohere; and things that are tied together, like those that are linked. A collectivity whose parts are organised to serve a definite purpose is also called one, as Ṭabarī's *History* [with its many volumes] is called one work, and the present discussion [with its multiple words] is also called one. Even a mixture is called one, as oxymel is, which is composed of vinegar and honey.[55]

The point that seems to excite Ibn Bājjah is not the unity of all souls, which he took to be Plato's teaching, but the possibility of a unity among spiritual beings that retain their individuality. Ibn Bājjah senses a breakthrough here, because preserving diversity within unity will allow retention of Plato's intellectualist argument for immortality without discarding individual accountability. The key to Ibn Bājjah's approach is the idea of organic unity, which is, of course, one of the great themes of the philosophy of Aristotle.[56]

Plato had wrestled with the implications of the intellectualism of the *Phaedo* in the *Republic* (609–17). He had clearly sought to establish the credibility of recompense and retribution for individual human souls, reasoning that if virtue is a strength, virtuous souls ought to enjoy immortality. The experience and propensities of choice that had formed their lives should set the stage for their future condition, as suggested by the symbolism of reborn souls choosing their own lots (*Republic* 617–21). But if souls are immortal, Plato reasoned (611), their number should never change; none are ever created or destroyed. It was here that Ibn Bājjah saw the opening for transmigrationism that was the apparent outcome of the Platonic line of reasoning. Individuality at that point seemed too strong, leading to the "absurd and untenable" view that souls flit from body to body, even occupying the bodies of animals. Plato had voiced such a view, at least on a surface reading; and Ibn Bājjah's critique of "certain of the natural scientists" who had misunderstood what Plato's imagery was meant to suggest might well refer to Rāzī, and his well-known penchant for naturalism and transmigration. The truth that the transmigrationists were reaching for, Ibn Bājjah urges, was not captured in the myth of metempsychosis. Rather, it was the subtler Neoplatonic idea that the "prime mover" in each of us is the universal rational soul, groping for the highest good. This is what is one and undifferentiated, although present in a variety of embodiments and soul-settings:

> The mind is a rational faculty, but "rational faculty" refers in the first instance to a spiritual form that takes on intelligence and, insofar as it does, is called actual intelligence. It was of this that al-Fārābī raised the question whether it was present in an infant but altered [and so made ineffectual] by the moistness of a youthful temperament, or whether it arises later.[57]

Ibn Bājjah answers al-Fārābī's question by arguing[58] that a human being is like a plant while in the womb, growing and taking nourishment. At birth, beginning to move about and use one's senses, one is like an animal. One is only potentially human (rational) in infancy. This account of the realisation of the potential for intelligence applies an Aristotelian, developmental narrative to the resolution of what is at bottom a Platonic question, that is, a question about innate ideas.[59] But Ibn Bājjah's reply avoids the suggestion that human intelligence is some sort of indestructible matter poured out and interchanged among individuals or even spilling across the boundaries of species. The unity of rational beings, like the larger unity of beings in general, is functional, organic, not merely qualitative, but not such as to negate the individuality of the diverse members of the overarching whole:

> If this mind is arithmetically one in every man, then clearly, from what has been sketched thus far, all people, past, present and future, would be one arithmetically, bizarre and perhaps absurd as that might seem. But if they are not arithmetically one, this Intellect is not one. In short, if there is one Intellect in all of us, then all the individuals who have it are one arithmetically – as if you held a magnet enveloped in wax and moved now this iron and now that, and then swathed it in pitch and it moved the iron the same way, and then in other bodies: All these moving bodies would be arithmetically one, as with the master of a ship [whose seamanship and purpose give unity and direction to the ship and can be transferred from vessel to vessel] – except that with bodies one cannot be in several physical locations at the same time, as these ideas can. That is what the transmigrationists believed, although they missed the mark.[60]

Strange as it might seem, then, all persons that share in the distinctive rationality of human beings are identical – not just qualitatively, but arithmetically.[61] They are in one sense the same individual. But this does not mean that they are the same person, nor that "soul stuff" is simply partitioned off from a single source and distributed among individuals, as imagined by those who take literally the image of transmigration and who think of souls in a materialistic manner. For rationality is shared not by partitioning but by the realisation of potential, the activation or actualisation of matter, or in the present case, the "enforming" of the animal spirit that plays the role of matter as the potential that underlies the work of intellect. Individuals do not lose their identity in the spiritual unity that links them with universal intelligence. For their unity is an organic or functional uniting of diversity. Individuality is maintained when each rational soul "becomes one of those lights that gives glory to God".

Ibn Ṭufayl adopts Ibn Bājjah's reasoning when he compares the soul in plants, animals, and human beings to liquids at different levels. He captures Ibn Bājjah's sense perfectly when he elaborates an Islamic sense for Plato's vision of beatitude, as undergone by Ḥayy Ibn Yaqẓān:

> Here too was an essence free of matter. Only this being had seventy thousand faces. In every face were seventy thousand mouths; in every mouth, seventy thousand tongues, with which it ceaselessly praised, glorified, and sanctified the being of the One who is the Truth. It was as though the form of the sun were shining in rippling water from the last mirror in the sequence, reflected down the series from the first, which faced directly into the sun.[62]

If the forms of all things are their reality, then in a sense all reality is one individual, as the idea of a macrocosm, so widely held among medieval philosophers, suggests. But what unites all beings as one, Ibn Bājjah argues, is not that plants, animals and persons are indistinguishable or interchangeable or even that all are "parts" of a larger whole but that all (in their different ways) share a common source of life and movement; all are animated, despite their diversity, by a common end – the Good Itself, as a Platonic philosopher would put it. Rationality in human beings, body heat or animal spirit in animals, and in the case of plants (as Ibn Ṭufayl writes), "whatever they have to fill the role of body-heat in animals"[63] is a principle of unity. Ibn Bājjah had closely studied the characters that plants have in common,[64] and what he found is again summed up by Ibn Ṭufayl. All things, even inanimate objects (as Ibn Bājjah's theories of motion and gravity reveal)

> must have some special thing to make them behave in their own peculiar way, and give them their particular qualities to the senses and their ways of moving. This is the form, or as philosophers call it, the nature of the thing.[65]

In keeping with the Neoplatonic appreciation of Aristotle's conception of the *pros hen* equivocity of being, Ibn Bājjah can see and can insist that the being that all things derive from their source is specific or indeed unique in each case. Although it has the same source it is not the same being. The form that gives being to all things and that gives life and insight to humans specifically does unite them but does not destroy the unique identity of each.

Philosophers before Ibn Bājjah had held that all forms flow from above, and some had held that the unity of human beings, resultant from their partaking of rationality, made all humans (at least potentially) one individual, identical with one another, with the Active Intellect, and thus, for some, with God. But the distinction of Ibn Bājjah was to have shown how the unity of forms in general and of rational minds in particular left room for the differentiation of individual identities, as particulars united in a common movement toward the good. Without such a possibility of differentiation, creation and emanation would have been impossible – since what was created or emanated would have no reality of its own – and immortality would have been valueless.

Spinoza shows the profit of Ibn Bājjah's argumentation when he insists that modes are differentiations of Substance, but not partitively. But the appreciation of Ibn Bājjah's telling riposte to materialistic images of the spiritual did not await the modern age. Despite his harsh criticisms of Ibn Bājjah's lifestyle, Ibn Ṭufayl welcomes and explicates his predecessor's approach to questions about the arithmetic of souls, and Maimonides quietly but appreciatively adopts Ibn Bājjah's approach as well. As a result of Ibn Bājjah's work and the foundations given it in the work of Avicenna, the Rambam becomes quite tranquil about the once-vexed issues of the number of souls that God will create and the possibility of their maintaining their individuality, even when they have lost the bodies that once differentiated them and have been, in the Rabbinic phrase, bound up in the bonds of life.[66]

— NOTES —

1. Goodman, *God of Abraham*, pp. 141–2, lists *kalām* ideas that Maimonides rejects in Saadiah.
2. See David Neumark, "Jehuda Hallevi's Philosophy", in S. Cohon, ed. David Neumark, *Essays in Jewish Philosophy* (Cincinatti: Central Conference of American Rabbis, 1929; repr. Amsterdam: Philo, 1971; the essay first appeared in 1908) pp. 219–300.
3. Parmenides, frag. 8, ap. Simplicius *in Aristot. Phys.* 78, 5; 145, 5.
4. Cf. Augustine, *Confessions* XI 9–21.
5. See John Philoponus, *Against Aristotle on the Eternity of the World*, trans. Christian Wildberg (Ithaca: Cornell University Press, 1987); R. Sorabji, ed., *Philoponus and the Rejection of Aristotelian Science* (Ithaca: Cornell University Press, 1987); Shmuel Sambursky, *The Physical World of Late Antiquity* (London: Routledge, 1962) pp. 154–75; Davidson, *Proofs for Eternity, Creation and the Existence of God*, pp. 86–116.
6. Al-Kindī, *First Philosophy*, trans. Ivry, pp. 73, 65.
7. Al-Kindī, *First Philosophy*, trans. Ivry, p. 67.
8. Al-Kindī, *First Philosophy*, trans. Ivry, p. 65.
9. See *Guide* III 12; Goodman, "Saadya Gaon on the Human Condition".
10. See Chapter 2 above; cf. Epicurus *VF* 63: "There is a limit even to simplicity, and one who ignores it is as much in error as one who goes too far."
11. See p. 57 above.

12. See Maimonides, "Eight Chapters", 4; Goodman, *Rambam*, p. 227; Goodman, "Rāzī", p. 209.
13. See M. Mohaghegh, "Rāzī's *Kitāb al-'Ilm al-Ilāhī* and the Five Eternals", *Abr-Nahrain* 13 (1973) pp. 16–23; Goodman, "Rāzī's Myth of the Fall of the Soul".
14. See Najm al-Dīn al-Qazwīnī on Fakhr al-Dīn al-Rāzī's *K. Muḥṣal Afkār al-Mutaqaddimīn wa-'l-Muta'akhirīn min al-'Ulamā' wa-'l-Ḥukamā' al-Mutakallimīn*, in Kraus, p. 203, where it is urged that for Rāzī matter is eternal but form is temporal and imparted.
15. See al-Ghazālī, *Munqidh*, trans. Watt, p. 55, where drunkenness is the example.
16. Galen seeks a balance between empiricism and rationalism in *On the Sects*, *An Outline of Empiricism*, and *On Medical Experience*. The three works are translated in Michael Frede's *Three Treatises on the Nature of Science* (Indianapolis: Hackett, 1985), the third work being Walzer's translation of the Arabic, the Greek original being lost.
17. *Guide* II 17; Goodman, *Rambam*, pp. 186–9; cf. 136–40; for the *kalām* resort to logic as a limit of possibility, see Munk vol. 1, p. 113.
18. *TF*, Discussions 3, 4, and 10.
19. See Goodman, "Ghazālī's Argument from Creation".
20. Cf. Proclus, *Elements of Theology*, Props. 18, 29, 70, 132, 145, 172–4.
21. Whether Plotinian emanation itself is indeed necessitarian remains a disputed question. See Plotinus, *Enneads* VI 8.
22. See *TF*, Discussion 3, Bouyges, 2nd ed., p. 97.
23. For this dictum, see Arthur Hyman, "From What is One and Simple Only What is One and Simple Can Come to Be", in Goodman, ed., *Neoplatonism and Jewish Thought*, pp. 111–35.
24. Modern anti-Darwinists took shelter from the idea of the genesis of one species out of another in an Aristotelian cosmos which they labelled Biblical. But ancient and medieval anti-creationists sheltered in the same Aristotelian cosmos, which they assumed was anti-Biblical, since it outlawed fundamental change in the course of cosmic history. See Goodman and Goodman, "Creation and Evolution: Another Round in an Ancient Struggle". Darwin's idea that natural selection is the driving force of evolution is ancient but clearly not Maimonidean or Ghazālian, and the systematic arguments that Darwin and Wallace urged on behalf of evolution by natural selection are, of course, very much their own.
25. See Goodman, "Maimonidean Naturalism".
26. Al-Fārābī, *On De Interpretatione* 9, trans. F. W. Zimmermann, *Al-Fārābī's Commentary and Short Treatise on Aristotle's De Interpretatione* (London: Oxford University Press, 1981) pp. 81–96; Goodman, "Al-Fārābī's Modalities"; Gilbert Ryle, "It was to be", *Dilemmas* (Cambridge: Cambridge University Press, 1962, pp. 15–35. My thanks to Alfred Ivry for relating al-Fārābī's argument to creation.
27. J. M. Rist, *Plotinus: The Road to Reality* (Cambridge: Cambridge University Press, 1967) p. 66.
28. See the final chapter of Goodman, *God of Abraham*.
29. Plotinus, *Enneads* II 9.12, where the inclusion of matter in the emanative scheme aims directly at the Gnostic doctrine of a rival force to that of the One and Being. Cf. Proclus, *Elements of Theology*, Prop. 72, ed. Dodds, p. 68 ll. 24–6.

30. Cf. *Guide* III 8; Goodman "Matter and Form as Attributes of God in Maimonides' Philosophy".
31. Al-Ghazālī, *Munqidh*, trans. Watt, pp. 78–9.
32. Ibn Ṭufayl, *Ḥayy Ibn Yaqẓān*.
33. Al-Kindī, *Risālah fī 'l-Ḥīla li-Daf'i 'l-Aḥzān*, "Essay on the Technique of Banishing Sorrows", ed. with Italian trans. H. Ritter and R. Walzer as *Uno Scritto Morale Inedito di al-Kindī* (Rome: Accademia dei Lincei, 1938) pp. 31–2; the translation here is my own. The essay will appear in L. Goodman, ed., *Philosophical Readings from the Arabic Tradition* (London: Routledge, 1999).
34. See Maurice Hayoun, ed., *Moshe Narboni* (ed. and French trans. of Narboni's Commentary on *Guide* I 1–50) (Tübingen: Mohr, 1986) p. 42, Hebrew, p. 132; cf pp. 35, 125; the translation here is my own.
35. Maimonides, "Eight Chapters", 8, trans. Gorfinkle, p. 47; Goodman, *Rambam*, pp. 246–7.
36. See *Guide* I 46, citing Genesis Rabbah 27 and Ezekiel 1:26; *Guide* II 11, 37–8.
37. See Goodman, "Jewish and Islamic Philosophies", esp. p. 50; Goodman, "Ordinary and Extraordinary Language".
38. Thus Ibn Ḥazm, in Kraus, pp. 170, 174–5.
39. *Munāẓarāt bayna 'al-Rāziyayn*, in Kraus, pp. 295, 301.
40. Maimonides, *Perek Ḥelek*, trans. Fred Rosner in Maimonides' *Commentary on the Mishnah: Tractate Sanhedrin*, p. 147.
41. See Jeffrey Macy, "A Study in Medieval Jewish and Arabic Political Philosophy: Maimonides' *Shemonah Peraqim* and al-Fārābī's *Fuṣūl al-Madanī*", Hebrew University doctoral dissertation, 1982.
42. See Goodman, "Maimonidean Naturalism", and Goodman, *Avicenna*, pp. 123–49.
43. See *Avicenna's Psychology*, *Najāt* II 6, trans. Rahman, pp. 38–54.
44. Rāzī's insistence that reason is universal comes as a rebuttal to the Mu'tazilite (quondam Stoic) claim that revelation is God's moral responsibility. Maimonides rejects the strong version of this claim, treating revelation not as God's obligation but as an act of grace, and hence not necessarily imparted to all alike. All healthy human beings do, however, share in some measure in the universal gift of natural revelation, that is, in reason.
45. Maimonides, *Commentary on the Mishnah*, Introduction, ed. Rabinowitz, in *Hakdamot le-Ferush ha-Mishnah*, pp. 28–9; trans. Rosner in *Maimonides: Commentary on the Mishnah – Introduction*, p. 63. See also Salo Baron, *A Social and Religious History of the Jews* (New York: Columbia University Press, 1960), vol. 6, p. 230, and *PAAJR* 6 (1934–5) pp. 25 ff., 96 ff.; for Baron's rendering of the passage cited here, p. 108. Baron qualifies Maimonides' commitment to the idea of progress, with a rightful eye to the Rambam's respect for the sources. But the relevant qualifications are stated clearly by Maimonides himself in the passage cited here. It was acceptance of the principles elicited from the founding figures of the canon that allowed the rabbinic tradition to progress. Otherwise, what ensued could not be deemed a legitimate continuation. Creativity depends on continuity.
46. For the general theme, see Stephen Benin, *The Footprints of God: Divine Accommodation in Jewish and Christian Thought* (Albany: SUNY Press, 1993).
47. See Goodman, *Avicenna*, pp. 149–72.

48. See al-Ghazālī, *Tahāfut al-Falāsifa*, Bouyges, 2nd ed., p. 55. For the claim that Avicenna himself succumbed to the monopsychist idea, see Chapter 1 above, note 33.
49. Herbert Davidson records Ibn Bājjah's reflections on al-Fārābī's reported rejection of the idea of immortality through *ittiṣāl*, contact with the Active Intellect. See Davidson's *Alfarabi, Avicenna and Averroes, on Intellect*, pp. 71–2. Ibn Bājjah seems to conclude that al-Fārābī did not ultimately reject that possibility.
50. See Tzvi Langermann, "The True Perplexity: *The Guide of the Perplexed* Part II, Chapter 24", in Joel Kraemer, ed., *Perspectives on Maimonides* (Oxford: Oxford University Press, 1991) pp. 159–74; A. I. Sabra, "The Andalusian Revolt against Ptolemaic Astronomy: Averroes and al-Biṭrūjī", in Everett Mendelsohn, ed., *Transformation and Tradition in the Sciences* (Cambridge: Cambridge University Press, 1984). Maimonides respectfully cites the astronomical work of Ibn Bājjah at *Guide* II 9, and there reports his own apprenticeship to a student of Ibn Bājjah's in the study of astronomical texts and argumentation; he cites Ibn Bājjah on the impossibility of epicycles at *Guide* II 24.
51. Ibn Bājjah, *Ittiṣāl al-ʿAql bi-'l-'Insān*, (Man's Contact with the Intellect), in *Opera Metaphysica*, ed. Fakhry, p. 155. The essay is found in Spanish translation in Miguel Asín Palacios, "Tratado de Avempace sobre la Union del Intellecto con el Hombre", *Al-Andalus* 7 (1942) pp. 1–47. My own translation is included in *Philosophical Readings from the Arabic Tradition.* The disciple whom Ibn Bājjah addresses is Abū 'l-Ḥasan b. al-Imām; see the MS note, Fakhry, loc. cit. Ibn Bājjah, plainly does not share al-Kindī's confidence that ideas cannot slip away from us; he refers to the elusiveness of his idea using the same word (*fawt*) that al-Kindī had applied to the elusiveness of temporal possessions.
52. Cf Ibn Sīnā's Floating Man argument and my discussion in *Avicenna*, pp. 155–8.
53. Ibn Bājjah, *Ittiṣāl*, ed. Fakhry, *Opera*, pp. 157–8. The naturalists here would include Rāzī; Ibn Bājjah's fellow Andalusian Ibn Ḥazm targets him on precisely this point. See note 38 above.
54. Ibn Bājjah, *Ittiṣāl*, ed. Fakhry, *Opera*, p. 162.
55. Ibn Bājjah, *Ittiṣāl*, ed. Fakhry, *Opera*, p. 156.
56. See Aristotle, *Metaphysics*, Zeta 4, 1030b 9, where the *Iliad* rather than al-Ṭabarī's *History* is the paradigm of organic unity; cf. *Posterior Analytics* II 10; *Poetics* 8.
57. Ibn Bājjah, *Ittiṣāl*, ed. Fakhry, *Opera*, p. 161.
58. Ibn Bājjah, *Ittiṣāl*, ed. Fakhry, *Opera*, pp. 159–60.
59. In consonance with Ibn Bājjah's Aristotelian stance here, we find him arguing as to reason: "That this faculty is not always in actuality is clear. For if it were, learning would be recollection and would certainly not depend on sense perception, and it would not be the case that when we are deficient in a particular sense we would be deficient in a corresponding kind of knowledge." Ibn Bājjah, *ʿIlm al-Nafs*, trans. after M. S. Hasan Maʿsumi (Karachi: Pakistan Historical Society, c. 1960) p. 117; Maʿsumi notes the parallel to Aristotle's *De Anima* III 8, 432a 6 and to Ibn Rushd's corresponding discussions. At issue, we observe, is not simply the old dispute between rationalism and empiricism, but the question of what it means for Intellect, which is in principle universal and eternal to become individuated and temporal. Ibn Bājjah, consistently with his treatment of

individuation and in the tradition of al-Fārābī and Ibn Sīnā, treats the temporalisation of rationality in terms of the realisation (actualisation) of the material intellect, the imparting of a form in which the individual mind participates but of which it constitutes neither the whole nor a "part".

60. Ibn Bājjah, *Ittiṣāl*, ed. Fakhry *Opera*, pp. 161–2.
61. Ibn Bājjah, *Ittiṣāl*, ed. Fakhry, *Opera*, p. 156.
62. Ibn Ṭufayl, *Ḥayy Ibn Yaqẓān*, trans. Goodman, p. 153.
63. Ibn Ṭufayl, *Ḥayy Ibn Yaqẓān*, trans. Goodman, p. 123.
64. See M. Asín Palacios, "Avempace Botánico", *Al-Andalus* 5 (1940) pp. 255–99.
65. Ibn Ṭufayl, *Ḥayy Ibn Yaqẓān*, trans. Goodman, p. 123.
66. See *Guide* I 70, 74, II 27; cf. al-Ghazālī, *TF*, ed. Bouyges, 2nd ed., p. 55.

Chapter 5

Friendship

Al-Ghazālī built his system of ethics on the framework established by the Persian courtier ethicist Miskawayh (936–1030). He relied on Miskawayh in recasting the command ethics of the *Qur'ān* and the exemplarist ethics of the *sunna* in the form of virtue ethics. But he did not simply take over Miskawayh's ethics. He sifted it critically, omitting what did not suit his needs and freely supplying ideas from other sources.[1] Pietist Sufi themes in particular dramatically alter the cast of al-Ghazālī's ethics. He filleted all that smacked of humanism and secularism from his ethical sources before adopting their ideas.[2] What I want to examine in this chapter is the impact of these modifications on his treatment of friendship. Our baseline is the Aristotelian conception of friendship as the cement of society, a secular ideal acculturated in the Islamic context by Miskawayh. Al-Ghazālī displaces this ideal in favour of a Sufi reading of the Qur'anic ideal of brotherhood.

In keeping with our comparative aims, I have set off al-Ghazālī's treatment against some reflections on Maimonides' ideas about friendship, since Maimonides, as we have seen, is in many ways a counterpart to al-Ghazālī. And, in keeping with our thematic focus, I have considered the scriptural and post-scriptural ideas of friendship and fellowship that intertwine with the classical ideals in the tradition that Maimonides and al-Ghazālī receive.

— 1. Friendship as reciprocated virtue —

In Aristotle's treatment of the moral virtues in the *Nicomachaean Ethics*, friendship (*philia*) either is or presupposes a virtue (*NE* VIII 1, 1155a 3). Friendship is more a matter of caring for another than of being cared for (*NE* VIII 8, 1159a 28). For it motivates us to regard the interests of others. Thus friendship is understood by reference to the love, respect and support that human beings offer one another. Aristotle ascribes the stability and strength of real friendship, its ability to withstand strains, to overcome spatial and temporal distance (within limits), and to generate rather than exploit and exhaust trust, to its disinterestedness. Disinterested friendship is not contingent on the utility or pleasure that any human association may engender. Real friends are "second selves" (*NE* IX 4, 1166a 32), respecting and protecting each other's interests as their own. Such friendship is possible, Aristotle argues, because virtuous friends serve the good they see in one another; they need not expect any direct return to themselves.

Gregory Vlastos found Plato's ideal of friendship wholly egoistic.[3] W. D. Ross said much the same of Aristotle.[4] But this seems wrong-headed on three counts. First, it makes nonsense of Aristotle's differentiation of disinterested friendship from the lower types, based on desires for gain or the simple appetite for (social) pleasures. Second, it ignores the dialectical posture shared by Aristotle and Plato, which always seeks to show that virtue is advantageous, never simply to define it as such, let alone to reduce the virtuous to what is commonly thought to be advantageous. Third, it ignores the fact that for Aristotle, as for Plato, no ground of motivation takes precedence to the Good itself. Goodness discovered in another makes as direct a claim on the energies and concerns of the virtuous as would any narrow interest. The virtuous recognise virtue when they see it and know that personal interest, rightly construed, is not diminished but enhanced by service to another – both through the complementarity of private interests that form a community and through the enlargement of one's identity when one takes another's interests as one's own. So friends will genuinely rejoice in one another's successes and achievements.[5]

D. J. Allan's reductionistic claim, then, that one who dies for his friend acts out of enlightened self-interest, since he gains nobility,[6] is a palpable analogue of the hedonistic fallacy. For if what Aristotle calls nobility counts as self-interest (on no better grounds than Aristotle's deeming noble actions to be intrinsically worthwhile and nobility to be the highest human motive, and praiseworthy as such) then the contrast between selfishness and unselfishness becomes meaningless. Only a pedant or a prig would distinguish acting out of nobility from acting unselfishly or, say, out of reverence for the moral law. And only a clod would place nobility, construed as an end worthy of choice for its own sake, on all fours with motives derived, say, from ordinary appetites or sensory passions.

W. F. R. Hardie cites Aristotle's own defence[7] to expose the equivocation involved in calling Aristotle's eudaimonism selfish:

> If we grasp the sense in which each party uses the phrase "lover of self", the truth may become evident. Those who use the term as one of reproach ascribe self-

> love to people who assign themselves the greater share of wealth, honours, and bodily pleasures; for these are what most people desire and busy themselves about as though they were the best of all things, which is the reason, too, why they become objects of competition ... if a man were always anxious that he himself, above all things, should act justly, temperately, or in accordance with any other of the virtues, and in general were always to try to secure for himself the honourable course, no one would call such a man a lover of self or blame him. But in fact such a man would seem more than the other a lover of self; at all events he assigns to himself the things that are noblest and best and pleases the most authoritative element in himself and in all things obeys this; and just as a city or any other organised whole is most properly identified with the most authoritative element in it, so is a man. (*NE* IX 8, 1168b 12–33)

Nowhere does Aristotle's enterprise of translating Plato's poetry into prose have greater effect than in his account of friendship. Plato had sought and found the meaning of eros on a cosmic scale when he wrote the *Symposium*, discovering behind all human desire, that is, all wholesome desire, a quest for immortality and perfection – biologically, morally, aesthetically, spiritually and intellectually. But, just as Socrates brought philosophy down out of the heavens, Aristotle here has a homelier question to ask than Plato's – not about the supernal, cosmically freighted and sexually charged idea of eros but about the more generic and down-to-earth notion of *philia*: what is it that binds human beings together? He answers that our regard for others may be interested, as with boon companions or friends of convenience. But the bonds among us, in the stablest case, rest on sheer regard for the other. In that case we still see Plato's underlying love of the good as the basic motive, presupposed, if narrowed, in the more self-serving types of friendship, but preserved in its purity and integrity when brought to focus in perfect friendship.

By offering a homelier and less super-heated account of friendship than Plato's cosmological quest, Aristotle can apply his insights about friendship directly, literally, to our daily relationships. We can see this even when Aristotle tries (without notable success) to sort out the thorny issues raised in his own social context, about the relations of a free man with a slave.[8] More valuably, the optimal form of friendship in Aristotle's description matches well with what we see as a sound marital relationship. Cultural biases common to the Greek social milieu[9] may inhibit Aristotle in naming marriage as the paradigm of friendship. Yet he is keenly aware of the role of *philia* in good marriages:

> Between man and wife friendship seems to exist by nature; for mankind is naturally inclined to form couples – even more than to form cities ... human beings live together not only for the sake of reproduction but also for the various purposes of life. For from the start the tasks are divided, and those of man and

> woman are different. So they aid each other by throwing their distinctive gifts into the common stock. Accordingly, both utility and pleasure seem to be found in this kind of friendship. But this friendship may also be based on virtue, if the parties are good. For each has its own virtue, and they will delight in the fact. (*NE* VIII 12, 1162a 16–27; cf. 1160b 32–6)[10]

Despite his brilliant and brilliantly elaborated, if late blooming, theoretical account of the metaphysics of *eros*, Plato never married. Aristotle, despite the gender bias that infects his biology and even his metaphysics, married twice, happily both times as far as we can tell, once to a princess and, after her death, to a freed-woman. His account, then, and his sensitivity to social differences within friendships, was informed by experience. Plato's characteristically, touched an ideal.

As Aristotle intends, the homelier account he offers is useful to social and political philosophy, precisely because *philia*, taken generically, is the name for whatever attachments bind us to the interests of others. Here Aristotle gives a name but also an explanation for the capacity that underlies our constructive social relations, a disposition as essential as our human disposition to laughter – since we humans are social animals. *Philia* grounds the possibility of politics: what makes man a *zoon politikon*, a social and civil animal, by Aristotle's account, is that humanity cannot realise itself as humanity without social cooperation, and cannot realise itself fully as human without the institutions of the city – schools, theatres, palaestras, baths, temples, markets, and indeed government. Only a beast or a god can live alone. But it is *philia*, our basic sociability, that enables us to live together. And that sociability is essential to our humanity not only at the minimal, subsistence level, but through the gamut of human activities and even at the highest levels of the realisation of our humanity. Good friends are the fairest gifts of fortune; no man would willingly live without them (*NE* VIII 1, 1155a 5–6).

Plato knew that societies are formed, in the first instance, around the need for cooperation. But he expressed that truth by way of a myth of origin, and he dramatised human interdependence by symbolising society as an organism. One by-product of the symbolism was his idealisation of organic unity in a manner that seemed to make the individual not a whole at all but a part within the organic whole of the state, as though the very being of individuals were subordinate and expendable, and as though individual human purposes meant nothing unless they served the purposes of the whole. Aristotle stripped away Plato's literary reliance on a myth of origin. He did not rest his case for the *polis* on the symbolism of the state as the individual writ large. He knew that the ethos of a society reflects its members' values, strengths and weaknesses. Indeed he argued that a state is a community of families and depends not only on spatial contiguity but on endogamy. But he had no use for the specious suggestion that the state is the real person. He answers Plato's *Republic* as though the living Socrates had just freshly argued his case:

> The error of Socrates must be attributed to the false supposition from which he starts. Unity there should be, both of the family and of the state, but in some respects only. For there is a point at which a state may attain such a degree of unity as no longer to be a state, or at which, without actually ceasing to exist, it will become an inferior state, like harmony passing into unison, or rhythm which has been reduced to a single foot. The state, as I was saying, is a plurality, which should be united and made into a community by education. (*Politics* II 5, 1263b 27–37)[11]

The irritant that provokes Aristotle's insightful condemnation of Plato's penchant toward collectivism is the idea of communism:

> Such legislation may have a specious appearance of benevolence; men readily listen to it, and are easily induced to believe that in some wonderful manner everybody will become everybody's friend – especially when someone is heard denouncing the evils now existing in states, suits about contracts, convictions for perjury, flatteries of rich men and the like, which are said to arise out of the possession of private property. These evils, however, are due not to the absence of communism but to wickedness. and it is strange that the author of a system of education which he thinks will make the state virtuous, should expect to improve his citizens by regulations of this sort, and not by philosophy or by customs and laws, like those which prevail at Sparta and Crete respecting common meals. (*Politics* II 5, 1263b 15–20, 37–41)[12]

Arguing that people can quarrel and wrangle just as much over property they hold in common as over property that is privately owned, Aristotle sets aside Plato's notion that if integration is a social good, maximal unity is the social ideal, dissolving households and families and submerging individual identities and aspirations in the all-embracing social good, now seen, somehow, as both subsuming and displacing private interests, rather than serving them.

We do not, Aristotle reasons, make all men friends by manipulating the rules of ownership. But we can do something very similar by giving them something to like about each other. And that can be done by education, that is, by making them better human beings, more capable of liking and more worthy of being liked – and by providing occasions for them to enjoy one another's company and profit from one another's fellowship. The friendship sought here is not some universal, utopian or celestial ideal, but a practical specification of the generic idea. People do not need to love each other as best friends do in order to live together harmoniously in a city.

> Goodwill [*eunoia*] is a friendly sort of relation, but not *identical* with friendship, since one may have goodwill towards people one does not know, and without their knowing it, but not friendship. Goodwill is not even friendly feeling. For it does not involve intensity or desire, whereas these accompany friendly feeling; and friendly feeling implies intimacy, while goodwill may arise of a sudden, as it does toward competitors in a contest; we come to feel goodwill for them and to share in their wishes, but we would not *do* anything for them, since ... we love them only superficially. (*NE* IX 5, 1166b 30–1167a 3)

Friendship, in the proper or specific sense, is for an individual, not for a collective mass. And it is for someone with whom one interacts. The athlete in the arena may be as impersonally related to us as an abstraction in a board game, and the mass of humanity or one's fellow citizens are abstractions too, perforce, although we interact with them. For the interaction is not personal. In loving a friend one loves the good in that person. But this does not mean simply that one loves the good in the abstract or at large. One loves this person's unique goodness. Not her haecceity, which is itself an abstraction, but the good as uniquely revealed in her. And one loves her not for the good one receives or takes from her, but for the good she has, to which one can contribute, because she uniquely deserves that good, in virtue of the goodness that she is.

Friendship proper is never without intimacy and particularity. Its nature changes crucially when affection or regard is generalised or made generic. And, even then, particularity and interaction remain a part of it – even when its nature is altered so as to enable it to be extended universally. One can, in an extended, generic, or metaphoric sense, be a friend to a nation, to humanity or to God. But one can no more be a friend to the universe than one can be a friend to Kant's categories, or Plato's Forms – hence Aristotle's good-humoured irony in referring to the friends of the Forms.

The *philia* that unites citizens does not fuse or merge their identities. Indeed, it presupposes the distinctness of those identities. True, it does not flare with the intensity of that kind of love or friendship that demands exclusivity. The *philia* of fellow citizens is attenuated and diffuse. Yet it is powerfully effectual.

> Friendship and justice seem to be concerned with the same objects and exhibited between the same persons. For in every community there is thought to be some form of justice, and friendship too; at least men address as friends their fellow-voyagers and fellow-soldiers, and so too those associated with them in any other kind of community. And the extent of their association is the extent of their friendship. (*NE* VIII 9, 1159b 25–30)

Friendship in the strict sense is a kind of justice. Justice, in the narrow or public sense is a specification of friendship in the broad, generic sense.

> To inquire how to treat a friend is to look for a particular kind of justice; for all justice in general is in relation to a friend. For justice involves a number of individuals who are partners, and the friend is a partner either in family or in one's scheme of life. For man is not only a political but a domestic animal, and his unions are not, like those of other animals, confined to certain times, and formed with any chance partner, male or female, but man has an inclination to partnership with those to whom he is by nature akin. (*Eudemian Ethics* VII 10, 1242a 19–30)

Political relations, then, depend on an attenuated form of friendship. But not just attenuated, also formalised and more strict in the weighting of earned desert or merit in calibrating the scales of reciprocity (see *NE* VIII 9, 11 and 7, 1158b 30–3). Formalisation can mean rigour as well as impersonality: the citizens of a virtuous society will die for one another, if the cause be just. Even brothers are seldom called upon to do that.

Custom is the basis of ethos, and ethos is the basis of action. It is here that we see the relevance of the idea of friendship societally. For friendship involves more than a quid pro quo. In a healthy society, all three levels of friendship operate. People do expect a fair return for what they spend or invest, and they expect that affronts, offences and injuries will be requited. Otherwise, "they would think their position mere slavery" (*NE* V 5, 1132b 22–1133a 1). The ideal of reciprocity is what is symbolised (thus taught in a peculiarly compelling, Platonic way) in the temples of the Graces. But at the same time, cooperation fosters fellowship, and good fellowship is the seed-bed of genuine, disinterested friendship.

Those who experience reciprocity, say indirectly, from the normal workings of a social system, will take the initiative themselves, as a result, and contribute to the commonweal (*NE* 1133a 2–5). Social virtues like philanthropy and public spiritedness, then, can grow through the learning that stems from modelling. As with any virtue, what begins from narrow motives expands to more generous, more spontaneous, higher motives, that pursue nobility rather than simply gain or pleasure as their end. Aristotle describes the outcome in the simple case of a friendship between two good people:

> Men wish well to those they love, for their sake, not because of feeling but because of character; and in loving a friend men love what is good for themselves; for the good man in becoming a friend becomes a good for his friend. (*NE* VIII 5, 1157b 31–4)

Similarly on a social scale, cooperation breeds cooperation, whether its basis be economic or more broadly social. We can add that courtesy breeds courtesy, and consideration breeds consideration. As a result of their shared life, the members of a virtuous society will enjoy each other's company and pursue each other's good. A diffuse but pervasive version of disinterested friendship will inform their interactions, not by dissolving but by extending their conceptions of their private interests.

— 2. BIBLICAL, RABBINIC, MAIMONIDEAN AND QUR'ANIC FELLOWSHIP —

In the Biblical tradition that complements the work of the Greek philosophers and contributes to the Islamic philosophical synthesis and agenda, the Aristotelian ideal of disinterested friendship is deepened and enriched by the idea of fellowship (*re'ut*), the target of the commandment in Leviticus (19:18) to love one's fellow as one's self. Both Aristotelian friendship and Biblical fellowship are conceptualised in terms of love; and both are operationalised in terms of action in behalf of another. Both, in effect, are social virtues. For just as Aristotle regards a diffuse form of friendship as what knits society together, Leviticus prescribes and seeks to inculcate *re'ut* as the bond of peoplehood.

Synthesising the Aristotelian and Rabbinic ideas of the social nexus, Maimonides, aided by the Aristotelian idea of friendship, transmutes Plato's idea of government as an adjudication among rival interests into a conception of government as a conciliation of human characters:

> It has been made as clear as can be [by Aristotle] that man is a social being by nature, that his nature is civil, unlike other animals that do not need to congregate in groups. Because of the immense complexity in the make-up of this organism, which, as you know, represents the final stage in the compounding of living species, individual differences abound – so much so that you are scarcely any more likely to find two individuals who match at all in any specific character trait than to find two who look alike physically. The reason is the diverse make-up of individuals: the matter is different, so the accidents attendant on its form will differ as well ... Such immense individual diversity is not found in any other animal species. In fact, the variation among individuals of every other species is not wide. But with humans you might find two individuals who are as different in every trait of character as if they belonged to different species: one might be hard to the point that he would slaughter his littlest child in the heat of anger, while the other might quail at killing a bedbug or some such insect, because his spirit is too soft to do it. And so with most accidents.
>
> But since the nature of our species dictates that there must be so much diversity among its members, and yet requires that we live together socially, we need someone, necessarily, to regulate our actions. For without this, our social existence could not be achieved at all – someone to tone down our excesses and tune up our deficiencies, to model actions and characters for us all, instituting more constant and consistent patterns of behaviour, to cover over the disparities of our natures with an abundance of conventional concord, so that society can

> function in an organised fashion. That is why I say that although the Law is not natural, it makes an entry into the natural order, and part of the wisdom of the Deity, in behalf of the survival of this species, which He was pleased to give existence, was to give it a nature such that its members have the ability to govern. (*Guide* II 40)

Maimonides is not here advocating artificiality, but he is explaining that civilisation needs convention, that concord is not natural but must be achieved. He may underestimate the individual differences in non-human species, but he values human diversity, despite the obstacle it presents to social accommodation; he believes that obstacle can be overcome, but only through institutions. Adam does not know that he is naked until he falls away from guidance by God's truth and begins to judge good and evil by his subjective notions of interest (See *Guide* I 2). But in the realm of nature such subjective judgements and the conventions that institute them socially are necessary conditions of our common life and the survival of any of us. Our socialisation is too vital to be left to the vagaries of individual amiability. It must be secured by institutions (such as language) that paper over our idiosyncrasies and make us behave, whether we are friends or not, as though we were friends.

Genuine friendship, of course, goes deeper. Commenting on Joshua ben Peraḥiah's advice, "get thyself a friend" (Mishnah Avot 1.6), Maimonides writes:

> He used the expression "get" and did not say "make yourself a friend" or "befriend others". For the point is the necessity of finding a friend to enhance one's actions and one's interests, as they said, "Friendship or death!" (B. Ta'anit 23a). If one does not find a friend, one should try with all one's heart to do so, even if one must draw the other to like him, until he return one's friendship. And one must not desist but constantly strive to please the other, to make the friendship firm. As the moralists teach: "Do not be a friend on your own terms but on those of your friend." When two friends both follow this precept, each will seek to sustain the other's purpose, and their aims will doubtless form a single purpose. Aristotle said well: "A friend is one with thyself".[13]

This union of wills, interpreting Aristotle's idea that a friend is a second self, is preserved in Spinoza's social ideal:

> We can never bring it about that we require nothing outside ourselves to preserve our being, nor that we live without give and take with things outside us … There are, then, many things outside ourselves that are useful to us. And of these none can possibly be discovered that is better than those that are in direct concord with our nature. For if, say, two individuals of just the same nature are joined together, they form a new individual twice as capable as either alone. Nothing, then, is more useful to man than man; nothing, I say, can be wished for

by men that would be more effective in preserving their own being, than for all their minds and bodies so to come together in every way, to form, as it were, one body and one mind, and, all together, in so far as this is possible, strive to preserve their own being and seek for themselves the common benefit of all. (E4P18S)

Spinoza may seem more sanguine than Maimonides about the complementarities of human natures. But he acknowledges the Rambam's point about diversity by specifying like and complementary natures in those who come together, in so far as their affinities are based on reason. "Only in so far as men live according to the guidance of reason", he cautions, "must they always agree in nature" (E4P35). He warns those who would be free against reliance on the ignorant: "A free man who lives among the ignorant strives, as far as he can, to avoid their favours" (E4P70). He leaves the institutional question of how diversities are reconciled for fuller treatment in his political writings.

Maimonides places a similar emphasis on caution. The wise leader, he remarks, will look upon all people:

in regard to their individual situations, in terms of which they are, no doubt, either like a flock or like predators. A perfect man who keeps to himself [a *mutawaḥḥid* or solitary who follows the ideal of Ibn Bājjah], if he thinks of them at all will do so only with a view to escaping the harm that the noxious ones might do him if he chanced to associate with them, or of benefiting from the helpful ones, as necessity may require. (*Guide* II 36, ed. Munk, p. 79b)

But a genuine leader cannot hold aloof, despite the risk of falling afoul of the more noxious members of humanity. A Moses will thus be found "advancing boldly to the great king with nothing but his staff, to save a nation from the yoke of slavery, undaunted and undismayed, because he has been told (Exodus 3:12), 'I shall surely be with you'" (*Guide* II 38).

A genuine leader must unite and conciliate the predators with the flock. For Maimonides, like Spinoza, understands the ultimate demands of friendship socially, and he casts his messianic vision (*Mishneh Torah* XIV, Laws of Kings and Wars, xii 1) in terms of the global consummation of that friendship:

Let no one think that in the days of the Messiah any of the laws of nature will be set aside, or any innovation be introduced into creation. The world will follow its accustomed course. The words of Isaiah (11:6) "And the wolf shall dwell with the lamb, and the leopard shall lie down with the kid", are to be understood figuratively, meaning that Israel will dwell securely among the (once) wicked of the heathens, who are likened to wolves and leopards, as it is written, "A wolf of the deserts doth spoil them, a leopard watcheth over their cities" (Jeremiah 5:6). They will all accept the true religion [some form of monotheism, derived from

> Judaism and respectful of it], and will neither plunder nor destroy, but together with Israel earn a comfortable and legitimate living, as it is written, "And the lion shall eat straw like the ox" (Isaiah 11:7).

For the character of the predaceous nations is a reflection of their mores, not vice versa, as Maimonides' references to the impact of individual situations and socio-economic conditions in fostering noxious or helpful characters makes clear. When cooperation supersedes predation, the warlike ethos will abate, replaced by a spirit of international friendship.

Maimonides follows Aristotle in dividing friendships, by their aims, into those of utility, pleasure and virtue. His paradigm of the friendship of utility is that of a king and his army; of pleasure, that of males and females; and of virtue, that of master and disciple. He preserves the idea of the friendship of virtue when he says that we need one another not only for the enhancement of our interests but also for the enhancement of our acts. Perhaps guided by the Epicurean thinking of Rāzī, Maimonides subdivides the friendships of pleasure into those based on enjoyment and those based on trust, mirroring the extent to which one (offers or) expects the benefit of the doubt. He justifies this odd invasion of the realm of pleasure by what may seem more like the friendship of the good, with the simple remark that it is a great pleasure to be able to trust another enough to let down one's guard, even about potential embarrassments. The theme, as we shall see, is shared with al-Ghazālī.

The Rabbinic norm that makes all Israelites responsible for one another is formalised beyond its Biblical roots and its Talmudic moral and juridical elaborations (B. Sanhedrin 27b, etc.) in the Qur'anic (2:77) principle of *zakāt*, one of the five Pillars of Islam. This general welfare tax on wealth is traditionally construed as a purgation that purifies and blesses one's remaining property, through the moral and spiritual merit of sharing the mandated portion with fellow Muslims: those too poor to owe a such a tax themselves, those with no property at all, debtors, slaves, wayfarers, *mujāhidīn* (those who wage holy war in behalf of Islam) and, to be sure, the tax collector.

The structural parallels and methodological differences between a virtue ethic and a legislatively instituted command ethic show up vividly in the concrete specifications of the *Sharīʿa* as to the proportions of one's camels, kine, horses, silver, gold, merchandise, ores, and produce payable as *zakāt*. There are threshold amounts that trigger a tax liability in each category, and there is a formally instituted manner in which the system is to be administered. Aristotle will sound far more liberal in saying simply that friends withhold nothing from one another:

> Friendship asks a man to do what he can, not what is proportional to the merits of the case; since that cannot always be done, e.g., in honours paid to the gods or to parents; for no one could ever return to them the equivalent of what he gets. (*NE* VIII 14, 1163b 13–18)

Yet when Aristotle tries to make a social or societal rule of this broad principle, his usual lucidity fades as soon as he departs from the economic model of proportion, and perhaps even sooner, when he asks who is to fix the value of a service (*NE* IX 1). As Hardie says, "In covering this kind of ground it is not possible even for Aristotle, nor did he try, to avoid a certain amount of platitude".[14] Aristotle's remark rolls easily off the tongue: "A friend is to be preferred to things and not things to a friend" (*Eudemian Ethics* VII 2, 1237b 30–4). But to interpret this in practice or even formulate it as a rule of conduct is not as easy as the words might make it seem. When Aristotle fumbles with issues in the casuistry of friendship – the ransom of captives, the priorities among friends, benefactors, family members and the like – the reason is not that the subject matter is inherently dull or irrelevant to practical ethical concerns. It is simply that he has stumbled into the proper sphere of legislation, custom, ethos and etiquette. Here virtue ethics issues no conclusive determinations but, as Kant recognised,[15] can only raise questions, to which law or custom must provide the best answers it can.

The strength of legislation lies in its institutional articulation – for the sake of enforcement and implementation by formal social agencies. Thus, with *zakāt*, societal support is most prominent where the need is greatest, and familial, tribal and other informal mechanisms of support are weakest. For the index case of a beneficiary of *zakāt* is the destitute stranger. But the weakness of the legislative approach to moral problems lies in its very strength. For institutions have a life of their own. The minimal requirements of sanction-bearing institutions are all too readily mistaken, as Ibn Ṭufayl complains, for the maximal demands of moral concern.[16] And legal institutions, as al-Fārābī warned, may be made the vehicles of narrow and invidious standards.[17] Crucially for our topic of friendship, the *Qur'ān* (5:51) will command: "O ye who believe! Take not the Jews and the Christians for your friends and protectors (*awliyā'*). They are but friends and protectors to each other. And he amongst you that turns to them. Verily Allah guideth not the unjust." I quote here not from my own translation, but from the King Fahd *Qur'ān*, published in Medinah under the auspices of The Presidency of Islamic Researches, *Iftā'*, Call and Guidance, sanctioned by *'ulamā'* diligently seeking the propagation of Islam. The accompanying commentary expounds on the warning against friendship or cooperation with Jews and Christians:

> Look not to them for help and comfort. They are more likely to combine against you than to help you. And this happened more than once in the lifetime of the Prophet, and in after-ages again and again. He who associates with them and shares their counsels must be counted as of them. The trimmer loses whichever way the wheel of fortune turns.[18]

Progressive minded Muslims read the *Qur'ān* here as making reference to a particular historical juncture in the career of the Islamic prophet. But in the Saudi sanctioned reading an ideal that ought to have been cosmopolitan and open-hearted becomes parochial and suspicious – divisive of humanity and dismissive or condemnatory of those who seek friendship or alliance beyond the narrow fold and amongst the alien "other" against the hardships of the human condition.

— 3. MISKAWAYH ON FRIENDSHIP —

Miskawayh, courtier, historian and physician, is sensitive to the social role of friendship, which he interprets, in very Aristotelian terms, as a kind of sociability or affability, the potential that allows Aristotle to treat humans as a social or civil species. Miskawayh opens his *Tahdhīb al-Akhlāq*, *On the Refinement of Character*[19] with a traditional Islamic foreword, setting out the task of an Islamic ethics. In this passage he applies a voluntaristic Mu'tazilite/Shi'ite gloss to one of the *Qur'ān*'s characteristic oaths: "By the soul and that which shaped it and breathed into it its wickedness and piety." The passage might seem a perfect proof-text for predestinarians. But Miskawayh reads on – "he who keeps it pure prospers, and he who corrupts it fails!" Accordingly, Miskawayh reads the verses (91:7–10) as mandating a Socratic tendance of the soul. One might, he explains, forge the same metal into a perfect or a worthless sword (*Tahdhīb*, 35). The Creator affords the matter of our humanity, but to work up that material through art and culture is our responsibility. The word *tahdhīb*, then, means improvement, correction, or refinement. The term points to an idea more often conveyed by another favourite term of Miskawayh's, *adab*, and its second form *masdar*, *ta'dīb*. *Adab* is literature; *ta'dīb* is discipline. But the meanings that link the two lie in the realm of connotation. For both connote culture, and culture is Miskawayh's great theme, as in some ways it was Plato's. The ideal of *adab* is courtesy, the refinement brought by literature. *Ta'dīb* is education conceived as moral discipline, our means to the refinement of character.

Miskawayh's commitment to virtue ethics, then, is no mere matter of meta-ethical theory or casebook morals. Rather it is an attempt to codify an ethos, guided by literary and historical models. It is in this respect that Miskawayh is an *adīb* – not merely a connoisseur of literary and historical traditions but a humanist who seeks in literature the vivid paradigms of action and character that will link the abstract ideals of philosophy with the concrete behavioural demands of scripture to generate a true *ta'dīb*, *paideia*.

Society, Miskawayh argues, is our means to this end. Each of us is necessary to someone else's perfection, and all of us must cooperate to provide the material base needed to humanise our existence (*Tahdhīb*, 14). Once the bare necessities are secured, higher and more intellectual plateaus are sought – each of us advancing in the measure of his capacities and all of us shoring up the weaknesses of the rest (*Tahdhīb*, 118, 123, cf. 64). This means that the social virtues of friendliness, affability and cooperativeness, are necessary to human well-being, as Aristotle argued in a strong sense. For we cannot achieve our fulfilment, accomplish our work, or actualise our nature as human beings without an intimate reliance on one another.

Ascetics, then, are mistaken in seeking perfection outside human society: the life of the anchorite or vagabond stunts our humanity and thwarts our nature. Such men are neither temperate nor just, Indeed, they lack the social theatre in which these virtues can be developed, let alone exercised.[20] In the spirit of his Christian teacher Yaḥyā Ibn 'Ādī, and in agreement with Aristotle (*NE* VIII 9), Miskawayh argues that love is the basis of all society – friendship being a more intimate and fellowship a more diffuse form of love. Humanity itself is named for fellowship, according to Miskawayh. For he derives the Arabic *'insān* from *'uns*, friendliness, sociability, treating the idea of humanity as the derivative notion and sociability as the basic one, rather than vice versa, as the linguistic givens might lead us to expect. He rejects the fanciful etymology of one embittered poet who pretends to derive the word from *nisyān*, forgetfulness.

Friendship in the strict sense is not generalisable: "It is a species of love, but more specific, affection *per se*. It cannot be shared with a large group, as love can."[21] In the young and those who share their nature, its basis is pleasure, Miskawayh writes, following Aristotle. Love based on pleasure is established quickly and dissolves quickly. Among the old, friendship is rooted in usefulness. Love based on usefulness is established slowly but dissolved quickly.

> Friendship among the good is for the sake of the good. The good is its cause, and since the good is something stable and unchanging in its essence the affections of those who are attached in this way grow to be unchanging and permanent. (*Tahdhīb*, 128)

Love of this kind is established quickly but dissolves slowly. However, a love founded on all of these – pleasure, mutual benefits and the good – is the stablest, established slowly, but extinguished only with difficulty. This love, which goes beyond friendship in the narrow sense, is the stablest foundation of a social order, allowing human beings to come together as one to overcome their individual deficiencies and act harmoniously to achieve a perfection that no one of us could achieve alone (*Tahdhīb* 123–4).

Even public worship is devised by the religious law, Miskawayh argues, to foster human fellowship – neighbourhood by neighbourhood, city by city, and (through the pilgrimage to Mecca) among Muslims throughout the world:

> One must understand that this natural human sociability is what we must cherish and cultivate in concert with others of our kind. We must bend every effort and capacity to ensure that it does not elude or escape us. For it is the basis of every form of love. The only reason that both the Law and good manners make it an obligation for people to extend invitations to one another and gather at parties (*ma'ādib*) is to make them sociable. Indeed, the Law may have imposed on people the duty of gathering in mosques five times a day, and preferred public over private prayer, solely to ensure that this inborn sociability, natural to us all as a potential, would be realised and emerge into actuality, confirmed by the sound beliefs that unite us.
>
> Such daily gatherings are not hard for the denizens of a single street or neighbourhood. But the proof that the Lawgiver's aim was as we have stated is that he made it an obligation for the entire populace of a city to gather once a week on an appointed day in mosques spacious enough to hold them, so that the denizens of every street and neighbourhood might assemble weekly, just as those from every household and dwelling gather daily. He further required that twice a year the people of the city join those of the villages and the nearby countryside in a broad, open place of worship that would accommodate them, to renew their fellowship with one another face to face and enfold themselves in the love that links them together.
>
> Finally, he made it an obligation, once in a lifetime, to gather at the holy site in Mecca, not appointing some specific time of life, so as to ensure latitude in finding the opportunity. Thus persons from the most widely distant cities would come together just as the people of a single city do, in the same sociability, love, joy, and good fellowship as do all those who gather every year, every week, every day, sharing in this unity the good things they have in common, renewing their common love of the Law, celebrating God for the guidance He has vouchsafed them, and rejoicing in the true and upright faith that unites them in piety and service to God. (*Tahdhīb*, 130–1)

It was with this thought in mind – that religion does not isolate but unites humanity – that the wise King Ardashir of Persia (r. 226–41, founder of the Sassanian dynasty) called religion and monarchy twin brothers (*Tahdhīb*, 125–8).

Miskawayh does not press a reduction of religiosity to social motives. On the contrary, he treats piety and credal correctness as gifts of God whose intrinsic value is enhanced and stabilised by participation in a socially integrated community. He accepts the prevalent medieval assumption that communities, whether local or far-flung, are not ethnic, linguistic, geographical, economic, historic or cultural but credal in their ideal form. But he does seek to explain the modalities of religious observance – public prayer, the neighbourhood and cathedral mosque, the pilgrimage – by reference to the Platonic and Aristotelian idea that practice actualises virtues that are otherwise only potential or ideal. Aristotle makes the same point about public worship, also without reductionist intention. Immediately after describing the geographic contiguity and genetic continuity of the polis, he writes: "Hence arise in cities family connections, brotherhoods, common sacrifices, and amusements which draw men together. These are created by friendship, for the will to live together is friendship" (*Politics* III 9, 1280b 35–9).[22]

— 4. FRIENDSHIP IN AL-GHAZĀLĪ —

The same theistic interests that make naturalism problematic for al-Ghazālī tug at the relations among human beings and lead him to reformulate the basis of our relationships. Unlike Maimonides (*Guide* III 43), he will none of the Peripatetic rationale, so welcome to Miskawayh, that treats religious assemblies as means of enhancing sociability. Like Galen and Rāzī (and in keeping with the Biblical obligation of reproof, which provides the original setting of the general admonition to love one's fellow as one's self), al-Ghazālī speaks of friends as a means of discovering one's faults, either by seeking their counsel or by learning from their plight. Naturally, children should be taught to respect their friends, just as they are taught not to boast of their parents' possessions or their own food and clothing.[23] But the primary role of friends is instrumental: no one but God can give without expecting a return. For al-Ghazālī, action for the sake of a heavenly reward has the same moral quality as sheerly disinterested action does for other ethicists. Acts of generosity toward one's friends, he argues, can be considered pure if done for the sake of a reward in heaven, or for the sake of cultivating the virtue of generosity. They need not be done for the friend's sake alone.[24]

Everyone needs help, so everyone needs friends. They are an aid in time of trouble and a necessity in time of need. But friends can be a source of temptations – to gossip, for example. And popularity can be a source of overweening pride. One must walk a narrow track indeed between the influence over others that one needs to survive in life – to repel the attacks of enemies and promote one's interests appropriately – and the temptation to arrogate to oneself the divine attribute of sovereignty – as though human power could go with one beyond the grave. The saintly do attract more influence than they need. But there is a right and a wrong way to acquire influence and use it.[25] To make friendship an end in itself is a secular and humanistic way of organising one's priorities. When saintliness (*ṣidq*) pursues detachment, al-Ghazālī argues, it seeks escape from the worldliness of valuing friendship for its own sake – or friends for themselves.

Friends may meet at school or in a prince's court, drawn together perhaps by appearance, pleasant conversation, or some chance of benefit.[26] Turning Aristotle on his head, al-Ghazālī pursues his aim of redirecting our intentions from intrinsic values to the service of God. If what we seek out of friendship, he urges, is some godly aim, like enhancing one's heavenly reward, or if the love one feels for another is based on that person's love of God, then one's love is in fact directed toward God. That is, the instrumental love of another is really "in behalf of God", *fī-'llāh*, for the sake of God; and the admiration of another's godliness is really directed toward God, *li-'llāh*. A godly motive legitimates feelings of attachment. An intrinsic basis for such feelings would delegitimise them. For pietism, the risk is that a relationship that is legitimate in so far as it is directed toward God and heaven might have some lesser aim. The danger can be grave. For al-Ghazālī legitimates the use of a friend as a kind of surrogate or stepping stone to the mystic's passionate love of God – a practice fraught with risks of abuse, both of God's sanctity and of the human surrogate taken in some Sufi poetry and practice as God's image.[27]

For humanism, there is a danger less insidious but more pervasive, in the exclusion of simple human warmth as a legitimate and primary focus of human interests. If all our attachments are placed so directly in the service of God, there may be little left of the original human motives for friendship. Aristotle finds a noble, humanising and ultimately divine aim (service of the good for its own sake) in the seeming anomaly of disinterested friendship. Pietism, in seeking to retain the priority that is God's due, creates a competition where humanism saw a complementarity. But such efforts to redirect human warmth toward God exclusively seem, by instrumentalising even friendship, to undermine the very purposes for which a humanistic theist would expect that God created us.

The difficulty, as we suggested at the outset, parallels that of horizontal causality in al-Ghazālī's radical monotheism. And the line of response in behalf of humanism and naturalism corresponds to the difficulties Maimonides raised against Ash'arism and occasionalism: if proximate (natural) causes do not act within the world, why did God bother to create them? Similarly here: if we can serve God only by pursuing godliness and not by the manifold cultivation of the human virtues, do we not fail in the very task of becoming as like to God as humanly possible – which, in terms of the Maimonidean parallel, would mean perfecting our God-given humanity in all its aspects? Can Ghazālī offer as adroit an answer here as he does to the question of causality? The concern I want to raise is that he cannot. Specifically, I want to raise the possibility that in very self-consciously removing the secular and humanistic elements from Miskawayh's account of the virtues in general and of friendship in particular, and in re-formalising virtue ethics in a Sufi pietist framework, to generate an explicit and thematically homogeneous prescriptive code, al-Ghazālī has rigidified, denatured, and in some measure dehumanised the core or basis of human fellowship, at the very moment when he sought to render it most intense and sacred, and by the very means that he had hoped would render it most effective morally and spiritually most satisfying.

We can see the strengths and weaknesses of al-Ghazālī's approach clearly in his account of the Duties of Brotherhood in the *Iḥyā' 'Ulūm al-Dīn*. As M. A. Sherif explains, in keeping with al-Ghazālī's own description, the *Iḥyā'* is a work of devotional praxis (*mu'āmalah*), not mystical knowledge (*mukāshafah*). Its four great divisions address outward and inner acts of worship and human relations. Its second quarter deals with human relations, and the fifth of the ten books in that quarter, with "The Ethics (*ādāb*) of Sociability, Brotherhood, Friendship, and Living with Diverse Sorts of Human Beings".

Al-Ghazālī opens this section by declaring, in the spirit of Aristotle and Miskawayh – although citing more traditional authorities – that "sociability is the fruit of a wholesome character; and isolation, the fruit of a bad character".[28] But as he moves forward in classifying the motives of friendship, the illustrations he gives allow glimpses of a social setting. We are in a Sufi conventicle. Gazing on a fair face, as one might gaze on flowers that please the eyes, may be forbidden or permitted, depending on the intent that motivates the gaze. But the love of a disciple toward his guide is love of God, if it is stirred by love of the supernal goods to which that guide's teaching points. And if a disciple's love is mingled with a yen for worldly success, that is only natural. For how can one be expected to long for well-being in the hereafter who does not desire it in the here and now?[29] Thus, the advice of one of the sages, that one should seek out as a friend either a person from whom one can learn or a person whom one can teach, and avoid all others.[30]

The discussion places us not in an open society – not even in such surroundings as we might have pictured when al-Ghazālī mentioned making friends in school – but in a closed environment. This is not a rich and multi-textured reality, but a rule-constituted system, whose all-defining norms seem to reach out to every possible choice and motion and inclination of the eyes. Nothing is casual or spontaneous here.[31] The bond of brotherhood, al-Ghazālī writes, is like the marriage bond. For both entail specific rights (*ḥuqūq*).[32] Brethren must share in good or ill fortune and unselfishly share their wealth – minimally, as a master cares for his slave; better, as equals; and ideally, in saintly fashion, placing the other's interest first. Thus the Sufi counterpart to Damon and Pythias, "Abū 'l-Ḥusayn al-Nūrī, who rushed forward to take his brother's place before the executioner".[33] The ideal of self-sacrifice is preserved and heightened, its motive fused with pietist zeal. Friendship is overlaid with the spiritual bond of Sufi brethren. But the gilt encrustation of aretalogy removes the ideal even further than in the ancient story from the immediacy of day-to-day altruism. Some Muslims, al-Ghazālī writes, became so elevated that "they would shun the fellowship of one who would say 'my sandal'" – since such a person had claimed the shoe as his own.[34] Here the ideal rises so high as to explode. For what can we make of an altruism so exalted and so exclusive that it refuses to reach out to a fellow human being simply on the grounds that he is no more than mortal?

The same tendency to substitute hagiography for moral immediacy is found in al-Ghazālī's discussion of meeting others' needs. He cites several sources who say that one should count as dead a fellow Muslim who refuses to accord needed help. In the glory days of early Islam, we learn, a Muslim would support his dead brother's wife and children for forty years. Al-Ghazālī quotes Ja'far b. Muḥammad as saying: "I make haste to satisfy the needs of my enemies, for fear that if I reject them they will find that they can get along without me." Al-Ghazālī ignores the wit in the remark and its accompanying show of ego, commenting simply, "If this is the attitude towards enemies, how then towards friends?"[35]

Reversing the fields of his initial modelling of duties to brethren on the marital bond, al-Ghazālī argues that brethren should be dearer to us than kin. Did not al-Ḥasan used to say, "our families remind us of this world; our brethren, of the hereafter"? Plainly the needs of brethren should be as compelling to us as our own – or more so. Such circularities and reversals – predicating altruism on a love of self that is alternately presumed and rejected – expose the rhetorical framing of the whole discussion, an artefact of al-Ghazālī's patchwork method. He does better when he gets down to cases.

We have an obligation to our brethren, he argues, to keep silent as to their faults, their private business, and their secrets. We must not contradict them, say anything unpleasant to them, or criticise those whom they hold dear. If we see any fault in brethren, we must remember that we too have faults and try to excuse their failings and avoid suspicious or uncharitable constructions of their acts: "The least degree of brotherhood is to treat your brother as you would wish to be treated; obviously you would expect him not to expose your shame but to keep quiet about your faults and failings."[36] Here the courtly virtue of discretion is applied not to the flattery of a prince but to the consideration of a comrade. Pietism has slipped quietly into the robes of courtesy. Accordingly we read:

> A certain cultured man (*ba'ḍu 'l-'udabā'*) was asked, "How do you keep a secret?" He answered, "I am its grave". It was said, "The breasts of the free are the tombs of secrets". And again: "The heart of the fool is in his mouth, but the tongue of the intelligent is in his heart." ... Another was asked, "How do you keep a secret?" and answered, "I deny even knowing the source, and I give my oath to the one who wants to know". Another said, "I conceal it and conceal as well the fact that I am concealing it".[37]

Here al-Ghazālī draws freely on the sources of *adab*, and imbibes its values as well: the free spirit is the role model now, taking the place of the spiritual guide or the Prophet's companions. Prevarication or even a false oath seem justified in defence of a friend's privacy and honour. The courtly values persist when Abū Yazīd is quoted as saying that a comrade should know as much of you as God does, and keep just as silent. Likewise when Abū Said al-Thawrī recommends testing a prospective friend by provoking him and then checking to see if he has revealed your secrets. This is the stuff of farce and light opera, or perhaps tragedy, or heavy opera. But al-Ghazālī does not seem to mind.

Counterbalancing the duty of discretion is the obligation to speak out: to express affection and concern, to greet a fellow Muslim warmly and address him by his preferred names, to praise his good qualities, his children and skills, to acquaint him with the praises of others, defend him in his absence and vigorously rebuke the fault finder: "How vile in a brother to see you savaged by a dog, tearing your flesh, yet remain silent."[38] Part of true Islam, al-Ghazālī argues, is that what one hates for oneself one hates for one's brother:

> Abū 'l-Dardā' once noticed two oxen plowing, yoked together. When one stopped to scratch itself, the other stopped too. Abū 'l-Dardā' wept and said, "So it is when two brothers in God are doing God's work: When one halts, the other does too".[39]

Here once again the secular ideal is sublimated by Sufism. Glossing the ideal of concord mooted by Abū 'l-Dardā', al-Ghazālī interprets the demands of fellowship in reference to the pietist ideal of *khalāṣ*, sincerity of heart and purity of motive: "Complaisance perfects sincerity, and to be a hypocrite means to be insincere rather than wholehearted toward one's brethren."[40]

In pietism, as we have already had occasion to remark, sincerity is a material rather than a purely formal virtue. It betokens not merely internal consistency, meaning what one says, but yearning and striving for the good. Part of the Stoic reconstruction of Cynic ethics was the supplying of a good intention where the Cynics had idealised sheer candour, unaffectedness, scorn for convention and outspoken openness about one's natural feelings and urges, whatever they might be. The idea that the formal virtue of sincerity entails a material virtue of good will is preserved among deontological philosophers down to Kant's claim that the only thing that is unqualifiedly good is a good will.[41] Whole-heartedness (*khalāṣ*) entails love as well as candour, and only benevolence can guide the choice between speaking out and keeping silent.

Accordingly, al-Ghazālī argues, one must speak out not only in praise and defence of one's brother, but also by way of instruction, advice and admonition. As in the Rabbinic construal of the Biblical obligation of reproof, public disgrace is not what is called for, but the use of private moments to hold a mirror to a brother's flaws – just as God will admonish the faithful on the Judgement Day, "under His wings, in the shadow of His veil", although He will publicly shame the despicable.[42] "The difference between censorious reproach and sincere advice is that between the public and the private, just as the difference between tact and flattery lies in the motive of one's indulgence."[43] Here al-Ghazālī offers genuine moral counsel. For the differences in question are subtle and rest on the intentions of the speaker and the one whom he might aid or alienate by a word:

> If you are indulgent out of religious scruples and because you judge it to be for your brother's own good, that is tact. But if you do so in your own behalf, to serve your own desires or avoid discomfort, you are a flatterer. Dhū 'l-Nūn said: "In fellowship with God, only acceptance; with man, only candour; with oneself, only criticism; and with the devil, only enmity!"[44]

Just as friends have a right to tact and candour, so they have a right to forgiveness. Abū Dharr advised one to break with a friend who obstinately persisted in wrongdoing: "Hate him as you used to love him!" But al-Ghazālī prefers the advice of Abū 'l-Dardā': "Do not desert him. For your brother might be crooked now and straight anon."[45] As many a *ḥadīth* teaches, a friend might be moved to repent, and a slip does not dissolve the bond of friendship. So Abū 'l-Dardā's is the subtler and more effective, albeit the riskier advice. Ultimately, fellowship, like kinship, is not a bond to be lightly abandoned. If it demands material aid, *a fortiori* does it demand moral and spiritual support for those who need it most. Al-Ghazālī's argument leans on the fact that fellowship is called brotherhood: Like kinship, it is an existential bond, not a mere convention, like some purely contractual relationship:

> Friendship is a relationship like blood kinship, and one cannot simply abandon a kinsman when he does wrong. That is why God told His prophet, as to his kin, "If they disobey you, say, 'I'll have nothing to do with your actions'" (*Qur'ān* 26:216). He did not tell him to say, "I'll have nothing to do with you".[46]

Love the sinner, hate the sin.

In the interest of piety, al-Ghazālī again subverts the ground he builds on, arguing that only a spiritual brother is a real brother, and that the brotherhood of faith is stronger than that of kinship, on which, only lines before, it was predicated. He even turns the secular scripture of proverbs to use in behalf of spiritual fellowship, by pressing into service the worldly remark: "Kinship needs affection, but affection does not need kinship."[47] His thesis: that spiritual brothers have a claim on us that does not dissolve even when they stray. But in fact, kinship has a more basic claim, only rhetorically denied. For, as al-Ghazālī acknowledges, we are free to avoid fellowship with reprobates, but we may not reject our obligations to our kin.

If spiritual failings and moral faults are to be forgiven, personal disappointments must be dealt with even more leniently. If one who feels no offence when provoked is an ass, one who takes no comfort when conciliated is a devil. Al-Ghazālī carves out a pietist mean when he follows al-Shāfi'ī in urging us to be neither. As the poet said, we must forgive the noble out of humility and the base out of nobility. The Prophet tells us, "A believer who is quick to anger is quick to forgive". But he does not, al-Ghazālī, explains, expect a believer never to be angry. An injury to the heart is no less painful than one to the body, and no more possible to ignore. "One cannot simply pluck it out. But one can curb and suppress it and countermand its dictates. For it demands redress, revenge, and recompense. But one need not act on these demands."[48]

We must pray for our brethren, as we do for ourselves, in life and in death, and hold steadfast to them, even – or especially after death. Death here is a test of moral purity, like aid to the helpless in the Mosaic morality, or support for the elderly in Confucianism. For the dead offer no requital. The fact that friendship transcends interest is appropriately signalled in the argument that it transcends death: "The Prophet said, 'Among the seven whom God shades beneath His tabernacle are two men who love each other in God, together or apart." The *ḥadīth* here becomes the vehicle of Aristotle's ideal of disinterested friendship, its orientation toward the good itself, translated into the technical phrase, "in God".[49]

Al-Ghazālī cites a *ḥadīth* about the warm welcome Muḥammad once gave an old woman, and the Prophet's explanation: "She used to visit us in Khadījah's time, and honouring old ties is part of religion." Here religion pays deference to the purely human worth of human warmth, as the Prophet of Islam is pictured remembering the friendships of the days of his young manhood, during his marriage to his first wife. But al-Ghazālī cannot let the matter rest at that: "Lasting affection is that which is in God", he adds. And then, as if to echo Aristotle or al-Kindī, but now in a Sufi mode: "That which has some other object passes with the passing of that object."[50] He avoids contradicting his claim that true friendship surmounts even death (and thus endures despite its focus on the friend rather than on the hereafter) by stipulating that the only true friendship is in God.

Friends have a right to generosity, support, even indulgence from one another, but they should not make demands. For friends also have a right not to be burdened or embarrassed. It is not contradictory of al-Ghazālī to argue that we have rights but should not demand their implementation. In the case of friendship, all one's rights rest on consideration and regard. They are no longer the rights of a friend when they must be exacted or extracted, let alone enforced. Only when freely given do they have their proper meaning. The point can be generalised, and it relates to one of the core differences between modern and pre-modern ideas of rights, an area in which the old texts can be informative to us, although their authors are in no position to profit from our instruction. For although rights may presuppose corresponding duties, the idea that those duties are not real unless they are enforced as formal obligations is a product of the litigiousness that a societal (as opposed to communal) model of human relations fosters. The Talmudic Rabbis address the point when they say, with a touch of seeming paradox, that Jerusalem was destroyed because its people insisted on their rights. A stable society needs generosity as well as formal fairness, and the same is true of the marriages and other friendships and fellowships that are molecular to the stability of a good society.

Al-Ghazālī's point is simply that friends do not impose on one another. Not in a sound friendship. They do not make one another uncomfortable or give one another constant reason to apologise for their actions. The asymmetry of human desires lies at the root of al-Ghazālī's thought here and links it to his pietist theme. For in God's eyes my flaw or merit or desert is no less nor more than yours. But individual human perspectives are myopic: "Why beholdest thou the mote that is in thy brother's eye, but considerest not the beam that is in thine own?" (Matthew 5:3). Applying the idea broadly to issues of tact, discomfort, and ease, Ghazālī writes:

> Ja'far b. Muḥammad al-Ṣādiq (may God be pleased with him and with his father), used to say, "The heaviest of my brethren for me is one who is artificial with me and with whom I must be reserved. The lightest on my heart is one with whom I can be just as I am when I am alone".
>
> A certain Sufi said, "Do not become close with people, unless their respect for you will not be augmented by your devoutness or diminished by your sins. That way your actions will be your own, for better or for worse, and you will be the same in your friend's eyes, regardless". The only reason he said this was because he thought it would provide a means of escape from artificiality and unnatural reserve ....
>
> Another said, "Do not make friends with anyone unless he will repent for you when you sin, make excuses for you when you do wrong, bear your soul's burden and not expect you to bear his own". But the person who said this drew the course of brotherhood too narrowly for people. That is not the way things are. On the contrary, one should seek to be the brother of any intelligent religious person, resolved to keep these conditions oneself but not imposing them on others. Then you will have many brethren. For you will be a brother for the sake of God. Otherwise, you will be one only out of self-interest.
>
> Thus a man said to al-Junayd, "Brethren are scarce these days. Where can I find a brother in God?" al-Junayd turned away three times without answering, but when the man persisted, he replied: "If you want a brother to take care of you and carry your burden, that kind is scarce indeed. But if you want a brother in God whose burden you can carry and whose hurts you can endure, I have a whole host to introduce to you."[51]

Peeking out from the Sufi latticework here, we see not just the pietism of the Sermon on the Mount but the Cynicism of Diogenes, searching for a man, and the Stoics' response to their Cynic forebears, couched in the language of duty and concern. The Cynic's cardinal, existential virtue of candour, naturalness, or sincerity, is preserved as well, transmuted from the mere rejection of convention, to a positive focus on God and devotion. Aristotle's distinction of interested from disinterested friendship is made canonical, as brotherhood in God. And Aristotle's central themes, that enlightened self-interest seeks the good for its own sake and that short-sighted self-interest is not genuine self-interest at all,[52] have also been preserved, by substituting action for the sake of God and the hereafter for the secular ideals of altruism and disinterest.

Has al-Ghazālī, then, subverted the humanism of Aristotle's account of friendship? In a sense he has. Clearly he has abandoned the worldly particularity of Aristotle's account, where disinterested friendship serves the good that it discovers in a genuine friend. In its place, he has set the more generalised service of the Good itself that Plato discovers as the theme uniting all varieties of love (*Lysis* 216, 218, 220; *Symposium* 204–13) – creating a conflict, where Plato saw a complementarity. Yet, curiously enough, in the moral casuistry of friendship that spells out this theme in the context al-Ghazālī gives it – of Sufi theory and practice – the idea of friendship regains much of its Aristotelian concreteness. Even the humanistic *paideia* of Miskawayh finds its place in the *adab* and *ta'dīb* of the Sufis.

In his rejection of artificiality, moreover, al-Ghazālī, following the lead of the great Sufi al-Junayd, seems to try to puncture the encircling dome of pietist formalism, which his own work did so much to complete. He asks his disciples, now that they have learned the code of friendship, to recognise that freedom is the only real basis of friendship. His aim is not that they should break that code but that they should break through its artificiality, so that their actions may be their own and so that they may relate to one another as adults and not as prigs or children. The ritual construct he has helped to build, for all that it does in behalf of piety, does not make that breakthrough easier. But, to al-Ghazālī's credit, just as he found a quiet corner in his philosophy of nature to acknowledge, alongside the causality that flows from God, the causality it engenders among events, so he found a place, in the heart of the *Revival of the Religious Sciences*, to acknowledge the precious liberty of friendship.

— NOTES —

1. See Richard Walzer and H. A. R. Gibb, s.v. *Akhlāq* in EI_2 vol. 1, p. 326; cf. Walzer's *Greek into Arabic* (Oxford: Cassirer, 1963) pp. 220–35. Walzer and Gibb wrote: "Miskawayh was fully excepted [*sic*] by such an influential theologian as al-Ghazālī and in this way was integrated with religious tradition." The typographical slip "excepted" for "accepted" is probably closer to the truth. Miskawayh was fully "excerpted" by al-Ghazālī. See Muhammad Abul Quasem, *The Ethics of al-Ghazālī: A Composite Ethics in Islam* (published privately in Petaling Jaya, Selangor, Peninsular Malaysia, 1975) and "Al-Ghazālī's Rejection of Philosophic Ethics", *Islamic Studies* 13 (1974) pp. 111–27; Mohamed Ahmed Sherif, *Ghazali's Theory of Virtue* (Albany: SUNY Press, 1975).
2. See Goodman "Morals and Society in Islamic Philosophy".
3. G. Vlastos, "The Individual as Object of Love in Plato", *Platonic Studies* (Princeton: Princeton University Press, 1981).
4. W. D. Ross, *Aristotle* (London: Methuen, 1966; 1st ed. 1923, 5th ed. rev. 1949) p. 231.
5. For a different but more detailed response to Vlastos, see A. W. Price, *Love and Friendship in Plato and Aristotle* (Oxford: Clarendon Press, 1989).
6. D. J. Allan, *The Philosophy of Aristotle* (Oxford: Oxford University Press, 1970) p. 138.

7. Hardie, *Aristotle's Ethical Theory*, pp. 325–8.
8. *NE* VIII 11, 1161a 35–1161b 5: "*Qua* slave one cannot be friends with him, but *qua* man one can; for there seems to be some justice between any man and any other who can share in a system of law or be a party to an agreement"; cf. VIII 10, 1160b 28.
9. See Robert Littman, *The Greek Experiment* (London: Thames and Hudson, 1974) pp. 16–20, 36.
10. Hardie gives prominence to these lines, rightly, I think, since the complementarities cited are not just gender differences but individual talents. Hardie's wife, we note, was a physician.
11. Aristotle's preservation of individuality within the social unity parallels and underwrites the metaphysical project that we examined in Chapter 4, pp. 109–14 above.
12. Cf. Goodman, *On Justice*, esp. Chapter 5.
13. Maimonides, *Perush le-Masechet Avot*, ed. Rabinowitz, pp. 13–14; the translation here is my own.
14. Hardie, *Aristotle's Ethical Theory*, p. 322.
15. See Immanuel Kant, *The Metaphysics of Morals*, trans. Mary Gregor (Cambridge: Cambridge University Press, 1991) pp. 210–32.
16. Ibn Ṭufayl, *Ḥayy Ibn Yaqẓān*, trans. Goodman, pp. 161–2.
17. *Arā'*, pp. 287–329.
18. *King Fahd Holy Qur'ān* (Medina: The Presidency of Islamic Researches, *Iftā'* [issuance of authoritative rulings or *Fetwas*], Call and Guidance [that is, Propagation of the Faith], c. 1990) p. 302.
19. *Tahdhīb*; Mohammed Arkoun, *L'humanisme Arabe* (Paris: Vrin, 1982); Mohammed Arkoun, *Contribution a l'étude de l'humanisme arabe au IV/Xe siecle: Miskawayh, philosophe et historien* (Paris: Vrin, 1970); M. A.-H. Ansari, *The Ethical Philosophy of Miskawayh* (Aligarh: Aligarh Muslim University, 1964).
20. *Tahdhīb*, 25–6, 139; cf. Saadiah Gaon, *ED* X 4.
21. *Tahdhīb*, Arabic, p. 128.
22. The *Politics* was not translated into Arabic, but the *NE* also refers to "religious guilds and social clubs", organised "respectively, for the sake of offering sacrifice and for companionship" (VIII 9 1160a 19–25). The *Ethics* passage makes a forward reference to the *Politics*.
23. *Iḥyā'* (Cairo: Aleppo Foundation and Publishing Companies, 1967) vol. 3, pt. 2 pp. 93–4; cf. Abul Quasem, p. 98.
24. *Iḥyā'*, vol. 3, pt. 7, pp. 323–4, with pp. 302–21; cf. Abul Quasem, p. 130.
25. *Iḥyā*, vol. 3, pt. 8, pp. 350–6; cf. Abul Quasem, pp. 132, 137.
26. *Iḥyā'*, vol. 2, pt. 5, pp. 205–7, 246–7; cf. Abul Quasem, p. 212.
27. See J. N. Bell on Ibn Abī Ḥajala et al. in *Love Theory in Later Hanbalite Islam* (Albany: SUNY Press, 1979) p. 183; Goodman, "The Sacred and the Secular".
28. *Iḥyā'*, vol. 2, pt. 5, p. 200.
29. Where, then, is al-Ghazālī's critical stance of the *Munqidh*, where he confesses and condemns the worldly motives that tied him to his post, when spiritually he needed to leave Baghdad? See *The Faith and Practice of al-Ghazālī*, p. 56.
30. *Iḥyā'* (Cairo, 1967) vol. 2, pt. 5, p. 219.

31. Cf. the closed world reflected in the glosses of Abravanel, Yonah, et al. on Avot 1.6, paraphrased in Abraham Chill, ed., *Abrabanel on Pirke Avot* (New York: Sepher-Hermon Press, 1991) pp. 43–6.
32. *Iḥyā'*, vol. 2, pt. 5, p. 220. Al-Ghazālī consistently refers to rights in discussing these interhuman relations. Scholars who suppose that there is no medieval idea of rights, if they are to make their point, must define the term so narrowly around the great declarations of 1688–1789 as in effect to beg the question. Cf. Muhtar Holland's translation, *On the Duties of Brotherhood* (London: Latimer, 1975). For medieval ideas about rights, see Goodman, *Judaism, Human Rights and Human Values*.
33. *Iḥyā'*, vol. 2, pt. 5, p. 221.
34. *Iḥyā'*, vol. 2, pt. 5, p. 221.
35. For this line I quote Holland's rendering, p. 31.
36. *Iḥyā'*, vol. 2, pt. 5, p. 227.
37. *Iḥyā'*, vol. 2, pt. 5, p. 228.
38. Trans. Holland, p. 51.
39. *Iḥyā'*, vol. 2, pt. 5, p. 231.
40. *Iḥyā'*, vol. 2, pt. 5, p. 231.
41. For more on *khalāṣ*, see Goodman, "Judah Halevi", pp. 198–9.
42. Al-Ghazālī's imagery here is Midrashic.
43. *Iḥyā'*, vol. 2, pt. 5, p. 232.
44. *Iḥyā'*, vol. 2, pt. 5, p. 232.
45. *Iḥyā'*, vol. 2, pt. 5, pp. 233–4.
46. *Iḥyā'*, vol. 2, pt. 5, p. 235.
47. *Iḥyā'*, vol. 2, pt. 5, p. 235.
48. *Iḥyā'*, vol. 2, pt. 5, pp. 236–7.
49. *Iḥyā'*, vol. 2, pt. 5, p. 238.
50. *Iḥyā'*, vol. 2, pt. 5, p. 238.
51. *Iḥyā'*, vol. 2, pt. 5, p. 241.
52. This was the thought that Aristotle summed up in calling Plato, "the only man or the first to show clearly by his own life and by the reasonings of his discourses, that to be happy is to be good".

CHAPTER 6

Determinism and freedom in Spinoza, Maimonides and Aristotle

Determinism is the belief that things must be as they are. Three types of determinism are distinguishable: logical, theological and causal. Logical determinism rests on the notion that a thing cannot be other than it is. Theological determinism is founded on the belief that God makes all things as they are. Causal determinism is the belief that things must be as they are because their causes make them so.

The three determinisms overlap – not only because a thinker might be led to determinism by more than one path but also because their terms are often explained by reference to one another and their claims are often made interdependent: God is treated as a cause in most theological determinisms. Or God is called a cause of causes, the fabric of causality read as an act of God. When the divine is assimilated to fate and fate to the underlying character of reality, causal, theological and logical determinism may coincide. Similarly, essentialism can make causality a matter of identity; and so a requirement of logic. The same movement between logic and metaphysics can be traced in some varieties of theological determinism. For some argue that God Himself cannot be other than He is or do other than He does. This chapter examines the affirmation of human freedom in three philosophers who championed moral philosophy but were all committed to determinism in one or several of our three senses: Aristotle, Maimonides and Spinoza.

I propose to proceed at first chronologically, to examine the sense given to necessity in each of the three, noting the philosophic rationales that give credibility to each position and especially the linkages between the causal, logical and theological considerations. Then I want to trace our way back from Spinoza to Maimonides to Aristotle, considering Spinoza's view that man is free to the extent that he is the adequate cause of his own actions, Maimonides' voluntaristic account of choice and character, and finally Aristotle's subtle account of the manner in which knowledge works and fails to work in making us morally free. All three of these philosophers are rationalists – and intellectualists in some sense. So Aristotle's conception of the limits of the contribution thought can make to action is critical to the project on which all three are embarked. In this project, Aristotle lays the foundation on which Maimonides and Spinoza build their conceptions of human freedom. And examination of the accomplishments of Maimonides and Spinoza in developing key Aristotelian commitments will in turn enhance our appreciation of what we might call Aristotle's theory of excuses.

— 1. ARISTOTLE'S DETERMINISM —

Aristotle's commitment to determinism is rooted in his logic, grows to metaphysical stature in his essentialism, and flowers in his theory and practice of scientific observation and speculation. The heritage is Parmenidean. For Parmenides had founded logic and metaphysics on the recognition that a thing must be what it is and cannot be otherwise. He interpreted identity as an implication of the law of the excluded middle and understood it to imply in turn the impossibility of change. Not distinguishing facts from things, Parmenides took any negation for the absolute negation (affirmation of pure nullity) that his primary metaphysical insight (non-being is unthinkable) took to be impossible. The law of contradiction, interpreted materially in favour of affirmation, seemed to imply the impossibility of plurality, process or even predication. For all differentiation depends upon negation.[1]

There was much for Aristotle to clear up. His crucial first move, the opening shot in the *Categories*, which sets forth his theory of predication, was to pinion the fallacy of equivocation. If diverse senses of the verb to be can be distinguished, then it can be shown that what is affirmed when one identifies Socrates is not negated when one denies that Socrates is Plato or affirms that Socrates grows musical. Aristotle distinguishes substances from their accidents in the interest of predication, plurality and change. At the same time, he frames the scheme of the categories in the interest of sustaining what he deems sound in Parmenides: absolute non-being and absolute genesis or destruction remain impossible. A particular can become what it is not, either accidentally (Socrates becomes musical) or essentially (Socrates dies). But no particular can become what is not absolutely (none can be annihilated), and none can come to be from nothing (there is no absolute creation).

A prime reason for Aristotle's differentiating substance from accident and assigning a certain ontic precedence to secondary substance (that is, species) is Aristotle's intent to preserve the Parmenidean thesis that what is (at least in the most primary way) cannot not be. Essences express the identity of things not as individuals, but as members of natural kinds; and essences (just as in Plato) do not change. Indeed, it is because individuals come and go that essences are necessary – both for science and for nature. Thus individuals (primary substances) can persist through change, and the logic of change does not demand absolute negation of the subject term. Species, for their part, exist eternally and unchangeably, allowing what is and what is known to be, at least in the rock-bottom sense, to remain as it is.

Aristotle is not averse to what we would call a somewhat statistical approach to natural laws. He knows of sports of nature; and his approach to all sorts of anomalies is far more open, say, than that of Hume, who founds his expectations on what is customary and familiar. Natural necessity for Aristotle is what is true always or for the most part.[2] Yet there is a striking excrescence of the Parmenidean heritage in Aristotle's thesis that there are no unrealised possibilities.[3] In his polemic with the Megarian heirs of Eleatic monism, Aristotle defends real possibility against the Megarian denial. To accept what seems the over-stringent Megarian interpretation of the law of the excluded middle (as applied to judgements about the future) would lead to the rejection of time and change and the complete undoing of all Aristotle's good work on predication. For potentiality is the bulwark of that work: A is not negated when it is claimed that the A that was ϕ is no longer ϕ but Ψ since A was Ψ potentially. Aristotle's affirmation of real potentiality would seem to commit him to the assertion that some potentialities are unrealised. For surely the potential of A to be Ψ before A was so was unrealised. But in the universal perspective of cosmic time, the Parmenidean logic takes over: if there is no time at which A is or will be Ψ, then it is senseless, Aristotle argued, to say that A is Ψ potentially. The concession plays into the hands of later Megarians like Diodorus Cronus, yielding a key premise of his celebrated master argument. But Aristotle takes this route nonetheless, because (like many logicians since) he inclines to equate necessity with universal tense quantification. His rationalism, specifically, leads him to equate what will never be with the impossible: if a thing will never be, it has no cause in nature, and what is uncaused cannot occur. Indeed, there must be natural reasons why it cannot occur.

Despite the "statistical" expression of Aristotle's naturalism, then, his notion of natural necessity is founded in logic – in the logical necessity of things' being what they are. This Aristotle interprets by reference to the idea of things' remaining true to their essences.[4] Species are not merely sets of particulars that we group together at our convenience. They are exemplars of a functional plan, held together by sets of characteristics in terms of which the members are what they are and act and suffer as they do. The characteristics that unite particular individuals in this way, the essential properties of things, are the subject matter of science. They are the intelligible natures of things, not just because they express what we most readily apprehend but because they express immutable natural principles. It is these principles that scientific understanding requires. Their constancy and generality are the reflex of their necessity and the food of scientific reflection. For there is no science of the unique as unique, or of the changeable *qua* changing.[5] Essential properties anchor natural necessity in the immanent logic of natural form, allowing Aristotelian science the goal it pursues: discovery of a very special necessity, the kind that makes comprehensible why things must be as they are.[6]

Aristotle edits the Parmenidean principle of identity and law of contradiction from notions that exclude all change to principles that mark the boundaries of possible change. He specifies that the law of contradiction requires that a thing cannot both be and not be at a given time, in a given sense and respect. The point is to differentiate the self-identical composite substances that persist through change and underlie predication and to mark the matter and essential form whose constancy allows such composites to persist. The result is a seamless vision of nature that shifts Eleatic necessity to the realm of becoming, giving pungent physical application to Plato's seemingly gnomic dictum (*Timaeus* 37d) calling time the moving image of eternity. For Aristotle, the continuity of causes is also the continuity of matter, form, time, and change. There are no interruptions in the causal fabric because there are no gaps in nature, no spots of nullity in being. The approach is naturalistic; but the thrust of Aristotle's naturalism always bears a distinctive, rationalistic and ultimately theological component, betokened here by the Eleatic fullness of nature and the Platonic inviolability of its rational pattern. Violation of the causal rhythm (as by absolute creation or destruction) is for Aristotle violation of the intelligible order that distinguishes the cosmos as divine from a mere chaos or Democritean whirligig.[7]

Accordingly we find a theological as well as a causal/logical determinism in Aristotle – not a doctrine of predestination, of course, still less any idea of special (that is, individual) providence, but a thesis that the divine intelligence guides all things for the best: the passing-away of this is the coming-to-be of that. So coming-to-be and passing-away will always be continuous, "For in all things, as we affirm, Nature always strives after the better". Being is better than not being, but particulars cannot have unqualified being. "God therefore adopted the remaining alternative and fulfilled the perfection of the universe by making coming-to-be uninterrupted

... because that coming-to-be should itself come-to-be perpetually is the closest approximation to eternal being" (*De. Gen et Corr.* I 3, 318a 13–318b 13). We have already had occasion to note how al-Fārābī expands this approach of Aristotle's into a doctrine of succession among natural forms.[8]

When Aristotle reaffirms Socrates' disappointment with the work of Anaxagoras for promising to show how all things are ruled by nous but failing to show how nous (as intelligence would require) governs all things for the best, Aristotle lays claim for his own metaphysic of nous (as it will unfold in the climax of the *Metaphysics*) to have overcome the weaknesses he cites.[9] Nous in Anaxagoras, Aristotle finds, has the character of a *deus ex machina*. It does not operate organically within the action of nature, as, say, in a tragedy a hero's character, working within the logic or dynamic of the action, brings about (and does not merely foreshadow) the inevitability of his fall.[10] Aristotle's nous is not tacked on to nature, to account for what the natural principles themselves cannot explain. It works in and through the natural principles, as the ultimate cause, the goal of all change. As the principle of pure actuality and perfection and the final cause of all motion, Aristotle's nous does direct all things toward the good. For Aristotle, this inevitably means *their* good, just as being means the being of each thing and kind of thing and is not an abstract and adventitious notion, externally stuck on, as it were, by a *deus ex machina*. Mechanically all things in nature are moved by other things and in some measure by their own natures and the supervenient motions of the spheres. The order of the cosmos is directed by the train of causation from the spheres to the meteora and the changing seasons of growth, reproduction and decay. But the spheres are moved telically by the divine intelligences, which, in so doing, express their recognition of the divine perfection of pure intelligence. All change (in so far as movement is a progress from potency to act) is a mimesis of perfection, each being pursuing its own good or persisting in its own nature and its own act and thereby pursuing realisation of its own character as a member of its species. And each species enacts (rather than merely pursuing) the perfect realisation of its nature as a species. The whole of nature, urged on and led by the movements of the heavens, is a vast choric dance celebrating divine wisdom given body and made flesh.

— 2. MAIMONIDES' DETERMINISM —

Maimonides grafts a scriptural predestinarianism and a Neoplatonic emanationism to the naturalism and essentialism of Aristotle, as developed and made more rigorous in the post-Aristotelian Peripatetic tradition down to the time of Maimonides' Muslim contemporary Averroes (Ibn Rushd). The expected effect might be to make determinism more oppressive, shifting from bonds of inner logic and nature to those imposed by divine causality, without relaxing their stringency. Yet, as we shall see, Maimonides maintains the Aristotelian balance and mutual interpretability of the logical, theological, and natural dimensions of determinism. When we turn to Maimonides' celebrated voluntarism, we shall see that, like Aristotle, he was undaunted by the notion that there might be a contradiction between determinism and human freedom. For the moment we focus on Maimonides' determinism. For we must comprehend the groundings of his affirmations of determinism if we are to understand how Maimonides, like Aristotle and Spinoza, judged determinism to be compatible with human freedom.

In the *Guide to the Perplexed*, Maimonides sees his philosophical task as that of interpreting the Torah in the light of the challenges of Neoplatonic Aristotelianism, in his view the most adequate, mature and responsible historical development of philosophy. No faith-straining dogmas were to be found in scripture, for the Torah (to be appropriated as a timeless law, founded on wisdom for all ages) must be open to constant reinterpretation, by the probing of its own dynamic[11] and by the exploration of its interactions with the requirements of reason, the findings of science, and the contrasting and complementary values and ideas of cultures alien to its own.[12] Philosophy too, and the natural science it included, must not be regarded as a closed book. "The sages of the nations" (as Maimonides echoes the Talmudic phrase) rightly triumph when natural science dismisses the idea of the music of the spheres.[13] But, by the same token, the findings of naturalists might be found wanting – as the Ptolemaic model, weighed down with epicycles, seemed clearly to be.[14] Just as creation itself must be yielded up and allegorised away as poetry if philosophy can demonstrate its untenability (*Guide* II 25), so it must be recognised that the dogmatic pretensions of some philosophers against creation do not constitute demonstrations. Neither scripture nor philosophy is a dead corpus. Both are living, and either may inform the other.

In the usage of the Torah, Maimonides observes, all events are ascribed to God – natural occurrences, acts of will, even the outcomes of pure chance (*Guide* II 48). All events, in fact, are causal. For nature is governed by causal law, wills are motivated by the ends they choose, and what we call chance is really the outcome of a superfluity of causes, a mere confluence, as Aristotle made clear, of causal streams not normally related.[15] If we were to read the Bible literally *in toto*, we might feel moved to adopt some species of occasionalism, as did many of the *mutakallimūn* who in one way or another ascribed all events directly to the act of God. For the Biblical idiom routinely elides reference to proximate causes. Such extreme versions of theological determinism are untenable, however. Theologically, Maimonides argues, as we have seen, that if there is no horizontal causality, then God's creation of apparent causes as the mere occasions of their effects (our perceptions, or our nourishment for example) is otiose and unbefitting the divine.[16] Philosophically, Maimonides refutes the notions of continuous creation and atomic time and space as incompatible with the principles of geometry and the practicalities of mechanics. Such atomism, he argues, is at odds even with the continuity and integrity of bodies, and more largely, with the very possibility of science.[17] Accordingly, the Biblical tendency to ascribe all events to God must be interpreted as referential to God's ultimate causality. That approach has the advantage of preserving scripture's frequent reliance on ordinary, naturalistic causal language, often side by side with its ascription of all events to God: God is the cause of all things, but not to the exclusion of the proximate causes we encounter in experience and study in the natural sciences. The metaphysics of emanation readily explains such seeming overdetermination. For here the vehicle of divine causality is the being or perfection that is the active essence of each thing. God's providence and governance act through the flow of forms to things, and even the special providence shed by God's grace – even prophecy – is the bestowal of form upon the mind and imagination.[18]

It is a central teaching of the Torah, clearly articulated by the Rabbinic sages, according to Maimonides, that the world's existence is tripartite, or as he puts it, that there are three kinds of created beings:

1. Prime matter and the natural bodies we encounter here on earth.
2. Celestial matter, the bodies of the spheres.
3. The disembodied intellects, natural forms or essences, energising forces or principles that mediate between God and nature.

These last form the link through which the non-physical and illimitable God governs finite, physical, changeable bodies. In Biblical parlance these intellects are called angels; but since scripture and the Rabbis take the reality of angels to be unproblematic, indeed axiomatic, Maimonides infers that the reference is not to some anthropomorphic figure but to the forms – some temporal and unique, others recurrent and thus properly construed as universal. Maimonides bolsters his naturalistic gloss of angelology with Biblical and Rabbinic proof-texts about the "angel appointed over lust" and the like.[19] The thrust of his argument is the appropriation of the Neoplatonic intermediary ontology. It is this that keeps medieval metaphysics from collapsing into a lifeless post-Cartesian mechanism where only ghosts seem able to animate the dead machine. Here what gives life, consciousness and form is the divinely imparted reality of each thing. This is the very principle by which each is governed causally, by God. But governed they are; all has been and continually is determined. The rejection of arbitrary divine intervention is not a rejection of determinism but is accomplished only by the consummation of a perfect, emanative causal determination.

Causal and theological determinism are reconciled, then, by way of emanation, and logical determinism follows suit. For the being that emanates to all things, giving them their determinate characters and dispositions, is the formal being of their essences, which we study in the sciences.[20] Prior to the bestowal of those essences there is, of course no inner necessity to their character. Only formal logic provides absolute boundaries to necessity and possibility. However, once the natures of things are given by God's will, in the act of creation, there is a settled order of nature,[21] and it is possible to infer soundly that things must behave in accordance with their given natures.[22]

For us human beings empirical study of nature is necessary because there is no necessity beyond that of logic to constrain the divine choice in its selection of underlying natural principles. Our natural sciences are necessarily a posteriori, attendant on the settled order of nature, which is itself a radically contingent fact. Yet such sciences hold good within the order of nature. The logic they discover is not that of categorical necessity, but an a posteriori logic of respect for the consequences of natural givens. God's knowledge, by contrast is a priori, like the inventor's knowledge of a clock before it has been built (*Guide* III 21; cf. III 19). God knows the natures He will posit and thus knows timelessly all that will follow from things' essences and identities (*Guide* III 20). The thought owes something to al-Ghazālī's meditations on the interface of temporality with eternity and is therefore fittingly complemented with a related thought elaborated by al-Ghazālī's metaphysical adversary Ibn Rushd: that it is in terms of God's a priori conception of the forms of things that philosophers can conceive of what theologians picture as continuous creation – that is, emanation, the vehicle of God's authorship and governance of the world.

— 3. SPINOZA'S DETERMINISM —

Spinoza argues vehemently in behalf of a strict determinism and carries forward the trend represented in his predecessors, Aristotle and Maimonides, of conflating logical, causal and theological determinisms.

Yet his cosmology is less constrained than Aristotle's by essentialism, and his denial of what he calls free will does not prevent him from affirming a remarkable doctrine of human freedom at the very climax of his philosophic exposition in the *Ethics*. What is the meaning of Spinoza's determinism, and how are his affirmations of human freedom compatible with his categorical assertion that all events are determined?

Like other rationalists – Descartes for example[23] – Spinoza treats causal determinism as an axiom (E1A3,4) and relates the principle of causality with that of identity to establish a thoroughgoing assertion of the intelligibility of all things: "What cannot be conceived through something else must be conceived through itself" (E1A2): Each thing can be conceptualised and thus understood, either in its own terms or in terms of the complex of external causes that condition its character. Causality is comprehensive: it necessitates, either from within or from without (E1P8S2, theses 3 and 4). The complementarity of internal and external causality fully determines the nature of each thing.

As in Aristotle, so in Spinoza, it is the law of identity, construed as a principle of logic, that lays the foundation of causal determinism. Determinism rests on the determinacy of all things. God Himself is both the subject and the object of causal determination. The absoluteness of His being and omnipotence of His power do not exempt Him from the logic of determinacy. On the contrary, God's eternal and necessary production of all that expresses reality is the sole and sufficient manifestation of divine power. Spinoza takes over the emanative thinking of the Neoplatonists, including their logicist penchant. For he says that God's acts "follow from" His nature, in the language of geometry, as the properties of a triangle follow from its definition.[24] The value of this imagery for Spinoza lies in the link it forges between causality and intelligibility. We can understand God through "what follows from Him", as we can understand a triangle through study of the implications of its essence;[25] or (taking a more cosmic perspective), causes serve as principles of explanation, allowing a perfect intelligence to comprehend nature a priori, from the underlying principles of being (see E1P16, 25–30).

Here causal determinism is elegantly fused with logical determinism, as in Aristotle by way of essentialism, now coupled with a newly energised rationalism that looks to causes (not merely internal essences) as essential principles of explanation and is thus more emphatically interactive than was Aristotle. The interactive character of his view of causality is perhaps most evident when Spinoza, in a striking echo of Aristotle's functionalism, finds individuals wherever (and in so far as) there is concatenated action (E2A7).

Two other features of Spinoza's determinism are new at least in thrust, and both were put to telling use by Leibniz.

1. In keeping with the nominalism of Renaissance philosophy, Spinoza has cut clear of Aristotle's dependence on Platonic universals. He defines the essence of each thing as its *conatus in suo esse perseverare*, its striving to persist in its own being. He writes: "*Conatus quo unaquaeque res in suo esse perseverare conatur, nihil est praeter ipsius rei actualem essentiam*" (E3P7, ed. Gebhardt vol. 2, p. 146, ll. 20–1) – "The striving by which each and every particular endeavours to persist in its own being is none other than the actual essence of that particular". Essences are no longer defined in terms that make unavoidable reference to species or other natural groups. Determinism, accordingly, is dissociated from logical dependence on the notion of natural classes. Things behave as they do because of what each of them is individually and what all of them are interactively. Causality stems not from the fatality of species membership, but from the active nature of all particulars.[26]

2. Partly because they are disentangled from the idea of species, Spinozistic essences are more dynamic than Aristotle's. What stays constant in Spinoza is a mode of organisation. Thus an organism (as in Aristotle) can grow (or metamorphose) without losing its essential form – and the universe as a whole can "vary in infinite ways without any change in the individual as a whole" (E2A3L7S). Looking to Spinoza's predecessors we can see this thesis as the triumphant conclusion to a refutation of the anti-determinist claim that essentialist determinism renders change and variation impossible. Spinoza has refined Aristotle's essentialism to allow temporal variation within nature at large without changing the essential face of nature, just as he has refined Parmenides' monism to allow unity in nature without compromising the variety of existents (E2A7). In terms highly relevant to Spinoza's contemporaries and successors (Descartes himself was a "discreet" evolutionist),[27] Spinoza's essentialism leaves room for evolution, which Aristotelian essentialism precludes as a matter of logic. For there are many forms that a thing may take, or that a mode of organisation may pursue in its striving to persist in its own being. In view of the individuality and the dynamism of essences in Spinoza, Richard Mason has argued that it is at least as appropriate to construe Spinoza's logicism causally as to think of his determinism in logicist terms.[28]

Theological determinism is, of course, again conflated with the causal cum logical determinism in Spinoza (E1P33). Since God is the whole of nature, including both the physical and the mental aspects of reality and infinite other manifestations that surpass our understanding because we have nothing in common with them, and since God or nature is not exempt from the universal law by which each thing is what it is and does what it does, God's infinite expressive power and claim upon reality are fully actual at all times. Everything that can be is, and the very laws of nature – the principle of determinacy itself – are the manifestations of God's power and act. God is not interpreted as that which acts – or to whom appeal must be made – when all else fails; for there is nothing else. God's infinity precludes all other being and action, not by stifling but by including all that there is. God's necessity of existence, as the sole substance, the sole self-sufficient existent, lays down the necessity of all existents that express God's diverse aspects. For God is the cause of their essences (*conatus*) as well as their existence, and God's essence is His existence (E1P25, 16, 7).

— 4. SPINOZA'S DEFENCE OF HUMAN FREEDOM —

Unlike Aristotle and Maimonides, Spinoza argues vociferously and repeatedly against the notion of free will. By free will, he understands an unconditioned mode of thought – a clearly incoherent notion (E1P32; 2P48). Working in the tradition of Averroes's reading of Peripatetic causality, Spinoza equates the assertion that a being might do other than it does with the specious claim that an existent might be other than the thing it is. What is undetermined, Averroes argued, having no cause, has no definite nature – so it does not exist.[29] Contingency is an illusion arising in ignorance (E1App.). There is no contingency in nature. All is determined, because all is determinate. Determinacy is the condition of existence, and the actions of all beings are expressions of that determinacy (cf. E1P35). Free will is just a projection arising from the illusion of contingency – treating our choices as though they were groundless and ascribing human unpredictability not to our ignorance of the springs of human action but to an imagined power of arbitrary, uncaused and unconditioned choice. Misconceiving arbitrariness as power, voluntarists project the same ignorance into their anthropomorphic notions of God, assigning God an arbitrary will and inventing a realm of unrealised possibilities over which the divine indeterminacy may range. But in fact will is a mode of thought, and like all modes it is determinate in each of its instances. There is no faculty or power of will in general. Such notions are mere hypostatisations, reifying and blurring the various instances of volitional thought, each of which is conditioned fully by the infinite array of other thoughts (mental processes) that come into associative contact with it.[30] Although infinite in infinite ways, God is as determinate as actuality and as determined as the world – because, of course, God is the world (E1P31–2).

Our penchant for investing God, ourselves and one another with free will stems from our proneness to various passive emotions – regret, vainglory, guilt and shame, to name a few. Whatever we perceive as causing us pain or pleasure, sorrow or joy, we think of as evil or good accordingly. We take a kind of perverse pleasure in focusing on such causes, isolating them from their concomitants and conditions, and investing them with independent powers, whose intensionalities and purposes, like their specious independence, are illusory, projections of our own anger or expectations, hopes and fears. Our notion of free will is in part a figment of such emotions of ours. We flagellate ourselves or one another with the notion that we might have done better. Or we translate our wishes and anxieties into the idea that God ought to have done better by us – or still might if rightly wooed. We sense our own power of action and ignore its limits and predisposing factors. Seeking praise for ourselves and disparagement for our detractors, we assign to allies and enemies alike an arbitrary absoluteness in volitions that is purely mythic. That is, its affirmation and indeed presupposition in our thought are artefacts of the irrational, associative psychology of the emotions, unwarranted and indeed negated by the evidence of science.

Yet the discourse of the emotions and of subjective valuation runs deep. Is it possible to dispense with the language of free will? Confronting the standard objection that without free will there would be neither praise and blame nor punishment and reward, nor human dignity, Spinoza answers as follows:

1. Praise and blame are impertinent. Our task is not to bemoan the human condition nor to congratulate ourselves upon it, but to understand it and to think and act in accordance with that understanding (E3Preface).

2. Punishment and reward do not logically require belief in arbitrary, uncaused choices. Punishment presupposes some measure of causal control over our actions. How else could we single out and differentiate whom to punish and whom to reward, and for what? But no notion of free will is required. We can (in keeping with what we now call strict liability) punish or reward persons for what they have done, without regard for what we may deem their ultimate motives. Punishment, Spinoza argues, may be justified by the rule of pestilence:

> You may ask at this point, "Why then are the wicked punished, for they act by their own nature and according to the divine decree?" But I respond: "It is equally at the divine decree that they are punished. And if only those ought to be punished whom we deem to have offended by their own free will, then why do men strive to extirpate poisonous snakes – for they too offend only by their own nature and cannot do otherwise."[31]

Criminals need not, of course, be extirpated. What the rule of pestilence warrants is their constraint, by whatever means prove most appropriate. The overriding concern of law, it can be argued, is not with motives or intentions but with actions. It is these we rightly punish and reward, and to do so we do not need to know that an individual had free will or was (as medieval philosophers might have put it) the sole and sufficient creator of his acts.

3. As for human dignity, it can well be argued that human dignity does not stand or fall with the affirmation of uncaused volitions, any more than the dignity of God profits from the imputation of arbitrariness. To please their fancies, human beings have abstracted from the little that they know about the causes that underlie their conscious motives. Just as we artificially abstract an item from its causal milieu when we call a finite mode a "substance", so we artificially abstract ourselves and our volitions from their thought environment when we call them "free" and mean "unconditioned" (E1P36). The effect of such illogic (treating modes as substances) is naturally a paradox. We make our choices appear simultaneously more rational and more irrational than they are, and we are left with no criterion by which to judge their rationality. Then we compound the affront to the determinacy of nature by projecting the same faulty model of human choices on to God, inventing a teleology in which God is made to act in the design of nature with the same pettish and arbitrary emotions that we imagine constitute freedom in ourselves. The pettiness and passions of our fancied deity (who wants only to be honoured by ourselves and jolts nature about to accommodate our every flattery or affront) reflect, on a grotesquely enlarged scale, the pettiness and passions of His creators. It can come as no surprise that this specious deity's chief interest is imagined to rest upon ourselves (E1App.; cf. *Guide* III 13).

It is after this wide-ranging denunciation of free will has been set out that Spinoza returns to the idea of freedom, which he has defined at the very outset of his *Ethics* (Def. 7) as belonging to that thing "which exists solely by the necessity of its own nature and is determined to action solely by itself". For the entire fifth part of the *Ethics* is devoted to delineating a path of human freedom by which we can release ourselves from the control of the passions and become, in some measure, the governors of our own destiny. The means by which Spinoza can affirm human freedom after categorically rejecting the very notion of free will and most of its familiar bastions of defence in psychology, theology, law and morals are most instructive for contemporary discussions of freedom and responsibility and too often neglected or misunderstood.

To begin with, what Spinoza rejects is not the same as what he reaffirms.

It is characteristic of Spinoza that he dissolves classic conundrums of philosophy by means of the careful distinctions he embeds within his definitions. Thus, it is by insistence on rigorous and unflinching application of the Aristotelian and Cartesian criteria of substantiality, which he combines, that he reaches his monistic interpretation of reality and obviates the fudging notion of his predecessors that there is a relative self-sufficiency in finite substances (E1P10C&S). He similarly eliminates anthropocentric and anthropomorphic teleology, to replace it with a more objective and universal teleology in which each being carries and develops in itself the goals focused as its *conatus*.[32] He inveighs against projective notions of good and bad, order and disorder, even perfection and imperfection, only to displace them with a more objective conceptualisation that identifies perfection with reality, introducing a new version of the Neoplatonists' hierarchically graded reality as an ontic and ethical scale (E1P11, 2D6).

Spinoza's keen analytic sense is reflected in his definition of the freedom he accepts as self-necessitation. This freedom is not and does not call for an exception to the universal causal law and the governance of nature by the determinacy (not fixedness) of all things' essences. Freedom is autonomy, self-causedness and self-determination, not indeterminacy or causelessness. Clearly God is free, since God is self-determined. Spinoza is prepared to argue that freedom as autonomy is worthier of God than free will. God is more nobly and dispassionately conceived as self-sufficing than as arbitrary (even if sense could be made of divinely perfect arbitrariness), and human choices are more nobly and dispassionately planned when related to an idea of necessity than when related to an idea of abstract and arbitrary positivity (a fiat, rule, or mere isolated fact).[33] But the question remains: is anyone free besides God?

Plainly, only God is free in an absolute sense, for only God is clear of all possibility of interference. But from the very outset Spinoza lays the groundwork for a partial or relative human freedom as well. Human beings are free to the extent that they are self-determined in their actions. In defining that branch of necessity which excludes freedom, Spinoza identifies those agents as coerced or constrained (*coacta*) "which are determined to be and to behave in a certain way by another" – by some thing or some one other than themselves (E1D7). All things, of course, are necessary, so Spinoza substitutes the term *coacta* here for *necessaria*, writing "*necessaria … vel potius coacta*" (necessary or, more properly, constrained) to distinguish as constrained that class of necessary actions which are externally determined. He thus leaves room for necessary actions whose causal determination is internal.

The latter are properly called free. It is true that the actions of finite beings (modes) are never wholly self-determined but always externally conditioned in an infinitude of interactions. Yet each determinate mode makes its own causal contributions to the interactive system and can be called free to the extent that its own character and identity are the determinants of its actions, rather than mere effects of the actions of others upon it. The *conatus* of each thing, be it remembered, is that thing's essence and identity. *Conatus* of which the subject is conscious is desire. It is called appetite when it pertains to mind and body alike. But considered as a mental affection, it is called the will (E3P9). Each of us is determined to action by a personal *conatus*, interacting with the impacts upon us of all other things; and our *conatus* is conditioned by all that we have undergone – conditioned, but not determined or created, for we are not the mere products of our history, reducible to what we have been. Each being participates in making itself what (or who) it is, and it is from what or who we are (from our *conatus*, not our history) that our actions flow.

Spinoza thus subscribes to a rigorous and unexceptioned determinism in all three of the senses we have identified, while maintaining human freedom. He adopts a strong version of the metaphysical reading of the law of identity that we have labelled logic-grounded determinism. He links this with his causal determinism via a modified (dynamic and individual) essentialism, setting all beings and events in thoroughgoing causal interaction. He sums up the whole in a classic reformulation of theological determinism worthy of being set alongside any other produced by a natural theologian when he argues that nothing occurs contrary to God's nature and that God Himself expresses His power not in arbitrary invasions of nature but by the flowing forth from His nature of all that takes place. This occurs with a necessity as regular and as intellectually transparent to absolute intelligence as the necessity of geometrical implication, and without any essential change in God or nature. Spinoza preserves freedom in the context of determinism by the simple but elegant expedient of distinguishing between uncaused and self-caused actions. The former are an illusion, and a pernicious one at that. The latter are real and are no exception to determinism, but a necessary component in it.

It has long been commonplace for proponents of free will to cite the self-evidence of human intentions. Opponents cite the concealment and uncertainty of our inner motives as evidence of the lack of rational control. Awareness of the hidden dimensions of the inner life does not begin with Freud, after all, but runs back, as we have seen, through Kant and his Pietist predecessors, into the Middle Ages and ultimately to the Biblical footings of Western spirituality.[34] In historical perspective, the triumphant observations of a Paul Edwards, discovering to his readers or listeners that human motivations have genetic and environmental precursors that can be read or pled as their determinants,[35] inevitably looks almost sophomoric. Clarence Darrow's archetypical defence speech, canonised in dramatic representations of his summation in the Loeb-Leopold trial or transmogrified by Hollywood in the famous summing up in the film *Knock on Any Door* – arguing that any member of the jury, given the wrong background, might have been the prisoner in the dock – has antecedents going back to the legal practice of the ancient Sophists. Modern sciences like psychology, sociology, genetics and endocrinology add props but alter little in the structure of the argument.[36] If the notion is that we can be victims of our past circumstances, Spinoza offers little disagreement; but if the price of understanding (which Spinoza does not believe entails exoneration) is adoption of a metaphysical denial of human freedom in the sense of self-direction, Spinoza vigorously dissents. What Spinoza contributes here is the exposition of a dynamic by which individuals can be seen as causally, rationally responsible for their own actions in some varying measure, dependent in part on their fortunes (the natural given), but dependent in part on choices over which we can exercise some measure of control. For in the complex array of determinants, one is oneself an actor.

Modern sociological accounts of human agency often overlook this feature. They tend to treat the human person as a product of heredity and environment whose every choice and motivating value is the product of external forces. Such an analysis, as I argued years ago in what I called the Point Zero argument, is self-undermining to the extent that it assumes other persons to be agents of the effects that it holds to determine a subject's choices.[37] That is, the familiar types of social and behavioural determinism presume upon the very kind of active agency they deny. The problem is that all causal agency is assumed to be external. However, if persons cannot act, much of the agency relied upon in the deterministic theory is vitiated or dissipated. We receive inputs but pass them on essentially unmodified by any distinctive contribution of our own. If that were possible, we would be unique in nature. Indeed, our identity would vanish to a point, to nullity. In Spinoza's terms (to express the reduction in his language of comprehensibility), nothing would be contributed to an understanding of our actions by an understanding of ourselves. Otherwise expressed: there would be only passivities, no actions. The spurious determinism founded on such a farrago defeats its own intention, if the intention was the Lucretian one of knowing the causes of things: it does not count human beings as causes, but only as the butts of causal effects.

Only the pragmatic and dramatic rhetorical uses of this spurious determinism keep it alive. Its images and appeals to external causation – of stars, or lots and destinies, or of genes, hormones and Oedipal conflicts – serve our passion for exoneration, just as the equally specious indeterminism of moral backgroundlessness serves our passion for vituperation. The truth lies in the middle ground: we humans are partially responsible for our own acts and choices, and much of the strength of Spinoza's psychology lies in its ability to show how this can be so. Like the Eastern sage in the fable who comforted a group of foolish monks who thought they had lost one of their number in crossing a river, he points out that in counting heads after crossing, each one of the weeping monks has forgotten to count himself. As Richard Mason puts it: "Among the causes that will bring about the future are decisions I make now, based partly on what I have been able to discover about how I arrived where I am."[38]

Three features of Spinoza's metaphysics aid his discovery to us of a power of action to be counterpoised against our passivity:

1. In logic, Spinoza's dynamic essentialism leaves room for a reflexive or reflective moment in human action, allowing us to be conceived as in some measure the authors of our own choices.
2. In theology, Spinoza's immanent God overcomes the externality of divine causal agency, breaking down the idea that if God acts we do not.[39]
3. In causality, Spinoza's recognition of the thoroughgoing interconnectedness of all things does not preclude but presupposes the activity of each particular. The psychophysical parallelism Spinoza salvaged from the dualism of Descartes, moreover, prevents the reduction of mental events to physical causes that has short-circuited so much of modern deterministic psychology.

1. Just as Aristotle recognised that without a distinction between essence and accident the principle of identity would freeze reality in immobility, so Spinoza saw that essences must be dynamic and in some measure self-constituting if provision is to be made for the organic complexity of life[40] and the reflexivity of consciousness.[41] This I take to be the real thrust for the problem of freedom, of Spinoza's transformation of Aristotelian essence into the more dynamic notion of the *conatus*. For Aristotelian essences were already related to process, but they did not change. It was Aristotle's belief that the life cycle of a plant or the changing purposes of a person could be accounted for by way of the varying material encounters of an invariant specific essence with diverse situations as a programme of development unfolds. In Spinoza's view, however, essences are not externally bestowed or Platonically static: the plan (or

"face") of nature as a whole is what does not change, and essences themselves, as *conatus*, can unfold or self-construct. Nowhere is this clearer than where *conatus* becomes self-conscious as desire.[42] Human consciousness, like all other things in nature, existentiates itself. Granted it does so within a causal context, but like all other things it expresses a nature that is not merely given to it. In some measure consciousness is self-creative – and that on a level higher than other things because of its reflexivity and self-transparency. It does not merely know, but it knows that it knows. That gives it some measure of control. Consciousness is not, Spinoza insists, like some picture painted on a screen (E2P43S) – not even like a moving picture on a screen. It is not merely a set of objective presentations whose subject must be sought somewhere else, in the back of the theatre; the subject is present in the representations. They are subjective. As Descartes urged,[43] they never appear without the I. What this means, in so far as consciousness is capable of choosing its own focus and attitude, is that consciousness constitutes itself.

Spinoza's account of freedom rests on his distinction between adequate and inadequate ideas, active and passive emotions. Indeed, his account of freedom rests on his account of determinism. A principal source of passive emotions (as Stoic and Pietist advocates of resignation had long argued) is the notion that other individuals and external events freely or arbitrarily – at any rate, extra-causally – conspire in behalf of or against one's imagined interests. Understanding the causes of events gives one freedom (as in the teachings of the Buddha) by freeing the mind of passions – the troubled and troublesome desires and fears that enslave us to external things (E5P2–10). To understand a thing adequately is to understand it in relation to its causes, and such understanding necessarily dissolves the passions. This renders us more free, more adequately the cause of our own actions, which are then to be understood more in terms of our nature and identity – the nature and identity we ourselves define and make by our own acts and choices.

It remains nonsense for Spinoza (except as a species of refined and rather misleading abstraction) to say that an individual can choose or act other than he or she does; but it is equally nonsensical and misleading to pretend that we are in no measure the cause of our own actions, for that is to make all actions passive. Spinoza, to be sure, does not draw the line between active and passive just where we might place that between coercion and non-interference. Nor does he identify an act as free merely because it bears the mark of individuality or idiosyncrasy. An axe murderer does not grow freer as he develops his own unique style or *modus operandi*; he remains a victim of compulsions. For Spinoza we are free to the extent that we act on the basis of adequate ideas. This is what makes us adequate causes of our own actions. To quote Richard Mason once again, "my capacity to predict and affect the future may be improved by the exercise of my understanding".[44] Nothing, for Spinoza, can be other than what it is or do other than as the causes of its acts require. But the programme of the self is not simply static and externally imposed; it is in some measure self-created.

2. Spinoza's God is not external to the world. It is not the *deus ex machina* that Aristotle smiled about. Rather, it is nature, conceived as broadly as the idea of infinite perfection will allow. Such a God does not interfere with the world. The traditional problems of miracles and predestination are dissolved, along with the more specifically Cartesian problems of the creation and governance of physical nature by an immaterial spirit. Neoplatonic emanationism and Aristotelian immanentism are here culled for the benefits they provide in resolving the age-old problems theologians even today would rather ignore than confront. Spinoza expresses the idea that God is not an *ad hoc* hypothesis, a god of the gaps, by saying that God is the immanent, not *transeunt* cause of things. *Transeunt*, as Spinoza uses the term, does not mean "transient" but external to the world, operative on it from without. Spinoza's God, like Aristotle's, works in and through the natures of all things, as the natures of all things, omnipresently, irrefragably impersonally, and intelligibly, not as an external engine, but as the distinctive essence (*conatus*) in which each thing simultaneously manifests its own nature and a determinate aspect of God.

In medieval scholastic theology and *kalām*, the boundaries of the dispute between voluntarists and determinists were generally marked out by the recognition that to assign more liberty to God was to give less to man and nature. In Spinoza, where the human being is part of nature and nature is identical with God, there is no such competition: God acts when each being acts (E1P16C1). God loves humans when they love themselves and one another (E5P36&C). To know nature (as in Aristotle) is to know God, since each thing in nature manifests God – each is a small epiphany.[45]

Our autonomy or relative independence is, of course, a part of the authenticity of our being, our being in God and God's being in us. In medieval terms it can be asked whether God's act of creation is real if God does not impart real being to His creatures. In Spinozistic terms the authenticity of our being and thus of the divine creative act is guaranteed by the fact that our being is God's presence in us, that God's being is His manifestation in us and in all other things. Medievally, human autonomy mirrors the divine aseity; morally and intellectually it is clear why humans are said to be created in God's image. Spinozistically, the analogy between

God and man is preserved, as Wolfson showed,[46] in Spinoza's retention of the image of the anthropic microcosm in his portrait of nature. For nature stands here in the place of God. Thus the mind–body problem as bequeathed by Descartes is resolved by Spinoza in parallel with the Maimonidean problem of the nexus between God and nature, and by way of the Maimonidean theory of the attributes of God.[47] Human freedom, construed by Spinoza as relative autonomy, is identical in kind and different only in degree from the absolute self-determiningness of nature as a whole.

3. Brilliant as Descartes was, Spinoza argues, he betrayed his own fundamental insight when he attempted to relate mind and body (thought, spirit, or idea, with matter, extension, the mechanical) in causal terms. That we conceive of the two distinctly, one as (subjective) consciousness, the other as (objective) extension, does not, as Descartes imagined, demonstrate that they are separate substances. For, as determinacies, even if infinite, thought and extension are not conceivable as wholly self-sufficient. The distinctness of their conceptions does demonstrate, however, that thought and extension cannot causally delimit (determine or condition) one another. For they have nothing in common in terms of which their connection can be conceived. Their unity must be conceived in terms of their parallelism, as dual manifestations of the infinite exuberance of the divine. Neither can be the cause of the other or provide the explanation of the other's determinations. Mind cannot make contact with matter, and matter cannot impinge on mind or even locate it. If it could, then the same gearbox through which perceptions are transmitted from the body to the mind, or volitions from the mind to the body, could be used as reduction gear by which the body could be made to force the mind.[48] However, we know from experience and from the example both of martyrs and of stubborn people that it is simply not possible to posit so positive a nexus. So while there is a necessary parallelism between the states of the human body and the states of the human mind, there is no possibility of reductively explaining the behaviour of either in terms of the principles of the other. Just as each is conceived in its own terms, each must be explained by its own principles.[49] The reductive presumption that gives colour of scientific authority to the notion that mental acts must be wholly passive to the affects of the body is systematically dismissed. Both mind and body can be either active or passive; and, in all finite beings, each aspect will be both active and passive in some degree. We act not to the extent that we escape the sway of causal determinations, but to the extent that we integrate our thoughts well enough to allow the dissolution of our passions and direction of our acts and thoughts by our adequate ideas.

Since the distinction between adequate and inadequate ideas is crucial to Spinoza's account of human freedom, a word more is in order about this: what is the relation between adequate or inadequate ideas on the one hand, and active or passive emotions on the other? How are we liberated from passivity to the extent that we are guided by our adequate ideas? To begin with, of course, adequate ideas do not free us of all passivity. They, do not, for example, directly and in themselves free us from illness, poverty or cold. They free us from passivity by freeing us from the hold of passive emotions. It is in this sense that they make us more adequately the causes of our own actions and less the victims of external circumstance. For Spinoza it is a truth of reason that adequate ideas dissolve the corresponding passive emotions. Rationalists from Plato to Freud have held a faith corresponding to Spinoza's thesis that to understand a passion is to dissolve it; but few have succeeded, as Spinoza has, in spelling out the grounds that underlie this faith.

Spinoza argues that a passive emotion is nothing more than a confused idea. To say that such ideas cease when they are clearly thought through and so subsumed within an adequate idea is thus an analytic statement. It follows that "in proportion as we know an emotion better it is more within our control" (E5P3&C). Rage, jealousy, spite, timidity, arrogance, groundless hate, servility, vindictiveness, cruelty and self-contempt – all passive emotions – are rooted in, or rather identical with, confusion of ideas (compare the Hebrew expression *timahon levav*). Cruelty, for example, is defined by Spinoza (E3Defs. 38) as a desire to harm one whom we pity. Spinoza's associative psychology can account for such an emotion as a projection of our own discomfort: we identify with the object of our pity, dislike the disturbance that our empathy produces in ourselves, and project the dislike upon the object of our pity – or perhaps on others whom we associate with that victim, making them associatively causes of our discomfort. Cruel thoughts or actions are the result. If we understand the source and basis of our emotions, the linkage that promotes them is perceived to be irrational. When such understanding founds our feelings, rather than irrational, merely reactive associative responses, our feelings are no longer malicious. The same model can be followed for all the passive emotions.

The mere ability to recite such a model does not, of course, dissolve the passions. Only actual understanding can dissolve the passions and displace them as foundations of our actions. It will take an Aristotle, as we shall see, fully to lay bare the divergence of mere formulaic or sentential knowledge from the embedded or imbibed dispositional knowledge that is relevant to ethics. But what Spinoza has accomplished, I believe, is to show (as almost all philosophers have somehow hoped to show) that the calmer, wider, rationally grounded form of thought is no mere anodyne to the passions, but an antidote to the loss of control, the loss of freedom, that negative emotions represent.

Spinoza says that in so far as we are freed from the control of the passions, we are more adequately the causes of our own actions; our actions become more truly our own. What exactly does this mean? In Spinoza's highly interactive universe, every act of every particular is both the cause and the effect of countless other events. No finite mode is ever wholly self-determining, and no act of a finite mode can be understood without reference to the individual nature of that mode. When an animal hunts or two chemicals react, they are expressing their own natures. What does it mean for a person to be more free? If there is a monster – a beast of a certain type, or some moral monster with strange and perverse desires or needs – does it not act out of the necessity of its own nature? In what sense is a moral agent more free?

Clearly, all things in some minimal sense act out of the necessity of their own nature. What consciousness makes possible, through its reflexivity, is some degree of self-control. A rock thrown in the air can only rise and then fall. Its trajectory is determined by its nature and the nature of the things around it. A human being's actions too are determined by his or her nature and environment, but in some measure the human is capable of altering both. A beast pursues the dictates of its appetites and other stimuli and cues. A moral monster is the victim of such appetites and cues. His or her emotions are passive in the sense that this person (*qua* monster) is powerless to modify the manner of his or her response to external stimuli. It is in this sense that these externals can be said, metaphorically, to act through their victim.

It is not (we have observed) the idiosyncrasy of our actions that makes them uniquely our own. (Imagining that this is so was the mistake of Plato's tyrant, who supposed that only through perversity could he manifest his presence and his power.) Rather, our actions are our own to the extent that our nature is in our own control, to the extent that our *conatus* is self-conscious, self-reflective, self-critical – in some degree self-made. The key to Spinoza's insight here is the recognition that the passions do not constitute an identity in the same sense that the active emotions do. The emotions that Spinoza calls passive are those that render us capable only of automatic, mechanical, or relatively uncontrolled responses like those of grief, rage, pity, complacency, concupiscence or scorn. The more reflective emotions are those that place us on a higher plane of action, in which we are more in control of ourselves, less under the control of external events and thus more undertakers and less undergoers of events. Adequate ideas are liberating because of their reflective nature, because of their foundation upon understanding and their resultant displacement of the inadequate ideas that render human behaviour, to the extent that they are its determinants, as mechanical and unreflective as the behaviour of mechanisms or brutes.

When we speak of human actions as capable of being raised to a less mechanical level and thus being less externally determined, we raise several problems that can be readily dispelled: like other rationalists, Spinoza does not believe we are free when we act viciously. He does not, however, fall into the trap of denying that we are causally responsible for our vicious acts. For Spinoza separates freedom (in the sense that he affirms it) from volition in general: the mind is volitionally responsible for actions that arise both from its confused or inadequate ideas and from its clear or adequate ideas. In both cases we express our own nature – our own *conatus* and will (E3P9&C); but we are more adequately the cause of our own actions when that *conatus* is informed by adequate ideas. It may be true that the moral wretch is more to be pitied than censured. But Spinoza holds little brief for either pity or censure and does not rest the case for charity (or control) any more on pity than he rests the case for punishment on censure. The fact is that even in passivity a person's actions still bear the mark of a uniqueness, the stamp of whatever complex, indeed unique variety of wretchedness is that person's own. The sense in which irrational acts are not one's own is simply that in which more thought or better thought might have rendered them abhorrent to the presumptive actor.

What are we to make of this "might have"? Does Spinoza accept alternative futures? This is certainly not the sort of language he approves. However, in keeping with our analysis, a distinction should be made (as in Aristotle it was made) between futures whose determinants are given, and futures whose determinants have not yet emerged. Spinoza's account of the dynamic and reflexive character of *conatus* clearly allows this and in turn allows a Bergsonian rather than Laplacean account of determination. That is, things on Spinoza's account must act in accordance with what they are; but they have not always been what they are, and they do contribute, through their own actions, to the making of what they are. Laplacean causality would be criticised Spinozistically not for being too deterministic, but for being too linear and static, not allowing feedback, reflexivity or recursion. Bergson's idea of an open future, based on giving a new emphasis to the idea of time, would be more welcome. For what Laplace ignores is that we act in the present, although we have been acted on in the past. In Maimonides, where divine omniscience might be called upon to play the same role as Laplacean predictability, the issue is more clear-cut, since what God knows (and creates) is a volitional being, with polyvalent capabilities of choice. Reflecting specifically on the Biblical idiom of divine omnificence, Maimonides writes:

> One further thing evident to me from the texts of the Torah is that His knowledge that a particular possibility will be realised does not at all remove that possibility from the realm of the possible. The possible retains its contingent character, and knowledge of which alternatives will eventuate does not make the existence of one of them necessary. (*Guide* III 20)

Spinoza's calls to reflection and self-mastery suggest that his own stridency about contingency might need to be mitigated somewhat in the same direction, invoking the Aristotelian distinction between the specious notion of alternative pasts and the legitimate notion of alternative futures. For, to paraphrase a great athlete, a decision isn't made until it's made.

Spinoza's commitment to universal causality, I would argue, is no more compromised by an open future than is the biblical commitment to God's universal agency. What is important to remember Biblically is Baḥyā's lesson, that God acts through and not despite natural events and human volitions. What we must remember in Spinoza's case is that the dynamism of the *conatus*, to act at all, must make a difference – not between what is and what must be but between what is and what otherwise (that is, in abstraction from its agency) might have been.

In an argument of much apparent rigour, Jonathan Bennett seems to propose that Spinoza's claims in behalf of autonomy are to be read either as a plea in behalf of independence of all things external to the organism, or as an appeal to independence of all things external in the Stoic sense – that is, of all that is not dictated by our own will.[50] But surely, Bennett argues, we cannot literally ignore the data of the senses, despite Spinoza's evident fondness for medieval-sounding denigrations. Nor can we simply ignore the opinions of others or merely cower within ourselves, rejecting any great undertaking because its success may lie outside our mastery. What Bennett seems to think Spinoza ought to mean in urging relative self-sufficiency is the value of making ourselves volitionally autonomous – that is, making our own will the cause of our actions. "It is a pity, therefore, that this revised theory" – the theory of "completeness of voluntary control" Bennett supplies to smooth over Spinoza's confusions and "incoherence" was "perfectly unavailable" to Spinoza, since it undercuts Spinoza's argument for egoism based on the idea that an individual's destruction cannot proceed from its own essence (p. 328). Bennett has already (pp. 234 ff.) dismissed this argument of Spinoza's: "Since the conclusion is false, the argument is faulty." Bennett does not believe that "a purely endogenous cancer" is impossible, nor does he believe that suicide should be described as other than self-destruction. To this he adds, by way of criticising Spinoza's notion that beings express their own essences and that such essences cannot produce their own destruction, "it is hard to know what 'essence' means in this context, but there is no chance of making it mean 'will' or having anything to do with voluntary control" (p. 328) – presumably because individuals may voluntarily destroy themselves.

Moreover, taking Spinoza's internal–external distinction volitionally "abolishes most of the demonstrations in Part 4: their appearance of being arguments at all depends on the morality's being based on the dictates of 'reason', with this understood in terms of causal self-sufficiency; take away that last concept, and the elaborate structure of mostly invalid arguments collapses into a shapeless pile of rubble". I'm not sure just where the vitriol here is coming from, or where it is directed, but it seems pretty clear, since Bennett has already ruled out the non-volitional interpretations of the internal–external distinction as well, that the shapeless pile of rubble is not just a rhetorical virtuality but Bennett's version of the actual outcome of Spinoza's efforts in this area. I am not convinced, however, that Bennett's painstaking analyses are as destructive as he seems to fear or hope.

First, the notion of sensory deprivation, which Bennett invokes, is a red herring. When Spinoza proposes less reliance on the senses, he is speaking germanely to the issue of passivity, in so far as the senses are understood traditionally as the avenues through which the passions make their appeal. The point is not to exclude sensory information from our deliberations but to avoid the sort of merely reactive behaviour that is observable in organisms for which sensory inputs are determinative of response. Further, it is part of Spinoza's programme to articulate insights that describe the means by which the wise overcome other, equally reactive modes of behaviour, in which our human reflective capabilities are employed only to echo, amplify, blindly associate, or otherwise non-rationally manipulate the sensory data, allowing it, as passively modified, to determine our responses. The problem is not with the senses but with unreflective reliance on the impulses they engender.

Second, there is no "purely endogenous cancer" because, for Spinoza no finite cause is ever "purely endogenous". This is a major theme in Spinoza. As for suicide, Spinoza does not consider it a form of self-expression just because it may be the choice of a human will. Suicide cannot express the essence or identity (that is, the self) of a human being, because that essence, like all essences, is self-affirmatory, a striving to preserve and promote its own reality. Accordingly, suicide is not an action but a passion.

The suicide is a victim, not a free-chooser. If Bennett or (Marsha Norman) wishes to dispute this thesis of Spinoza's they are of course welcome to do so, but when they do, I think it will be readily observed that they do so not by discovering an incoherence in Spinoza's claims, but by removing themselves from the ambit of his central premises. The Spinozistic thesis is not that suicide is impossible, but that suicide is not a means of self-fulfilment.

Third, as to "complete volitional control". This is, of course, not a project of Spinoza's. A sound goal of human action, inasmuch as we are rational beings, lies in our maximising our freedom. But this does not mean simply getting what we want or think we want as often as possible. Rather, it entails having more adequate notions of what is worth wanting. The acquisition of more adequate ideas is, by Spinoza's account, both possible and desirable. It is not automatic. Acquisition of adequate ideas is possible in part because we are not required to invent or discover for ourselves *de novo* every idea we may entertain. As cultural beings who read books and (at least as important) encounter the trials and outcomes of many and varied moral experiments, we have rich experiential and imaginatively developed materials available to us among which to choose, refine and develop the working hypotheses of our moral lives. As conscious beings, we both order and appropriate the mental premises on which those lives are conducted.

A crucial difficulty in Spinoza's account of freedom, by Bennett's account, is the apparent gap between Spinoza's concept of will and the idea of essence Spinoza employs in arguing that an individual's destruction cannot proceed from its essence. Quoting once again, "it is hard to know what 'essence' means in this context, but there is no chance of making it mean 'will' or having anything to do with voluntary control". Yet Spinoza does define the essence of a thing as its *conatus* – that is, its striving for self-preservation (and, by implication, self-expression, self-fulfilment); and, as we recall, he defines "will" as *conatus* relative to the mind, "appetite" as *conatus* relative to the mind–body complex, and "desire" as self-conscious appetite.

If the question is asked, then, how characters are to be informed and trained so that the exercise of human freedom in Spinoza's sense becomes actual rather than a mere virtuality (that is, how do we break the cycle of moral ignorance and bad example that seems to lock the doors against the moral advance of all but the most fortunate?), Spinoza's answer is intellectual and cultural – very much of a piece with the tradition of Aristotle, Plato and Socrates from which his thought springs. To begin with, as I have intimated, we are not as ideationally deprived as we sometimes like to make out. The point is Aristotle's, as we shall urge further on, but it is certainly not inaccessible to Spinoza. A rich array of exemplars of human strengths and weaknesses stands and moves before our eyes in every human environment; and logic, imagination and personal reaction readily ring the changes on what we observe directly, generating an infinite array of moral possibilities for emulation or rejection. The mind is the theatre in which this array is projected, but it is not just a theatre: it is also the observer and the chooser – it is the self.

What I think Bennett's analysis does touch on is the fact that Spinoza uses a shifting conception of human identity when he expresses the idea of pursuing our own best interest. That is, the self that is the subject of human freedom, its author and its beneficiary, is not identifiable with the empiric ego or with the empirically volitional self. When Spinoza speaks of choices we can make that make us more the author or more the victim of our acts, he is following a well-established tradition of Pietist moral philosophy that thinks of a higher and a lower self, only one of which at any given moment can be identified with the empiric self of choice. When I choose wisely, in these traditional schemes, which were modelled for us by Baḥyā, the higher self is said to act – in that I am choosing as I would have done had I known my own best interest. When I choose unwisely, the lower self, sometimes called spirit or by some other distinguishing term, is said to act: I was not the real chooser, because I did not choose what I really wanted (at least by the Aristotelian axiom that we all desire our own objective felicity). I did not choose my own best interest as I would have conceived it had I been adequately informed. The empiric self acts in the foreground, but a second self, higher or lower than the empiric self which chooses, remains virtual in the background, as the object created by the choices of the empiric self. For wise and foolish choices form the character: they make me a better or a lesser person, more capable or less capable of choice, on the dynamic and reflexive Mu'tazilite model of human freedom that Spinoza inherits from Maimonides and Saadiah Gaon. Thus the fact that I am the author of an act in the common-law sense that the event was uniquely modified by my participation does not imply my being the author in Spinoza's sense. I am active or passive on a relative scale that depends not on the extent to which I momentarily appropriate a given choice, but on the extent to which that choice contributes to the formation of an identity that may never empirically be mine but that I would recognise as my best self if my ideas were adequate enough to allow me to perceive its virtuality within me. This, I think, is Spinoza's sense when he justifies retaining (or reorienting) the ideas of good and evil on the grounds that "we desire to form an idea of man as a model of human nature that we may look to" (E4 Preface, Gebhardt p. 208 ll. 15–24).

In fairness to Bennett, be it said, Spinoza does not feel the need to spell out in detail the curious (but to moralists of the tradition all too familiar) piece of dialectic by which he addressed the higher self. He did, however, embed it at the core of his philosophy, when he equated the essence or identity of each thing not with what that thing has been (statically, empirically), but with a tendency, the tendency of each thing to persist in, express, promote and develop its own being.[51] The key assumption of Spinoza's scheme, as of the traditional literature whose categories he adapts, is that I am not necessarily who I think I am. I am also who I might become, a better (i.e. more perfect) or a lesser being, whose identity I acquire and indeed define in the appropriation of the choices I make, and whose identity I entrench in the habituation of those choices. My freedom rests on the intellectual access I have to what traditionally was called a higher self, but what Spinoza prefers to refer to (via the notion of wiser choices) in terms of adequate ideas.

Human consciousness is, by Spinoza's account, a reflexive and self-transparent idea, dynamic rather than static, and capable of access to its own content in practical and speculative ways. To deny this is to deny the mind's activity, and the burden of proof in such a case passes to the critic to explain in other terms (that is, without reference to an active and reflexive mind) the phenomena of consciousness and volition.

Spinoza's account is anything but a heap of rubble. Does this mean that the house, although habitable, is perfect? Spinoza died young, and it would be foolish to pretend that he left his philosophy flawless. There are many points at which the account could be criticised, ranging from the radical rejection of his premises to the detailed quibbles that might no more than add a nuance to his terminology or to the critic's understanding. To develop fully each major or minor point and to be fully candid about which criticisms reflect lacunae in Spinoza's philosophy and which project values or insights at variance with his own – which are constructive relative to his project and which relate to our own philosophic interests – would take us far beyond the project of the present book. Some misapprehensions can be readily cleared up. One miscue begins and persists, at least in part, through a persistent mistranslation: the two key emotions, upon which love and hate and all the more complex emotions are founded, are *laetitia* and *tristitia*. These terms, as any Latin student knows, mean joy and sorrow, not pleasure and pain. Spinoza defines them as transitions of the mind to a greater or lesser state of perfection. As mere transitions, both are passive; they happen to the mind, although in the special case of the joy that we can foster through developing our adequate ideas, joy involves an activation (self-awakening) as well.

Spinoza has names for pleasure and pain: *titillatio* and *dolor*, also regularly mistranslated to cover up the mistranslation of *laetitia* and *tristitia*, preserving the fiction that Spinoza's naturalism resolves to some form of hedonism. Spinoza defines *titillatio* and *dolor* as a localised joy or sorrow, referential to some particular part of the mind–body complex (E3P11S; Defs. 2–3). Readers who doubt that *laetitia* and *tristitia* are joy and sorrow should attempt to explain why Spinoza defined pleasure or pain as a transition of the mind to a state of greater or lesser perfection. This transition is a matter of moral development, not sensation. Those who doubt that *titillatio* and *dolor* mean what the Latin says they do, pleasure and pain, should endeavour to explain how these feelings could be localised, as Spinoza says they are, unless they had the nature of pleasures and pains.[52]

Spinoza did not imagine that adequate ideas make us proof against pain, as some faith-healers or exponents of positive thinking propose that illness can be held at bay by "good thoughts" or "visualisation". Nor was it Spinoza's hope to banish passions in the sense of neutering the mind to joy, grief or anger. Finite beings in an interactive world will experience passive emotions whether they like it or not, regardless of their mental strategies. The project of the *Ethics* is not to immunise us to the emotions, but to unfetter the mind from those passive emotions over which it can exercise control by exposing the roots of such passions in inadequate ideas. Adequate ideas are not a mental novocaine that dissolves or numbs our human feelings. But they do provide us, much as the Epicurean, Stoic and medieval monotheistic moralists claimed, with means of freeing ourselves from the obsessive grip of those passions whose tight hold derives from the passive collaboration of our own mental powers. Spinoza's brief is less to show that this is so than to provide a theory explaining the possibility of this well-known (if less systematically practised) power of the mind.

The model is this. When I nurse my wrath to keep it warm, harbour a grudge, cultivate my prejudices, succumb to my appetites or fears, or otherwise become a victim to my emotions and show signs of what earlier philosophers had no compunction in calling vices – that is, moral flaws – I am being less active and less adequate as a person (Spinoza argues). In effect, I am less myself, because I am not subjecting certain of my thoughts – irrational thoughts based on inadequate ideas – to the rational scrutiny that would dissolve them. The point is readily seen in the case of prejudice. When one harbours malice toward a person because that person is arbitrarily associated with some negative quality or experience – with my own discomfort at the thought of weakness, poverty or victimhood, for example – one is investing the object of one's prejudice with properties whose actual origin is one's own error. The harm to oneself (for such emotions are never harmful solely to their object) is a direct consequence of a negligence that is perhaps remediable. One ought to scrutinise the grounds of one's emotions, just as one should scrutinise the grounds of one's beliefs. For prejudice or bigotry has much the same logical structure as an unwarranted belief.

In Spinoza's metaphysics, given the critical role that monism and determinism play in that system, one can say that whenever human emotions gain the sort of power over the mind that is likely to limit our effectiveness as human agents (whenever they are passions or passivities in the ethically germane sense), we fall victim to a precise analogue of prejudice. Fear becomes unwieldy when the mind flounders in its own fascination with an object of terror, viewing that object as the sole and sufficient controlling factor in a situation or in our lives. A more holistic perspective, Spinoza is confident, would also be more wholesome. Hatred, sexual obsession and power mania all share the same structural anatomy. Grudges, spite, grief and regret commit the same fallacy in a dynamic framework: they presume contingency – which is, for Spinoza, just another way of falsely isolating a particular or a set of particulars or events from their causal environment. Monism and determinism, the outlooks advised by reason, allow, indeed require, a more detached, objective viewpoint, in which we would not crudely identify the good with our own immediate goal and from which we would perceive our comrades' goals as well. The larger perspective, Spinoza argues, is inherently cooling to the passions. It is the perspective Marcus Aurelius strove to adopt when he pleaded with himself to remember with whom he had to deal, admonishing himself: "Say to yourself in the early morning: I shall meet today inquisitive, ungrateful, uncharitable men. All these things have come upon them through ignorance of real good and ill."[53] Even if to understand is not to forgive, at least understanding will dissolve the most vicious hold upon us of our inability to forgive, the paralysing hatred, cruelty, anger or remorse that grow demonstrably from lack of understanding.

Spinoza's central thesis here is open to two lines of criticism. The first is that his monism and determinism might not be true. This requires a reversion to metaphysics that few ethicists are eager to undertake, unless with the question-begging goal of establishing that determinism obviates ethics or renders it impossible. For our present purpose, that journey really is not necessary. Determinism need not be true or even believed in order to be useful in the moral tactics of mastering the passions. Baḥyā, as we saw in Chapter 3, fields a superb version of the "philosophy of as if" in behalf of moral mastery, using determinism to minimise human regrets and wishfulness while simultaneously marshalling the idea of human freedom to maximise the scope of our moral responsibility. Kant, for his part, developing and secularising a related Pietist tradition, does something very similar, while avoiding commitment on the metaphysical issue almost as scrupulously as Baḥyā does. For ethics, the critical issue is not whether determinism is true or false, but whether belief in determinism or monism, or to generalise, any conviction we may hold, can actually give us power over our emotions. Spinoza, to be sure, is far too earnest a philosopher to rely on any notion he does not take to be true categorically, and in this I think he is right. Even the pragmatic value of a mere posture rather than a committed belief is questionable, and Spinoza would hardly be the philosopher to recommend inuring ourselves to a belief, as Pascal and James do, for the sake of its reputed benefits. But the monism and determinism required by Spinoza's ethical prescription amount to little more than the recognition of the inter-connectedness of all things in a single scheme or system and the correlative recognition that the events that harm or aid us did not conspire to do so but follow a logic and dynamic of their own. That is the heart of the understanding that Spinoza is confident will give us peace of mind. Do we in fact battle against a determinism of the emotions that makes such peace of mind impossible?

Most modern critics of rationalism are romantics in the precise sense that they believe the power of the emotions to be primary, perhaps insuperable, certainly inaccessible to the pleas of reason – a fact or purported fact that is reveled in or more tragically celebrated with an unwholesome and sometimes unholy mingling of grim acceptance and delight that Baḥyā would recognise as the outcome of the whisperings of inclination; that Spinoza, in another language but with a kindred moral clarity, would pinion as the flickering and oscillating of moral ambivalence and a conflicted and confused moral sensibility; and that a modern moralist, preserving the same diagnosis but again using the language of the day, would ascribe to an over-eager quest for excuses.

The Spinozistic model, which relies upon a continuum between reason and emotion (since all of these are really only thoughts), is dismissed by romantics as bad psychology. Knowing appeals to the power of the emotions, the uniqueness and complexity of each, and their Humean inaccessibility to reason underlie many an over-subtle and arid effort at critique of rationalism. But Spinoza does not deny the power or distinctness of the emotions. The burden of his intellectualism and indeed of much of his monism and determinism is to deny their omnipotence by showing how better thinking and broader understanding can overcome the paralysis engendered by inadequate ideas.

The second line of criticism arises from the first and rests on psychodynamics. Spinoza, like Freud and perhaps like Plato, assumes that consciousness can access the unselfconscious processes of association by which a blind striving for self-preservation might mask our intentions to us and trip up our higher interests. Spinoza's Mosaic heritage here, like Freud's, denies the inevitability of tragedy and affirms the power of reason not merely to control the irrational within ourselves, but indeed to sublimate it and transform it into reason. There is evidence for the possibility of such alchemy; but as individuals and as a species we are far from mastery of its techniques, and we have many reasons to doubt the completeness of any prescription for its practice. We do know that no mere mechanism or recipe, no mere combination of thoughts or words or sentiments, can guarantee the reform of human character. The personality is too complex, too mercurial, too capable of receding and settling into its own depths, to allow doubts to be dispelled entirely. Complacency is just another of the protean traps which the mind, blindly seeking life, throws up about itself to defend itself from effort and liability to risk.

The evidence that consciousness can gain some measure of self-mastery – freedom in Spinoza's sense – comes from the lives of ordinary and extraordinary individuals who achieve some degree of inner peace and integration without withdrawing from the arena of active and creative engagement with nature in general or humanity in particular. The difficulty and depth of the process are reflected in the equally commonplace and extreme cases of human moral weakness. The issue of moral weakness affects Spinoza's claims, as it affects all rationalism in morals, because it challenges the rationalist's model of the relationship between consciousness and action. Specifically, Spinozists must confront the recalcitrance surrounding the efforts of character toward self-definition. In seeking intellectually to perfect our human dispositional matter, we operate in a context that is anything but purely intellectual. Spinoza did not develop a full and circumstantial account of this interface between reason and the emotions – partly because he believed that human weakness, as exemplified, say, in suicide, eludes the grasp of philosophy, and partly because he could rely on the work of predecessors, whose insights he had no need to repeat.

To be specific, in assaying the prospects of gaining control of our own character, Spinoza follows in the footsteps of Aristotle and the Maimonidean tradition – despite his sense of greater rigour in determinism and despite his outspoken disappointment and impatience with the flaws in the tradition. For this reason, just as we can use Spinoza to gain insight into what an Aristotelian can mean in calling the human subject a small prime mover, we can use Maimonides to gain insight into what it means for an individual to be responsible for the constitution of an individual moral character, and we can use Aristotle to gain further insight into the possibility of moral failure, despite the seeming presence of the knowledge that intellectualist (Socratic) accounts of virtue seem to tell us renders such failure impossible.

— 5. MAIMONIDES ON CHARACTER AND FREEDOM —

Looking over his shoulder at the Islamic heritage of predestinarian theology, Maimonides, as we recall, thanked God that the premise of free choice had never been questioned within his own confession (*Guide* III 17). Human freedom, he argues, is a Biblical axiom, implicit in the very syntax of the imperative mood in which the Torah addresses its commands. Rejection of fatalism – the notion that human actions make no difference to the outcome of events – is presupposed, Maimonides argues, particularly in the logic of the precautionary commandments – the commandment, for example, to place a parapet on one's roof as a precaution against tragic accidents. How can there be a law of negligence without the assumption that human precautions prevent what would otherwise have occurred?[54]

God, Maimonides argues, is not determined by His own nature – not determined, for example, to create. In arguing (*Guide* II 21, 22) that the idea of creation seems to make no real difference in an eternal world and that God's absolute simplicity can hardly be conceived to give rise to complexity if the divine creative act works solely by necessity,[55] Maimonides shores up the groundwork for what will become Leibniz's and later Kripke's doctrine of alternative possible worlds. Causal necessity, as we have seen, acquires the logical authority of essentialism when essences are given, but such is the case only within "the settled order of nature". And part of that settled order, Maimonides insists, is human choice.

Thus Maimonides is a voluntarist within the context of his determinism. Is he a soft determinist? He certainly does not go easy on the *mutakallimūn* who attempted to combine occasionalism with human freedom: the Muʿtazilite voluntarists were inconsistent in affirming that we are the authors of our own actions while maintaining that God is the cause of each particular atom, with all its accidents, at every instant. Maimonides calls occasionalism a mockery of the divine creative act. The Ashʿarite doctrine that we "appropriate" our actions by our choices (and thus acquire moral responsibility for them, a doctrine modelled on Stoic theory) he labels a piece of double-talk, in view of the corresponding Ashʿarite view that our acts of acquisition (like the Muʿtazilite created capacities for action) are themselves directly created by God (see *Guide* I 73.6, III 17.4, I 51).

A soft determinist, as defined in Paul Edwards's now-classic explication of William James's original notion, is one who is prepared to concede that the determinants of our choices are predetermined by forces external to our control.[56] The "softness" consists in willingness to invoke moral categories – as of punishment and blame – despite the concession, in cases where overt constraints are not operative. Physical force and extreme threats of violence are taken as coercive, but inducements or even warnings coupled with the predispositions of our character are not, even though it is admitted that the combination predetermines choice. Strong blandishments and sanctions short of intimidation often remain in a somewhat murky or mushy area, of relative freedom (semi-determination?). Perhaps here too there is some softness; but if so, it seems to be a logical softness – since all outcomes of choice are conceded to be predetermined by external factors. The intention (often overtly expressed) is simply to provide for the convenience of moral philosophers and social (e.g. penal) agencies by making a rather *ad hoc* distinction between remote or overwhelming determinants of choice or action, over which an individual is formally expected to exercise no control, and proximate determinants of choice, which are socially sanctioned, even though there are in fact no real alternative futures.[57] The distinction, then, between sanctioned and unsanctioned acts is arbitrary, and the decision to describe such acts in the language of freedom or fatality is purely rhetorical: all such language is a mere system of cues for haranguing juries, almost as readily deployed in prosecution as in defence, but in no case to be earnestly intended scientifically, in view of the presumed psychosocial, genetic or physiological givens. It is to the Rambam's credit that he steers clear of such concessions, and it seems philosophically worthwhile to see how he manages to do so.

Maimonides' assertion that human freedom was never questioned within Judaism is startling in view of the testimony of scripture, whose idiom, as he observes, is one of universal theistic determinism. Scripture, to be sure, as Baḥyā remarked, can be quoted on both sides of the issue, which the Rabbis address gnomically: "Everything is overseen, and leave is given", or "All is in the hands of Heaven except the fear of Heaven".[58] Among Jewish philosophers these two sayings were understood to mean that humans are delegated freedom of choice not just in faith and devotion but, by extension, in all ethical areas, where human actions might express the tenor of our intentions. But can God be a universal creator and governor of nature, while yet affording His creatures independence of choice and action?

Maimonides answers this question with the same sort of causal account that he used against occasionalism: God acts by way of intermediaries, which include not only the celestial intelligences that guide the spheres but the substantial forms of all things. In human beings the clearest manifestation of these divinely imparted forms is in the rational soul, whose affinity with God is clear in its intellectual apprehension of the objective essences of things, its governance of the body, and its reflection (in a finite way) of the perfection and stability that reason teaches us belong absolutely only to God. The human subject does choose, as the Muʿtazilites held, via a "created capacity".[59] But the human capacity for action is not monovalent and instantaneous (as the Ashʿarites proposed), but polyvalent and enduring, in keeping with the theory of character and dispositions that Aristotle developed from the ethical psychology of Plato: natural causes may have just one effect; choices confront alternatives (*Metaphysics* Theta 2, 1046b 1–24; 5, 1048a 8–12).

Dispositions are the key to any Aristotelian theory of human freedom. So it is crucial for Aristotle to observe that human dispositions are polyvalent. To establish freedom, it is necessary to show that choice is rational – not merely calculative, but self-constituting, reflexive and reflective. Here the Spinozistic way of speaking and analysis inform our understanding. For Spinoza understood Maimonides as Aristotle understood Plato or as Kant understood Hume, and the concepts of the later philosopher shed light on the assumptions of his predecessor. Spinoza's reflective *conatus* stands in the place of Maimonides' polyvalent dispositions. The original conception is Aristotelian.

Yet, as Guthrie remarks: "There is nothing in Aristotle of the philosophical debate between free will and determinism, which appears to have made its first entry with the Epicureans."[60] It was the Epicurean usage of *voluntas* (paired in the poetry of Lucretius with *voluptas*) that stuck in our vocabulary of volition. And it was Epicurus' mistrust of the Democritean determinism taught by his teacher Nausiphanes that made the debate between determinism and voluntarism a philosophic topos. Aristotle, for his part, saw no threat to voluntarism in scientific determinism. He was not unaware of freedom as an issue. But he tended to pack the rational criteria of freedom into his terminology, by defining choice, as rational, considered, and deliberative. Thus, in the discussion of the Sea Battle, Aristotle presumes and does not prove that we might choose other than as we do.[61] He returns to make what I think are his subtlest and most valuable contributions on this issue in his discussion of *akrasia*, as we shall see in the sixth section of this chapter. For in dealing with moral weakness, Aristotle confronts the issue of self-conscious wrongdoing and the tenability of his teachers' intellectualism. As Guthrie explains: "Aristotle's whole discussion of voluntary and involuntary action is avowedly an attempt to come to terms with the Socratic and Platonic dictum that virtue is knowledge and ignorance the whole cause of wrongdoing".[62] Aristotle's treatment of *akrasia* thus forms a critical missing piece of our puzzle, since it is moral weakness that Spinoza confessed his own rationalism inadequate fully to explain (E2P49S, Gebhardt, vol. 2, p. 135, ll. 30–1). But, taken in isolation, Aristotle's discussions of the voluntary and involuntary, or of choice and deliberation, seem to leave the key theses still embedded in the terminology.

The dialectic of confessional debates demands greater explicitness. Thus Maimonides directs his discussion to a broad, not an esoteric public and opens with a rejection of the notions of original sin and astral as well as physiological determinism, much in the spirit of the Rabbinic rejection of hereditarian notions of destiny. For the Talmud argues (B. Sanhedrin 38a) that humanity was created from a single stock, "So that the righteous should not say, 'We are the descendants of a righteous ancestor', and the wicked, 'We are the descendants of a wicked ancestor'", grounding complacency in the one group and a sense of futility or irresponsibility in the other. Maimonides outspokenly rejects appeals to the stars and their controlling influences on the humours. He dismisses all appeals to overwhelming fate – whether derived from God or from nature – insisting that the stars afford no excuse to adulterers or fornicators, and that fate provides no excuse to criminals. We humans retain moral and legal accountability for our actions because we are responsible for them causally. We act by a delegated power, just as natural causes do:

> If it were the case that man is compelled to act as he does, all the commands and admonitions of the Law would be voided ... it would put an end to teaching, studying, and training in the arts ... since it would be impossible in any case for one not to perform the foreordained act. All preparations and precautions would be wasted effort ...
>
> The saying of the Sages, "All is in the hands of Heaven except the fear of Heaven" (B. Berakhot 33b) is true and in concord with what we have stated. For we have shown that the commandments and prohibitions of the Torah regard only those actions a man may choose to do or not to do. And in this aspect of the soul is found the fear of Heaven, which, accordingly, is not "in the hands of Heaven" but entrusted to human choice ...
>
> The widely held popular doctrine, however, found not only in the words of the Sages but also in those of the Prophets, is that a man's sitting or standing – all his movements – are according to the will of God and at His pleasure. This doctrine is true, in a sense. For when a stone is tossed into the air and falls, we say rightly that it fell in accordance with God's will ... But it is not the case that God wills this bit of earth to fall at the time it falls, as the *Mutakallimūn* would have it. We do not believe this, but that the willing took place in the six days of creation and that all things continue forever in accordance with their natures, as

> it is said, "What has been done shall be done ..." (Ecclesiastes 1:9) ... "The world follows its accustomed course." ...Thus, when it is said that a man's sitting or standing is at the will of God, it must mean that man's nature was made such at his original creation that he could sit or stand by his own free choice ... just as God willed man to have fingers, to be broad at the chest, and to stand erect, so He willed that he should be self-moving, should come to rest of his own accord, and should act by his own free choice. ("Eight Chapters", 8)

The physiology of the humours, Maimonides urges, predisposes but does not predetermine choice. The argument in support of Maimonides' thesis is grounded in the Aristotelian analysis of virtue and vice as dispositions. The habits we single out for praise or blame are those in which choices are made that both manifest and entrench a certain tendency of character. It is habit that makes the tenor of our actions dependable, perhaps predictable in a probabilistic way. It is rational consciousness that makes them free. All things are determined, but we ourselves are participants in the process of determination. We can reject and overcome our inner urges and tendencies, combat and conquer our own nature, regardless of the depth, intensity or direction of its thrust. Thus Ben Zoma defines heroism as the conquest of our (lesser) nature: "Who is mighty? He who masters his nature" (Avot 4.1). Islamic pietism similarly calls self-conquest the true *jihād*. Neither tradition assumes that human nature is evil, but only that natural inclination is too readily followed and too facilely pled as an excuse.

The course of ethical habituation – that is, the acculturation and psychic assimilation, appropriation in the proper sense – of an ethos is not comparable to what a post-Pavlovian age would call conditioning. Conscious alternatives are always present; we are never so secure or so lost that we cannot alter our moral status, and indeed our heading, for better or for worse:

> Power (*reshut*) is given to every man. He may, if he wishes, direct himself toward the good and become just (*tzaddiq*), or toward evil and become wicked. Do not even entertain the notion of the foolish among the nations and among the mass of senseless Israelites, that God ordains from the outset of a person's creation that he will be righteous or wicked. It is not so. Every one of us is capable of growing as righteous as Moses or as wicked as Jeroboam. One can become wise or foolish, merciful or cruel, tight-fisted or liberal, and so for all the virtues and vices ... This thesis is axiomatic [*'iqqar gadol*] and foundational to the Torah, as it is said: "Behold, I set before thee this day a blessing and a curse" (Deuteronomy 30:15) ... that is why God says, "Would that they had such a heart as this always" (Deuteronomy 5:26), implying that the Creator does not compel or predestine human beings to do good or evil but cedes to them control of their own hearts ...
>
> Do not be puzzled at the thought that a person can do whatever he pleases and

> that his actions are left up to him, even acts that are not permitted by his Maker and not pleasing to Him, or that Scripture says, "All that the Lord pleaseth hath He done, in heaven and on earth" (Psalms 135:6). You must realise that God does do all that He pleases. Yet, all the same, our actions are our own. How so? Just as it was the Creator's pleasure that fire and air would ascend, earth and water descend, and the sphere revolve – and likewise, that all created things behave according to the pattern He was pleased to assign them – so it was His pleasure that human beings hold in their own hands the power to choose; it was His pleasure to turn over to us all our own actions, so that without coercion or compulsion but by our own Godgiven discretion we would do all that a human being can do. (*MT* Hilkhot Teshuvah v 1–4)

The argument for Maimonides' denial that characters are fore-ordained is supplied by Aristotle (*NE* II 1, 5): we are not praised or blamed for our emotions or our inborn liabilities to affect but for the traits of character that are acquired through our own participation, socialisation, habituation, indulgence and inurement – in the Stoic phrase, what we appropriate, not just in our actions but in our character. What is praiseworthy or blameworthy is not the nature we are born with but the nature we acquire, second nature, our habituated dispositions.[63] To quote from Maimonides again:

> Just as it was the pleasure of the Creator that fire and air should rise upwards, earth and water descend downwards, and the sphere revolve in a circle, and that all other creatures should be in their accustomed ways, which it pleased Him to assign, so He was pleased that man should have leave in all the actions which a human being can perform, to act freely, of his own accord and God given reason, without being pushed or pulled.[64]

The story of Adam and Eve, then, does not portend our long-consummated and inevitably tragic fall from grace. Rather it portrays the radical openness of the human future at every instant – we could, as we have seen already, reach out at this very moment and pluck eternity from the Tree of Life.[65]

The cowardly, like the courageous, can confront danger. But partly because of habit, partly because of temperament (this means the humours, for which we might read the hormones, substituting adrenalin and its releasing factors, antagonists and analogues for the medieval sanguine, phlegmatic, melancholic and bilious humours), it is harder for the cowardly to be brave than for the courageous. The courageous can become cowardly or the cowardly courageous. Either can self-transform, by pursuing actions that conduce to bravery or timidity. And so with any moral trait. For moral traits are those specifically which we acquire through our choices and which predispose us in turn to choosing further in ways that seem to call for encouragement or discouragement. As a result of habit we make such choices readily, but not mechanically, when we act virtuously, non-calculatively, as an expression of the nature that we continually acquire, modify and manifest through our actions.

Maimonides vividly models his Aristotelian theory of ethical dispositions by glossing a celebrated locus of the Biblical deterministic idiom, the passages where God reveals to Moses that He will harden Pharaoh's heart against the pleas of Israel ("Eight Chapters", 8, ad Exodus 14:4, Genesis 15:14). If God hardened Pharaoh's heart, the classic question is asked: why was Pharaoh's punishment justified? Maimonides' response is that Pharaoh's initial sin was the freely made choice to pursue a genocidal policy against the Israelites. This was a deliberate and coolly considered decision: "Let us deal wisely with him" (Exodus 1:9–10). The stereotypic use of "him" to designate all Israelites reveals the prejudice at the base of the proposal, and the phrase "lest he multiply … and he too be added to our enemies" reveals related passions of fear, suspicion and isolation. However, the deliberative context equally clearly precludes treating these motives as necessary determinants: the proposal might have been rejected. Other counsels might have been introduced or given greater weight. This policy was chosen; conscious intelligence hid from its own criteria and made genocide and oppression its icons of rationality. There were consequences not only for the Israelites. Adoption of a policy or appropriation of a choice entrenches habits in an individual. In a nation or society habits become trends, and trends become institutions. Maimonides analyses the outcome in keeping with the teaching of the second-century Tanna Ben Azzai: the wages of sin are sin, while those of duties fulfilled are the power to fulfil further duties.[66] As interpreted by Saadiah, this means that the abuse of freedom by the wicked restricts their degrees of freedom in the future.[67] That is the punishment brought upon them by their own acts. God's hardening of Pharaoh's heart, as Maimonides understands the passage, refers to Pharaoh's progressively diminished power to extricate himself psychologically and his nation politically from the dynamic that his choices and their outcomes had tightened about the monarch and nation.[68]

— 6. FREEDOM AND *AKRASIA* —

In a model speech that Gorgias wrote in defence of Helen of Troy, the famous Sophist argued (frag. 11) that if Helen was persuaded into adultery, she was as guiltless as if she had been abducted by force. Here, in its proper context of special pleading, is the central notion of soft determinism: that motives in a sense compel us and are determined ultimately by factors entirely beyond our control. Socrates, in his characteristically parodistic mode, was aping and inverting the contention of the Sophists when he argued (see *Protagoras* 345e) that no man willingly does evil, turning the Sophists' mockery, in effect, back into a silent sincerity. The outcome, when the Socratic claim was subjected to the rigour of Socratic analysis rather than being used in one context and then set aside or inverted in another, was the recognition of a deeper sense of willing (and of knowing) than the Sophists had been prepared to explore: wrongdoers plainly do not know what they are doing, although they may suppose they do. Right action always rests on knowledge, even when the understanding used does not belong to the actor.[69]

For Aristotle, the compatibility of freedom and determinism seemed clear, at least at the outset: the Aristotelian account of potentiality seemed sufficient to unfreeze nature from the cast of logical determinism and allow change to proceed in a world of unchanging essences. The account of God's immanent action seemed sufficient to release nature from the hold of an arbitrary *deus ex machina* imposing external decrees. The account of human rational dispositions seemed sufficient to dissolve the idea that human character was unalterably fixed and fatally fixative of our whole future course. It was because Aristotle saw no fundamental problems in these areas that we are forced to look to Spinoza for the recognition that *conatūs* – essences themselves – can be dynamic and self-changing; to Maimonides for the refutation of fatalistic versions of the idea of divine determination, which transformed God from a *deus ex machina* to a *deus mechanicus*. We look to both Maimonides and Spinoza for the further spelling out of the dialectics of the emotions and human character beyond what Aristotle had worked out. For Aristotle is penetrating and subtle about the interactions of the ethical dispositions with social and cultural influences, but frustratingly elliptical about the inner psychology of ethical *hexeis* and the internal dynamics of the emotions – their relationships with one another and with duties.

Yet it is Aristotle who provides the richer and philosophically more critical account when it comes to the assumption built into the rationalistic idea of freedom, that a certain kind of knowledge is sufficient to our freedom – that if we have that knowledge we are guaranteed control and not only can act freely, but in effect can do no wrong. Aristotle deals with the curious rationalist notion that free actions can never be wrong by way of a sophisticated reformulation of the Socratic paradox in unparadoxical terms. That is the function of his theory of *akrasia*, "incontinence" or moral weakness. Having settled or dismissed the more elementary problems of human freedom, Aristotle here reverts to the issue on a higher plane and contributes the cap-stone to our account of Maimonides' and Spinoza's theories of the compatibility of freedom and determinism, revealing (where Spinoza and Maimonides had shown how knowledge makes us free) how knowledge can fail to be operative while we yet exercise the will. This final stage is crucial, for on it hinges the success of the response to the Sophist use of internal or soft determinism.

Aristotle accepted the Socratic thesis that knowledge of a sort underlies the exercise of virtue. He defines virtue as a disposition toward action in accordance with a mean (between excess and deficiency of certain prima facie goods and ills) as determined by right reason – that is, sound thinking, modelled in the *phronimos*, the person of practical wisdom (*NE* II 6, 1106b 36–1107a 2). The cognitive component is essential if virtue is to refer to thoughtful moderation of action, rather than mere mechanical modulation of behaviour. The middles that virtue finds can be ascertained only by good judgement as habitually applied in diverse and varying circumstances, either as a practical expression of one's own practical wisdom or as the attunement of one's character to the standards of some common practical wisdom embedded in the mores of one's community (at the level of family, peers, or the culture at large). For the means virtue seeks and tends to find are not mathematically calculable; they involve sensitivity, tact and insight into what is appropriate in given circumstances – knowledge of roles, intentions, needs and deserts, the consequences of alternative choices for oneself and others (*NE* II 6, 1106a 26–1106b 27). What is ostentatious in a private home may be only decorous in a public building or a monument. Proper pride in one circumstance is arrogance or superciliousness in another (*NE* IV 2, 3). Insight is required into oneself and one's social circumstances if one is to steer one's course evenly or even safely. Vices involve a corresponding lack of insight – for the human condition is always social and thus always cultural. It is because we need insight that it is harder and rarer to live well than badly. And it is because knowledge underlies the virtues that lead to the good life (*eudaimonia*) that living well is like an art rather than an accident of fortune.

Aristotle's virtues, like those dealt with by Plato and implicitly by Socrates, are not merely bits of knowledge, however. They are habituations, dispositions of the practical side of character. This point is spelled out in Aristotle. Plato preferred only to suggest it, and Socrates apparently preferred to leave the matter tangled in *aporia*, as a trap-door escape from verbal earnestness and full disclosure, lest he seem to preach or to attempt to teach excellence as the Sophists did, selling recipes for success. It is because Aristotle has worked out the logic of the nexus between knowledge and virtue that he is capable of resolving the Socratic paradox, teasing out the senses of its discrete assertions to unsnarl the apparent contradiction between them.

It is clearly true in one sense that no one willingly does evil. For no one wittingly does what is bad for him, and it is clear from the great thrust of the *Republic* and from Aristotle's own conception of *eudaimonia* that to live well is to live the life of the virtues, fulfilling our human social, moral and intellectual nature. Wrong choices are not conducive to living well and are therefore not in our best interest. The vicious person does not know this, but has given precedence to less worthy and less fulfilling goals, laying down habits of choice founded on some kind of misconstruction of the good life. One who gave as much thought to ends as to means (to express in Aristotle's terms an argument that Socrates uses against Thrasymachus: *Republic* I, 344e; cf. *Apology* 38) would know that a vicious life is a fool's chase of unexamined objects, ends that will not withstand scrutiny if critically tested for their external consequences and inner implications or for their intrinsic worth. In that sense, all vice is self-deception, and the first onus on the morally unsound person is that of negligence: one has not given thought to the worth of the goods whose pursuit one's choices have ingrained within the character, compared with those one has habitually ignored or undervalued. Such a life at best is self-impoverished; or, in the extreme, perverted.

Vice, however, is not the only human failing, perhaps not even the most common. Most people have some notion at least of the broad outlines of right and wrong – enough that the values of the many are as needful a canon in orienting moral discourse as the disquisitions of the wise,[70] and enough that Aristotle can beg off on the expectation that he will be a teacher of virtue: if your parents and your peers have not taught you something of how to live, then formal moral discourse will be of little value to you, and you are more to be pitied than preached to (*NE* I 4, 1095b 5–14). Philosophy is of greater value in working out the syntax of the virtues (e.g. as dispositions) and of happiness (as a synthesis of activities together making up a life) than it is at formulating the actual modulations of right choice in every circumstance. That is better left to experience – to practical wisdom, culture and example, art and poetry – rather than to theory. That is why Plato steadfastly refused to write formulaically about the good life and Aristotle said of ethical and political discourse that a science should not be more precise than its subject matter (*NE* I 3, II 1, X 6). The common human goal of happiness can orient us toward the life of virtue, because virtue is the means to happiness, and we can observe in our own experience and that of others what sorts of character and behaviour seem most likely to lead to human fulfilment and what sorts to self-frustration, self-stultification or the self-satisfaction of a moral solipsist's fool's paradise.

Vice, we say, is not the only or the common human failing. If vice were as common as moral weakness, human societies could scarcely get by. Our common problem is that we do know at least what we are supposed to do and find ourselves time and again doing something else. Paul says: "For the good that I would I do not; but the evil that I would not, that I do" (Romans 7:19). Having known guilt, remorse and moral conflict, Paul is an eloquent spokesman for the phenomenology of choice against conscience. As a trained rhetorician, adept in the methods of argument taught by the Sophists, he also offers a rationale not unlike the apology of Gorgias for Helen, but even more closely akin to the poetic plea put in the mouth of Agamemnon by Homer himself: "Not I was the cause of this act [appropriating Achilles' captive girl], but Zeus and my lot, and the Fury who walks in darkness. It was they who in council put wild desire in my understanding the day I took Achilles' prize from him."[71] Paul argues: "Now then it is no longer I that do it but sin that dwelleth in me. For I know that in me (that is in, my flesh) dwelleth no good thing. For the will is present with me, but how to perform that which is good I find not." And as the underlying explanation: "I am carnal, sold under sin. For … what I hate that I do" (Romans 7:17–18, 14–15).

Paul's purpose is to demonstrate his utter helplessness before sin, the inability of the Law to save him, his need for an external eschaton. For the grace that would give him salvation depends on his recognition of his human powerlessness to find his way to right action. He is overwhelmed not because he does not know what is right – indeed he has been told (Micah 6:8) – but because conscience does not rule in him. The point, the guilt, is crucial to Paul's argument. If it is necessary rhetorically to overstate his helplessness, as though it were categorical, and write off the body utterly, as containing no good (at least in the present context, but see 1 Corinthians 6:15, 19), Paul is prepared to do so. Rhetorically the body is only a haven of sinful desires. Rational will does not rule in us; we are victims of our passions, as Agamemnon was of the destiny that gave him his.

Aristotle's brief is to answer such appeals to the irrational. His thesis that the good life is possible for human beings depends on this rebuttal. So ultimately does Maimonides' monotheistic rejection of the notion of dark and evil powers determining human fate and suborning nature and our motives. So does Spinoza's affirmation of the liberative power of adequate ideas. If Aristotle is to succeed in treating rational choice as a capable determinant of human actions, he must explain not the occasions where rational choice is not the basis of our actions, but the occasions where rational choice seems to break down – that is, where we say that we knew what was right, but somehow did not do it. Guilt, regret, remorse, mixed feelings and mixed motives are the common symptoms (*NE* VII 1, 1145b 12–13; 8, 1150b 29–30). We might regret an action, saying in a moral sense that we did not really know what we were doing; but remorse more often takes a different and perhaps more candid tack, admitting that we knew all along that what we chose was wrong. The remorse arises because we did it anyway, despite our better judgement. How is this possible within the intellectualist parameters of Aristotle's ultimately Socratic model of moral choice?

On the face of it, it is not possible. If Socrates be taken strictly at his word, he held knowledge in us to be sovereign and thus, in effect, denied the possibility of *akrasia*. But such a denial flies in the face of experience (*NE* VII 2, 1145b 20–8). The fact is that Socrates often said strange and paradoxical things, overstating one point to suggest another. Setting out to find the subtler truth behind the outspoken Socratic pronouncement, Aristotle argues that we might "have" knowledge in the sense of being able to state propositions correspondent to what is the case (e.g. "my best choice is philosophy"), yet not have it in the sense that it does not provide the practical foundation for a given choice or sequence of choices (*NE* VII 2, 1147b 6–19). This is not the case with vice. The vicious think they have a better maxim than virtue provides, although they are mistaken.[72] However, one whose head is willing but whose will is weak makes no such pretension. What is the status of this person's knowledge?

Obviously, a distinction must be made between having knowledge and using it. Socrates might be loath to say that someone who did not use his knowledge was acting knowingly. Yet it would be misleading to say that a person who, say, had learned and not forgotten that high-cholesterol meats are a health risk acted in ignorance by eating such meats. A rather special sense of knowledge and ignorance are needed to make that Socratic claim credible. Differentiating common usage from such Socratic usage, Aristotle can resolve the Socratic paradox by saying that one who violates what he knows to be a healthful diet has not acted on his knowledge. He remains responsible and aware. But if knowledge is taken to be fully actual or active only when it is maximally invoked in the formation of our decisions, a sense can be found in which *akrasia* does involve a rather special (yet common) form of ignorance: acting without the full benefit of our knowledge, acting on the basis of ignorance, even when we are, in the common acceptation, not ignorant at all.

One way of setting aside our knowledge (which the vicious person more systematically and wilfully spurns in favour of false opinion) is failure to apply our principles to ourselves. This might be called the "just this once" type of *akrasia*: I know that this sort of thing is good (or bad) for me, but I don't apply that knowledge in my choices, refusing to act in recognition of the various appropriate minor premises that mark the right course for me now. Such wrong choice is blameworthy, since I am responsible for focusing my general principles on concrete situations and remaining sensitive to every point of pertinent application for the principles of reason that serve to promote my happiness or fulfilment, *eudaimonia*. Yet in one sense I did not act with full knowledge, although I did not give full weight to my recognition that high-cholesterol meats may contribute to arteriosclerosis. I cannot say that my judgement was overwhelmed, but it was overruled when I gave precedence to some other claims upon my action.

As with vice, I set aside a relevant truth in favour of some distracting appetite or passion. But I did not substitute another maxim on the specious grounds of its superiority (*NE* II 3, 1104b 3–13). In *akrasia*, it is true to say that we know what we are doing in a sense of knowing that does not truthfully apply to vice. Yet in the intensified practical sense that Socrates gave to knowing we can still be said not to know at all: the moral and material knowledge we have has not been replaced with ignorance, but it does not form the basis of our action.

To this calm variety of *akrasia*, Aristotle adds a special case that he compares with drunkenness or madness, where in an excess of passion one seems somewhat more literally not to know what one is doing. Outbursts of anger or responses to other powerful emotions may actually seem to blot out what we know – for instance, about the consequences and implications of our acts. Indeed, such passions may seem to blot out all consciousness beyond the immediacy of the act they imperiously demand. In fact, however, consciousness is not obliterated, and such actions only superficially resemble those of madness, drunkenness or sleep-walking, with which they are figuratively compared. What actually is blotted out is the weight assigned to moderating or mitigating considerations. No new analysis is required: we have knowledge when we act in what we call a fit of passion, but the knowledge we have does not fully inform our decisions.

Maimonides' analysis of the failing of Moses ("Eight Chapters", 4) can profitably be read in the light of Aristotle's discussion of *akrasia*. For it would seem strange to assign a vice to one who was "the master of Antiquity but also of Posterity". Moses' failing, according to Maimonides, was his loss of patience with the Israelites "when he exclaimed, 'Hear me rebels!'" Moses failed to honour God in failing to retain his composure toward a people "the least woman of whom, as the Sages put it, was on a par with Ezekiel" (*Mekhilta* to Exodus 15:2). God was strict with Moses, Maimonides argues, as we recall, because for a man like him to be angry was tantamount to blasphemy – especially since the people took him to have no faults and modelled their actions upon his. In deviating only slightly from the mean, Moses did not acquire the corresponding habit, the vice of irascibility. His action, then, might be accountable to *akrasia.* He knew what was right and how it applied to himself and others, but in this instance he did not act upon his knowledge. His Socratic ignorance did not diminish his responsibility, since he was responsible for allowing himself to reach a state where the pressures of the moment overruled his usual better judgement. He gave vent to anger not from an uncontrollable rage (to be unable to control his rage would have been a weakness of character; that is, a vice), but from a momentary lapse of rational control – an instantaneous but conscious decision to express an emotion whose expression gave no place to the relevant considerations that might have controlled it.

Socrates presumes a close pragmatic integration between what we know and what we do. The Socratic man is very direct. If he deceives himself or holds his knowledge in abeyance, then he is presumed not to have given knowledge sufficient weight, not to have regarded it or treated it as knowledge really, but as mere opinion that could be set aside. Aristotle accepts this analysis on one level, but at the same time recognises that Socrates's words can be misleading to those still using the word 'knowledge' in a less rarefied – or, should we say, a less down-to-earth – sense.

The most distinctive feature of our ability to choose among alternative goods is our ability to determine for ourselves what premises to adopt in our moral deliberations, what weight to give each value, what syllogisms to pursue with practical intent, what to de-emphasise or drop. In building his analysis of *akrasia* on his recognition of this fact, Aristotle succeeds, where many other analysts of human agency have failed, in accounting for the possibility of wrong choices as well as right ones. The tendency in rationalist accounts, from Socrates to Kant, is to describe freedom in terms so intellectual that free choice of improper ends seems virtually impossible. That clearly was the suggestive tenor of the Socratic paradox, and of Spinoza's normativised definition of freedom as liberation from the passions. Spinoza adopted a spiritualised definition of freedom, whereas Socrates employed an almost private conception of knowledge. Aristotle's account has no quarrel with either of these but insists on their distinctness from the common conceptions of knowledge and freedom, since the common conceptions remain viable. Spinoza himself retains what is needful and valid from the common idea of freedom under the name of volition. And Aristotle will keep the common notion of knowledge as well. Given its head, the intellectualist notion of freedom, like the Socratic notion of knowledge, will undercut the very applicability of the idea of freedom in the moral and legal spheres, vitiating its usefulness most in the areas where it is most often needed.

Aristotelian deliberative choice is so Socratically rational that even the Peripatetic's analysis runs the risk of suggesting that wrong choices are never free (in the common sense), because those who make them do not fully know what they are doing. The fact is that we always know, in some measure, what we are doing. That is a corollary of Aristotle's social conception of human nature, in much the same way that Spinoza's recognition that all actions of finite beings are externally conditioned is a consequence of his holistic and interactive conception of being at large. Culture without some moral notions is impossible, so we always have at least some rudiments of moral knowledge and some reference by which our own intelligence can orient itself in its social environment vis-à-vis the ethos and range of ethical choices it presents.

Wrong choices in practice have as much to do with the application of major premises – that is, values – as they have to do with our appropriation of styles and modulation of passions and desires – that is our adoption of specific maxims as springs of action. But we act in a social setting and can never be wholly oblivious of cognitive pronouncements regarding right and wrong. If we took absolutely seriously all the sound moral notions we encountered, wrong choices would be virtually impossible. If we scoffed at all of them, our viciousness would preclude right choices (*NE* VI 12, 1144a 13–20). Socrates was right in regarding the vicious person as in way morally blind – although the Aristotelian analysis shows this person crucially to be self-blinded. Most wrong choices, however, result not from blindness, but from a tendency we have to close our eyes or blink when confronting powerful appetites or emotions. We forget ourselves, we say, when we are, figuratively speaking, overcome by appetite or anger. That is, we neglect to act on our principles, although they remain our principles – in much the way that we might neglect to apply a rule of grammar or arithmetic that we know very well and have not rejected, when we are distracted in our work by some extraneous concern. In living, as in other arts, not only speed but also excellence is of importance. That is why Aristotle says that the incontinent person may be clever but does not have practical wisdom (*NE* VII 9). The incontinent do not lose the ability to deliberate about means and ends and pursue a presumptive goal, but they do not keep steadily in view the rightly identified goal of human life. It is in this sense that they can be said to be unwise.

— 7. CONCLUSION —

We have considered three philosophers who are central figures in the tradition of Western rationalism that is the spine of Western philosophy. All three are committed to varieties of determinism on logical, causal and theological grounds. None is a soft determinist in Paul Edwards's sense. Yet each upholds a version of human freedom as a central thesis of his philosophy. None is willing to compartmentalise as Kant or Baḥyā did, or to make freedom a pure postulate of morality or law. Each grounds the idea of freedom in a naturalistic psychology. And each in his own way shows that human freedom is not incompatible with every variety of hard determinism. If every human action is antecedently determined by external forces, so that there can be no present control by the self over our choices, then there is, of course, no human freedom. But Spinoza, who is zealously protective of the individual effectiveness of each interactive mode, is careful to say that all actions of modes are externally conditioned, not externally determined. The causes of an action include those contributed by the self. Persons are capable of formulating rational foundations for individual action that extend directly to the present determination of choice. Similarly, Aristotle and Maimonides, in arguing that we are responsible for the constitution of our own character, sustain both a universal causal determinism and a clear commitment to voluntarism. Human selves in the Aristotelian scheme can act in some measure as a kind of volitional prime movers – not unconditioned by external givens, but undetermined by them, capable of rational, self-determining choice.

Human freedom is incompatible with soft determinism. For in conceding (or demanding) that all our motives are externally determined and treating motives as the monovalent causes of our actions (while pretending that such external determinations are irrelevant to questions of responsibility – by which it means accountability), soft determinism has in fact closed the door on human freedom. Aristotle is particularly telling in his exposure of soft determinists' favourite evasive haunts. His affirmation of our freedom and responsibility is expressed most importantly not in his well-known and rather strenuous exclusion from the realm of the involuntary of all actions over whose outcomes we exercise some measure of control (*NE* III 1), nor in any discussion of the term "will", which we have seen is an issue for Epicurus and Lucretius in a sense that never arises as a problem in the works of Aristotle, but rather in his insistence that the objects of our passions and our appetites are not by themselves the determinants of our actions. The point is made in the context of Aristotle's discussion of *akrasia*, which functions, in effect, as an argument against the claims of soft determinism, holding, contrary to the pleas of Helen and Agamemnon, that we can be responsible for our own motives, even when they seem overwhelming.

Vital to all ethical understanding is the Aristotelian recognition that choice stands at the helm of the causal linkage that governs the formation of character. As Aristotle puts it bluntly: "It is stupid not to recognise that states of character are the product of individual actions" (*NE* III 5, 1114a). Maimonides makes a similar point when he argues that no person is born innately virtuous or vicious. To imagine that such is possible is to misconstrue the notion of virtue. For virtue is a habit and can only be acquired; and, as a habit of rational choosing, it cannot be automatic or mechanical. The whole force of moral discourse addresses those aspects of character that are susceptible of improvement or decline. But to appeal to moral (or scriptural) discourse and its presuppositions is to argue dialectically, leaving untouched the question of whether those presuppositions themselves are warranted. Spinoza is of help here, since he shows, as well as can be shown, that the most rigorous determinism does not exclude some measure of autonomy for all finite agents.

Aristotle holds that all things in nature act out of their specific essences but that human nature gives us rational choice over a variety of alternatives whose modulation will modulate our character in turn. Maimonides, following and filling in the insight of Aristotle and synthesising it with the Biblical and Rabbinic tradition as read by his great philosophic and exegetical predecessor Saadiah Gaon, finds the authenticity of God's governance and creation in the bestowal of natures upon things, which can then act in their own behalf (*Guide* III 13), monovalently in the case of inanimate objects, polyvalently in the case of persons. Emanation of form upon all things (including intelligence in human beings) is both the vehicle of God's governance and the gift of independent action in nature and liberty in human subjects. Spinoza's contribution to the discussion of freedom is perhaps the most instructive. His determinism is the most uncompromising and his affirmation of freedom the most outspoken, and his account of the possibility of freedom in the context of determinism is the most circumstantial. He clearly and explicitly states the assumptions necessary to others in the same tradition: essences must be construed as dynamic and in the human case reflective; divine causality should be immanent, not hit and run. Above all, natural causality should not be construed exclusively as external. We too, along with all other things, are actors in the drama in which we are cast.

— NOTES —

1. See Parmenides, frags 6, 7, 8 ap. Simplicius *in Phys.* 117, 4; Plato *Sophist* 237A; Sextus *Adv. Math* VII 114; G. S. Kirk, J. E. Raven and M. Schofield, *The Presocratic Philosophers* (Cambridge: Cambridge University Press, 1985) items 291–9. For the continuing conflict between logic of the "strict" or Parmenidean type and the non-extensional (ultimately, intensional) notions of time (tense) and modality, see Alan Code, "Aristotle's Response to Quine's Objections to Modal Logic", *Journal of Philosophical Logic* 5 (1976) pp. 159–86.
2. See Aristotle *Physics* II 5, 196b 10 and II 8, 198b 32; *Metaphysics* Epsilon 2, 102b 26–34; *Prior Analytics* I 13, 32a 18–21. Contrast the Peripatetic empiric interest in collecting accounts of rare, unlikely and unique events with Hume's assertion that certain types of event are so unprecedented that he would not believe accounts of them – even though beliefs about the past have no logical bearing upon beliefs about the future. Compare the Peripatetic *De Mirabilibus Auscultationibus* and Aristotle's *De Divinatione per Somnum* with Hume's *Of Miracles*.
3. See *De Caelo* 110–12, cf. *Physics* III 4, 203b 30 and *Metaphysics* Theta 8, 1050b 9–24; but Aristotle qualifies this view at *Metaphysics* Theta 3, 1047a.
4. Thus Aristotle can say of necessity in mathematics and in nature that they are "almost the same". *Physics* II 9, 200a 15.
5. *Metaphysics* Epsilon 2, Lambda 4, 1078b 16–17. See also *Posterior Analytics* I 31, 87b 28 33, 88b 31–2, I 13, 32b 18–20, *Metaphysics* Zeta 6, 1031b 6–7, Alpha 6, 1003a 14–15; *NE* VI 6, 1140b 31–2.
6. *Posterior Analytics* I 2, 71b 9; *Metaphysics* Iota 2, 1053b 25–1054a 12 and *Physics* I 2, 185b 20–5, as applied in Ibn Rushd, *TT*, Bouyges, pp. 520–1; trans. Van den Bergh, p. 318, quoted at note 20 below.
7. See *De Gen. et Corr.* II 10, 336b–37a; *Metaphysics* Alpha 3, Delta 1, 1013a 22, Lambda 1075a 12–24.
8. See above p. 27.
9. See *Metaphysics* Alpha 3, 984b, 985a 18 *De Part. An.* IV 10, 687a 7 ff.; cf. Plato *Phaedo* 97–99, *Laws* 967c). Aristotle indeed reapplies the charge to Plato: see *Metaphysics* Alpha 9, 991a 12–14, 991b 1. Guthrie translates: "The Forms are of no assistance either to our knowledge of other things ... or to their existence, if they are not inherent in the objects which are said to participate in their being ... How can the Forms be essences when they exist apart? ... Granted there are Forms, the things that 'share in them' cannot be produced without a motive cause." *A History of Greek Philosophy*, vol. 6, p. 244; cf. 1080a 2.
10. See *Poetica* 15, 1454a 26–b 8; 9, 1452a 4–5; 35; 14, 1453b 1–2; cf. 9, 1450b 36, 1451b 34.
11. *Guide*, Epistle Dedicatory; I 2, II 2, cf. I 50; Goodman, *Rambam*, pp. 210, 77.
12. See *Guide*, e.g., I 34, III 29–32; Goodman, *Rambam*, pp. 413–24.
13. *Guide* II 8; Goodman, *Rambam*, p. 340.
14. *Guide* II 11. See above, Chapter 4 note 50.
15. *Guide* II 12, Goodman, *Rambam*, pp. 343–6; and see note 61 below.
16. *Guide* II 17, 13; Goodman, *Rambam*, pp. 311–18, 262–77.
17. *Guide* I 73–76; Goodman, *Rambam*, pp. 124–55.
18. *Guide* II 12, 48, III 23, with III 17.5, II 37–8, 45.

19. *Guide* II 2–7, 10; Goodman, *Rambam*, pp. 330–40. See Goodman, "Maimonidean Naturalism".
20. Cf. Averroes: "It is evident that things have essences and attributes that determine the actions specific to each. These are the characteristics in terms of which the natures of things are differentiated, and their names and definitions assigned. For if each being did not have its own specific mode of action it would not have its own specific nature, and if it did not have its own specific nature it would not have its own specific name or definition – all things would be one and the same thing and not one and the same thing ....". Ibn Rushd, *TT*, ed. Bouyges, p. 521 ll. 10–15; trans. Van den Bergh, p. 318.
21. *Guide* II 17; Goodman, *Rambam*, pp. 186–9.
22. See al-Ghazālī, *TF*, ed. Bouyges, 2nd ed., p. 197.
23. Thus, "it is manifest by the natural light that there must be at least as much reality in the efficient and total cause as in its effect". *Meditations* III, in E. S. Haldane and G. R. Ross, trans., *The Philosophical Works of Descartes* (Cambridge: Cambridge University Press, 1967) vol. 1, p. 162.
24. Thus Spinoza's usage of *sequitur* at *Cogitata Metaphysica* II viii, ed. Gebhardt, vol. 1, p. 264, ll. 6–7, and E1P15, Gebhardt, vol. 2, p. 60, ll. 10–12; E1P16, ll. 17–19, E1P36, p. 77, l. 13; E2P49S, p. 136, ll. 10–12: "Omnia ab aeterno Dei decreto eadem necessitate sequuntur, ac ex essentia trianguli sequitur, quod tres ejus anguli sunt aequales duobus rectis", etc. Compare Proclus, *Elements of Theology*, which is also organised in Euclidean style. Neoplatonic principles (*archai*) are both ontically and intellectually primary; they both produce and explain their effects. Proclus interprets geometry itself metaphysically See his Commentary on Book I of Euclid's *Elements*, trans. Glenn R. Morrow (Princeton: Princeton University Press, 1970). So the geometric organisation of Proclus's *Elements* is no more a mere metaphor than is that of Spinoza's *Ethics*. Maimonides too adopts the idea that God's effects (i.e. His works) are what follow from Him. He glosses the Biblical notion of God's back accordingly: Moses is enabled to see God's back in the sense of being given to understand "all the objects of My creation"; see *Guide* I 38, 54, Goodman, *Rambam*, pp. 70, 86–9. However, Maimonides rejects the idea that what follows from God follows automatically or mechanically; see *Guide* II 22, Goodman, *Rambam*, p. 201.
25. Maimonides similarly argues that although we cannot know God directly ("see His face") and although He has no proper essence or attributes distinct from His identity, we can know God through His works, recognising what we apprehend as God's "attributes" relative to our finite perspectives: in the mercy, wisdom and concern upon which nature is founded. These we can imitate. We model ourselves not on God's impersonality, but on those aspects of nature that manifest what would be perfections in us.
26. In the *TTP* Spinoza writes: "The universal power of nature at large is none other than the power of all individuals at once ... and the highest law of nature is that by which each and every thing, insofar as in it lies, strives to persist in its own state – ruled by no other principle than its own accustomed one." Here Spinoza fuses his determinist essentialism once again with his particularism/individualism – and with his doctrine of political liberty, for he infers: "Whence it follows that each

individual thing has the highest right to do this, that is, as aforesaid, to exist and act as it is naturally so determined." *TTP*, cap. 16, Gebhardt, vol. 3, p. 189, ll. 21–30.

27. See Descartes, *Principles of Philosophy* III 54, 61, 140, 146, IV 1, 2, 14, 44, 71.
28. Richard Mason, *The God of Spinoza.*
29. See E2P17C&S, P32–3; *TT*, ed. Bouyges, pp. 34–6, trans. Van den Bergh, pp. 18–20.
30. E1P32; 11, 48; 49C, Gebhardt p. 131, E2P49, *Objections*, esp. pp. 134–6.
31. *Cogitata Metaphysica* II cap. 8, Gebhardt, vol. 1, p. 265, ll. 18–24; cf. E4P51S.
32. The key to Spinoza's shift is his recognition that "the perfection of things [to be taken in an objective sense] must be evaluated solely in terms of their own nature and capability". E1App., Gebhardt, vol. 2, p. 83, ll. 22–3; cf. *Guide* III 13, 268–9. See also *De Intell. Emend.*, Gebhardt, vol. 2, p. 8, l. 22; p. 9, ll. 12–15; p. 12, ll. 23–4.
33. See E5P5–9. The polemical point, that God is more nobly conceived as self-constrained than as arbitrary, is made in the E1App., by the reference to projecting ignoble emotions upon God. The point was a standard piece of Averroistic invective against the notion of God as what the more modern cliché would call an "Oriental despot", and it is rooted in the natural theology of Aristotle and Alexander of Aphrodisias.
34. See above, p. 69.
35. See Paul Edwards, "Hard and Soft Determinism", in Sidney Hook, ed., *Determinism and Freedom in the Age of Modern Science* (New York: Macmillan, 1974, first ed. 1958) pp. 117–25.
36. For evidence against biological determinism of the sort that excludes the self, see Goodman and Goodman, *Sex Differences*, pp. 2–7, 72–73, 80–81, 86–107, etc. For biological determinism as a methodological bias, see Goodman and Goodman, "Is There a Feminist Biology?"
37. See Ibn Ṭufayl, *Ḥayy Ibn Yaqẓān*, trans. Goodman, pp. 17–21; cf. pp. 72–86.
38. Mason, *The God of Spinoza*, p. 67.
39. See E1P18; Letter 73, Gebhardt, vol. 4, p. 307, ll. 5–11.
40. Thus the *conatus* of a living being is its endeavor to persist in its own organic arrangement. See E2P13L7, Gebhardt vol. 2, pp. 101–2.
41. E2P22, cf. 5P29, 30, 31.
42. E3P9S, Defs. 1, '*cupiditas*'; *Cogitata Metaphysica* I cap. 6, Gebhardt vol. 1, p. 248, l. 6.
43. See Descartes, *Meditations* II; cf. Augustine, *De Trinitate* X iii, 5; John Philoponus in *De Anima* III 2, 425b 12, ed. M. Hayduck (Berlin, 1897), 13 ff., trans. in F. Rahman, *Avicenna's Psychology* (Westport, CT: Hyperion. 1981, 1st ed. 1952) pp. 111–14.
44. Mason, *The God of Spinoza*, p. 63
45. E5P31, 38–9, with P7–9; cf. Aristotle *NE* X 7–8; *Guide* I 54, 59.
46. See H. A. Wolfson, *The Philosophy of Spinoza: Unfolding the Latent Process of His Reasoning* (New York: Schocken, 1969, 1st ed., 1934), vol. 2, pp. 7 ff.
47. See Goodman, "Matter and Form as Attributes of God".
48. See E5Pref., Gebhardt, vol. 2, p. 278, l. 3, p. 280, l. 21 with E3Pref., p. 137 l. 25–138 l. 5; cf. Descartes, *Principles of Philosophy* I 64. Descartes' work was rightly

dedicated to Princess Elizabeth, since his correspondence and conversation with her led Descartes to a far subtler position than that of the denouement of the *Meditations*. The letters are translated in John Blom, ed., *Descartes: His Moral Philosophy and Psychology* (New York: NYU Press, 1978).

49. For an alternative interpretation, see Edwin Curley, *Behind the Geometrical Method: A Reading of Spinoza's Ethics* (Princeton: Princeton University Press, 1988).
50. Jonathan Bennett, *A Study of Spinoza's Ethics* (Hackett, 1984), esp. chaps 13–14.
51. Baḥyā's language about the suborning of the self gives a inkling of the sort of complexity that is at issue when Spinoza undertakes to think about selves, essences, the *conatus* in dynamic rather than static terms. See above, p. 71.
52. Curley (p. 642 of *The Collected Works*) corrects Elwes' hundred-year-old mistranslation. But Samuel Shirley unaccountably retains it in *The Ethics and Selected Letters* (Indianapolis: Hackett, 1982) p. 111; Henry Allison comes down firmly on both sides of the fence in *Benedict de Spinoza: An Introduction* (New Haven: Yale University Press, 1987) pp. 136–7, rendering *laetitia* "pleasure, or joy"; and *tristitia*, "pain, or sorrow".
53. Marcus Aurelius, *The Meditations* I 1, trans. A. S. L. Farquharson (Oxford: Oxford University Press, 1944) p. 21.
54. Maimonides, "Eight Chapters", 8, Goodman, *Rambam*, pp. 242–3.
55. See above, pp. 97–99.
56. See Hook, *Determinism and Freedom*, pp. 121–2.
57. I cite Paul Edwards's definition of soft determinism, since James assigned at least three distinct notions of freedom to those whom he called soft determinists: "acting without external constraint", "acting rightly", and "acquiescing in the law of the whole". See William James, "The Dilemma of Determinism", in *The Will to Believe and Other Essays in Popular Philosophy* (New York: Dover, 1959, lecture of 1884) p. 149. Our present exploration only tangentially concerns freedom as acquiescence or as recognition of necessity. Nor does it centrally address the question whether only rightful acts are free – although it does conclude with some reflections on the problem that rationalists may have in calling wrongful acts free. But my central concern here is with the confinement of freedom to the absence of external coercion. This is the sense that I find most commonly in those who wish to move on rapidly to issues of social or legal accountability and skirt the problems of human agency. The idea is to concede external determination of all human motives but to find sufficient grounds for accountability in the lack of overt coercion or overwhelming constraints upon our choices. Hobbes was a soft determinist; and his approach, adopted by Hume, gains a peculiar hold on English-speaking philosophers, who are prone to confuse it with the positions of the Stoics or Spinoza. "Liberty, or Freedom", Hobbes writes, "signifieth, properly, the absence of opposition; by opposition, I mean external impediments to motion … *Liberty* and *necessity* are consistent: as in the water, that hath not only *liberty*, but a *necessity* of descending by the channel; so likewise in the actions which men voluntarily do: which, because they proceed from their will, proceed from *liberty*; and yet, because every act of man's will, and every desire, and inclination proceedeth from some cause, and that from another cause, in a continual chain, whose first link is in the hand of God the first of all causes, proceed from necessity."

See *Leviathan* pt. 2, ch. 21 and "Of Liberty and Necessity" in Molesworth ed., 1839, vol. 4, pp. 239–78. As Ralph Ross succinctly sums up Hobbes's position: "A man may do as he wants, but he must want what he wants." See "Some Puzzles in Hobbes", in R. Ross et al., eds, *Thomas Hobbes in His Time* (Minneapolis: University of Minnesota Press, 1974) p. 43.

58. R. Akiba in Avot 3.15; cf. Jeremiah 10:23 with Deuteronomy 30:19; B. Berakhot 33b; Josephus, *Antiquities* XVIII i 3 and B. Niddah 16b.
59. See *Guide* I 73.10; Goodman, *Rambam*, pp. 136–8, Maimonides, "Eight Chapters", 2, 8; cf. *Guide* III 17.4–5; Saadiah, *ED* IV 3, trans. Rosenblatt, p. 186.
60. Guthrie, *A History of Greek Philosophy*, vol. 6, p. 361; cf. Martha Nussbaum, *The Fragility of Goodness* (Cambridge: Cambridge University Press, 1986) pp. 283–9 and her Aristotle's *De Motu Animalium* (Princeton: Princeton University Press, 1978). For *prohairesis* see *NE* III 2; for *boulesis* III 3.
61. That Aristotle presumes rather than arguing for free will at *De Interpretatione* 9 is clear from 18b 5–17 and vividly shown in al-Farabi's commentary ad loc., *Sharḥ fī 'l-'Ibāra*, ed. W. Kutsch and S. Marrow (Beirut: Catholic Press, 1960), 83 l. 24–84, l. 21, trans. F. W. Zimmermann (Oxford: Oxford University Press, 1981) pp. 76–7: see Goodman, "Al-Fārābī's Modalities". Aristotle's commitment to future contingency is evident in the *Metaphysics* (VI 3), where he argues that not all things are of necessity, since for some their causes have not yet come to be. Yet he rejects indeterminism: events are not fortuitous; they happen in accordance with their causes and as those causes require. Chance is the intervention of a causal train whose necessities are not regularly associated with those we are attending to. It is not an alternative to causality, but, as Maimonides put it, results from a superfluity of causes. See *Metaphysics* 1027a 30–b16; *Physics* II 6; Maimonides, *Guide* II 48, ed. Munk, vol. 2, p. 101a.
62. Guthrie, *A History of Greek Philosophy*, p. 359.
63. See *MT* I, *Sefer ha-Mada'*, *Hilkhot Teshuvah* 5.2, cf. 5.1 and 5.4 viii.
64. *MT* I, ed. and trans. by M. Hyamson as *Maimonides: The Book of Knowledge* (Jerusalem: Feldheim, 1974) 86b–87b. "Pushed or pulled" seems here to allude mechanistic determination and psychologic compulsion; cf. Aristotle, *De Anima* III 10, 433b 25, *Physics* VIII 2, 243b 15
65. Maimonides, "Eight Chapters", 8; Goodman, *Rambam*, pp. 246–7; MT I, Hyamson, 86b, 5.1. See above, p. 106.
66. Ben Azzai defines the dynamic of entrenchment: "One commandment draws another after it, and one sin draws another after it. For the reward of a commandment fulfilled is another, and the price of a transgression is another transgression." Avot 4.2; cf. Mekhilta ad. Exodus 15:26, ed. Lauterbach (Philadelphia: JPS, 1933) vol. 2, p. 97; cf. B. Makkot 10b, B. Shabbat 104a, B. Yoma 39a; cf. Ben Azzai at B. Yoma 38a.
67. See *ED* IV 5, 6.2. trans. Rosenblatt, p. 195, ad Proverbs 19:3, and 198 ad Isaiah 6:10, Deuteronomy 28:29, Job 5:13–14, 12:24–25. Saadiah's thesis is founded in Mu'tazilite *kalām*.
68. See Chapter 7 below.
69. See Plato, *Republic* IV 443–5, VI 484c, IX 589–90; cf. *Protagoras* 323–4, *Laws* VI 768b.

70. Hence Plato's practice of opening his Socratic dialogues with ostensive (almost Ryleian) lists of illustrations of the notion sought. Such a list does not constitute a definition; it is not a formula. But it does orient the discussion and provide a steady source of test cases from the pool of common notions. Hence too Aristotle's deference to the opinions of the many – in general and as the repository of the ethos from which (and not from theory) he expects our moral tendencies to arise. Cf. Chapter 2 above, p. 58.
71. *Iliad* 19:86, cited in E. R. Dodds, *The Greeks and the Irrational* (Berkeley: University of California Press, 1964) p. 3.
72. Aristotle argues that the saying "No one is voluntarily wicked" is false: "Otherwise … we shall have to deny that man is a moving principle or begetter of his actions, as of children …." *NE* III 5, 1113b 15–20. Aristotle does maintain that no one is involuntarily happy. For happiness, by Aristotle's standards, requires skill; it cannot be achieved by accident. Nor can one be voluntarily unhappy, since unhappiness is a goal that no one would choose voluntarily (*NE* I 1). If viciousness can be an art, it cannot be an art of living well and wisely in accordance with human nature. Vices are weaknesses, not strengths of character. The vicious person, then, in a salvageable sense of the Socratic dictum, does not know what he is doing, since he does not (ultimately) want what he is choosing. Such a person is responsible for his actions, just as a father is responsible for begetting children: he knows what actions he performs. But the vicious person does not choose his actions with full knowledge in the sense to which the Socratic dictum was allusive, because he mistakenly regards them as conducive to the good life.

Chapter 7

Ibn Khaldūn and Thucydides

Both Ibn Khaldūn and Thucydides rummage in the data of history, seeking patterns that reveal the nature of man as a political and social being. Like Machiavelli, both historians are survivors, but failed men of action. Both reach a cyclical rather than linear vision of history, and both enunciate a qualified relativism that affords them grounds, as we shall see, for a cautious acceptance of history, a naturalist's, perhaps a pessimist's historical theodicy.

— 1. A science of history and civilisation —

Initially what strikes us in both authors is a demand for clarity, realism, critical thinking, a reaction against the *naïveté* or *fausse naïveté* of traditional and sacred history.[1] This critical demand stands forth more vividly in the methods used and standards applied than any mere critique of prior work could be. Each of the two historians makes veracity his goal, bracketing *parti pris* and personal motives. Each is ready to make sacrifices for truth.[2] And this commends them to us. Studying the "archaeology" of Thucydides, or Ibn Khaldūn's efforts to situate history in its natural environment – or contemplating both men's relative dispassion as they review the events of their own full lives – we are struck by the power of the critical historiography that marks the achievement of each and makes kindred spirits of the two, across the gaps of time and cultural distance.

Yet, when we are given the distillate of a lifetime's thought and experience, a book composed in exile or isolation from the literary marketplace and the corridors of patronage and power,[3] we rightly expect more than a purely descriptive, albeit critical, narrative. Thucydides insists that he wrote his history as a possession for the ages.[4] His narrative speaks to a futurity far beyond the horizon of its first audience. Ibn Khaldūn wrote the first draft of his *Muqaddimah* in five months in 1377, "with words and ideas pouring into my head like cream into a churn", and without access to a library.[5] He takes credit, on the last page of the work, for founding a new field of study. Both writers think of history as bearing a meaning that the historian should discover and impart. Ibn Khaldūn indeed titles the universal history to which the *Muqaddimah* forms an introduction, *Kitāb al-ʿIbar*, the Book of the Lesson.[6] What lessons have the two historians set out to teach?

The message, in each case, is rooted in the method. For critical thinking demands critical standards, and realism demands criteria of reality. What standards of realism do the two historians accept? Evident immediately is their common search for what we might call scientific, that is, naturalistic standards. Thucydides' terminology and his attitude toward the war of which he writes, his respect for material causes and specifically for environmental and climatic factors, his careful watching for symptoms and crisis points, and his explicitly prognosticating stance link his work with the Hippocratic writings. Thucydides often appeals to empirical observation and never offers a supernatural explanation where natural causation will suffice. His treatment of the plague at Athens becomes a model of his method and a marker of his goal. As John Finley writes:

> The identifying mark of a body of writings from the late fifth century usually called Hippocratic – notably the *Prognostic*, *Regimen in Acute Diseases*, and *Epidemics* I and III – is that they substitute alike for religious dogma and philosophic theory an exclusive regard for the symptoms and circumstances of disease ... It is natural that the adherents of the school should have taken stock also of local and atmospheric conditions. This practice, particularly marked in the *Epidemics*, as in an earlier work possibly by the same hand, the famous *Airs, Waters and Places*, has given rise to the name "*meteorologische Medizin*" as a designation for the whole school, and like the practice of noting periods of crisis, is strongly observable in Thucydides' description of the plague ... the author's cool impersonal tone is in keeping with his method. From Thucydides' description of the plague, there can be no doubt that he was thoroughly acquainted with this school of thought.[7]

Thucydides' thinking hardly remains as clinical or as dismissive of the great philosophical questions as his affinity for medical naturalism might suggest. Nor, we find, are his ironies as cool and impersonal as they are detached. But the reductive moment is clearly prominent in his thought, and is, in fact, one source of his historiographic authority. The same is true, *mutatis mutandis*, of Ibn Khaldūn.

"Poverty", Thucydides writes, "was the real reason why the achievements of former ages were insignificant, and why the Trojan War, the most celebrated of them all, when brought to the test of facts, falls short of its fame and of the prevailing traditions to which the poets have given authority."[8] Hearsay and the poets should not be trusted,[9] especially not in quantitative matters; but the literary and physical remains of past times, if questioned critically, will offer answers that can be taken as foundations.[10] Oracles are of interest primarily for their psychological impact. Thucydides is amused and touched by men's willingness to bend an oracle to fit their present plight: "men's memories reflected their sufferings." Future generations will probably again rewrite prophecy, so as to fit the case.[11] But Thucydides' naturalism and empiricism are not destructively reductionistic. He dismisses no realm of experience out of hand. Indeed, the subtle irony of his tone often leaves us wondering if there is not more in what he means than what he says, more in history than meets even the most critical eye.

In Ibn Khaldūn again there is mistrust of the tradition;[12] again, a critique of the quantitative accuracy of traditional reports.[13] The absurdity of old claims is repeatedly urged on empirical grounds.[14] Again there is respect for physical as well as literary remains.[15] Thucydides' caution about ruins[16] has disappeared. In place of the thought that lack of major public works is no sure proof of an undeveloped society comes Ibn Khaldūn's theory that monuments are an index of power.[17] Taxes and expenditures bespeak political integration, like GNP for a modern economist[18] – or sea power for Thucydides.[19]

Like Thucydides, Ibn Khaldūn uses linguistic evidence to make sociological points.[20] Both men take pains to gather first-hand information and discount for bias in received accounts.[21] Ibn Khaldūn even suggests empirical tests for his theories: one who doubts the priority of country life has only to perform an impromptu survey, asking contemporaries about their family origins.[22] Ibn Khaldūn smiles at the unworldly scholars who mistake their own abstract constructions for realities.[23] And, like Thucydides, he is led by his empiricism into naturalism, setting aside the Philosophers' a priori talk of essences along with the *kalām* rejection of causality. Following al-Ghazālī, he contextualises the causal order within the divine milieu to render his naturalism at home in the Islamic environment.[24] But respect for material causes and for the air-waters-and-places line of thinking is here even more evident than in Thucydides.[25] Cities, Ibn Khaldūn urges, should be sited to take advantage of earth, water and air resources.[26] Crowding people near a swamp or polluted water, or where there is fetid or stagnant air leads to plague as surely as the decay of farming or the neglect of planning leads to famine.[27] Human racial characteristics are biological responses to diverse climates. They are not the scars of Noah's curse. For they vary with environment and indeed may change with a change of habitat.[28] Nor do the personality traits associated with the races reflect innate differences in mentality, as Galen and Kindī supposed. They are simply the natural responses of body and spirit to differences in climate and diet.[29] Ibn Khaldūn may have his prejudices;[30] his physiological psychology may be primitive. But he rebuts fantasies not with feelings but with natural facts as he understands them.

Facts, for Ibn Khaldūn, however, are not an end in themselves. As Baali writes,

> Although he is considered by Sorokin, Flint, Barnes, Schmidt, de Boer, Simon, Watt, Enan, and Khalife the founder of a scientific history, Ibn Khaldūn believed that the *inner* meaning of history "involves speculation … and therefore is firmly rooted in philosophy. It deserves to be accounted a branch of philosophy".[31]

Part of what we must ask is how is this so?

The general plan of the *Muqaddimah*, as Ibn Khaldūn explains,[32] is a gradual progress from the foundations of life to the highest products of civilisation, the arts and sciences that render humanity unique. The work's structure of theses and arguments and the expository progress from elements to complex theorems shows a Euclidean form. And, as in Euclid, the elements are starting points in an expository, not an epistemic sense: conceptually, they are the products of a prior analysis that began where the work ends, with Islamic society in its full blown realisation.

From its most elemental to its most rarefied, that society is drawn at full length in the *Muqaddimah*, like some great plant specimen. Taking its chapters in reverse order, the book is readily seen as the dissection of an entire civilisation: functionally, the sciences come last. Having no obvious pragmatic value, yet bearing within them the means of preservation and the seeds of future growth, they are the flowers, a luxury fostered for the sake of the fruit that arises from them and is their pragmatic goal.[33] The arts, for Ibn Khaldūn, are the fruit of society. Crafts, he points out, calling a spade a spade, are means of making a living. As in Plato, it is economic activity – ultimately grounded in the quest for the necessities of human life – that sustains (but does not perfect) any culture.

Urban civilisation is the leaf and branch, giving shelter and support to the arts and crafts; for only a large, settled, institutional society allows the diversification of effort needed for the efficiency of the crafts and efflorescence of the sciences. Power is the trunk that gives structure, upholds, preserves and protects social and economic institutions, fostering the continuity of culture that allows art, science and institutions to proliferate and thrive.[34] Desert culture, rural life in general and subsistence farming and nomadism in the extreme, are the roots, "the basis and reservoir of cities and city life".[35] The earth is the soil in which these roots grow; and the character of the earth, climate and topography – waters, airs and places – are crucial in determining what form societies will take and what level their civilisations will reach. Ibn Khaldūn's six chapters, then, deal with

1. The earth.
2. Primitive life, life at the subsistence level.
3. Sovereignty and kingdom.
4. Urban civilisation.
5. The arts.
6. The sciences.

Each chapter sets each grade in the hierarchy on the base of all that has gone before.

Like Plato and Aristotle before him, Ibn Khaldūn here employs a genetic or developmental model as a tool of analysis.[36] Plato had sketched the outlines of society and the structure of the state from a fictive genealogy based on calendaring human needs (*Republic* II 369–75). Aristotle had found the boundary marks for the science of politics in his historical studies of 158 Greek constitutions, observing their workings in action, rather than seeking to contemplate them in pure theory. Ibn Khaldūn, for his part, makes his analytical sketch of history the evidentiary prologue to his meta-historical study, even as he makes the *Muqaddimah* itself the conceptual prologue to his Study of History.[37]

But each phase in the development of the social organism has its own nature; none is dismissed as a mere disguised form of another, and the whole is always greater than the mere aggregate of its parts. Accordingly, Ibn Khaldūn places revelation among the elements of social structure, discussing "the sorts of human beings who reach awareness, whether through special gifts or by training".[38] Prophecy and true visions are causally distinct from divination. For true prophecy and mystic awareness demand real contact with the divine; but divination is a craft, dependent, at best, on human skill.[39]

Positivistically, prophecy and divination are alike. For they have similar pragmatic impacts. But Ibn Khaldūn finds empirical, even medical sounding, criteria for drawing a clear distinction between religion and superstition.[40] Like Thucydides, he seems amused by historical fables brought to the service of religious sensationalism. He laughs at the notion that starlings supply Rome with olive oil[41] and smiles at the credulity of worldly writers in repeating "storytellers' gossip" about the so-called City of Copper or the City of Ten-thousand Gates.[42] He compares the legend, retailed by

Qur'ān commentators, that the lost city of Iram still survived in their day with the facetious interpretations of a well known humorist.[43] He does not merely ridicule, however, but offers refutations that are consistently empirical in method and naturalistic in outlook.

Yet Ibn Khaldūn takes the *Qur'ān* seriously and quotes it sincerely.[44] He has faith in miracles[45] and respect for Sufism, at least in an orthodox form.[46] He cheerfully admits (even against the bent of the argument) that Muḥammad does not fit within his model of leadership.[47] Obviously, Thucydides is not so well at ease with received tradition, but the parallel holds. For he too is no doctrinaire positivist: the distortion of an oracle is not a serious matter unless an oracle is more than a fraud, unless it represents something more than any oracle can be. The care both men use in following up on prophetic predictions[48] reveals an interest beyond mere mention of the curious. A work on history need not be peppered with scripture or orchestrated with Delphic utterances, after all, if its sole purpose is to chronicle or regulate the chronicling of events.

The critical standards adopted by both historians, we have observed, are deployed in a quest for the message of history. But history will not yield up its meaning until its laws are known,[49] and critical principles are needed to uncover those laws. For that very reason, a critical method must not import hidden assumptions as to the content of historical laws. Thus, while both Ibn Khaldūn and Thucydides are decidedly empiricist epistemologically and naturalistic ontologically, it would be question-begging for either to write as a materialist.

The heart of scientific method from antiquity to the birth of nominalism was not materialism (*a fortiori* not phenomenalism) but universality. Only the law-like proposition can be scientific, and only universal statements can be law-like. Men who know only particulars might know that a thing is so but never why. Rational understanding, professionalism, control, teaching and communicating, invention, and above all explanation, are possible only when the subject is "first principles", that is, fundamental causes, about which generalisations can be formed.[50] Just as legislation cannot be fair unless the rules are universal (and not changeable with the moment, as some children take the rules of a game to be), so observations cannot be scientific unless they are universalisable. An experimental result that cannot be reproduced is no result; a principle that cannot be reapplied does not have the objective rationality to commend acceptance by the internal rationality of the mind.

What guides us in forming generalisations and discriminating law-like regularities from happenstance are rules of relevance drawn from experience and generalised to delimit the universe of hypotheses seriously to be considered. Skill, insight and timing are critical here: to ignore the very small, to defer to the influence of the stars, to confuse heritable with environmental factors or (as we have seen) arbitrarily to limit the universe of causes to these alone, ignoring the role of the self – all are damning to science. The limitations placed on causal relevance are critical to metaphysics as well. For to have no effects is the mark of the non-existent. Materialism offers one way of systematically delimiting the realm of relevance. Applied a priori to an uncharted field it is likely to be wrong and certain to be arbitrary.

Neither Ibn Khaldūn nor Thucydides is willing to limit causal relevance a priori to the material world. Both leave open the door to confirmation or reinterpretation of religious hypotheses. Each has an idea of the matter of history, the substrate and subject of historical change and bearer of the dispositions that set the parameters of historical possibility and delimit the range of credible hypotheses. Neither identifies that substrate with matter.

For Thucydides the substrate underlying all historical events is human nature.[51] Beyond floods, earthquakes, storms and pestilence, human motives must be deemed primary causes. The spark and damper of human drives are contained within human nature. Human nature may be many things, of course. But Thucydides' interest is aroused by times of trouble, when human nature bares its teeth.[52] Then that nature, "which is always ready to transgress the laws" sees them "trampled under foot" and takes perverse delight in flouting justice and all values.[53]

The oppressed, Thucydides writes, are "naturally animated by a passionate desire" for revenge; the poor covet "their neighbours' goods".[54] The dialectic of hatred, anarchy, atrocity, massacre and counter-massacre – "every form of wickedness" – has its origin in desire: "The cause of all these evils was the love of power, originating in avarice and ambition and the party spirit which is engendered by them when men are fairly engaged in a contest."[55] What could be more natural? "Party spirit" arises from the same sort of motives as other passions: "For party associations are not based upon established law nor do they seek public good; they are formed in defiance of the laws and from self-interest."[56] The argument rests on the Sophist dichotomy of *nomos* and *physis*: law and restraint are conventional; violence and aggression are natural.

As Finley shows, Thucydides sees human nature through the lens of Sophist thought, coloured and prepared by the tragedy of Sophocles and Euripides[57] and confirmed by the experience of history itself: man is selfish by nature, and self-destructive when his selfishness grows short-sighted. Overbearing, self-seeking, self-centered, and self-deceiving, man is above all a sophist to himself. To explain man to himself, Thucydides must become a sophist; enter into the realm of expediency, *ta deonta*, "the things called for" by a situation.[58] Verisimilitude and Realpolitik, after all, are of the realm of the Sophist, whose trade is not to demonstrate but to convince or teach the art of convincing, presenting not existence itself but plausible arguments and appearances. The realism of Sophist parlance is not reality but an image of reality. It is only this that the orator need create. Within his situation and role (for a speaker has more in common with an actor than with a scientist), a shared assumption will do as well as an axiom. In the frenzy of mistrust and fear that arise in times of cataclysm, no assumption more readily wins credence than one that errs on the dark side. For those who have learned to expect the worst are ever ready to believe the worst. Thus, in Thucydides's time and the times of which he wrote, no suasion was more plausible, as explanation or apology, than the Sophists' "likelihood" argument,[59] couched as an appeal to subjective expedience: "men tend to do what profits them" – it is only human nature. And who can be expected to resist nature?[60]

To explain the course of history Thucydides must view events from the standpoints of the participants, constantly traversing the line between what is right and what seems right or can be made to seem right. Hence his reliance on the method of speeches. For in a speech or debate all sides of a situation can be made explicit and counterpoised against each other. Thus the speeches of Thucydides are full of concessives and minority reports. Each position is put on its most rational footing.[61] For even Medea has not just her grievances but her reasons.

It is highly effective for the historian to make maxims and intentions explicit in the way that the students of the Sophists articulate the interests of their clients, or the tragedian articulates the intentions of his protagonists. For to make human motives explicit is to lay bare the principles of human nature. Just as the scientist or physician needs to understand the nature of pestilence and disease,[62] so the citizen or statesman needs to understand human reactions. The stages of the terror at Corcyra and its aftermath were "such as have always been and always will be while human nature remains the same".[63] And the laws of human nature, exposed to view by such extreme conditions, are what make Thucydides' *History* "an everlasting possession", "useful" in grasping not only what has happened but "like events which may be expected to happen in the future in the order of human things".[64]

To desire empire is natural. So are fear, honour, and interest – three all-powerful motives that no natural man can ignore.[65] War has a nature; its substrate is not matter at large but the human material that is the stuff of politics. But, given an understanding of human nature and the mesh or clash of the forces that drive it, the dialectic of history becomes transparent, and the causes and course of war become as clear as physics becomes with the disassembly of matter.

Wars begin in optimism, in a confident, expansive, sanguine and ambitious mood.[66] No one who goes to war expects it to last long. Ambition breeds fear,[67] expansion confirms it,[68] and fear breeds fear in turn.[69] An anticipated blow is met by defensive preparations, or a pre-emptive strike. An actual blow meets retaliation. Once hostilities commence, terror breeds terror;[70] and atrocity foments atrocity.[71] Security, authority and trust disappear. Men imitate nations, and nations act the part of beasts,[72] setting aside "all law, human and divine".[73] But, unlike beasts, states do not disengage, even when they see themselves locked in an embrace from which neither party will escape intact. The dialectic of fear and vengeance has momentum now. Each side struggles for the last blow, as bickerers fight for the last word. Gestures of conciliation are read as signs of weakness,[74] promising a victory only scarcely out of reach.

Readers have divided in interpreting Thucydides' history, some seeking a *parti pris*, others finding a detached and neutral scientific observer. But these views are overly polarised, as so often happens when narrower agendas are brought to the great works of human thought. As Clifford Orwin's masterful analysis confirms, the *History* proves neither positivistic nor moralistic.[75] Thucydides's narrative strategy mutes but also reflects the escalating savagery of the war in the subtle interplay of principle and expedience still visible in the speeches. Thucydides tells us that the speakers did not actually use the very words he puts in their mouths. But his technique of dramatic irony – like that of Plato, another master ironist – sets up a crosslight that vividly highlights authorial intentions, alongside the intentions of the original actors. The speakers are, as we might expect, both self-serving and (when it suits them) self-righteous. They paint themselves as driven by necessity, even when necessity, in the case of Athens, includes the natural penchant of states for empire. They all appeal to justice, even when justice, in the case of Sparta, envelops in its legalism actions and arguments that consistently serve state expediency. In Orwin's words: "The parties are not black and white but more or less equally gray."[76] Thucydides does not refrain from judgement. He is not a scorekeeper or cheerleader, but neither does he descend into the role of referee or executioner. The readers are the jury, as they compare one rationale and rationalisation with another and detect the self-betrayals with which the text is salted. Justice falls, as in a tragedy, heavily, inexorably – predictably but not as any of the parties might have expected or demanded. History does judge, and the parties themselves, along with the nature they appealed to, are the executioners, betrayed as much by their self-righteous postures as by their self-serving motives.

There are laws here, patterns and reactions. But the forces, momenta and inertias are those of human nature. The events they determine and define are not reducible to physics. They are *sui generis*, the events of history. As Ibn Khaldūn frequently remarks, giving a powerful and concrete sense to the famous words of Aristotle, habit or custom is second nature,[77] a nature that acts and responds by laws of its own.

Man's character, Ibn Khaldūn argues, is conditioned by his way of life.[78] That in turn is delimited in large measure by environment.[79] The elemental motives for Thucydides are the dispositions and incapacities of human nature. They reflect but are not reduced to the natures of the material elements. The human dispositions play, if anything, a larger role for Ibn Khaldūn.[80] The fear-dialectic that Thucydides views with the diagnostic-prognostic eye of an ancient medical observer, Ibn Khaldūn – himself a doctor of states who was not afraid to tinker with political forces – expands into the basis of a theory of sovereignty.[81] The model was more fully developed by Hobbes, who had himself no small experience of civil upheaval and who translated Thucydides' *History* in 1628. Ambition, for Ibn Khaldūn, retains its pivotal role, at the nexus between the individual and the group. Thucydides' "party spirit"[82] has metamorphosed into the *ʿaṣabiyya* of Ibn Khaldūn.

Thucydides reasoned from the sophist axiom "men tend to do what profits them" to a natural appetite for empire. Ibn Khaldūn, correspondingly, invokes a postulate: "kingdom is the goal of *ʿaṣabiyya*."[83] He is not content here with a blanket appeal to elemental human nature, declining to reduce political questions to matters of psychology. The political must be considered in its own terms.[84] Indeed, Ibn Khaldūn cites as critical a number of religious, dynastic, socio-political, linguistic and other factors that are not reducible to (or deducible from) the primary givens of our social nature or of the basic ethnic and climatic variables of his account. "Everything that comes into being", he urges, "whether an entity or an event, must have its own special nature determined by what it is and by the conditions to which it is subject."[85] If man is the political animal, human character must have its uniquely political aspects. If we are to live together in groups, there must be distinctively political motives that moderate and modulate our egoism.[86]

For Ibn Khaldūn not friendship but *ʿaṣabiyya* is the political fact *par excellence*. Etymologically, the root word means "nerve", the fibre or sinew that binds a group together. Ibn Khaldūn has a clear idea of the make-up of that fibre, and this idea is one of his chief contributions to the theory of politics: the political relation is based on subjective identification. It is this that enables human beings to subordinate their individual honour, interests, rights, advantage, privileges, power or wealth, to group interests or expectations. Governance, in a state or any other social organisation, from a loose-knit confederation to a family or clan, is the art of gaining effective assent in behalf of the needs or demands of others.[87] It is thus the art of fostering identification with the interests of others. If motives like fear and ambition (Hobbes' "vain-glory") were all that men considered, or if fear and ambition themselves had no recourse, politics would be impossible. Men would remain isolated monads, never overcoming the centrifugal thrust and irritability of primitive human nature.[88] Life would be a war of all against all; or, as Ibn Mas'ūd (seventh century) put it, echoing a tradition that goes back to Pirkei Avot (3.2), "men would devour each other".[89] Without the group, individual survival would be impossible.[90] But, given the egoism inherent in human nature, Ibn Khaldūn reasons, men can subordinate themselves to a group (or even pursue their own collective interests) only in so far as they identify with one another, effectively linking their personal hopes, fears, pride, wants, needs, or for that matter their own shame, guilt and responsibility, with those of the group.

The bond of loyalty arising from such identification is *'aṣabiyya* in the broadest sense.[91] Its paradigm case is in the family,[92] where identification of self with other is most natural and least often called into question. But by various fictions and extensions the relation grows to encompass wider groups – the clan and tribe.[93] For *'aṣabiyya*, in some form is, in Ibn Khaldūn's view, the foundation of all social cooperation. It is critical in political relations. For "only through *'aṣabiyya* can any claim be enforced".[94] By skilful management and cultivation, *'aṣabiyya* may be transmuted to a bond of loyalty among strangers, along lines that Weber would classify as traditional, rational or charismatic. It is such an extended bond of *'aṣabiyya* that forms the basis for a built-up civilisation.[95]

Were the idea of *'aṣabiyya* to rest at the level of theory, we might have no more here than a nominal explanation, a circularity disguised in the wrapper of technical jargon, like the classic claim that opium induces sleep through the *virtus dormativa*: society is held together by *'aṣabiyya*, namely social cohesiveness. But that is not the level of Ibn Khaldūn's analysis. The idea is to locate the peculiar strands and strains of identification (and alienation) and to put the knowledge to work in understanding events and patterns of events. Thus, for example, Ibn Khaldūn uses the idea of *'aṣabiyya* in explicating the first Islamic Civil War, the *Fiṭna* of 657. Unlike many another historian, he does not simply colour his narrative with sympathy for one party or another but follows the threads of *ʿaṣabiyya* in explicating the causes of the revolt.[96] His own favourite case for the historiographic use of his model is the fall of the Barmecides.[97] Fitting evidence to model and model to evidence, he uses the concept of *ʿaṣabiyya* as a tool of analysis. By following the bonds of loyalty and noting where they fray or hold, he hopes to expose underlying political causes. The metamorphoses of *ʿaṣabiyya* are the metamorphoses of politics. The potentialities and limitations of *ʿaṣabiyya* mark the possibilities of political change, and the laws of *ʿaṣabiyya* will be the laws of history.[98]

By making *ʿaṣabiyya* the nerve of political relations, Ibn Khaldūn's analysis transcends the confines of rational choice theory without sailing into the misty heights of an organismic conception of the social group. Coercive power is clearly present in any society.[99] But what is needed, in all economy, for the cooperation that underlies any social effort is not massive force but a shared sense of purpose, a sense of community. Identification of the individual with the group underlies such a sense, Ibn Khaldūn reasons.[100] Identification then, loyalty, is the connective tissue of politics and the energy of history. How is identification achieved?

The assumption that all human motives aim at personal pleasure falls short of the subtlety and universality of Ibn Khaldūn's analysis. The strict hedonist ignores the varied motives of human action; the rational-choice theorist too readily ignores the fact that sane men almost never conceive their identities atomistically. They never wholly isolate their interests from those of at least some other human beings. A theorist who confines both identity and interest to the subject monad can always explain the containment of human irritability and thus the possibility of social cooperation by citing the manifest pragmatic benefits of cooperation. Ibn Khaldūn certainly does so.[101] Such explanations have been widely familiar to Europeans at least since the time of Hobbes. As pragmatic apologies for politics and dialectical warrants for government they typically accomplish what they set out to achieve rhetorically. But as social theory they underrate human interdependence. Nor do they adequately explain why some will make sacrifices for a group, or die for it. Critically, they fail to explain human selectivity about groups as foci of cooperation, loyalty or self-sacrifice.

In the abstract, any social body might expect cooperation, or even devotion, from anyone, merely in virtue of its being a social body. But human beings do not cooperate with simply anyone but among "themselves". Sacrifices are never made for a group *qua* group, but *qua* "us". Once subjective identification is recognised at the roots of group action (as such), the question is no longer, "How is it that aggregates of individuals come to function as effective groups?", but "Why is group loyalty focused in one group or transferred to another, shrunken or enlarged, weakened, strengthened, or shifted to some new basis of identification?" These for Ibn Khaldūn are the core questions of social and historical inquiry.

'Aṣabiyya in the narrowest and most familiar sense, is the bond of cohesion among the members of that primitive political grouping, the tribe. Living at a subsistence level and without the benefit of entrenched political institutions, elaborate systems of legal authority – or of walls – exposed not only to the elements but to enemies, tribesmen can rely on no one but one another. Tribal life is inherently cohesive, and the bond of cohesion must be intense, personal, and (if the group is to survive) pretty unwavering. It must be as like as possible to the familial bond. But *'aṣabiyya* is not left behind in the more advanced stages of political development: it is a lowest common denominator, underlying and thus surviving all political change. Ibn Khaldūn, accordingly, speaking with blunt realism, expands the scope of the term: "In every human activity, whether prophecy, founding a realm, or appealing for support of a cause, nothing can be won without fighting for it (for it is the nature of men to resist); and, in fighting, *'aṣabiyya* is a *sine qua non*."[102] Only if men effectively enlarge their subjective identities can they be expected to risk death, to stand and fight rather than "slink away".[103] Like Hegel, Ibn Khaldūn finds that the ruler, when it comes to that, is the man who is least afraid to die.

The aim and end of *'aṣabiyya* is kingdom.[104] It is for this reason that nations are born; and for this reason they die. For *'aṣabiyya* relaxes its grip when it has attained its goal. The sickness and death of states and civilisations is for Ibn Khaldūn no metaphorical matter. In calling social "senescence" irreversible,[105] he is not merely arguing from analogy or pressing a conceit but explaining the facts of history, using the laws whose workings he has observed. An "accident" pertaining to human affairs, *'aṣabiyya* cannot be eternal. It has a minimum and a maximum effective level. For politically men cannot do less than act or more than die. There is a limit beyond which *'aṣabiyya* cannot be distended. It may take many forms, but it can no more be wholly transmuted than it can be left behind. It has a nature of its own governing and limiting its development. That fact alone suffices to show that it must die. For all things that come to be must perish.[106]

'Aṣabiyya is as old as human culture, of which it is at once an epiphenomenon and a mainstay. The childhood of *'aṣabiyya* is tribalism. But *'aṣabiyya* is restless, with a motion of its own. It is, after all, the stuff of human loyalties. Religion is the adolescence of *'aṣabiyya*, transforming and in a way creating *'aṣabiyya* as a broader social bond. Viewing the *Muqaddimah* as a dramatic structure, the first chapter sets the scene. The

inclusion of revelation (in the place of fire, as it were) along with, water, earth and air, presents the motive force, as in a Greek drama, just before the entry of the *dramatis personae*, in Chapter 2. Religion attaches the self to the transcendent viewed as such. It is therefore the natural agency for bringing coherence to the otherwise diffuse energies of particularistic *'aṣabiyyāt*. To put the matter in military terms – since *'aṣabiyya* is ultimately a military issue – it is religion that aligns and unifies the otherwise mutually destructive forces of rival *'aṣabiyyāt*, transforming "bands of savages" into an effective striking force.[107] By an appeal that is at once concrete and universal, religion can broaden the purview of identification beyond the horizon of immediate or obvious interdependency. And only religion (through its appeal to the unseen and its supplanting of exclusive standards of identity with inclusive ones) can offer fulfilment to the groping aspirations of *'aṣabiyya* in search of horizonless worlds to conquer.

The target of *'aṣabiyya* in its drive for power is not, of course, the Absolute or the universal as such, but "the possessions of others". The dynamic of religiously channelised *'aṣabiyya* is one of expansion: the political effect of religion on *'aṣabiyya*, regardless of its effects on men as men, is to give real force to the otherwise idle expansionism of the tribe. For, in any language, the *'aṣabiyya* of an enemy is fanaticism – just as the religion of an enemy is superstition. The political impact of universal religion is, of course, a mere by-product of its transformation of man and society. But strictly politically, at the elemental level, it is this by-product alone that matters. Religion transforms the base and focus of *'aṣabiyya*. This in turn allows the formation of a society that extends its reach beyond the primitive interdependencies of the tribe. In the metamorphosis of primitive cultures into civilisations, and the corresponding transformations that must be undergone by every conqueror or creator of civilisations, religion is the critical growth factor, expanding the sense of self beyond family, clan or tribe. Only through such an expansion of the sense of self can tribesmen slip on the new, impersonal social bonds so critical to urban life and so vital to the transition from heir or founder to possessor of a city.

Culture in our broad sense, "life" as Ibn Khaldūn calls it, is, like *'aṣabiyya*, found in all human societies. But civilisation and *'aṣabiyya* are at odds. Each seems to retreat where the other advances. For the institutionalised, rationalised foundations of civil society, as distinguished from the direct personal relationships of the family or tribe, are more efficient, more fair – at any rate necessary in a large, urban society with a money economy and a written, universally applicable law. But even in the city, *'aṣabiyya* grounds all political relations. It has not been transcended – any more than culture, which grounds its antithesis, can be left behind by a human group.[108] With the coming of civilisation, however, *'aṣabiyya*, the protean stuff of political relations, has undergone another metamorphosis. It reaches maturity with the development of the state.

Only in the state, where institutions are impersonal, office-holders interchangeable, laws immutable, can the claims of *'aṣabiyya* be made public, explicit and enforceable. That is why the state – the kingdom or dynasty, in Ibn Khaldūn's language – is the *telos* of *'aṣabiyya*.[109] But kingdom, ironically, is an end in more ways than one. For when *'aṣabiyya* requires enforcement, it is no longer *'aṣabiyya*. Men continue to identify; they must. They continue to subordinate their atomic interests to those of others. But they no longer identify directly with the other members of their group. Rather they tender such sacrifices as they make in the name of some principle or ideal, the group itself as an abstract, corporate entity, some institution, individual or symbol representative of the group. *'Aṣabiyya* has been sublimated. Its rationale is still at work, and its effects persist, still relating its subject to its object. But both subject and object have greatly changed, and the modalities governing acceptable and unacceptable expressions of identification and alienation have been transformed. Crime in the streets is the nobility of the tribe.

'Aṣabiyya in the broadest sense can never be wholly absent in any group that functions at all differently from a mere collection of individuals. For any such group must somehow command identification in a pragmatically significant number and combination of its members. And *'aṣabiyya* has a minimum effective level. A group that cannot command allegiance or bring feelings of identification to the pitch of action cannot function as a group. Action, of some kind, we have seen, is the least expression of effective identification; dying is the greatest. These define the upper and lower limits of political claims. The tragic fact of history, which Ibn Khaldūn insists on bringing before us, is that in politics whatever can be demanded will be demanded: in the nation, as in the tribe, *'aṣabiyya* becomes a matter of willingness to die.[110] It is because this is so that nations and tribes, and the families, states or dynasties that rule them, have finite lifespans. Unless individuals are prepared to die for their group, the group itself will die. It is for this reason – a specification of the metaphysical fact that all things perish under the sun – that all political institutions must die, and that there is such a process as history at all.[111] Willingness to die itself may die.

Empire is the goal of *'aṣabiyya*, because *'aṣabiyya* is fundamentally a force for self-enlargement, in a broad and rather subtle sense of "self" and a crude and rather narrow sense of "enlargement". As aspirations go, the aspirations of the tribesman are easily satisfied. For the primitive is not a romantic; he wants to live otherwise than as he has. He wants property and the leisure and security to enjoy it. He wants the permanence, order and organisation that can make him master of time, space and the elements, instead of their victim. In short, he wants the city. By implication, although he may not know it, and cannot know at the outset the full implications of his desires, he wants laws, institutions, sedentary life, and the division of labour. But when these are achieved – even while they are being won – what becomes of the power that secures them? Ibn Khaldūn's answer is neither delicate nor equivocal: "The reliance of sedentary people upon laws destroys their courage and power to resist."[112] The same effect is produced by education, whether in the arts by which civilisation is upheld or in the sciences, secular or religious, by which it is refined.[113] Of course there are institutions now to fill the power gap. Indeed, the development of such institutions in urbanised society is the chief cause of the decline of tribal *ʿaṣabiyya*. But although state institutions supplant tribal *ʿaṣabiyya*, they cannot completely replace it. And civilised institutions, by their very nature (as *telos* of *ʿaṣabiyya*, at once its target, its goal, its satiation and its end), lack the savagery[114] that made possible life in the open desert:

> By its nature, kingdom demands peace. When people grow used to being at peace and at ease, such ways, like any habit, become part of their nature and character. The new generations grow up in comfort, in a life of tranquillity and ease. The old savagery is transformed. The ways of the desert which made them rulers, their violence, rapacity, skill in finding their way in the desert and travelling across wastes, are lost. They now differ from city folk only in their manner and dress. Gradually their prowess is lost, their vigour is eroded, their power undermined ... As men adopt each new luxury and refinement, sinking deeper and deeper into comfort, softness, and peace, they grow more and more estranged from the life of the desert and the desert toughness. They forget the bravery that was their defence. Finally, they come to rely for their protection on some armed force other than their own.[115]

Once this happens, in Ibn Khaldūn's view, a group's rule is ended and its very survival hangs in the balance.

Sublimated *ʿaṣabiyya*, allowing identification with others not just as one's fellows but as office-holders or possessors of the various specific and general rights and privileges that arise in a religiously regulated society with a diversified, money economy and a sedentary civil population, is necessary in any fully elaborated civilisation. But, being sublimated, it bears within it the seeds of its own destruction. For it operates through the medium of principles. In human conscience and consciousness these are abstract. As such, they are subjective. They may, to be sure, have some higher reality, objectivity and canonisation in some court beyond our earthly interactions. But within our human affairs, any principle or ideal is subject to misprision and compromise, either publicly or by that most self-deceiving of tribunals, human nature. Regardless of its many drawbacks, such was not the case with primitive *'aṣabiyya*. In the tribe it does not much matter how one feels about one's obligations; the painful and immediate consequences of dissociation from the group or rejection of its expectations are all too present and pressing. But in civilisation obligations have proliferated and ramified. Multiple substitutions of doer and recipient are possible, and multiple layers of mediation are active. For in institutions it is the function, not the agency that counts. Institutions afford a thick cushion against the consequences of omission, inefficiency or neglect. The rise of wealth, the products of industry, including leisure – which is at once the most precious and most dangerous product of human industry – have opened the door to the most persuasive enemies of duty (for sublimated *'aṣabiyya* in the most general sense is duty), namely personal ease, personal safety and personal pleasure. Civilisation beckons invitingly, even before its portals are fully opened, to the confidence artist and the free-rider.

Individualism is perhaps the most ambiguous of all the ambiguous by-products of civilisation. In primitive life the ambiguity was held in check by necessity. But with the growth of wealth and leisure, the individual grows eager to defend the new freedom of his person afforded by the sublimation of *'aṣabiyya*. The thin line grows blurred between the liberal, who believes one can do better (even for the group) if left alone, and the permissive, whose demands sound the same *in abstracto*, but whose motive is affection for his own pleasures and vices. Pleasure and vice are not equated by Ibn Khaldūn.[116] But pleasure is the commonest ground for self-deception, the commonest cause for obfuscation of motives and distortion of moral perspectives. Its nexus to dissolution and corruption will be intimate. And the slide from a life of pleasure to a life of vice, as Ibn Khaldūn insists, will be almost impossible to abate. For once pleasure has become a prime desideratum, it is demanded in ever larger doses and ever more exquisite, exotic or perverse variety.[117]

All this would matter little politically, were it not for the fact that both within and outside the walls of any society there are those who do not share in the dilemmas of affluence and those who esteem themselves to be above civil demands for responsible action and commitments. To the opportunist, whether political or intellectual, civilisation (even while it lives) seems a bloated and moribund body whose riches (and last vigour) exist only to be sapped – often under the guise of response to its own desperate cries for help. Perhaps partly for this reason, the infusion of a new spirit of resolution may for a time forestall the inevitable decline of a society but cannot prevent it. For highly organised, urban societies, by their very nature, seek remedies to their problems in professionalism and expertise. They thus seek remedies that only deepen their dependence on specialists and laid-off responsibilities. As civilisational crises grow more acute, the bounty of civilisation offers itself as bait to charlatans – and to religious, political, ultimately military, opportunists.

Brute militarism, demagoguery and the intellectual authority of the pseudo-prophets whom the situation calls forth are as destructive to the fabric of society as decadence itself.[118] But all the while, outside the cities, to the primitive, whose main concern remains survival, whose social, legal and even familial status remain intertwined, whose *ʿaṣabiyya* is still direct, personal, unquestionable, still a matter of life and death, the affluence of urban civilisation (once a religion or some religion surrogate has sparked the expansion of *ʿaṣabiyya*) beckons temptingly. For the urban individualist has lost the ultimate sanction of *ʿaṣabiyya*, lost it willingly, by his eager entry into the more comprehensive but less personally demanding bonds of civilisation. He has forgotten, as Ibn Khaldūn puts it, how wealth and power, the sources of his pleasure and security, were won.[119] That is, he has lost what the desperate man and the most dangerous members of a primitive society have in common: willingness, if necessary, to die.

It is the willingness of some to die, then, that renders history so like a drama, with the players ever changing while the roles remain the same. In propounding the thesis that "nations, like individuals, have life spans"[120] Ibn Khaldūn is simply drawing an inference from the fact that *ʿaṣabiyya*, as it is widened, is weakened. He infers that there must come a point in the attenuation of the social bond when it will snap.[121] Given the existence of alien, naturally hostile *ʿaṣabiyyāt* that seek to subordinate one another, and given the natural selfishness of man, it becomes apparent that the balloon will be burst long before the internal breaking point is reached. Nor is confirmation of the hypothesis far to seek. For as Carl Sandburg observed, in *The People, Yes*, "the world is strewn with the burst bladders of the puffed up". Nations are born, grow to maturity and die in a regular pattern that echoes the rhythms of physical nature and reflects the ceaseless motion of material being in its restless striving and constant failing to reach changelessness and perfection.[122] The pattern Ibn Khaldūn finds in history, then, is neither extrapolated from the laws of natural science nor superimposed from the projected image of a higher principle – the knowledge a priori that all things less than God are ever moving, ever imperfect, rising, falling, growing and dying. Rather it is perceived (for all sound metaphysics rests on observation) in the expanse of history. The patterns of historical change follow lines of growth and decay inherent in a nature that pertains specifically to politics and history.

Like Thucydides, Ibn Khaldūn grounds his notion of the laws of history on his conception of human nature and rests the credibility of those laws on a certain pessimism, at least regarding the propensities of human nature in adverse circumstances. Like Thucydides, he observes that historical forces can grow in magnitude and momentum beyond the powers of the actors themselves to contain or control them, and by increments that are not purely arithmetic. Pressing his analysis, Ibn Khaldūn discerns in the dialectic of history a political nature analogous to the "party spirit" of Thucydides but more comprehensive in function and effect, underlying all political affiliations. Grasping the peculiar nature of *ʿaṣabiyya* and the unique laws of its growth, development, transferral and decay, Ibn Khaldūn is in a position to write comprehensively of the laws of history at large.

— 2. GOVERNANCE IN HISTORY —

A historian today might feel little need to delve as deeply as Thucydides does into human nature and motivation for an understanding of historical events and their "principles". A contemporary political scientist might feel it was enough to go as far as Ibn Khaldūn does when he discerns a pattern in events. For Ibn Khaldūn and Thucydides, however, it is not enough merely to discern a pattern or a law in history. Both men are after bigger game, which their hard-won empirical grasp of historical patterns and laws can satisfy. In seeking a meaning behind the patterns and laws of history they are probing for evidence of a governance beyond the governments of human beings.

Both men were, in a way, cut off from comfortable acceptance of the most familiar varieties of religious (and political) myth and hyperbole. But neither rejected out of hand the values that such acceptance expressed. A reflective inquirer could see well enough how the divine does not take part in history: for Thucydides the gods of Homer were dead; and so, for that matter, was the God of primitive faith for Ibn Khaldūn. Yet neither Ibn Khaldūn nor Thucydides was prepared to assert dogmatically that the divine plays no role in human events. In asking after such a role and questioning whether and in what sense right or divine justice can triumph, both men were doggedly determined to be empiricists.

Both historians viewed the past from what they saw as the end of an era; each in his own way sought to weigh up history for a kind of outcome. The answers that each found through his long engagement with history, in the flesh and in the ashes, were probably not what he had expected. They were more complex than a young man might have suspected, and subtler, perhaps, than previous inquirers had realised – not to be stated baldly, but to be raked out of the dialectic of events.

Ibn Khaldūn's cyclical view of history arose from the same sort of bitter experience that forced Thucydides to retreat from the expectation of inevitable progress,[123] recognition of deep conflicts among values that history itself does not resolve. In a finite world of more than one participant, to act at all is to have interests and a point of view, thus to risk becoming an aggressor or a victim, or both. The sophists and the tragedians, in their different ways, had been struck by the recognition that no human act is without its explanation – indeed its justification. It is this awareness that gives the players in Greek tragedy their depth and colours the value-theory of the sophists so deeply with relativism: the very fact of intersubjectivity, underlying human aggressiveness and vulnerability, made crime, in the doing or the being done by, the inevitable human condition.

Both Ibn Khaldūn and Thucydides are troubled by the dilemma of action and passivity implied in any widespread acceptance of sophist "likelihood" assumptions, the elevation of the vulgar motto "Do unto others before they do unto you" into a universal norm of action. Neither historian endorses that standard. But both are keenly aware of the urgency that expedience demands with individuals, and all the more with nations, parties and tribes, since groups have no conscience of their own yet often bear grave responsibilities. So although both Ibn Khaldūn and Thucydides reject the sophist morality and repeatedly reject the opportunity it affords for the evasion of value judgements, both have learned from it. For both are seeking a standpoint from which to assay a world where partisanship has become the norm, and where the rhetoric of justice, of faith and of truth itself has been pressed into the service of partisan causes.

In a world of conflict the sophist notion that no action is either right or wrong in itself seemed only narrowly to miss the truth. Not that actions, for Ibn Khaldūn or Thucydides, are somehow stripped of moral weight by their partiality. On the contrary, all acts take on a taint of moral ambivalence and complexity, the very ambivalence that Euripides found in all great human undertakings: the same act was at once right and wrong. In defending one's interests, or aggressing to secure further interests to defend, one was almost certain to be right, and almost equally certain to do wrong.

When Thucydides finds the human passions of vengeance and greed exposed with the "trampling of all laws under foot",[124] he confirms to himself and his readers the sophist maxim that laws are an artificial constraint on the underlying aggressiveness of human nature. In this perspective, conflict among contested values seems inevitable. And, since there is no external standpoint, no uninterested party, such conflict seems ultimately irresolvable. Similar assumptions are even more explicit in Ibn Khaldūn's view of the ruler as a "restraining force" holding human appetites and passions in check. Neither the sophists nor the tragedians, neither Ibn Khaldūn nor Thucydides, imagines that the ruler himself will be immune to the fear dialectic or above the arena of conflict, interest and aggression. Any finite viewpoint, in subject, ruler, people or state, is only partial, liable to be wrong as well as right, and, most likely, being one-sided, to be both wrong and right. There are, as the sophist advocate would say, two sides to every case. Creon is as liable to be wrong as Antigone. Athens has no more claim than Sparta to be the injured party. The greatest conqueror is as much the victim of history as he is its curse.

What we find in Ibn Khaldūn, as in Thucydides, is a tragic vision of history. The notion of progress is pushed back by the ever-mounting evidence not of decline but of moral ambiguity, the chronic and ineradicable affliction inherent in every human undertaking. Neither Ibn Khaldūn nor Thucydides adopts the sophist posture as to the relativity of all values, absolute relativism as it were. But both recognise, inasmuch as values are subject to human notions, desires, passions and fears, that no ideal will be untainted, no principle uncompromised. Ideals as such have not the sort of being that can be tarnished; but institutions have. No law or principle by which men endeavour to live, regardless how nobly conceived, is immune to distortion, perversion, "trampling underfoot".

In a complex world of action and reaction, cause and effect, where the jostling of human subjects produces complex and ungovernable outcomes, where events move with a lurching inertia and momentum of their own, ever threatening to break loose from the slender reins by which we hope to control them, every action begins to appear double-edged, every accomplishment imponderable. Acts and institutions, programmes, laws and wars slip their moorings and take on a life of their own. The paths of possibility and necessity branch in a labyrinth of confusing directions. As the motives and consequences of action grow increasingly complex, it seems increasingly clear that the greater and more impressive an undertaking, the greater its moral ambiguity.

Against such a backdrop, objective values become not the guide but the test of human history. Historical denouements now appear as inconclusive endgames, in which the inadequate (and inadequately justified) forces of countervailing powers seem to fight to a standstill or a stand-off – ignorant armies clash by night. The triumph of right is found now not in the victory of one myopic force over another but in some higher justice. Justice here becomes the stand-in, where right will not entirely prevail. Or perhaps what prevails will be poetic justice, with justice itself falling by default to the province of the poet, the contriver of situations. The historic forces seem now to cancel one another, the good and evil of each undercutting or distorting those of the other. Indeed the cancellation may be found internally, with each event, value, and action bearing within its ambiguity the seeds and force of its own moral cancellation: each act becomes at once its own crime and its own punishment, its own virtue and its own reward. Such was the tragic vision of life. Such, I submit, was the image that both Ibn Khaldūn and Thucydides reflect in their visions of history.

Thucydides opened his history with the affirmation that the war he had witnessed would be the greatest event in the history of Hellas, or perhaps the world.[125] All prior Hellenic history seemed a ramp to the political powers and military forces that rendered the Peloponnesian War possible – indeed, inevitable.[126] But the vision of the past as a cumulative progress to the present was not to be extrapolated to the future. The very achievements that gave present events their "greatness" had planted deadly ambiguities in greatness itself. Thus, "of all Hellenic actions which took place in this war, or indeed, as I think, of all Hellenic actions which are on record", the last great action of the war, the Sicilian expedition (and the reprisals that answered it) "was the greatest – the most glorious to the victors, the most ruinous to the vanquished".[127] The dialectic of this greatness is no progress in the happy sense, but an escalation that strips away not only tactical restraints but every moral or religious inhibition to the perpetration of ever more egregious crimes. And in the background, echoing the rising pitch of violence, inhumanity and impiety, as if in some ominous counterpoint, again and again Thucydides records oracles, omens, natural disasters.

Men had committed crimes not only against each other, but against the gods.[128] Thucydides studiously notes the:

> earthquakes unparalleled in their extent and fury, and eclipses of the sun more numerous than are recorded to have happened in any former age. In some places there were great droughts which caused famines, and, lastly, there was the plague, which did immense harm and destroyed numbers of people. All these calamities fell upon Hellas simultaneously with the war.[129]

Were the natural disasters a response to human crimes? Surely, "never before had so many cities been depopulated and resettled, never had exile and slaughter been more frequent".[130] Thucydides states no *propter hoc*. His general sophistication, if not his naturalism, does not allow him to attribute the calamities observed to direct intervention of the gods. But he knows that such attributions were precisely what much popular and popularising thought were indulging.[131] What then is his purpose in the careful parataxes by which he juxtaposes or records the juxtapositions (for the method of speeches allows him to do both) of the crimes of men with what popular opinion widely held to be divine retribution?

The first actions of the war arose from treachery and deceit.[132] The very outbreak of hostilities meant the breaking of oaths; and, as the fighting continued, more oaths were broken. Fourteen years into a planned thirty-year peace, the war resumed.[133] The peace itself must have been no small achievement. But it somehow lacked that elusive quality of "greatness". With the mounting dialectic of deceit, it gradually grows clear what form the vengeance of the gods will take. All the elements of the dialectic Thucydides perceives are present in the affair of Plataea: fifth-column treachery, the self-deluding ambition that demands a pre-emptive strike, the crimes against both human and sacred law, by the Thebans' aggressing in time of truce, and by the Plataeans, in murdering their prisoners, violating the oath or understanding by which they had induced the Theban forces to withdraw. Accompanying these events, we hear the ominous mutterings of the oracle-mongers and soothsayers. The threats immanent in the situation have not yet made themselves overt, but by the time the many little dramas of Thucydides' history have been played out, covert ambition has metamorphosed to blatant hubris. Frequent and flagrant violations of oaths, of sanctuary, of the rights of prisoners are now expected. Crimes against all laws of mankind and the gods have become the norm. Ambition and the fear dialectic have now fashioned a juggernaut that neither side has the power or the will to stop. And the gloomy predictions of the prophets, the mouthpieces of the gods, are fulfilled, not only in natural disasters but by the doings of men, whose nature contains the nemesis of self-destruction.

When the tables are turned on the Plataeans,[134] they must pay with compound interest for their crimes, their broken oaths and violated prisoners.[135] The stakes of violence have risen. Men have lost their fear of the gods.[136] Indeed, it has become possible to fell fruit trees and mount a massacre in the name of the gods.[137] The Thebans and Lacedaemonians can convince one another, and themselves, that justice and truth are served by the destruction of Plataea and the massacre of its people.[138] They see nothing barbarous in the slaughter of a surrendered populace,[139] since massacres are now almost the rule.[140] It no longer seems strange that the possessions of the betrayed should be made over to Hera.[141] The crimes of others have turned the crimes of ego into inspired acts of vengeance.[142] Sophistry and self-love blind the perpetrators to the meshes that increasingly ensnare them.

With each new atrocity, each new act of self-deception and mutual destruction, Thucydides' irony rises and his distance grows more pronounced. Tragedy is evident long before the last blow is struck. The vantage point of hindsight and the detachment of exile allow the historian to see what the adversaries still in the heat of battle cannot: that war has a force and justice of its own, that a crime against another people is a crime against one's own, because of what it makes of us, and, in a way that no sophistry or blasphemy[143] can hide, because of what it makes of the victims too. The Plataean massacre brings that of Corcyra in its train. And even today, the shades of Plataea and Corcyra still haunt the killing fields of Bosnia and the Congo, Kosovo and Ruanda.

It is not by chance that the model act of hubris in Thucydides' history, Pericles' funeral oration, is juxtaposed with the historian's description of the plague at Athens. Nor is it mere casual chronicling that places the historian's development of the Corcyran débâcle, the model internecine disaster, only a page before chronology demands mention of the recurring plague, now accompanied by earthquakes and tidal waves. It is not Thucydides' purpose to repeat the gossip of the common folk or to gape journalistically at the fulfilment or non-fulfilment of yesterday's oracles – any more than it is Thomas Hardy's purpose to commit the pathetic fallacy by attributing to nature concern or unconcern in the affairs of men. But Thucydides uses his parataxes of natural with historical disasters (as Hardy juxtaposes natural with personal upheavals) to signal and underscore the true causes of the trouble. Neither the objective pattern of events described by Thucydides nor the subjective framework into which he sets them warrants attribution of the slightest tinge of supernatural intervention to the gods or assignment of the slightest taint of superstitious imagination to the mind of the historian. Thucydides' intention is far subtler. His parataxes, show (as thunder in the theatre re-echoes and amplifies hidden passions that are not easily seen or heard) just where the hidden causes of destruction lie. They lie where some might least expect to find them, in the fine words, grand ideals, and lofty reasoning of a Pericles. And they lie where others might be most ashamed to seek them, in petty motives of self-seeking, or in natural instincts like fear and ambition, love of self, or "party spirit".

What the historian has discovered is what the tragedian creates, an internal logic and dynamic in human events that does the work of the gods, furies or fates, but far more subtly, directly and inevitably than would be done by the gods of myth, or the *deus ex machina* of the theatre. In history, as in physics, every act bears within it its own consequences. Every choice comes at its own price, carries its own consequence and brings in train its own reaction. Thus the subtle irony of the historian (and the polite absence of the tragedian from the stage). It is not necessary for either to do more than the gods do: let the players write their sentences in their own hands, damn themselves out of their own mouths.

Pericles' funeral oration, that masterpiece of Attic clarity, so inept to the occasion, as hindsight would come to know, so insensitive, in its brilliance, to human feelings and human grief, yet so keenly perceptive of the main roads and short-cuts of civic flattery. Even to the modern reader, identifying as an Athenian, side by side with the others among the throng, the speech remains so skilful in its appeals to chauvinism and self-love, so lofty in conception, lucid in design, noble in the standards it sets forth to be died for, that many are tempted to read it as Thucydides shows us Pericles would have wished the Athenians to have heard it – as a stirring appeal to ideals to be fought for[144] – and modern readers feel ready to enlist, and even to do battle, as honorary Athenians. Only little hints like the proud tone, or the showmanship of Pericles in arranging his rostrum – or, above all, the immediate juxtaposition of Thucydides' description of the Athenian plague – bring us to our senses, remind us of what every original reader of Thucydides knew, that Pericles' speech was the prelude and invitation to disaster.[145]

The abutment of the speech with the horror of the plague tempts us to wonder (as Greek readers must have wondered): does Thucydides mean to ascribe the plague to the hubris of Pericles and the Athenians? If not, why did he contrive to link the two events? But in studying the description of the plague, the answer becomes patent: this wondering and inquiring were just what Thucydides desired – to raise the question, and to raise it in this context. The popular and inevitable hypothesis was that divine vengeance struck out against specific human crimes – the breaking of oaths, the atrocities that had already occurred, the horrors blasphemously performed in the name of the gods, above all the hubris of empire. Having raised the question, Thucydides could allow a subtler hypothesis to form in the reader's mind, one that did not reject but that reinterpreted the thinking of popular piety: that the real punishment came within and through the crime itself. For what made the plague unbearable, beyond the dying and the suffering, was the depth of human bestiality and impiety that it unleashed.[146]

To desire empire is natural. So is the desire to defend it. Empire can be won only by aggression and defended, as Cleon argues,[147] only by severity. Thus the massacres, the suppliants dragged from the altars,[148] the women and children enslaved,[149] the cities razed.[150] The whole gamut of terror and treachery that goes by the name of war starts from natural human desires. As policy these may be debated, compromised, even denied. But the underlying drives seem never to be wholly suppressed. And beyond the drives and the policies they promote are further consequences, reactions, dialectics of destruction and self-destruction. In the end, the drives, the policies and the consequences can hardly be distinguished. These dynamics are the punishment of crime as surely as attainment of its object is its reward. They are not the punishments that folk religion might expect. But they are not alien to the forces its myths may symbolise or personify. And they are clearly as inexorable as the furies in pursuing the guilty. For no act can be divorced from its consequences or isolated from its logic. No criminal can be free from the consequences of his act – from his conscience if he has one, or from what he has become if he has not; from what he has made of himself and what his actions have made of his enemies. No criminal can reverse the transformation he has brought about in his entire universe, until his act is itself somehow cancelled or avenged.

Thucydides traces the complex dialectics of such actions and reactions, paradigmatically, in describing the Corcyran blood-bath. He shows how human beings vied with rumour in devising atrocities.[151] They discarded all "higher motives", for (as an Ibn Khaldūn might have said) "their characters were assimilated to their conditions".[152] They submerged all social and even familial bonds for partisanship and the fellowship of crime.[153] That the pattern is self-sustaining and self-aggravating is obvious. But, with a poet's touch Thucydides makes the Corcyran atrocities and sacrileges a model foreshadowing what is to come.[154] The renewal of the plague in its natural cycle and the coincidence of earthquake and tidal wave become devices to alert us to the subtle nemesis at work, a divine justice, like that spoken of in popular rumour, but not working in the traditional way. For, in reality, retribution is immanent in each act, much as the divine order is immanent in nature. Nothing may overstep. The limits of each finite being become its destruction when it overreaches. As in Anaximander (ap. Simplicius *in Phys*. 24, 17), each actor, by necessity, pays the penalty of its injustice according to the sentence of time. Just as Heraclitus cautioned, character takes the place of destiny.

The irony of Thucydides is neither cheap nor facile. He does not need to expose the inner natures of the men of whom he writes; they do that well enough for themselves. His purpose, like that of the tragedian, is to add a profundity and subtlety to our understanding of human motives and action. Like the tragedian, he offers a moral purge. And, like the tragedian, his narrative offers a form of secular theodicy. He gives voice to the human incapacity to live in the same universe with evil, first by the attempt, god-like, to see every side of the issue; and then – for what cannot be forgiven – by recognising within history an inexorable and supremely even-handed justice, the immanent work of the gods.

What Thucydides saw in the Peloponnesian War, Ibn Khaldūn, hoped to see in the whole of human history open to his view. The lesson

Thucydides extracted from his archetypal war was the equivalent philosophically to the lesson Ibn Khaldūn drew from history at large. Thucydides began his work with the famous digression on ancient history, which set the critical tone by parting the curtains as it were, broadening the scope of the work beyond the flat, peep-hole view of those narrative histories that see the past as a dimly lit staircase leading inevitably upward to the present. His method was to provide a summary account of ancient life, drawing out the contrast between the highly organised, urban, commercial civilisation his readers knew and the migratory subsistence of their forebears in primitive social groups, rude in knowledge and technique. The contrast heightens the complexities of the life his contemporaries know and allows him to candle the present for the moral ambiguities that will show up so vividly when the actors begin to speak in the main body of his drama. As in tragedy, the ambiguities lend depth and verisimilitude to the author's vision. But they are also constitutive at the core of his message.

By Ibn Khaldūn's time historiography is a well-developed discipline. The introductory passages, in which the historian is now expected to defend his craft and outline his method and assumptions, have become traditional and have been augmented with the riches of the *isagoge* genre and encyclopedia literature.[155] The image of two contrasted ways of life – one in which arts, leisure and the law prevail,[156] the other in which even ordinary men wear arms in their day to day routine[157] – has opened up from a glimpse of the remote past and exotic present[158] to fill the universe of present and future possibility. The settled and unsettled lives are now archetypes of societies and individuals as well. Plato had early observed how one social type might metamorphose or die into another, and Ibn Khaldūn was quick to note how social types verge into one another at their temporal or geographic frontiers. Man himself bends with the ebb and flow of history.

Both the Greek and the Muslim experiment had failed before Ibn Khaldūn or Thucydides took up their pens. The state of the *Laws* had not been built on earth; and the *umma* of Muḥammad seemed far less real than his warnings and fears. History as Ibn Khaldūn saw it was clearly not a progress. Rather, it was the endless interaction of the desert and the city. And that interaction is no mere contest of forces but a moral drama. The socio-economic types that Ibn Khaldūn marked take on moral qualities, since human characters are conditioned by their social and economic situations. As a value typology, Ibn Khaldūn's categories make it possible, even necessary, for the historian to ask and answer evaluative and metaphysical questions. What he finds is that the values represented in the two great human types are complementary. The rhythmic interplay of those values, as now one, now the other type prevails, is the closest approach to perfection to be found in a world of conflict.

The bedouin (paradigmatically) is untamed,[159] greedy,[160] courageous,[161] healthy,[162] self-reliant,[163] easily moulded.[164] He lives at a lower cultural level,[165] but is "closer to being good" than a city dweller.[166] Urban man is civilised,[167] law-abiding,[168] spiritual,[169] flaccid[170] and superstitious.[171] He depends on professionals for everything from his daily wants and luxuries[172] to his personal protection.[173] He is sensual, prone to illness[174] and easily corrupted.[175] Urban society is humanity's only means of accomplishing anything truly great.[176] But its denizens are not typically as superior as the achievements of civilisation (that is, primarily of others) may lead them to suppose.[177] Civilisation is the custodian of the arts and sciences.[178] But in language,[179] poetry[180] and pedigree,[181] where nature must take artifice by the hand, it is the bedouins who excel. Ibn Khaldūn's judgement as to the quality of people and the quality of life is succinctly expressed in a single one of his theses: "Bedouins are closer to being good than settled people."[182]

There is a cleavage, then, among the values that human beings may represent. One set of strengths is incompatible with the other. Civilisation, the highest, best, and most beautiful product of human efforts, does not nurture the purest, simplest, bravest spirits. Each way of life has its own virtues and vices. Indeed, the vices are the natural diseases of the virtues. For nothing good in a world of becoming will lack its own mode of decay. So the vices and their virtues will be inseparable from each other, complementary facets of the same bivalent human material. And the excess of either set of traits – the overreaching of civilisation or the overstepping of the bedouin – casts the die that marks the inevitable death of either into the other.

Like Thucydides, Ibn Khaldūn is never a dogmatic relativist. His "realism" never brings him to declare all values and ideals nugatory or subjective. But he never ceases to believe that men are judged by standards that it is at best unrealistic to expect they can live up to. Richard Walzer was fond of saying that Ibn Khaldūn was no Plato in Arab dress. By this he meant that it was wrong to look to Ibn Khaldūn as the projector of radical social and societal reforms. But if Ibn Khaldūn lacked Plato's disaffection with politics as it was practised, neither was he nothing more than an opportunist or apologist and agent of opportunists. In his eager and repeated participation in the art of the *coup d'état*, he was playing the game that he would describe far more brilliantly and insightfully than he played it. In giving aid and information to Tamerlane, he was failing at the same game. But such failures are far more common than successes. Had it not been Thucydides' failure as a general that made him a spectator rather than a player at history? Perhaps in his zealous stewardship of his tasks as *qāḍī* in the last years of his life, Ibn Khaldūn rose at times above the partialities that the *Muqaddimah* transcended only intellectually. But his political efforts, halting though they proved to be, were at the core of his life's activity; his idealism stood at the margins, as is plainly revealed by his opportunism in turning on his patron Barqūq and his obsequious reversal when Barqūq was restored. For Plato the proportions are reversed: the political attempt was a spectacular failure; but Plato's broad disaffection from Athenian politics led him to an idealism that would long outlive its author. Ibn Khaldūn was perhaps too much a worldling to reach that plane.

The content of history, as he came to see it, was the struggle of two ways of life against one another, and each against itself. The message of history was that in that struggle – in the expression of the virtues of each aspect, their overarching into vices, and their suppression by their own internal logic and the dialectic of their interaction – debts were cancelled, injustice overcome. Human inadequacies were met and matched by their opposites. Each flourish of glory had its moment, paid its price and gave way to an alternative that was strong where the other was weak and weak where the other was strong. The meaning of history was not in the outcome but in the process.

Ibn Khaldūn's dialectical vision made room for a naturalistic theodicy. In place of a vision of progress or a steep descent toward judgement, his cyclical vision of history confronts the empirical realities and exonerates God and being at large from charges of injustice without accepting the odious and manifestly false doctrine that whatever is is right. As in Condorcet's account of progress, every event has its place, but the warrant now is not in leading from good to better to best, but in the partiality of each action and event.

The energies of human and social nature bring men into conflict, cause them to overstep. Each man in his society pursues a partial vision and reaches partial goods, developing virtues that bear vices within them and bring on their own retribution. For societies, as for individuals, crime and punishment, virtue and reward are mutually inextricable. Caligula must live the life of Caligula and die the death of Caligula, and so must every empire or horde live the life that is in its nature and die the death that is of its nature. For nations, like individuals, pay for their crimes, and for all their natural desires. To know these things implies obligations but does not guarantee that they will be met – since there is, as Aristotle saw, a knowing that is deep and intuitive, embedded in action, and a knowing that is self-conscious, reflective, and for that very reason, such that it can be set aside.

Even the best of men cannot encompass all that is good, nor can the best society embody all possibilities.

Finite being is never wholly satisfied with finitude; and, as al-Fārābī suggests, it is that dissatisfaction that keeps the natural world spinning. A thinker seeking spheres of action for the divine on higher planes than those assigned by popular religion might view as an act of God the maintenance of the inner equilibrium that makes this so. That, in fact, is what Ibn Khaldūn does when he makes his model of generational decline not merely an application of Plato's dialectic of states and personality types but an application of Exodus 20:5 (which he quotes in Arabic from a translation of the Vulgate): "God, your Lord is powerful and jealous, visiting the sins of the fathers upon the children to the third and fourth (generations)", reading the words of God's epiphany to Moses as proof of his own thesis: "This shows that four generations in one lineage are the limit to which ancestral prestige can be extended."[183]

With numerous quotations from the *Qur'ān*, Ibn Khaldūn spells out his model at length.[184] Baali, then, overstates his case in arguing that Ibn Khaldūn "did not appeal to God as an explanatory principle underlying the whole of history".[185] It is true that Ibn Khaldūn does not ascribe each outcome of a seemingly contingent juncture to God's direct intervention. Such explanations would be futile. For God is omnipotent, and all events are in God's hands. There would no explanatory force in appeals to God's efficacy. For every outcome would be equally an expression of God's will. But it is wrong to suggest that Ibn Khaldūn's God plays no underlying role in history. Ibn Khaldūn relies on the pervasive (but not invasive) agency of God.

Shehadi reasons:

> That the principle of moral retribution is not generalised as a principle of historical explanation (beyond the unusual, occasional intervention of God) is evident from the fact that in Ibn Khaldūn's account of history all dynasties rise and then fall, not just those that transgress against justice or God's will. There is no attempt to fit the process of history into some grand moral scheme with such retribution as a guiding force.[186]

This is true, if the moral scheme is construed as a partisan – or even a triumphalist Islamic one. But the description fails to take account of Ibn Khaldūn's larger view, which regards all dynasties and all things human as flawed and failing. Retribution touches all human acts, and all human works. We know that the overarching scheme is moral, since the vitality of any regime is proportioned to its virtue. Here we see the religious significance of the idea of civic virtue, operating in a context that refuses to ignore the impact of all natural and social effects. In the words of the *Qur'ān* (17:16): "And if We wish to destroy a city, We order the affluent to transgress in it, and the verdict is justly passed against it, and we destroy it utterly."[187]

Ibn Khaldūn's answer to the problem of evil, and of failure in history, was found in the tragic finitude of men and all that they create, a finitude at once noble and degrading, which God in His wisdom and grace bestowed upon men and nations, allowing them to live and causing them to die through a nature of their own. Only so, in the light of all that Ibn Khaldūn wrote, can we read the words by which he opens his *Muqaddimah*:

> Praised be God, whose is the Kingdom of Heaven and in whose hand are all earthly rule and dominion. His are the most exquisite names and attributes, and nothing, be it whispered or left unsaid, is unknown to Him. He is all powerful, and nothing in heaven or on earth is impossible for Him or escapes Him. He raised us up from the earth as spirits, let us live on earth as nations and generations, gives us our portion and sustenance from the earth. The wombs of our mothers and our houses were our shelters. Food keeps us alive. Time wears us out, and our fate comes, which has been fixed in the Book. But He endures. He lives and does not die.

— NOTES —

1. For Ibn Khaldūn's naturalism, see Nassif Nassar, *La Pensée Réaliste d'Ibn Khaldūn* (Paris: Presses Univeritaires de France, 1967).
2. Ibn Khaldūn does shade and colour, suppressing, for example, his own role as a signatory of the *fetwa* used in deposing his patron Barqūq, whose favour was vital to Ibn Khaldūn when Barqūq was restored. See Walter Fischel, *Ibn Khaldūn in Egypt* (Berkeley: University of California Press, 1967) pp. 75–6.
3. As Ibn Khaldūn observes, "State and empire are the world's marketplace, attracting the produce of science and industry alike" 1 *Muqaddimah* Introduction, pp. 46–7. (In what follows, references to the *Muqaddimah* comprise an Arabic numeral for the volume of Franz Rosenthal's translation, then the title of the work, chapter, section, and page – where appropriate – in that translation. Translations here, for the most part, are my own.) For Ibn Khaldūn's periods of forced retirement, see Fischel, *Ibn Khaldūn in Egypt*, p. 4.
4. Thucydides, *The Peloponnesian War* 1.23, trans. Benjamin Jowett (New York: Bantam Books, 1960) p. 34. (Following references to page numbers are to the Jowett translation.)
5. 3 *Muqaddimah* concluding remark, p. 481; cf. 1 *Muqaddimah* Preliminary Remarks, p. 77; and see Ibn Khaldūn's *Autobiography*, p. 229, quoted in Rosenthal's introduction to the *Muqaddimah*, p. liii; cf. pp. lv–lvi. Ibn Khaldūn finished the *Muqaddimah* in Tunis in the course of four more years, now with the benefit of a library. For his further revisions of the work in Egypt, see Fischel, *Ibn Khaldūn in Egypt*, pp. 4–5.
6. For the resonances of the term, see *Qur'ān* 12:111, regarding the histories of the prophets: "There was a lesson (*'ibra*) in their stories for those with hearts to

understand ..." Vividly contrasting the inscrutable *Dahr* of the *Jāhilyya* with the history of the *Qur'ān*, where, "By sheer dint of repetition, fact becomes parable", Tarif Khalidi writes, in *Arabic Historical Thought in the Classical Period* (p. 9), that in the *Qur'ān* time itself becomes parabolic: "Events acquire their moral significance from their *'āqiba*, or outcome, and this *'āqiba* is at the same time the *'ibra*, or moral, of the narrative, a key word in later historiography." M. Talbi glosses Ibn Khaldūn's term *'ibar* as an expression for the "meaning and deep significance of history", EI_2 vol. 3, p. 828b.

7. John Finley, *Thucydides* (Cambridge: Harvard University Press, 1947) pp. 68–70. The same thesis was laid out earlier in C. N. Cochrane, *Thucydides and the Science of History*, (Oxford, 1929); cf. Moses Hadas' introduction to the Jowett translation, p. 13.
8. Thucydides 1.11, p. 29.
9. Thucydides 1.22, p. 33.
10. Thucydides 1.7–13, pp. 26–28.
11. Thucydides 2.53 ff., pp. 124–25; cf. 2.8, p. 101; 5.26 f., p. 308. Thucydides' suspicion that oracles are back projections exemplifies what Peter Kosso calls a coherentist (non-foundationalist) structure of justification; "Historical Evidence and Epistemic Justification: Thucydides as a Case Study", *History and Theory* 32 (1993) pp. 1–13. Evidentiary claims for Thucydides, as for Ibn Khaldūn, must pass through a fine hermeneutical sieve. This does not entail that no claim is ever made foundational. It does mean that any claim is subject to critique.
12. 1 *Muqaddimah* Introduction, pp. 15–65, and Preliminary Remarks, p. 72.
13. But Ibn Khaldūn, himself an eyewitness, balks at numbering the forces of Tamerlane in the siege of Damascus. As Fischel writes (*Ibn Khaldūn in Egypt*, p. 99): "While some contemporary sources estimate the strength of the whole army of Tamerlane at 240,000, including 30,000 fighters, some even as high as 800,000, Ibn Khaldūn states only: 'The people are of a number which cannot be counted; if you estimate it at one million it would not be too much, nor can you say it is less. If they pitched their tents together in the land they would fill all vacant spaces, and if their armies came into a wide territory the plain would be too narrow for them.'" Here Ibn Khaldūn's scepticism is reduced to a mere reticence at hazarding more than a very round estimate. He falls back on rhetoric and keeps vague about the visual impressions that prompt his estimate.
14. 1 *Muqaddimah*, pp. 16 ff. In keeping with Islamic juridical tradition, with its well known suspicion of a priorism and arbitrariness in formal reasoning, Ibn Khaldūn's empiricism extends to a distrust of rational argument, see 1 *Muqaddimah* Introduction, p. 58; cf. 3 *Muqaddimah* VI 41, pp. 308–10.
15. 1 *Muqaddimah* Introduction, p. 57; cf. 2 *Muqaddimah* IV 3– 4, pp. 238–43; 7–11, pp. 266–76; 19, pp. 297–301 etc.
16. Thucydides 1.8–11, pp. 27–8.
17. 1 *Muqaddimah* III 16, pp. 356 ff.
18. 1 *Muqaddimah* III 16, pp. 359 ff. Eugene Myers, *Arabic Thought and the Western World* (New York: Ungar, 1966) calls Ibn Khaldūn "the first thinker to treat economics as a special discipline outside the fields of ethics and philosophy"; see his "Ibn Khaldūn: Forerunner of New Science", *The Arab World* (March, 1966) p.

5. The claim is a bit strong, but we can see how Ibn Khaldūn systematises economic ideas when we compare his treatment of what is now called the Laffer curve (the decline of productivity as tax burdens become excessive) with Plato's original statement of the theme, in the *Republic*, VIII 567a.
19. Thucydides 1.5–18, pp. 25–31.
20. Thucydides 1.3, p. 24; 2 *Muqaddimah* IV 22, pp. 305–7.
21. Thucydides 5.26 f., p. 308; cf. 1.23, p. 33; and, typically, 1 *Muqaddimah* I Introduction, pp. 40, 19.
22. See 1 *Muqaddimah* II 4, p. 253; II 14, p. 279. For Ibn Khaldūn, as Aziz al-Azmeh points out, "The anteriority of beduinism to urbanism is not only a serial anteriority ... but is also a conceptual anteriority, a sort of logical presupposition", *Ibn Khaldūn* (London: Routledge, 1982) p. 55. Plato used a thought experiment to make the corresponding point.
23. 3 *Muqaddimah* VI 41, pp. 308–10.
24. See 3 *Muqaddimah* VI 30, pp. 246–51, 257; cf. Nassar, *La Pensée Réaliste*, pp. 62, 73–5, 99; Baali, *Society, State and Urbanism*, p. 7.
25. 1 *Muqaddimah* I iii–v, pp. 167–83.
26. 2 *Muqaddimah* IV 5, pp. 243 ff.
27. 2 *Muqaddimah* III 49, p. 136.
28. 1 *Muqaddimah* I 3, pp. 167–71.
29. 1 *Muqaddimah* I 4, pp. 174–75.
30. See Goodman and Goodman, "'Particularly Amongst the Sunburnt Nations ...'".
31. Baali, *Society, State and Urbanism*, p. 9, quoting 1 *Muqaddimah* Foreword, p. 6. Baali italicises *inner* to highlight the contrast with a more conventional idea cited by Ibn Khaldūn: "on the surface, history is no more than information about political events, dynasties, and occurrences of the remote past, elegantly presented and spiced with proverbs."
32. 1 *Muqaddimah* Introduction, pp. 84–5.
33. As Muhsin Mahdi points out, not all the disciplines that bear the name of sciences are pure quests for intellectual satisfaction. Legal and religious sciences, medicine, Aristotle's "political science", (and Ibn Khaldūn's own science of culture or civilisation) mingle practical with conceptual interests; *Ibn Khaldūn's Philosophy of History*, pp. 97–100, 34. It is an Aristotelian thought that the higher and more disciplined arts, those that can be taught by way of rational explanation, are scientific at the core.
35. See e.g. 1 *Muqaddimah* II 14, p. 278.
36. 1 *Muqaddimah* II 3, p. 252
37. Cf. Mahdi, *Ibn Khaldūn's Philosophy of History*, pp. 187–90, 260–9.
38. As Mahdi remarks (*Ibn Khaldūn's Philosophy of History*, p. 171): "In the sequence through which the mind achieves knowledge, the science of culture comes *after* history: it reflects on, and explains the external events ascertained by history. The historian cannot, however, ascertain external events without a minimal acquaintance with their nature and causes. In the art of the historian, history and the science of culture should be combined. Finally, in the order of being, the object of the science of culture comes *before* the object of history. Historical events are the product of the nature and causes underlying them."

38. 1 *Muqaddimah* I 6, p. 184
39. 1 *Muqaddimah* I 6, pp. 185 ff., 226 ff.
40. 1 *Muqaddimah* I 6, pp. 184–90. The "positivism" sometimes remarked in Ibn Khaldūn's historiography is in fact nothing of the sort. Ibn Khaldūn's naturalism would run counter to his religious commitments only if it were part of a general positivist theory of knowledge; see Fadlou Shehadi, "Theism, Mysticism and Scientific History in Ibn Khaldūn", in M. Marmura, ed., *Islamic Theology and Philosophy* (Albany: SUNY Press, 1984) p. 270. Charles Issawi takes up the claim that Ibn Khaldūn is a positivist only to turn it on its head: "His Theory of Knowledge shows him to be an Empiricist and Positivist … But, like Kant, he excludes Philosophy only to make room for faith"; *An Arab Philosophy of History* (London: John Murray, 1950; repr. Princeton: Darwin Press, 1987) p. 14. Although the terms here may be used somewhat loosely, the parallel with such figures as Ibn Ḥazm is striking.
41. 1 *Muqaddimah* Introduction, p. 74.
42. 1 *Muqaddimah* Introduction, p. 75.
43. 1 *Muqaddimah* Introduction, pp. 26–7. Archaeologists of our own day believe that they may have rediscovered the lost city of Iram.
44. The *Muqaddimah* quotes the *Qur'ān* several hundred times, citing most of the Surahs, not merely for pious phrases or embellishment but frequently to bolster a theory or underline an outlook. *Ḥadīth* too is heavily used, albeit more selectively.
45. 1 *Muqaddimah* I 6, pp. 188–91.
46. 3 *Muqaddimah* VI 16, cf. 17. Ibn Khaldūn was not an unqualified Sufi-sympathiser. He endorsed orthodox and Sunnī Sufism but condemned as heretical the Sufism of such moderns (*muta'akhkhirūn*) as Ibn 'Arabī. See his fetwa in M. al-Tanji, ed., *Shifā' al-Sā'il fi Tahdhīb al-Masā'il* (Istanbul, 1958).
47. 1 *Muqaddimah* II 14, p. 279.
48. E.g. Thucydides 5.26 f., p. 308, 2.7–8, p. 101; 1 *Muqaddimah* I 6, e.g., pp. 202 f., 207 f., 226 f., etc.
49. 1 *Muqaddimah* Introduction, esp. pp. 6 ff., 56–65; Thucydides 1.23, pp. 33–4.
50. See Aristotle, *Metaphysics* Alpha 1, 981a 15 ff.; cf. 1139b 14 ff.
51. Cf. Finley, *Thucydides*, p. 70.
52. Cf. Thucydides 3.82 f., pp. 198 ff.
53. Thucydides 3.84, p. 201.
54. Thucydides loc. cit. Many scholars regard 3.84 as an interpolation, but its theses, although perhaps more explicit and outspoken than the text elsewhere permits itself to be, are not out of keeping with its outlook.
55. Thucydides 3.83, p. 200.
56. Thucydides 3.82, p. 199.
57. Finley, *Thucydides*, pp. 51 ff.; cf. pp. 43 ff.
58. Cf. Finley, *Thucydides*, pp. 95–100.
59. Finley, *Thucydides*, p. 48.
60. See Finley, *Thucydides*, pp. 51, 54–5.
61. Thucydides 1.23, p. 33.
62. Thucydides 2.48, p. 122.
63. Thucydides 3.82, pp. 198–9.

64. Thucydides 1.23, pp. 33–4.
65. Thucydides 1.77 f., pp. 60 f.; cf. 3.9.39–40, pp. 176–7; 4.11.6 ff., pp. 250–1; 6.18.17–20, pp. 360–1.
66. See Thucydides' accounts of the arguments for war among the Spartans, 1.87 ff., p. 65; the Corinthians, 1.121 ff., pp. 80 ff.; and above all the Athenians, where the cool rationality of Pericles, "the greatest politician and public speaker" of his day, initiates the events that will lead to the self-destruction of Hellas, 1.140 ff., pp. 92–6.
67. Cf. Thucydides 1.24, p. 34.
68. Thucydides 1.90, p. 66.
69. Cf. e.g. Thucydides 1.103 f., p. 72.
70. Cf. e.g. Thucydides 2.50 ff, pp. 123–4.
71. Thucydides 2.66–7, pp. 132–3.
72. Cf. Thucydides 3.75, pp. 196 ff.
73. Thucydides 2.52, p. 124.
74. Thucydides 4.17, pp. 228–9; 39 f., pp. 240–1; 5.15.13, p. 301, etc.
75. Clifford Orwin, *The Humanity of Thucydides* (Princeton: Princeton University Press, 1994).
76. Orwin, *The Humanity of Thucydides*, p. 74.
77. 2 *Muqaddimah* III 44, p. 117.
78. 1 *Muqaddimah* II 1, p. 249; cf. I iii–v, pp. 167–83; and e.g. II 4, 5, 6, pp. 253–61.
79. 1 *Muqaddimah* I 3, p. 167–73; cf. 4, 5, pp. 173–83
80. 1 *Muqaddimah* I 1, p. 90; cf. Mahdi, *Ibn Khaldūn's Philosophy of History*, pp. 173–9.
81. 1 *Muqaddimah* III 21, pp. 380–1; cf. the references collected in Rosenthal's introduction, p. lxxv and n. 102.
82. Thucydides 3.75 ff., pp. 196–200.
83. 1 *Muqaddimah* II 16, pp. 284 ff.
84. 1 *Muqaddimah* Introduction, pp. 56–62; cf. Mahdi, *Ibn Khaldūn's Philosophy of History*, pp. 180–3.
85. 1 *Muqaddimah* I Preliminary Remarks, p. 72; cf. Introduction pp. 55–6, and I vi, p. 195.
86. 1 *Muqaddimah* I i, p. 89, 2 *Muqaddimah* III 3, p. 417; cf. 1 *Muqaddimah* II 16, p. 284.
87. Cf. 1 *Muqaddimah* II 11, pp. 269 ff., 16, pp. 284.
88. 1 *Muqaddimah* II 26, p. 305, cf. 25, p. 304; II 7, p. 262.
89. Quoted in Rosenthal's Introduction to the *Muqaddimah*, p. lxxiv, n. 99; cf. 1 *Muqaddimah* I Preliminary Remarks, pp. 79–82; 2 *Muqaddimah* VI 4, pp. 419 ff. The remark in *Avot* is ascribed to Rabbi Ḥanina, the Vice-High Priest, a loyalist of the days before the destruction of the Temple in Jerusalem in 73 CE.
90. 1 *Muqaddimah* I i, p. 89; cf. 1 *Muqaddimah* III 21, pp. 380 ff.; 2 *Muqaddimah* VI 3, p. 417.
91. 1 *Muqaddimah* II 8, pp. 264 ff.; 2 *Muqaddimah* IV 21, pp. 302 ff.
92. 1 *Muqaddimah* II 8, p. 264.
93. Loc. cit.; 1 *Muqaddimah* III 18, p. 374.
94. 1 *Muqaddimah* II 16, p. 284; 1 *Muqaddimah* III 1, p. 313; III 6, pp. 322 ff., III 26, p. 414; 1 *Muqaddimah* II 7, p. 263.
95. 1 *Muqaddimah* II 26, p. 305; cf. 1 *Muqaddimah* III 18, pp. 374–5, 2 *Muqaddimah* IV 3, p. 238, IV 21, pp. 302–5; cf. 1 *Muqaddimah* Introduction, p. 55.

96. See M. M. Rabīʿ, *The Political Theory of Ibn Khaldūn* (Leiden: Brill, 1967).
97. 1 *Muqaddimah*, Introduction, pp. 28–36; cf. Richard Bosley, "Empiricism and Traditionalism in the Philosophy of History of Ibn Khaldūn", *Dialogue: Canadian Philosophical Review* 6 (1967) pp. 166–80.
98. See, e.g., 1 *Muqaddimah*, II 16, pp. 284–5; 1 *Muqaddimah* III 7, p. 328; cf., e.g., 1 *Muqaddimah* III 9, 21, 22, 23; 2 *Muqaddimah*, III 43, etc.
99. 1 *Muqaddimah* II 6, pp. 258–9; cf. 1 *Muqaddimah* III 15, pp. 353–5; 18,19, pp. 374–8; 22, pp. 382–5.
100. Coercion is never a sufficient political foundation. For even coercion, to be effective, requires the identification of some with the goals or values it serves. Elemental identification thus underlies all more complex (including coercive) social structures. See 1 *Muqaddimah* II 6, pp. 258–61; III 6, pp. 322–7; 8, pp. 330–2; 2 *Muqaddimah* IV 21, pp. 302–5, etc. Identification will arise variously from state to state – *a fortiori* will accounts of it differ from theorist to theorist. But in the mass, over the long run, humans do nothing wholly unwillingly. As Max Weber made clear, every lasting relation of control over large numbers of individuals must be based on "a certain minimum of voluntary submission; thus an interest (based on ulterior motives or genuine acceptance) in obedience". *The Theory of Social and Economic Organisation*, trans. A. M. Henderson and Talcott Parsons, (New York: Oxford University Press, 1947) p. 324. In a society based ultimately on the tribe, it was natural for Ibn Khaldūn to think of "voluntary subordination" on the model of familial identification. Weber, equally naturally, phrased the matter in terms of interests. The common insight might well represent the thread of truth: what is needed is (some form of) acceptance. Cf. 1 *Muqaddimah* III 23, p. 386.
101. 1 *Muqaddimah* I, Preliminary Remarks, pp. 79–82; cf. 2 *Muqaddimah* III 50, pp. 137–56.
102. 1 *Muqaddimah* II 7, p. 263.
103. 1 *Muqaddimah* II 7, p. 263.
104. 1 *Muqaddimah* II 16, pp. 284–6.
105. 1 *Muqaddimah* III 12, pp. 273–6; 2 *Muqaddimah* III 44, pp. 117–18.
106. 1 *Muqaddimah* II 14, p. 279; cf. Goodman, "Ghazālī's Argument from Creation".
107. Cf. 1 *Muqaddimah* II 26, pp. 305 ff.
108. Reflecting on the experience of Morocco, Gellner remarks that tribally based powers displaced city-based ones (themselves typically tribal in origin) throughout the Middle Ages. The pattern, "well described by Ibn Khaldūn", persisted, *mutatis mutandis*, into the modern era: "if the ultimate doom of the *ancien régime* were the dissident [or refractory] tribes, so the ultimate doom of the *nouveau régime* was the dissident shanty town outside the new city. But the world of Karl Marx did not replace the world of Ibn Khaldūn: the two existed side by side within one country." Ernest Gellner, "From Ibn Khaldūn to Karl Marx", *Political Quarterly* 32 (1961) p. 386. Baali remarks, "Gellner observed that as late as the 1950s the Moroccan tribes joined political parties, and swore an oath of loyalty to them, *as* tribal units", *Society, State and Urbanism*, p. 50.
109. See 1 *Muqaddimah* II 16, p. 284, III 1, p. 313; 2 *Muqaddimah* IV 18, p. 291.
110. 1 *Muqaddimah* III 1, p. 313.

111. 1 *Muqaddimah* III 12, p. 344; 2 *Muqaddimah* III 44, p. 117.
112. 1 *Muqaddimah* II 6, pp. 258–61.
113. Loc. cit., p. 254.
114. See 1 *Muqaddimah* II 26, p. 305.
115. 1 *Muqaddimah* III 11, pp. 341–2; cf. Khalidi on Balādhurī, *Arabic Historical Thought*, p. 61; Ecclesiastes 2:18–21; Goodman, "Arabic Universal History".
116. Cf. 1 *Muqaddimah* III 14, p. 351.
117. See 2 *Muqaddimah* V 16, p. 347; 2 *Muqaddimah* VI 8, p. 434; cf. Oswald Spengler's analysis in *The Decline of the West* trans. C. F. Atkinson (New York: Knopf, 1932).
118. Cf. 1 *Muqaddimah* III 15, pp. 355 ff.; 17, pp. 372 ff.; also 3 *Muqaddimah* VI 27–32, pp. 156–280; 35, pp. 290–1; 41, pp. 308–10.
119. 1 *Muqaddimah* III 12, pp. 343–6; cf. II 14, pp. 351–5.
120. 1 *Muqaddimah* III 12, II 14; 2 *Muqaddimah* III 44.
121. 1 *Muqaddimah* III 7, p. 327; III 11, pp. 339 ff.
122. See *Arā'*, ed. Walzer, pp. 144–7, quoted above at p. 27.
123. Cf. Finley, *Thucydides*, pp. 84 ff.
124. Thucydides 3.83, p. 201 ff.; see also the passages immediately preceding and 2.51, p. 124 ff.; 3.11, p. 161.
125. Thucydides, on the first page of the *History*.
126. Thucydides 1.2–25, pp. 24–34.
127. Thucydides 7.87, p. 463.
128. Thucydides 2.51 ff., 3.81, pp. 123 ff., among many others.
129. Thucydides 1.24, p. 34.
130. Loc. cit.
131. Loc. cit.
132. Thucydides 2.2–9, pp. 97–101.
133. Thucydides 2.1, p. 97.
134. Thucydides 3.9 and 10.50–69, pp. 183–93.
135. Thucydides 3.66, p. 191.
136. Thucydides 2.52, p. 124.
137. Thucydides 2.74, p. 137; for the protection of fruit trees by divine law, cf. Deuteronomy 22:19.
138. Thucydides 3.62, p. 191.
139. Thucydides 3.66, p. 193.
140. Cf. e.g. Thucydides 3.34 ff., the near massacre of the Mytilenaeans.
141. Thucydides 3.66, p. 193.
142. Thucydides 2.66 ff., pp. 132–3.
143. Cf. Thucydides 5.32, p. 311; and, for an earlier stage, 1.127 ff. pp. 84–5.
144. See Thucydides 2.34 ff.
145. For the response of the disheartened Plato to Pericles' oration, see his *Menexenus*. As Orwin notes (*The Humanity of Thucydides*, p. 15): "The funeral oration spoken by Pericles at the end of the first year of the Peloponnesian War is the best known passage in Thucydides. It is widely held to express the author's views as well as the speaker's." Among those whom Orwin cites for such readings are Regenbogen, Finley, Romilly, Grene, Parry, Farrar, and Yunis. "The list", he adds, "could be extended indefinitely."

146. See Thucydides 2.53, p. 124.
147. Thucydides 3.37 ff., pp, 174 ff.; cf. 1 *Muqaddimah* I i, p. 90.
148. Thucydides 3.81 ff., p. 198.
149. Thucydides 3.68 ff., p. 193.
150. Loc. cit., *inter alia*.
151. Thucydides 3.82, p. 199.
152. Loc. cit.
153. Loc. cit.
154. Thucydides 3.81, pp. 198–9.
155. For the two genres, see F. E. Peters, *Aristotle and the Arabs* (New York: NYU Press, 1968) pp. 15–16, 20, 104–20.
156. Thucydides 1.4 ff., p. 25.
157. Thucydides 1.5, p. 25; cf. 1 *Muqaddimah* Introduction, p. 36.
158. Thucydides loc. cit.
159. 1 *Muqaddimah* II 25, pp. 302 ff.
160. 1 *Muqaddimah* II 14, 15, 16, pp. 278–86; 18, pp. 287–90, etc.
161. 1 *Muqaddimah* II 5, pp. 257–8.
162. 2 *Muqaddimah* III 49, pp. 135 f.
163. 1 *Muqaddimah* II 3–7, pp. 252–65.
164. 1 *Muqaddimah* II 4, pp. 253–7.
165. 1 *Muqaddimah* II 28, pp. 308–10.
166. 1 *Muqaddimah* II 4, pp. 253–7.
167. *Muqaddimah* IV,V, VI *passim*.
168. 1 *Muqaddimah* II 6, pp. 258–61.
169. 3 *Muqaddimah* VI 16, pp. 76–103.
170. 1 *Muqaddimah* III 2, pp. 314–17; 11–15, pp. 339–55; cf. 2 *Muqaddimah* V 4–6, pp. 319–34; 11, pp. 339–40, etc.
171. 3 *Muqaddimah* VI 31, esp. p. 262; and in general VI 27–32, where Ibn Khaldūn attacks the false intellectual authorities of the pseudo-sciences – including philosophy.
172. 2 *Muqaddimah* V, pp. 311–407.
173. 1 *Muqaddimah* III 2–3, pp. 314–19; 11–12, pp. 339–46; 17, pp. 372–4; 2 *Muqaddimah* III 44, pp. 117–18, etc.
174. 2 *Muqaddimah* III 49, pp. 135–7.
175. 2 *Muqaddimah* IV 18, pp. 293 ff.
176. 1 *Muqaddimah* III 8, p. 330; 10, p. 336; 13, p. 347; 16, p. 356, etc.
177. 3 *Muqaddimah* V–VI with II. Civilisation, with all its complexities and ambiguities, must somehow be weighed against its counterpart.
178. 3 *Muqaddimah* VI; cf. 2 *Muqaddimah* V 20, p. 353.
179, 3 *Muqaddimah* VI 43, p. 318; 45, pp. 342 ff. 47, pp. 351–2; but cf. VI 33, p. 283 – there is no "natural" language.
180. 3 *Muqaddimah* VI 50–53.
181. 1 *Muqaddimah* II 9, pp. 265–7.
182. 1 *Muqaddimah* II 4, p. 253.
183. 1 *Muqaddimah* II 14, p. 281; as Rosenthal notes, it was De Slane who traced Ibn Khaldūn's quotation textually, since the word "powerful" is added in the Vulgate.

184. 1 *Muqaddimah* III 11–15, pp. 339–55.
185. Baali, *Society, State and Urbanism*, p. 16.
186. Shehadi, "Theism, Mysticism and Scientific History", p. 276; cf. pp. 274–5
187. I translate following Khalidi, *Arabic Historical Thought*, p. 11.

Bibliography

Altmann, Alexander, *Studies in Religious Philosophy and Mysticism* (London: Routledge, 1969).

Asín Palacios, Miguel, *Islam and the Divine Comedy* (London: Cass, 1968; 1st Spanish ed., Madrid, 1919).

Baali, Fuad, *Society, State and Urbanism: Ibn Khaldūn's Sociological Thought* (Albany: SUNY Press, 1988).

Baḥyā ibn Pāqūdā, *K. al-Hidāya ilā Farā'iḍ al-Qulūb*, ed. A. S. Yahuda (Leiden: Brill, 1912); trans. M. Mansoor (London: Routledge, 1973).

Davidson, Herbert, *Alfarabi, Avicenna and Averroes, on Intellect: Their Cosmologies, Theories of the Active Intellect, and Theories of Human Intellect* (New York: Oxford University Press, 1992).

Davidson, Herbert, *Proofs for Eternity, Creation and the Existence of God in Medieval Islamic and Jewish Philosophy* (New York: Oxford University Press, 1987).

Fakhry, Majid, *Ethical Theories in Islam* (Leiden: Brill, 2nd ed., 1994).

Al-Fārābī, *K. Mabādi' Arā' Ahlu 'l-Madīnatu 'l-Fāḍila* (The Book of the Principles underlying the Beliefs of the People of the Virtuous State), ed. and trans. R. Walzer as *Al-Fārābī on the Perfect State* (Oxford: Clarendon Press, 1985).

Al-Fārābī, *The Book of Letters*, ed. Muhsin Mahdi (Beirut: Dar el-Mashreq, 1969).

Al-Ghazālī, *Tahāfut al-Falāsifa* (The Incoherence of the Philosophers), ed. M. Bouyges (Beirut: Catholic Press, 2nd ed. 1962).

Al-Ghazālī, *K. al-Munqidh min al-Ḍalāl*, trans. W. Montgomery Watt in *The Faith and Practice of al-Ghazālī* (London: Allen Unwin, 1963; 1953).

Goodman, L. E., "Ghazālī's Argument from Creation", *International Journal of Middle East Studies* 2 (1971) pp. 67–85, 168–88.

Goodman, L. E., "Al-Fārābī's Modalities", *Iyyun* 23 (1972) 100–12, in Hebrew with English summary.

Goodman, L. E., "Rāzī's Myth of the Fall of the Soul: Its Function in His Philosophy", in George Hourani, ed., *Essays on Islamic Philosophy and Science* (Albany: SUNY Press, 1975) 25–40.

Goodman, L. E., "Saadya Gaon on the Human Condition", *JQR* NS 67 (1976) pp. 23–9.

Goodman, L. E., *Rambam: Readings in the Philosophy of Moses Maimonides* (New York: Viking, 1976).

Goodman, L. E., "Maimonides and Leibniz," *JJS* 31 (1980) pp. 214–36.

Goodman, L. E., Review of Eric Ormsby, *Theodicy in Islamic Thought: The Dispute over al-Ghazālī's "Best of all Possible Worlds"* in *JHP* 25 (1987) pp. 589–91.

Goodman, L. E., "Ordinary and Extraordinary Language in Medieval Jewish and Islamic Philosophy", *Manuscrito* 9 (1988) pp. 57–83.

Goodman, L. E., "Matter and Form as Attributes of God in Maimonides' Philosophy", in J. Hackett, R. J. Long and C. Manekin, eds, *A Straight Path. Studies ... in Honor of Arthur Hyman* (Washington: Catholic University of America Press 1988) pp. 86–97.

Goodman, L. E., "The Rational and Irrational in Jewish and Islamic Philosophy", in S. Biderman and B. Scharfstein, eds, *Rationality in Question: On Eastern and Western Views of Rationality* (Leiden: Brill, 1989) pp. 93–118.

Goodman, L. E., *On Justice* (New Haven: Yale University Press, 1991).

Goodman, L. E., "Three Enduring Achievements of Islamic Philosophy", in Eliot Deutsch, ed., *Culture and Modernity* (Honolulu: University of Hawaii Press, 1991).

Goodman, L. E., "Six Dogmas of Relativism", in M. Dascal, ed., *Cultural Relativism and Philosophy* (Leiden: Brill, 1991).

Goodman, L. E., Review of Richard Popkin, *La Peyrère* in *JHP* 29 (1991) pp. 131–5.

Goodman, L. E., *Avicenna* (London and New York: Routledge, 1992).

Goodman, L. E., ed., *Neoplatonism and Jewish Thought* (Albany: SUNY Press, 1992).

Goodman, L. E., "Maimonidean Naturalism", in L. E. Goodman, ed., *Neoplatonism and Jewish Thought* (Albany: SUNY Press, 1992).

Goodman, L. E., "Jewish and Islamic Philosophies of Language", in M. Dascal, D. Gerhardus, K. Lorenz and G. Meggle, eds, *Sprachphilosophie* (Berlin: DeGruyter, 1992) pp. 34–55.

Goodman, L. E., "Rāzī", in O. Leaman and S. H. Nasr, eds, *History of Islamic Philosophy* (London: Routledge, 1993) pp. 198–215.

Goodman, L. E., "The Sacred and the Secular: Rival Themes in Arabic Literature", in Mustansir Mir, ed., *Arabic and Islamic Studies in Honor of James A. Bellamy* (Princeton: Darwin, 1993) pp. 287–330.

Goodman, L. E., *God of Abraham* (New York: Oxford University Press, 1996).

Goodman, L. E., "Ibn Bājjah", in S. H. Nasr and Oliver Leaman, eds, *History of Islamic Philosophy* (London: Routledge, 1996), vol. 1, pp. 294–312.

Goodman, L. E., "Morals and Society in Islamic Philosophy", in B. Carr and I. Mahalingam, eds, *Encyclopedia of Asian Philosophy* (London: Curzon, 1997) pp. 1000–24.

Goodman, L. E., "Judah Halevi", in O. Leaman and D. Frank, eds, *History of Jewish Philosophy* (London: Routledge, 1997) pp. 188–227.

Goodman, L. E., *Judaism, Human Rights and Human Values* (New York: Oxford University Press, 1998).

Goodman, L. E., "Arabic Universal History", in *Islamic Humanism* (forthcoming).

Goodman, Madeleine and Goodman, Lenn E., *Sex Differences in the Human Life Cycle* (Los Angeles: Gee Tee Bee, 1986, 1st ed., 1980).

Goodman, Madeleine and Goodman, Lenn E., "Is There a Feminist Biology?" *International Journal of Women's Studies* 4 (1981) pp. 393–413.

Goodman, Madeleine and Goodman, Lenn E., "Creation and Evolution: Another Round in an Ancient Struggle", *Zygon* 18 (1983) pp. 3–43.

Goodman, Madeleine and Goodman, Lenn E., "'Particularly Amongst the Sunburnt Nations ...' – The Persistence of Sexual Stereotypes of Race in Bio-Science", *International Journal of Group Tensions* 19 (1989) 221–43, pp. 365–84.

Guthrie, W. K. C., *A History of Greek Philosophy* (Cambridge: Cambridge University Press, 1967–81) 6 vols.

Hadas, Moses, *Hellenistic Culture – Fusion and Diffusion* (New York: Columbia University Press, 1963).

Hamori, Andras, *On the Art of Medieval Arabic Literature* (Princeton: Princeton University Press, 1974).

Hardie, W. F. R., *Aristotle's Ethical Theory* (Oxford: Oxford University Press, 1988).

Al-Ḥujwīrī, *Kashf al-Maḥjūb*, trans. R. A. Nicholson (London: Luzac, 1911; repr. 1967).

Ibn Bājjah, *Opera Metaphysica*, ed. Majid Fakhry (Beirut: Dar an-Nahar, 1968).

Ibn Khaldūn, trans. Franz Rosenthal as *The Muqaddimah: An Introduction to History* (New York: Pantheon, 1958) 3 vols.

Ibn Rushd (Averroes) *Incoherence of the Incoherence*, ed. M. Bouyges (Beirut, 1930); trans. S. Van den Bergh (London: Luzac, 1954).

Ibn Sīnā, *K. al-Shifā'*, Psychology, Arabic ed. F. Rahman, as *Avicenna's De Anima* (London: Oxford University Press, for the University of Durham, 1959).

Ibn Sīnā, *Najāt*, Psychology, trans. F. Rahman (London: Oxford University Press, 1952; repr. Westport, Conn.: Hyperion, 1981).

Ibn Ṭufayl *Ḥayy Ibn Yaqẓān*, trans. L. E. Goodman (Boston: Twayne, 1972; repr. Los Angeles: Gee Tee Bee, 1984).

Ikhwān al-Ṣafā', *The Case of the Animals vs Man*, trans. L. E. Goodman (New York: Twayne, 1978; reissued, Los Angeles: Gee Tee Bee, 1989).

Khalidi, Tarif, *Arabic Historical Thought in the Classical Period* (Cambridge: Cambridge University Press, 1994).

Al-Kindī, *Risālah On First Philosophy*, ed. and trans. A. Ivry as *Al-Kindī's Metaphysics* (Albany: SUNY Press, 1974).

Al-Kindī, "Uno Scritto morale inedito di al-Kindi", ed. H. Ritter and R. Walzer in *Studi su al-Kindī II*, in *Atti della Academia dei Lincei* 8 (1938) pp. 5–63.

Kirk, G. S. and Raven, J. E., *The Presocratic Philosophers* (Cambridge: Cambridge University Press, 1962; 2nd edn, with M. Schofield, 1983).

Mahdi, Muhsin, *Ibn Khaldūn's Philosophy of History* (Chicago: University of Chicago Press, 1957; repr. 1964).

Maimonides, *Dalālatu 'l-Ḥā'irīn, The Guide to the Perplexed*, ed. S. Munk (Paris, 1856–6; repr. Osnabrück: Otto Zeller, 1964) 3 vols.

Maimonides, *The Eight Chapters of Maimonides on Ethics (Shemonah Perakim): A Psychological and Ethical Treatise*, annotated and trans. Joseph I. Gorfinkle (New York, 1912; repr. New York: AMS, 1966).

Maimonides, *Commentary on the Mishnah*, Introduction, in M. D. Rabinowitz, ed., *Hakdamot le-Ferush ha-Mishnah* (Jerusalem: Mossad Harav Kook, 1968); trans. Fred Rosner in *Maimonides: Commentary on the Mishnah – Introduction to the Mishnah Commentary and Commentary on Tractate Berachot* (New York: Feldheim, 1975).

Maimonides, *Commentary on the Mishnah: Tractate Sanhedrin*, trans. Fred Rosner (New York: Sepher-Hermon, 1981).

Maimonides, *Perush le-Masechet Avot* (Commentary on Avot), ed. M. D. Rabinowitz (Jerusalem: Mossad Harav Kook, 1961).

Mason, Richard, *The God of Spinoza: A Philosophical Study* (Cambridge: Cambridge University Press, 1997).

Merlan, Philip, *Monopsychism, Mysticism and Metaconsciousness* (The Hague: Nijhoff, 1963).

Miskawayh, *Tahdhīb al-Akhlāq* (Beirut: Hayat, 1961); trans. Constantine Zurayk (Beirut: American University of Beirut, 1968); annotated French trans. Mohammed Arkoun, *Traite d'Ethique* (Institut Francais de Damas, 1969).

Ormsby, Eric, *Theodicy in Islamic Thought: The Dispute over al-Ghazali's "Best of all Possible Worlds"* (Princeton: Princeton University Press, 1984).

Proclus, *Elements of Theology*, ed. E. R. Dodds (Oxford: Clarendon Press, 1964; 1st ed. 1933).

Al-Rāzī, *Abi Mohammadi Filii Zachariae Raghensis (Razis) Opera Philosophica Fragmentaque quae supersunt*, ed. Paul Kraus (Cairo: Fouad I Faculty of Letters, 1939; Pars Prior, all that was published; repr. Beirut: Dār al-Āfāq al-Jadīda, 1973).

Al-Rāzī, al-Tibb al-Rūhānī, trans. A. J. Arberry as *The Spiritual Physick of Rhazes* (London: John Murray, 1950).

Al-Rāzī, Philosophical Life, trans. A. J. Arberry as "Rhazes on the Philosophical Life", in *Asiatic Review* 45 (1949) pp. 703–13.

Rosenthal, Franz, ed., *The Classical Heritage in Islam*, trans. Jenny Marmorstein (London: Routledge, 1975; German original, Zürich, 1965).

Ryle, Gilbert, "It was to be", in *Dilemmas* (Cambridge: Cambridge University Press, 1962) pp. 15–35.

Saadiah Gaon, *Kitāb al-Mukhtār fi 'l-Āmānāt wa-'l-'I'tiqādāt* (*Sefer ha-Nivhar ba-Emunot ve-De'ot*) (The Book of Critically Selected Beliefs and Convictions), ed. J. Kafih (Jerusalem: Sura, 1970); trans. S. Rosenblatt as *The Book of Beliefs and Opinions* (New Haven: Yale University Press, 1948).

Saadiah Gaon, *The Book of Theodicy*, trans. with commentary L. E. Goodman (New Haven: Yale University Press, 1988).

Schechter, Soloman, *Aspects of Rabbinic Theology* (New York, 1909; repr. 1972).

Spinoza, *Opera*, ed. Carl Gebhardt (Heidelberg: Carl Winter, 1925); trans. Edwin Curley, *The Collected Works*, vol. 1 (Princeton: Princeton University Press, 1985).

Urbach, Ephraim E. *The Sages*, trans. Israel Abrahams (Jerusalem: The Magnes Press, 1975).
von Arnim, H. F. A., ed., *Stoicorum Veterum Fragmenta* (Stuttgart, 1968)
Wensinck, Arent Jan, *La Pensée de Ghazzali* (Paris: Maisnneuve, 1940).

Index